vol. 4

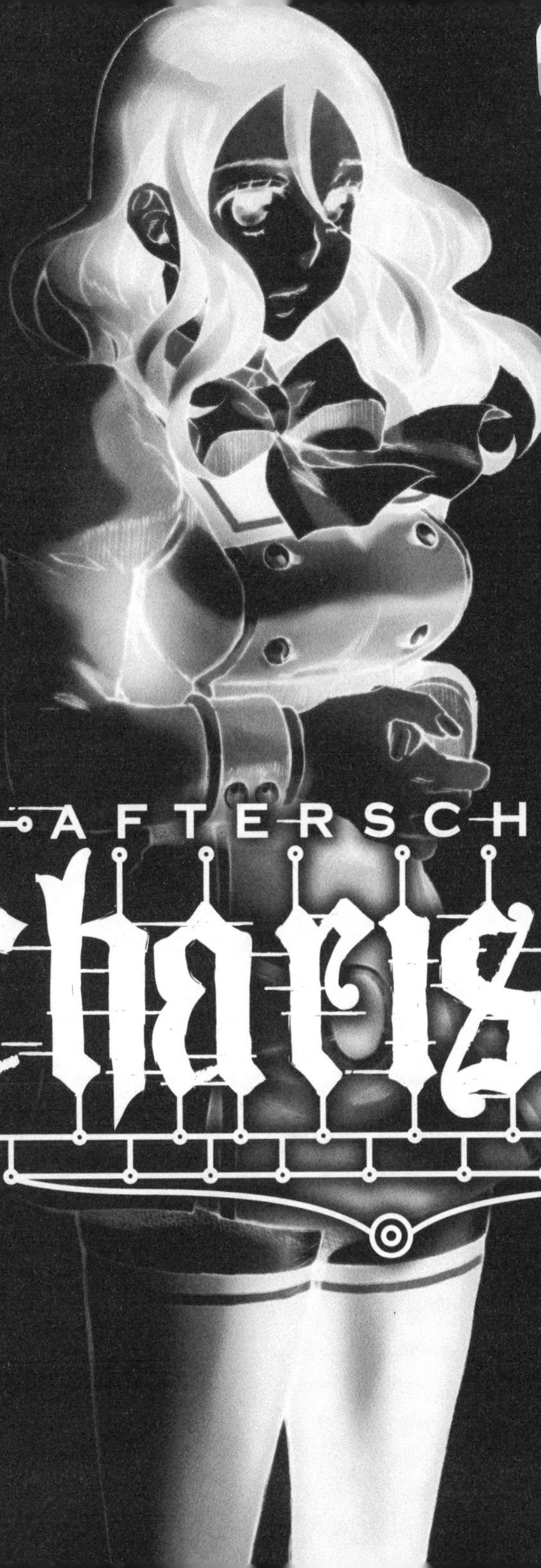

AFTERSCHOOL charisma

KUMIKO SUEKANE

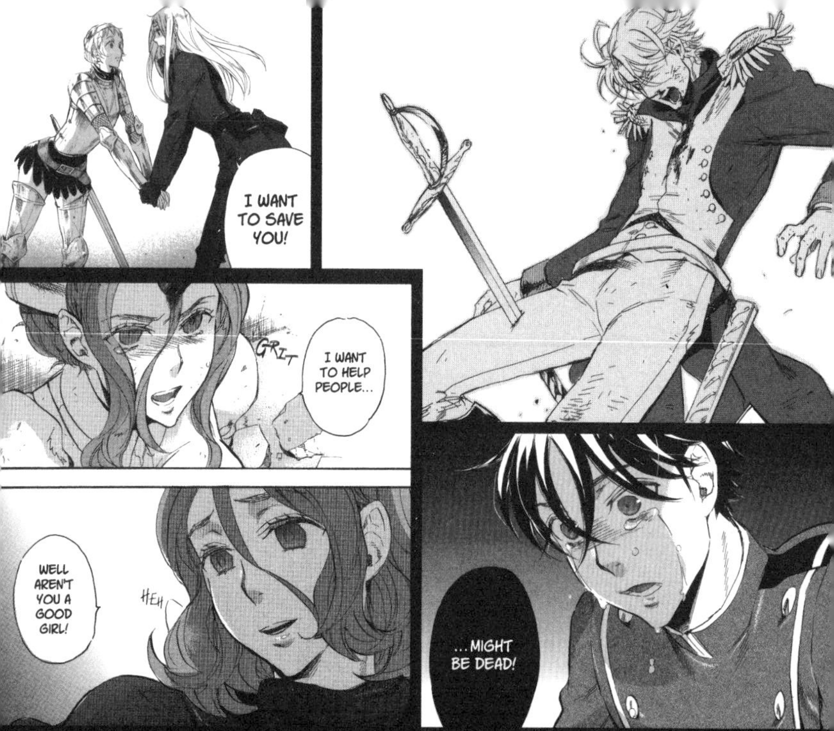
I WANT TO SAVE YOU!
GRIT
I WANT TO HELP PEOPLE...
...MIGHT BE DEAD!
WELL AREN'T YOU A GOOD GIRL!
HEH

story

The year is 2XXX, and at St. Kleio Academy, a school for the clones of famous historical figures, Shiro Kamiya is the only non-clone. While Marie Curie, Mozart, Joan of Arc and the other clones struggle to live their lives in the shadows of their Originals, sometimes seeking solace in a little sheep totem called "the Almighty Dolly," Shiro grapples with how different he is from his classmates.

But then Shiro meets a young man named Kai who's almost identical to Shiro. Kai maintains that he's a clone, but that he doesn't know who his Original is or what his relationship is to Shiro. Shiro doesn't know what to think—could it be that he is a clone after all?

Meanwhile, the students prepare for an Academic Exposition in which visitors from the outside society will gather to witness the clones' achievements. But in the midst of Rasputin's presentation, a bomb goes off in the auditorium. Pandemonium ensues as the students scramble to escape, pursued by a group of terrorists made up of...St. Kleio alumni! The attackers are also clones, and of the same historical figures!

But what do the attackers want? And what will become of their targets?

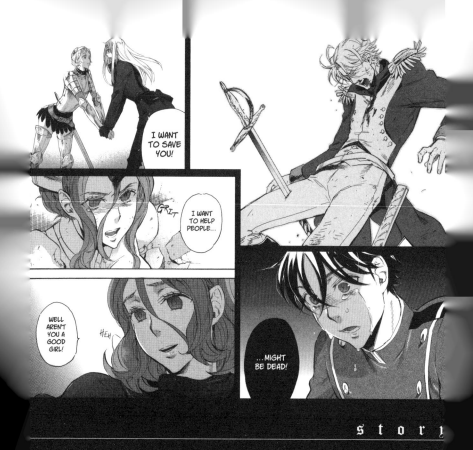

character

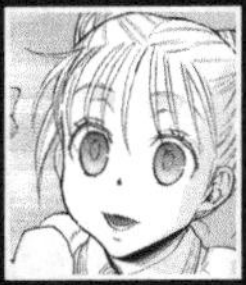

PANDORA
Clone of
Marie Curie

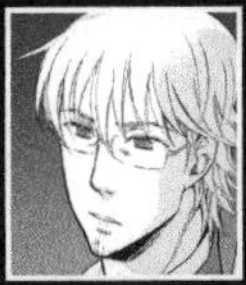

DR. KAMIYA
"Father" to Shiro
and professor at
St. Kleio

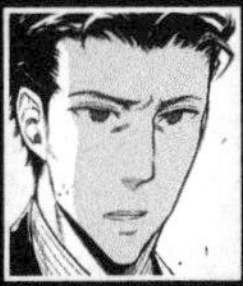

KUROE
Professor at
St. Kleio

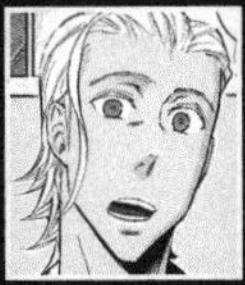

ROCKSWELL
Director of
St. Kleio

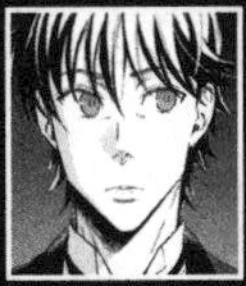

KAI
Graduate of
St. Kleio

students of st. kleio academy

(CLONES OF HISTORICAL FIGURES)

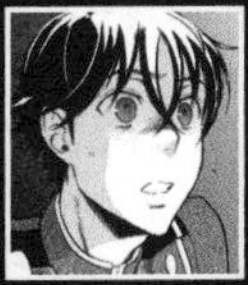

SHIRO KAMIYA
The only non-
clone at St. Kleio

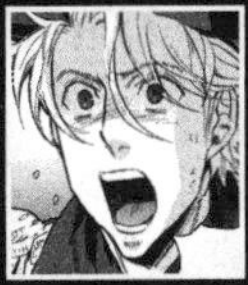

NAPOLEON BONAPARTE

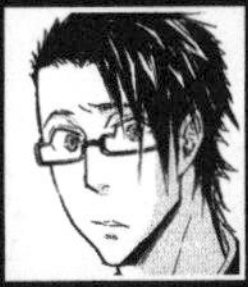

IKKYU SOJUN

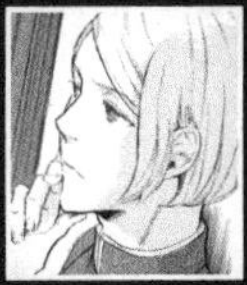

SIGMUND FREUD

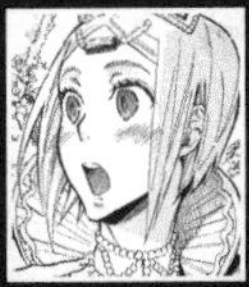

ELIZABETH I

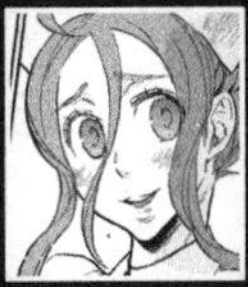

FLORENCE NIGHTINGALE

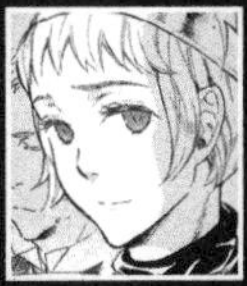

JOAN OF ARC

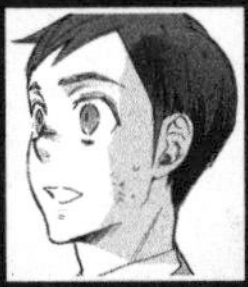

ADOLF HITLER

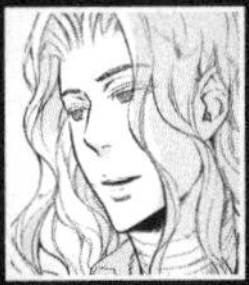

WOLFGANG AMADEUS MOZART

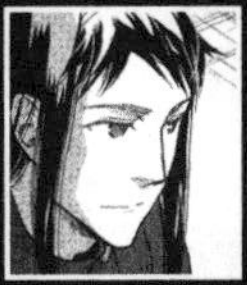

GREGORI YEFIMOVICH RASPUTIN

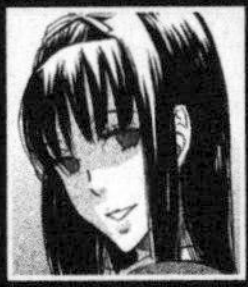

HIMIKO

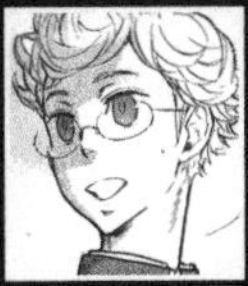

ALBERT EINSTEIN
*shot to death
by a sniper

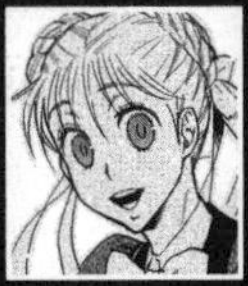

MARIE CURIE (MADAME CURIE)
*transferred to
another school (?)

St·K·L·F10
4

afterschool
charisma

c o n t e n t s

CHAPTER **nineteen**   7

CHAPTER **twenty**   39

CHAPTER **twenty-one**   71

CHAPTER **twenty-two**   105

CHAPTER **twenty-three** 137

CHAPTER **twenty-four** 169

SHORT COMIC   202

CHAPTER nineteen

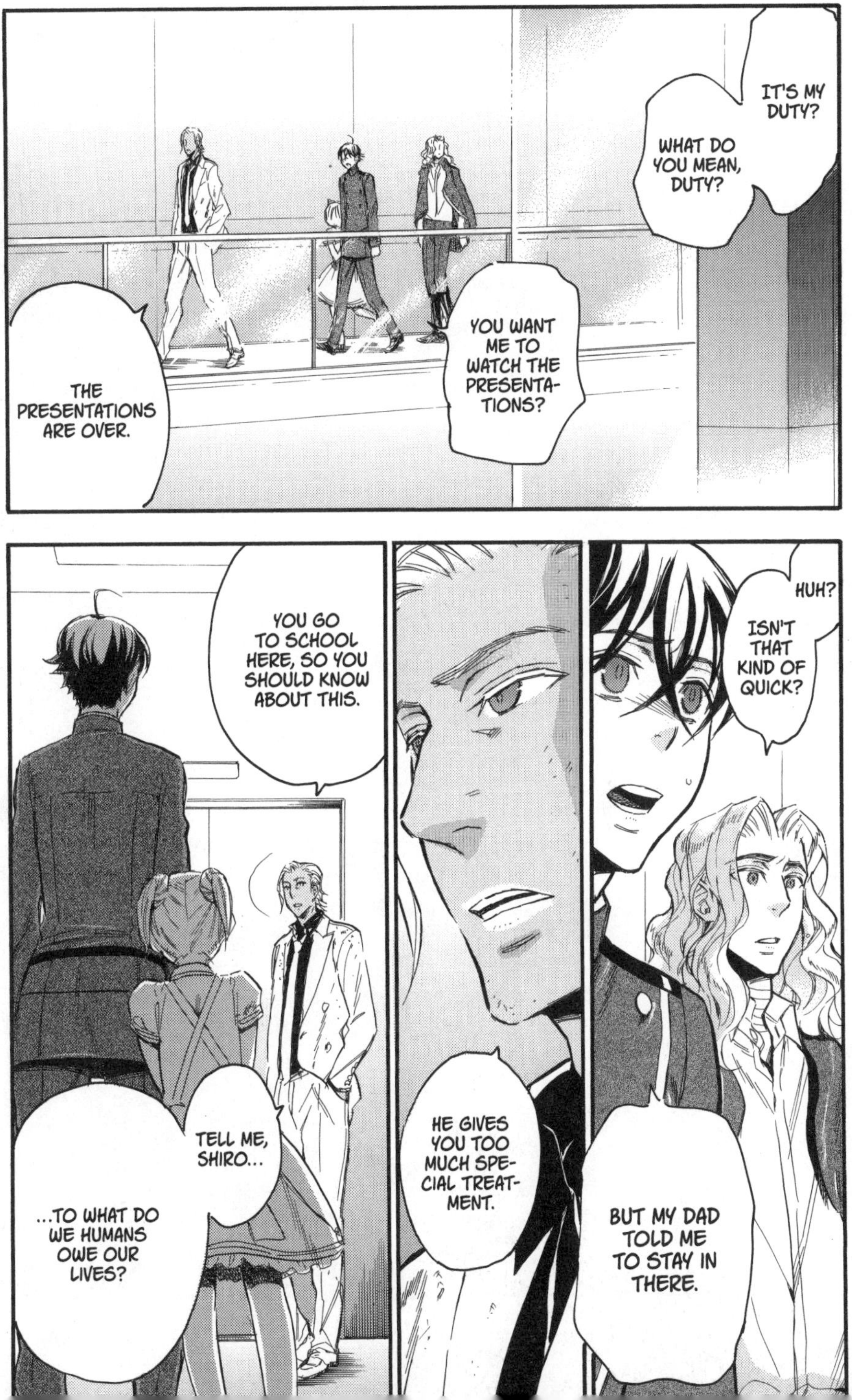
IT'S MY DUTY?
WHAT DO YOU MEAN, DUTY?
YOU WANT ME TO WATCH THE PRESENTATIONS?
THE PRESENTATIONS ARE OVER.
HUH?
ISN'T THAT KIND OF QUICK?
BUT MY DAD TOLD ME TO STAY IN THERE.
HE GIVES YOU TOO MUCH SPECIAL TREATMENT.
YOU GO TO SCHOOL HERE, SO YOU SHOULD KNOW ABOUT THIS.
TELL ME, SHIRO...
...TO WHAT DO WE HUMANS OWE OUR LIVES?

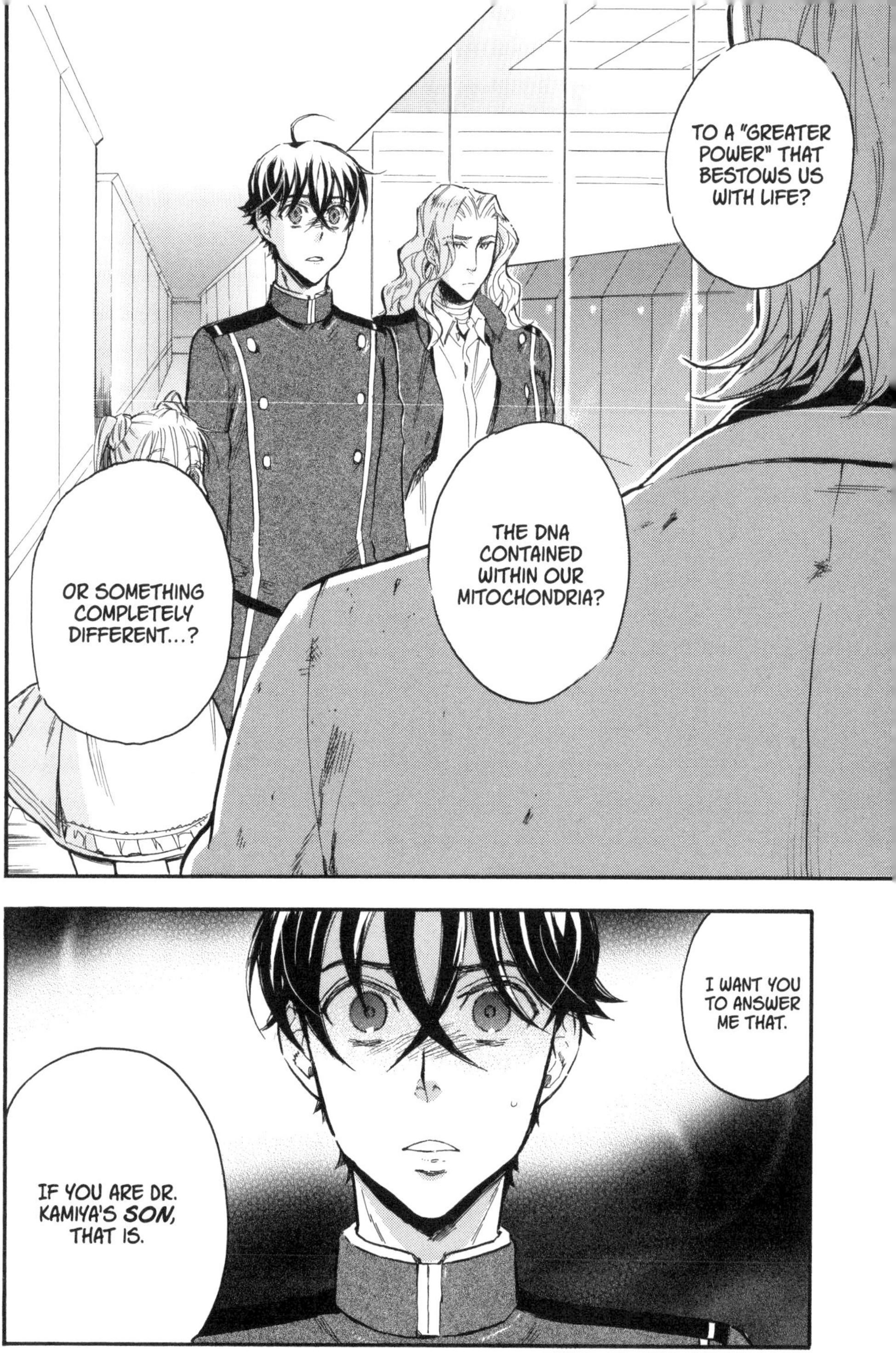
TO A "GREATER POWER" THAT BESTOWS US WITH LIFE?
THE DNA CONTAINED WITHIN OUR MITOCHONDRIA?
OR SOMETHING COMPLETELY DIFFERENT...?
I WANT YOU TO ANSWER ME THAT.
IF YOU ARE DR. KAMIYA'S *SON*, THAT IS.

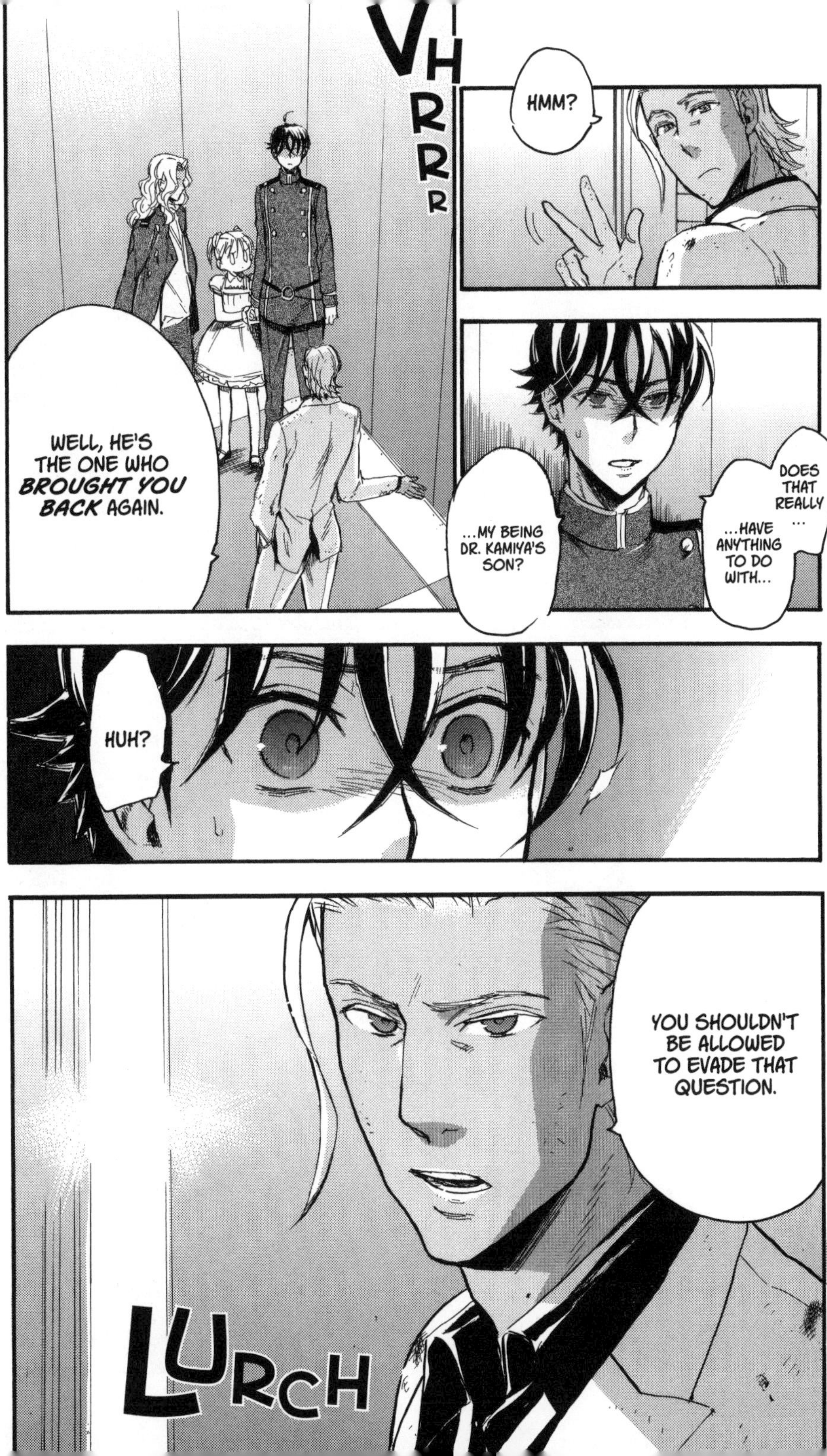
HMM?
DOES THAT REALLY ...
...HAVE ANYTHING TO DO WITH...
...MY BEING DR. KAMIYA'S SON?
VHRRR
WELL, HE'S THE ONE WHO *BROUGHT YOU BACK* AGAIN.
HUH?
YOU SHOULDN'T BE ALLOWED TO EVADE THAT QUESTION.
LURCH

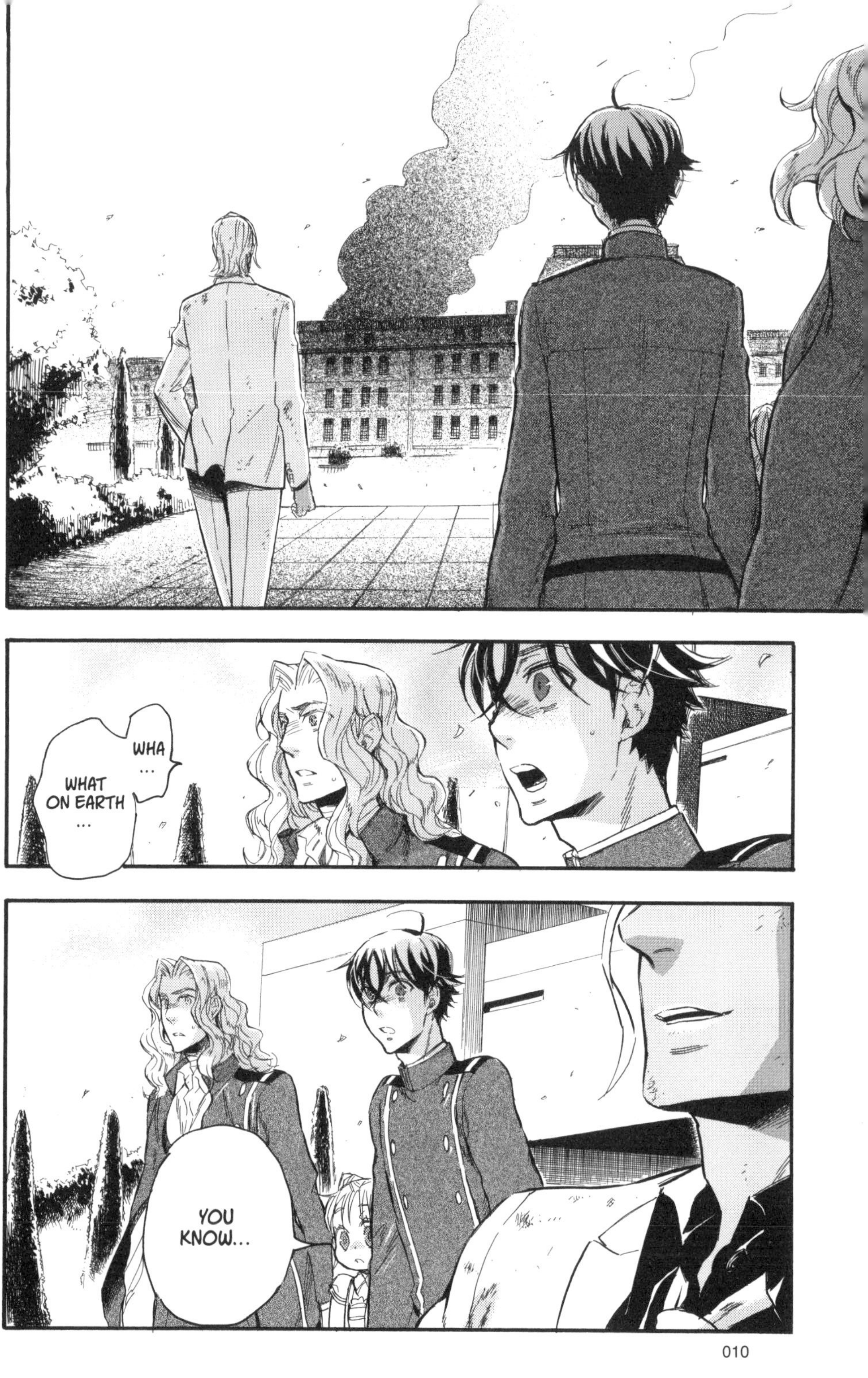
WHA ...
WHAT ON EARTH ...
YOU KNOW...

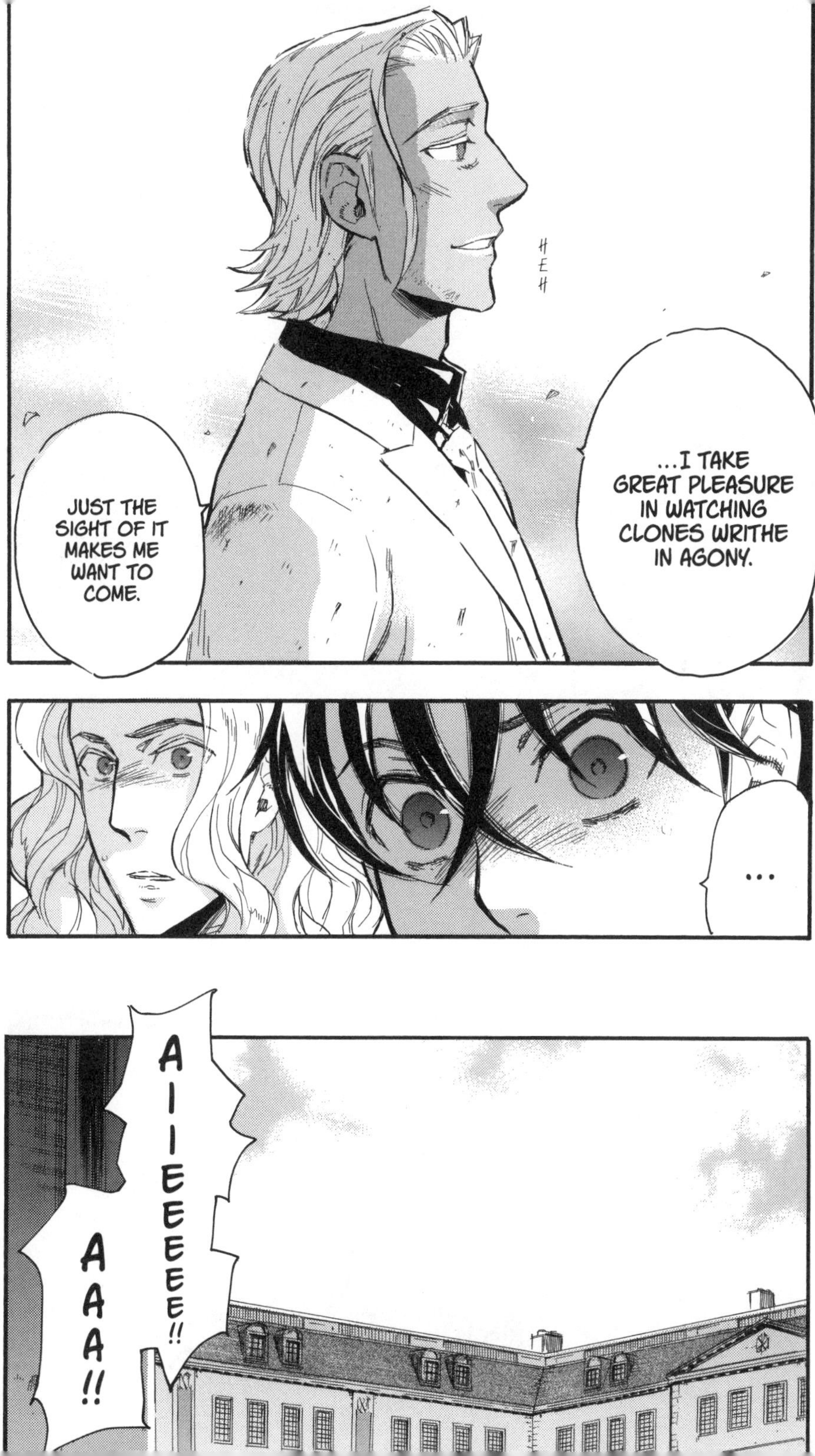
HEH
...I TAKE GREAT PLEASURE IN WATCHING CLONES WRITHE IN AGONY.
JUST THE SIGHT OF IT MAKES ME WANT TO COME.
...
AIIEEEEEE!!
AAAA!!

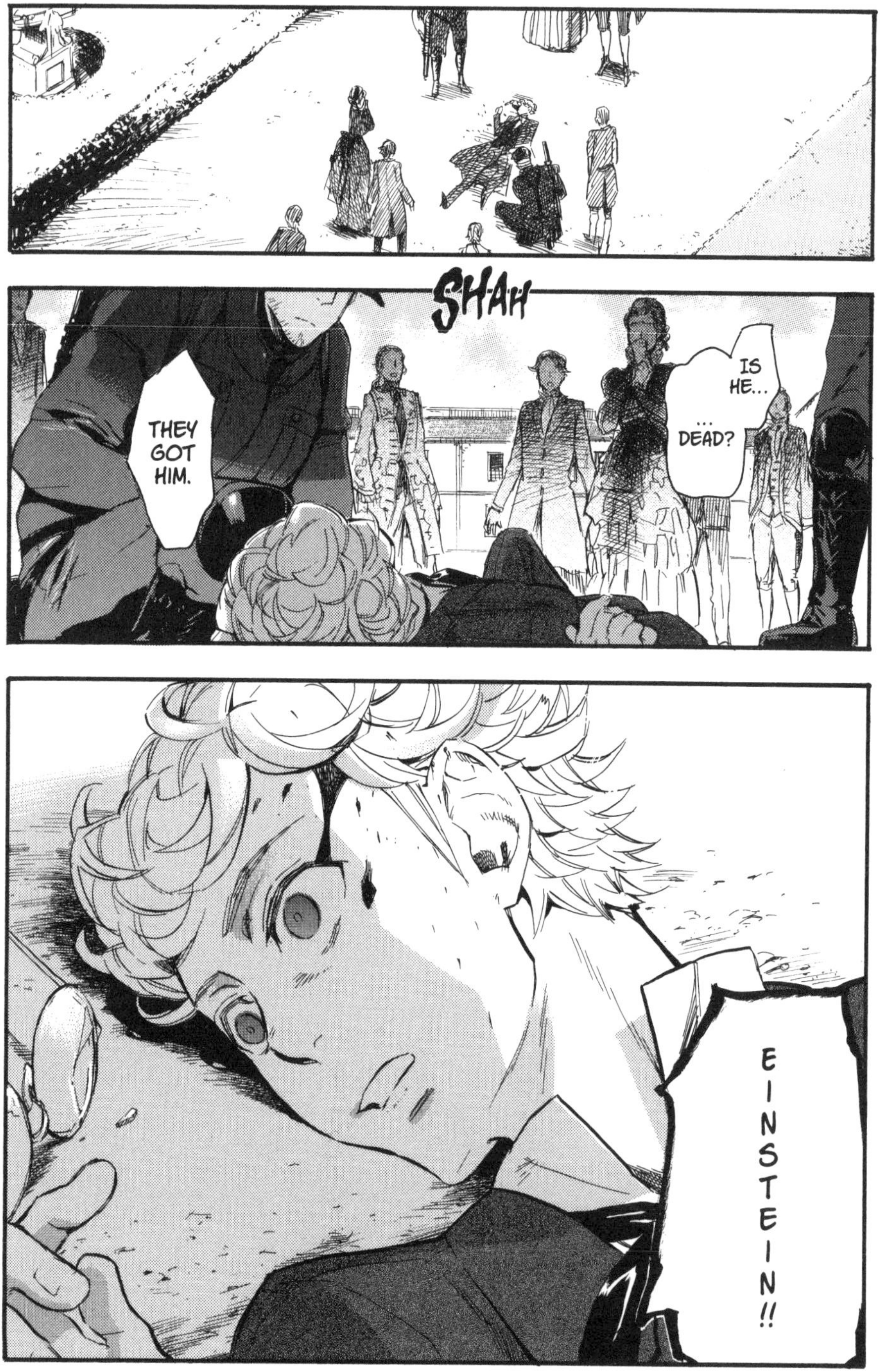
SHAH
IS HE... ...DEAD?
THEY GOT HIM.
EINSTEIN!!

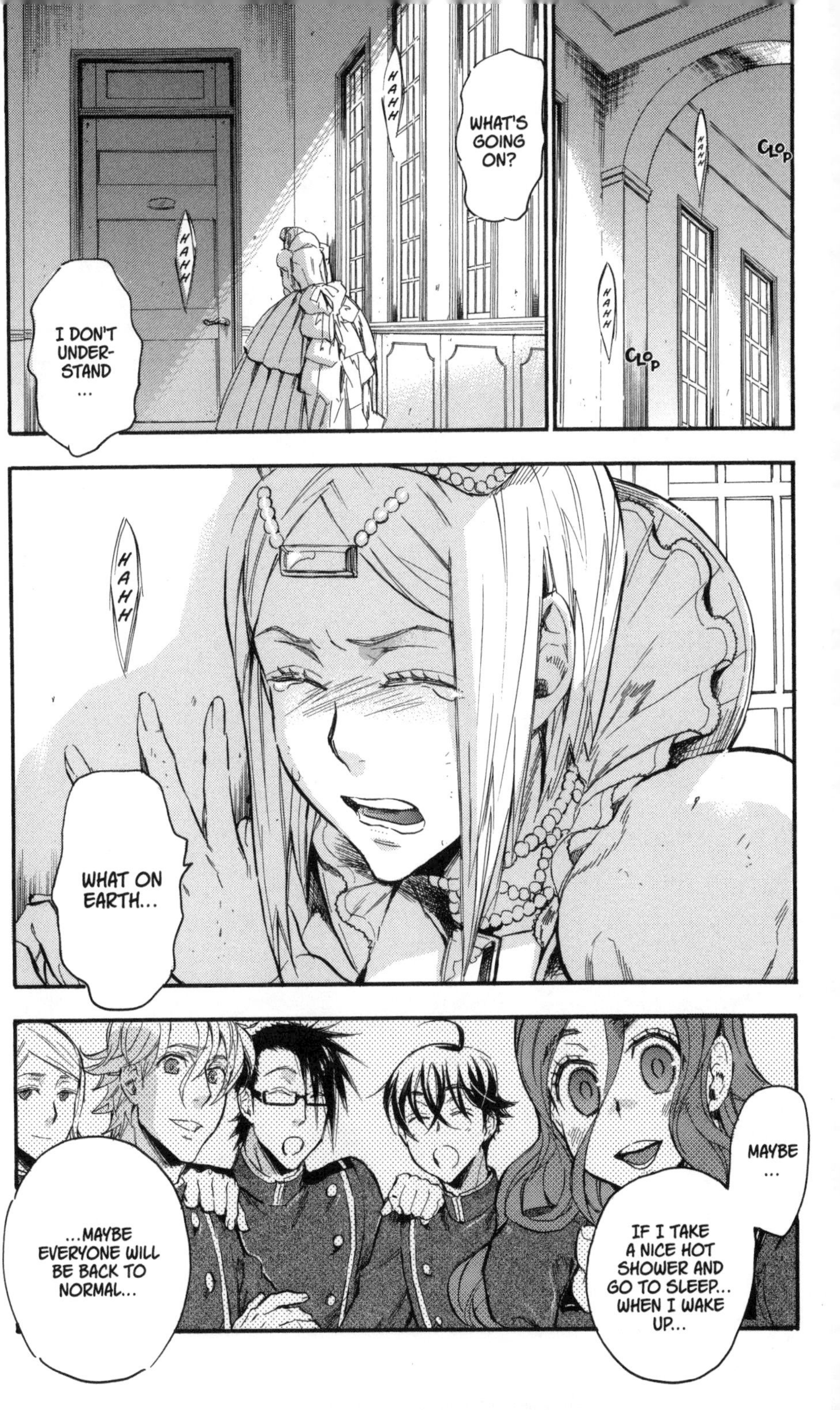
HAHH
CLOP
HAHH
CLOP
WHAT'S GOING ON?
HAHH
HAHH
I DON'T UNDER-STAND...
HAHH
WHAT ON EARTH...
MAYBE...
IF I TAKE A NICE HOT SHOWER AND GO TO SLEEP... WHEN I WAKE UP...
...MAYBE EVERYONE WILL BE BACK TO NORMAL...

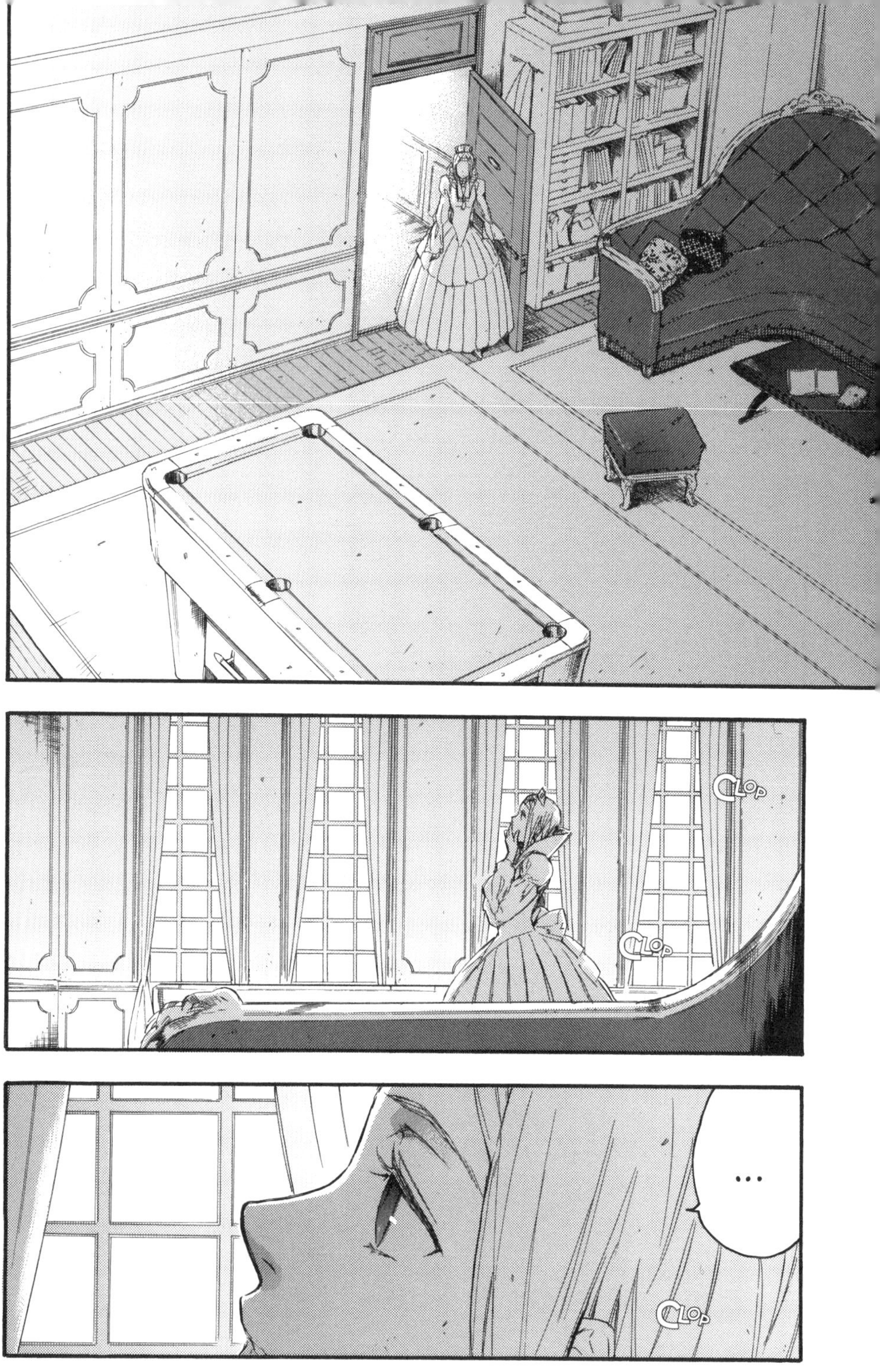
CLOP
CLOP
...
CLOP

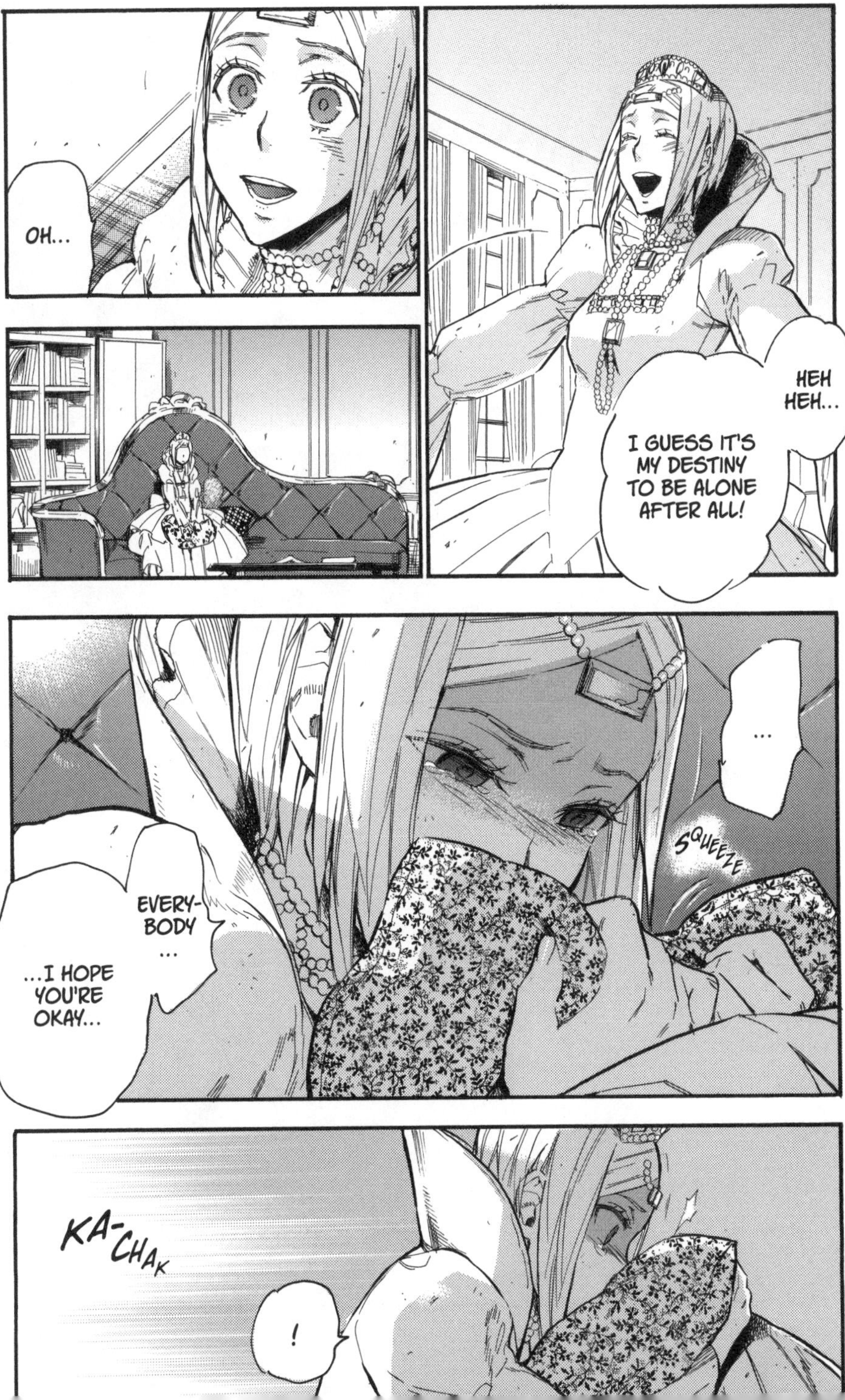
HEH HEH...
I GUESS IT'S MY DESTINY TO BE ALONE AFTER ALL!
OH...
...
SQUEEZE
EVERY-BODY ...
...I HOPE YOU'RE OKAY...
KA-CHAK
!

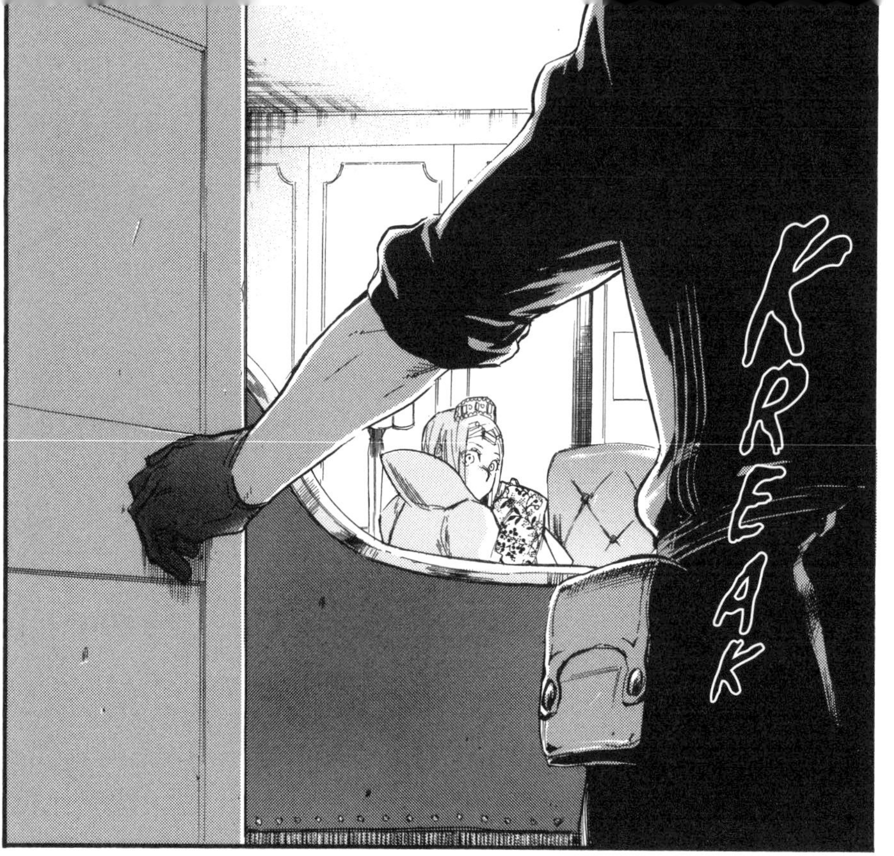
KREAK
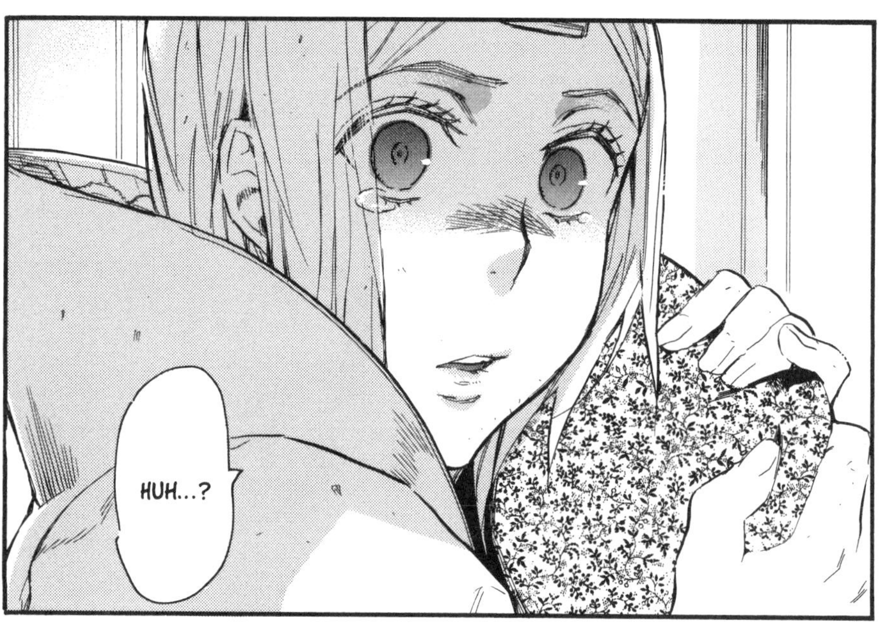
HUH...?

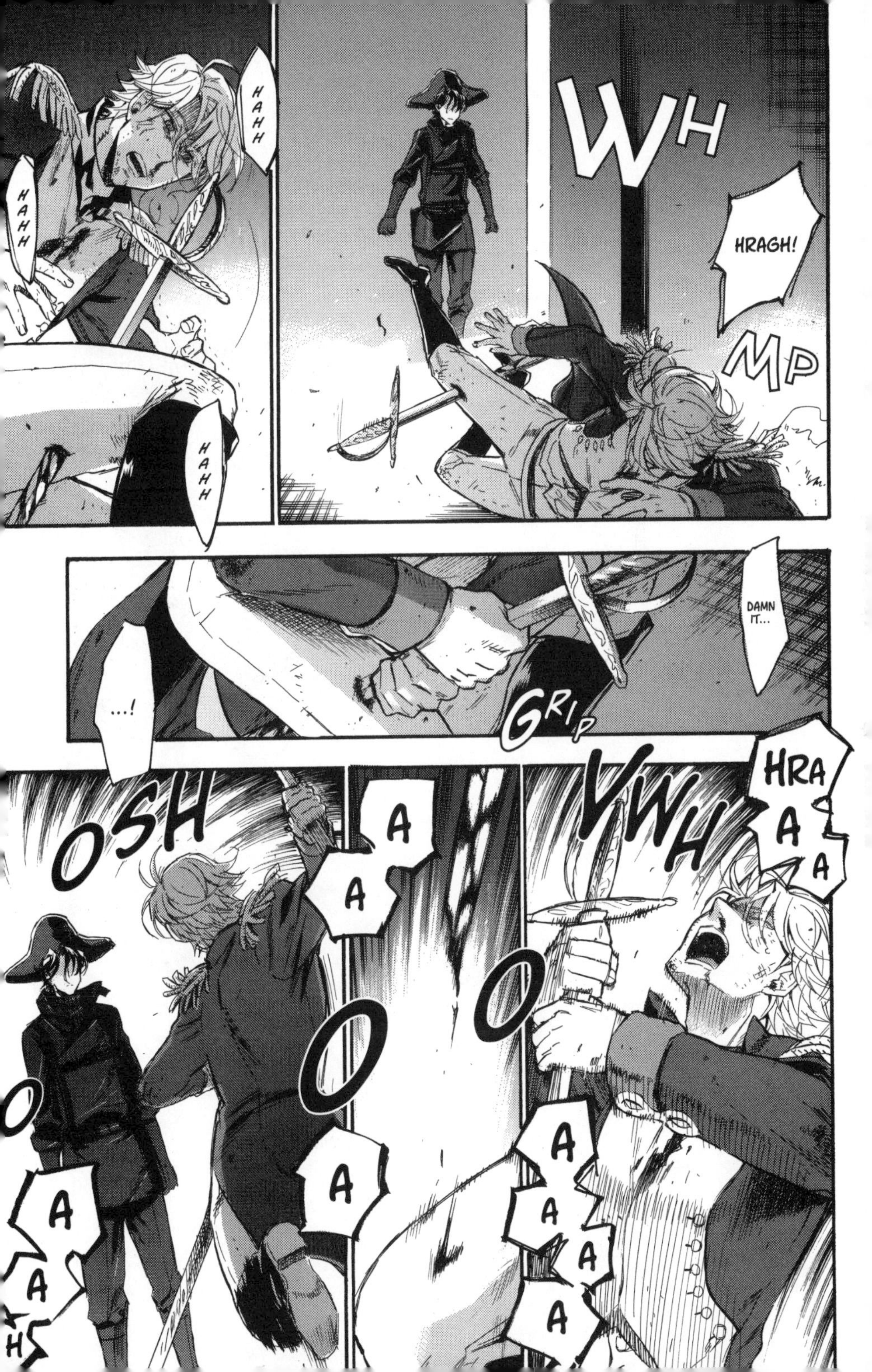
WH
HRAGH!
MP
HAHH
HAHH
HAHH
DAMN IT...
GRIP
...!
HRA A A
VWH
O
A
A
A
A
A
A
A
O
A
OSH
O
A
A
H

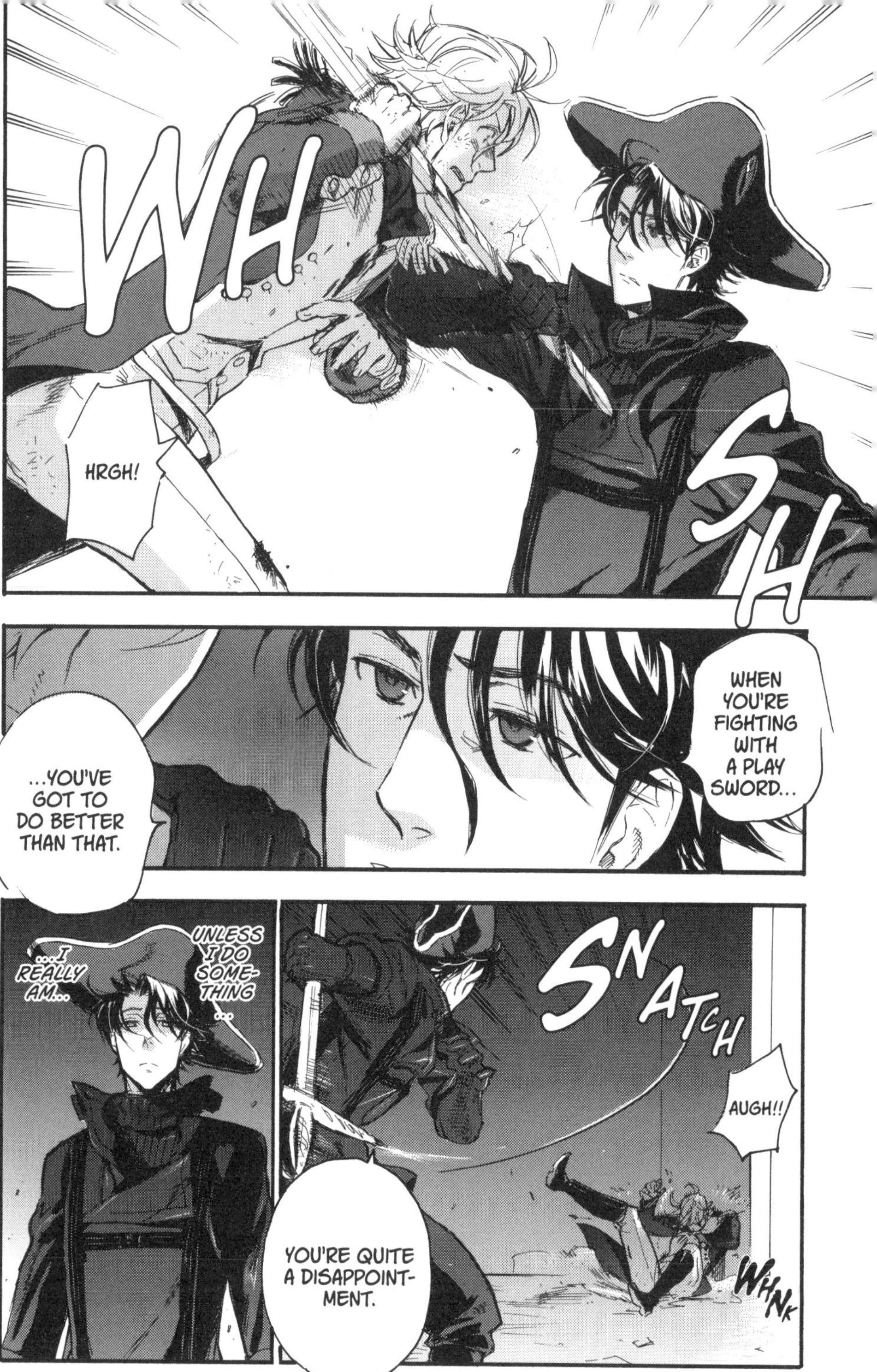
WH
SH
HRGH!
WHEN YOU'RE FIGHTING WITH A PLAY SWORD...
...YOU'VE GOT TO DO BETTER THAN THAT.
SNATCH
AUGH!!
YOU'RE QUITE A DISAPPOINT-MENT.
WHNK
UNLESS I DO SOME-THING...
...I REALLY AM...

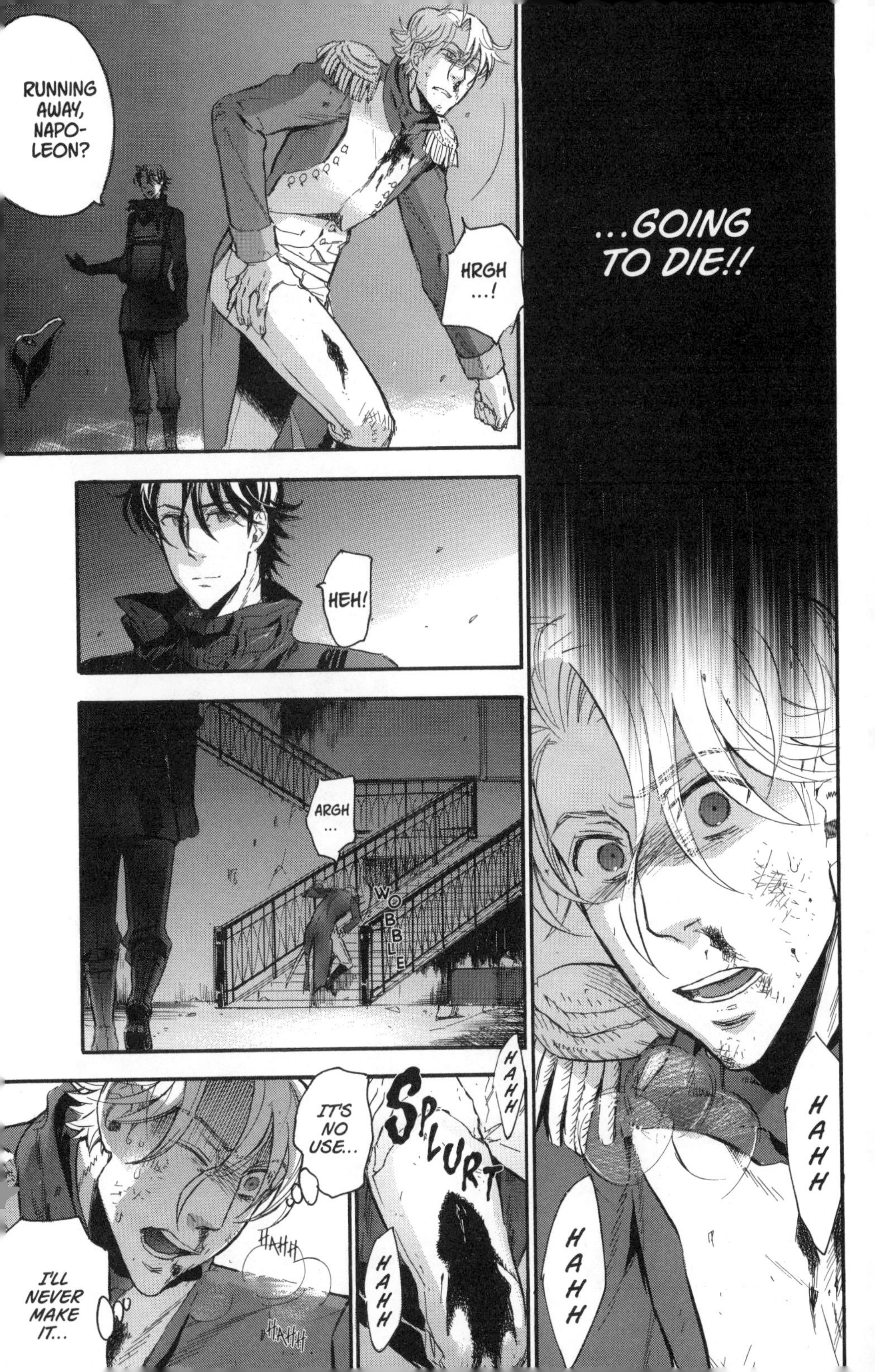
...GOING TO DIE!!
HAHH
HAHH
HRGH ...!
RUNNING AWAY, NAPO-LEON?
HEH!
ARGH ...
WOBBLE
HAHH
SPLURT
HAHH
IT'S NO USE...
HAHH
I'LL NEVER MAKE IT...
HAHH

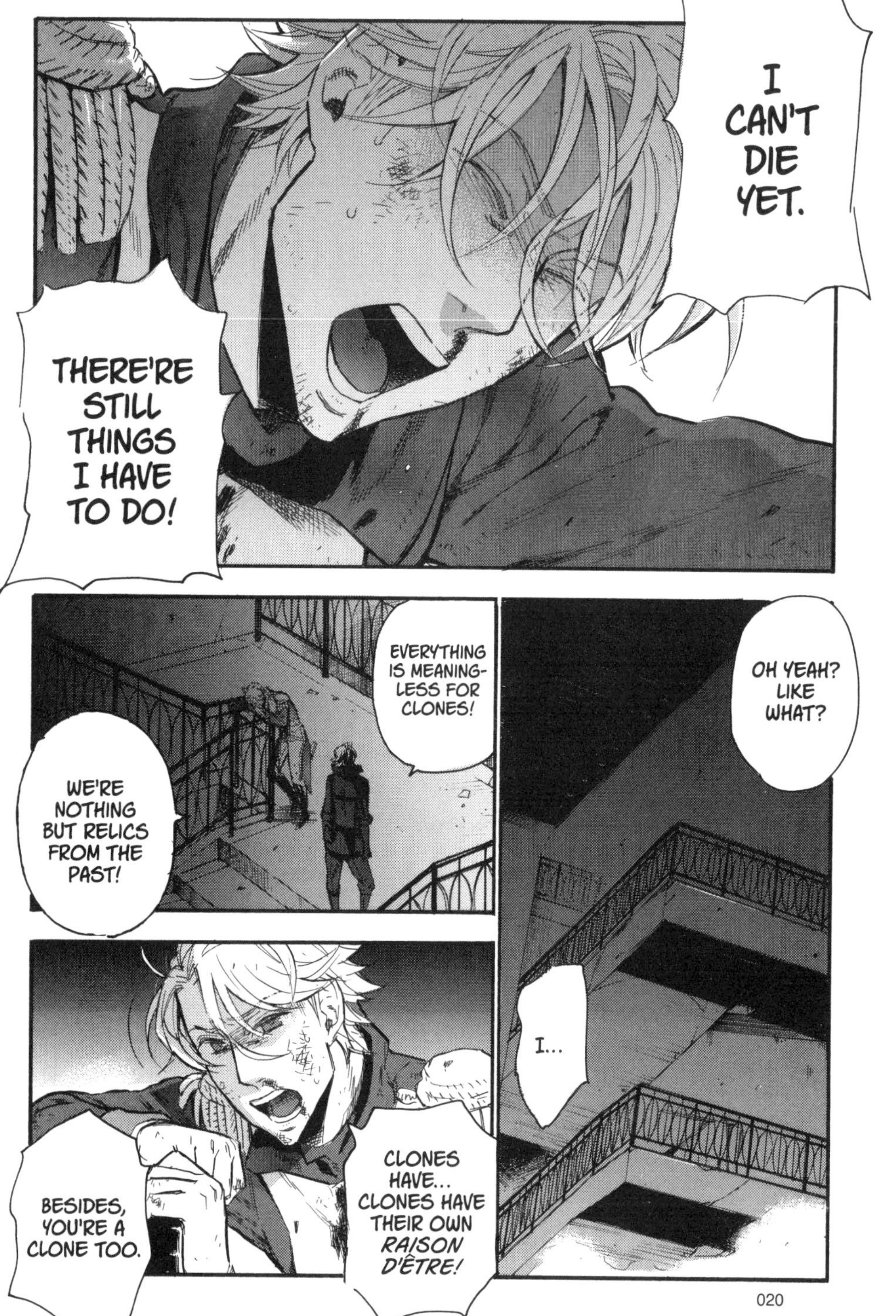
I CAN'T DIE YET.
THERE'RE STILL THINGS I HAVE TO DO!
OH YEAH? LIKE WHAT?
I...
EVERYTHING IS MEANING-LESS FOR CLONES!
WE'RE NOTHING BUT RELICS FROM THE PAST!
CLONES HAVE... CLONES HAVE THEIR OWN *RAISON D'ÊTRE!*
BESIDES, YOU'RE A CLONE TOO.

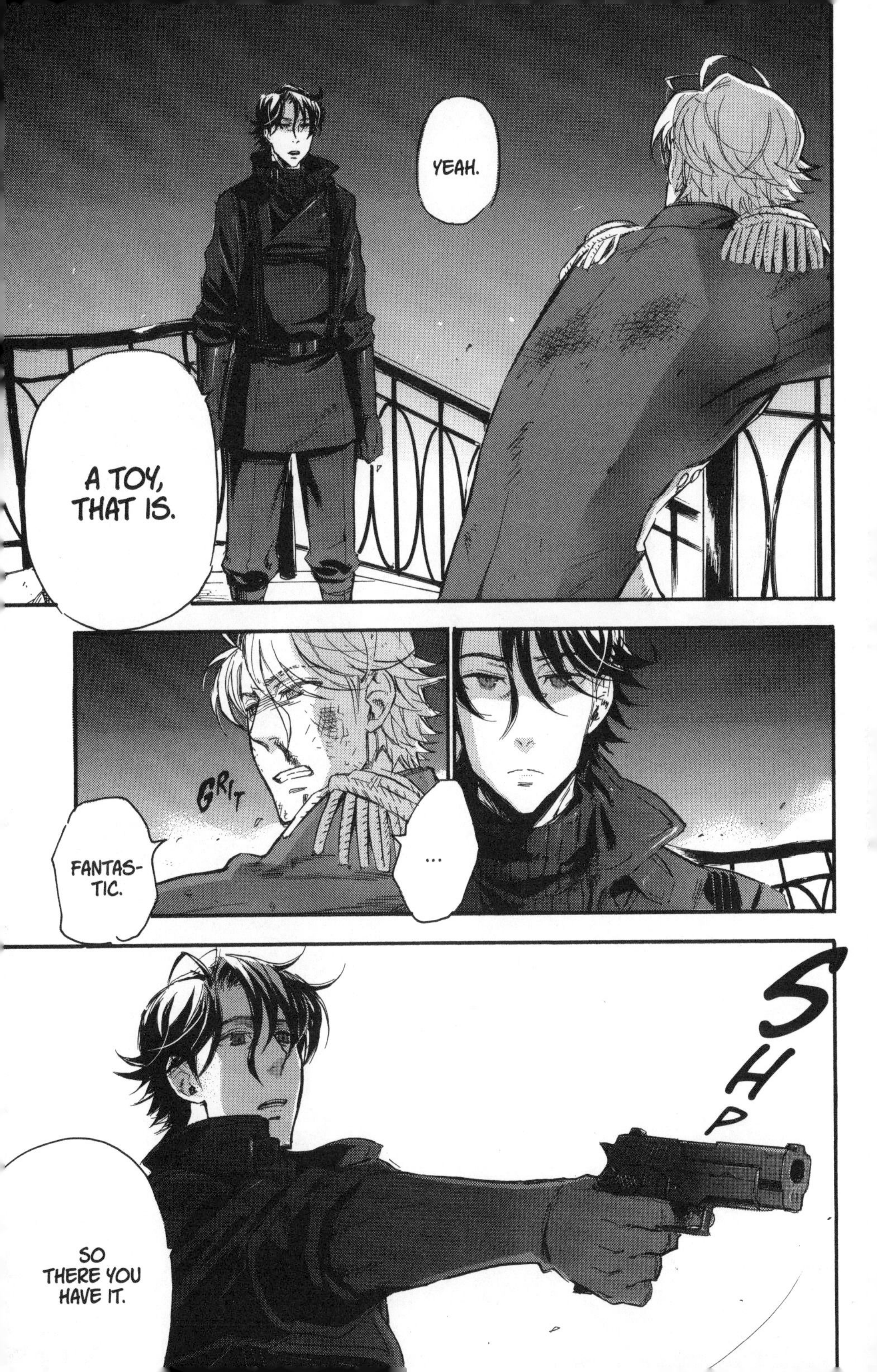
YEAH.
A TOY, THAT IS.
...
GRIT
FANTAS-TIC.
SHP
SO THERE YOU HAVE IT.

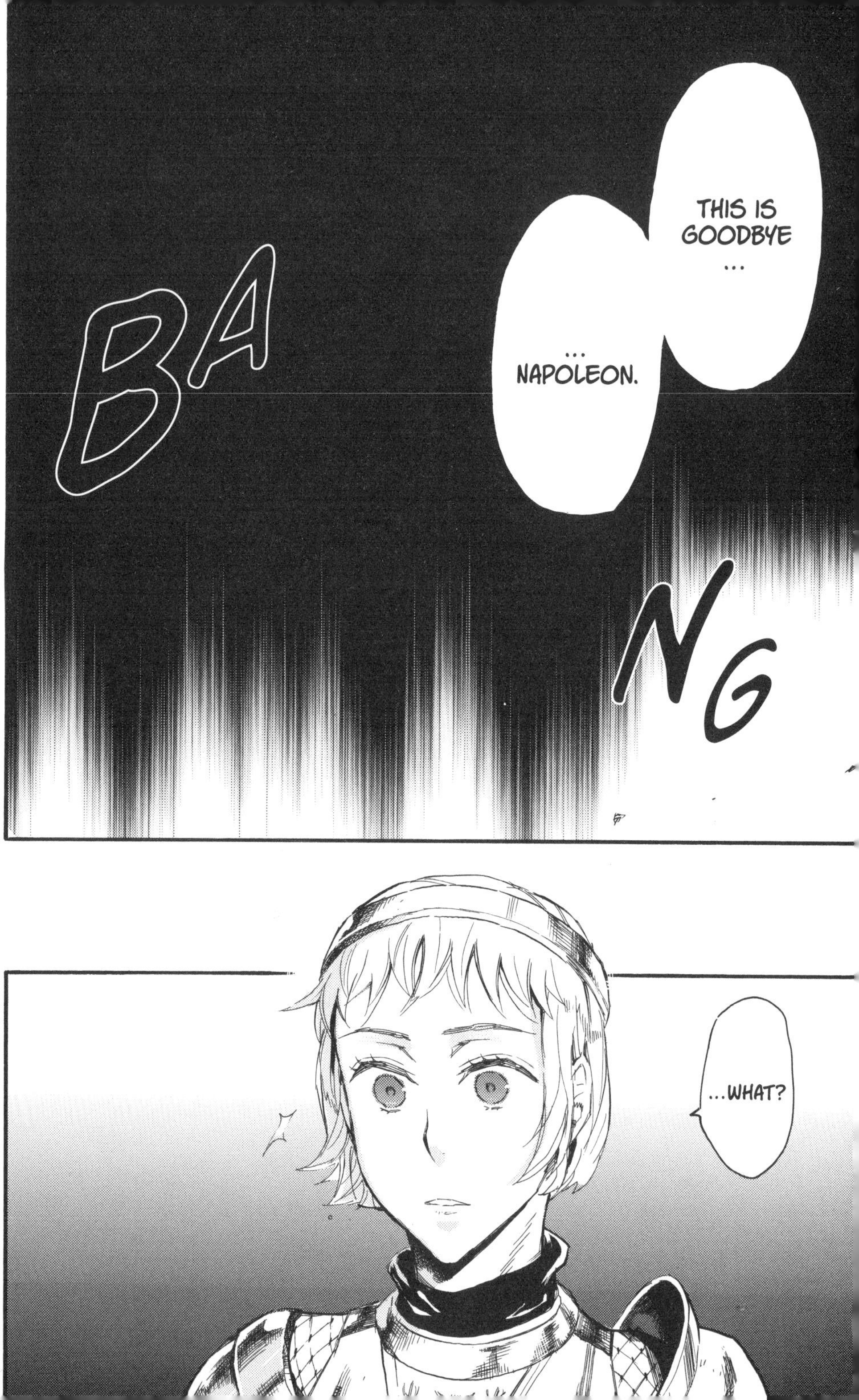
THIS IS GOODBYE ...
... NAPOLEON.
BANG
...WHAT?

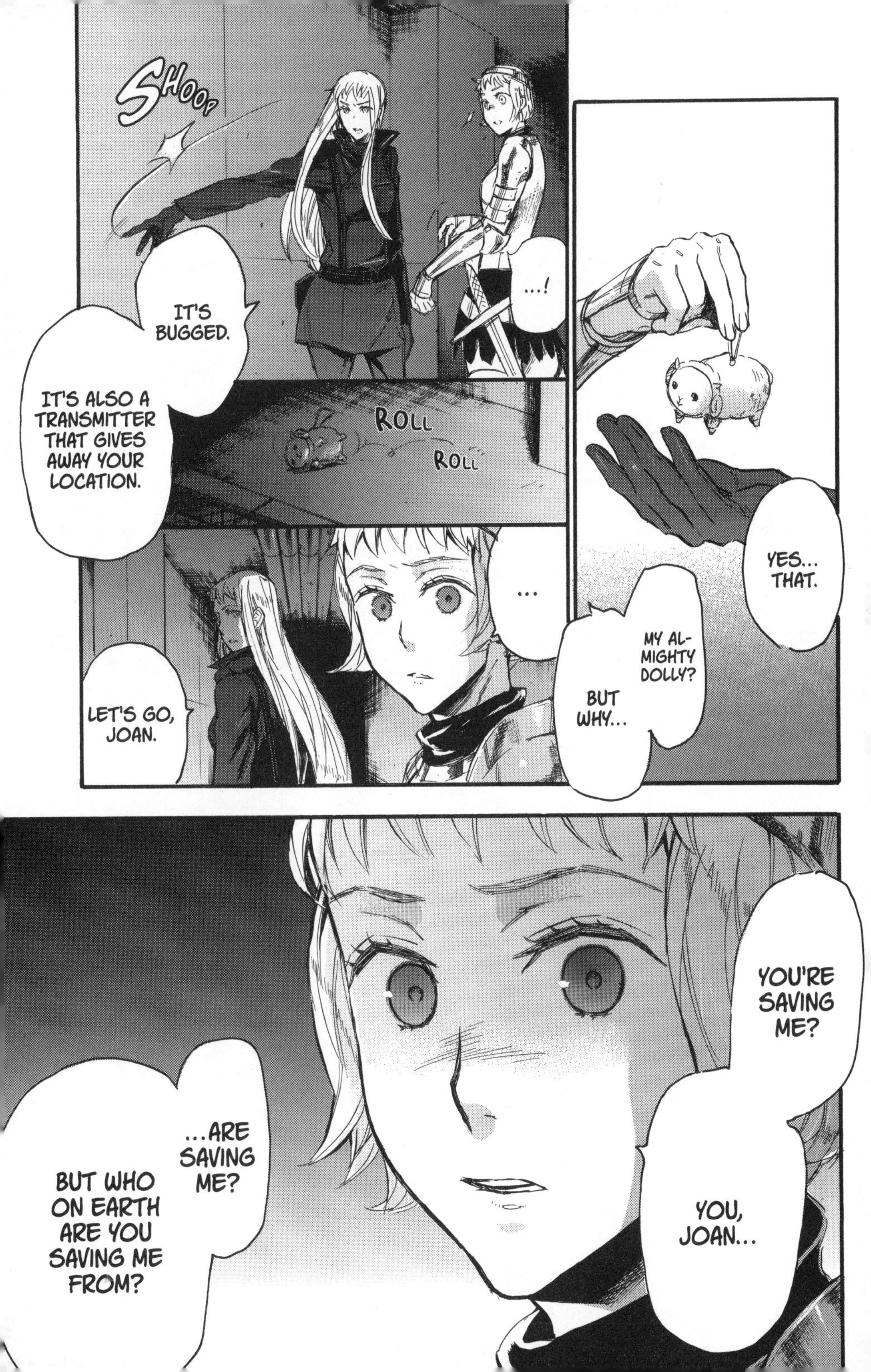
YES... THAT.
MY AL-MIGHTY DOLLY?
BUT WHY...
SHOOP
IT'S BUGGED.
...!
IT'S ALSO A TRANSMITTER THAT GIVES AWAY YOUR LOCATION.
ROLL
ROLL
...
LET'S GO, JOAN.
YOU'RE SAVING ME?
YOU, JOAN...
...ARE SAVING ME?
BUT WHO ON EARTH ARE YOU SAVING ME FROM?

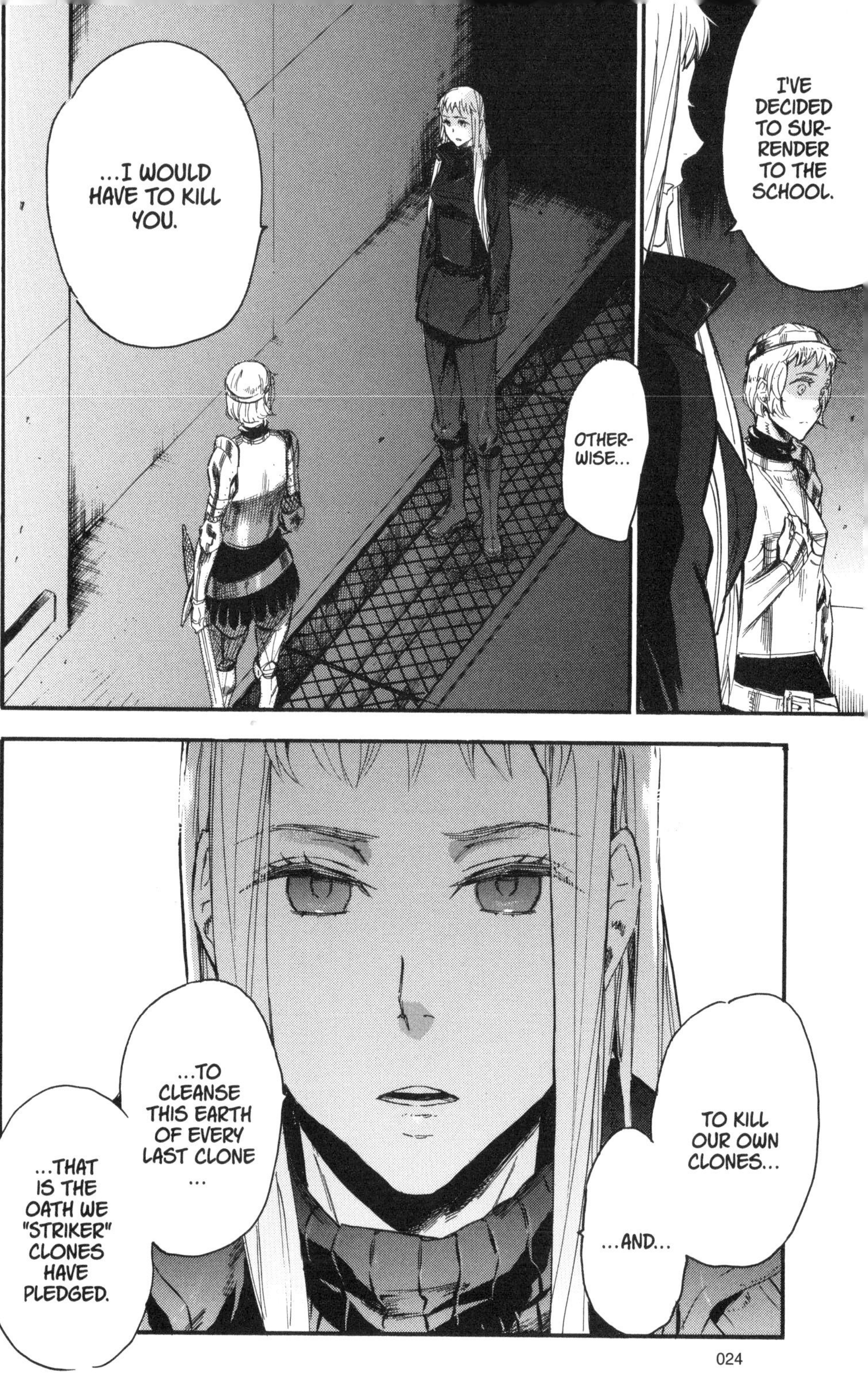
I'VE DECIDED TO SUR-RENDER TO THE SCHOOL.
OTHER-WISE...
...I WOULD HAVE TO KILL YOU.
TO KILL OUR OWN CLONES...
...AND...
...TO CLEANSE THIS EARTH OF EVERY LAST CLONE ...
...THAT IS THE OATH WE "STRIKER" CLONES HAVE PLEDGED.

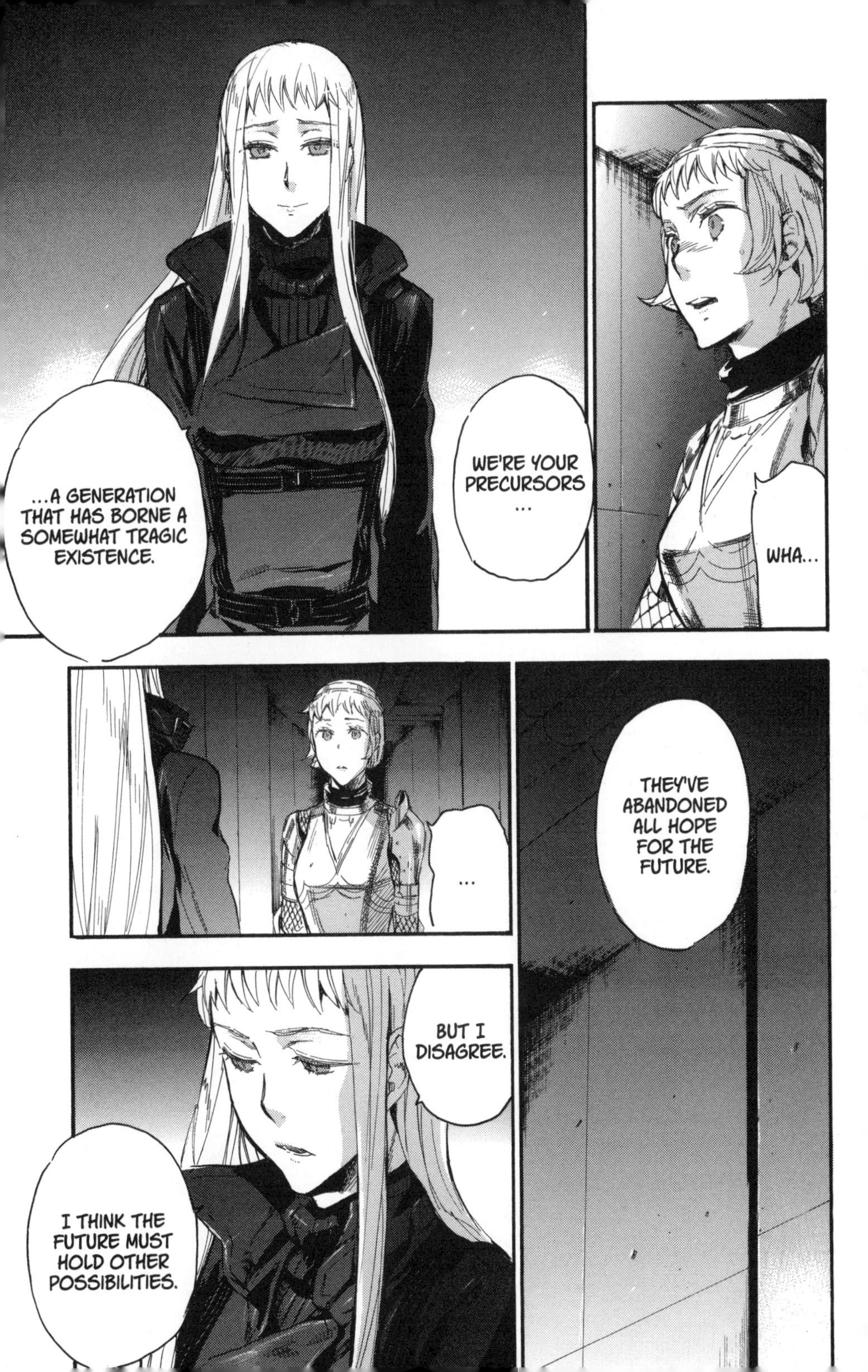
WHA...
WE'RE YOUR PRECURSORS ...
...A GENERATION THAT HAS BORNE A SOMEWHAT TRAGIC EXISTENCE.
THEY'VE ABANDONED ALL HOPE FOR THE FUTURE.
...
BUT I DISAGREE.
I THINK THE FUTURE MUST HOLD OTHER POSSIBILITIES.

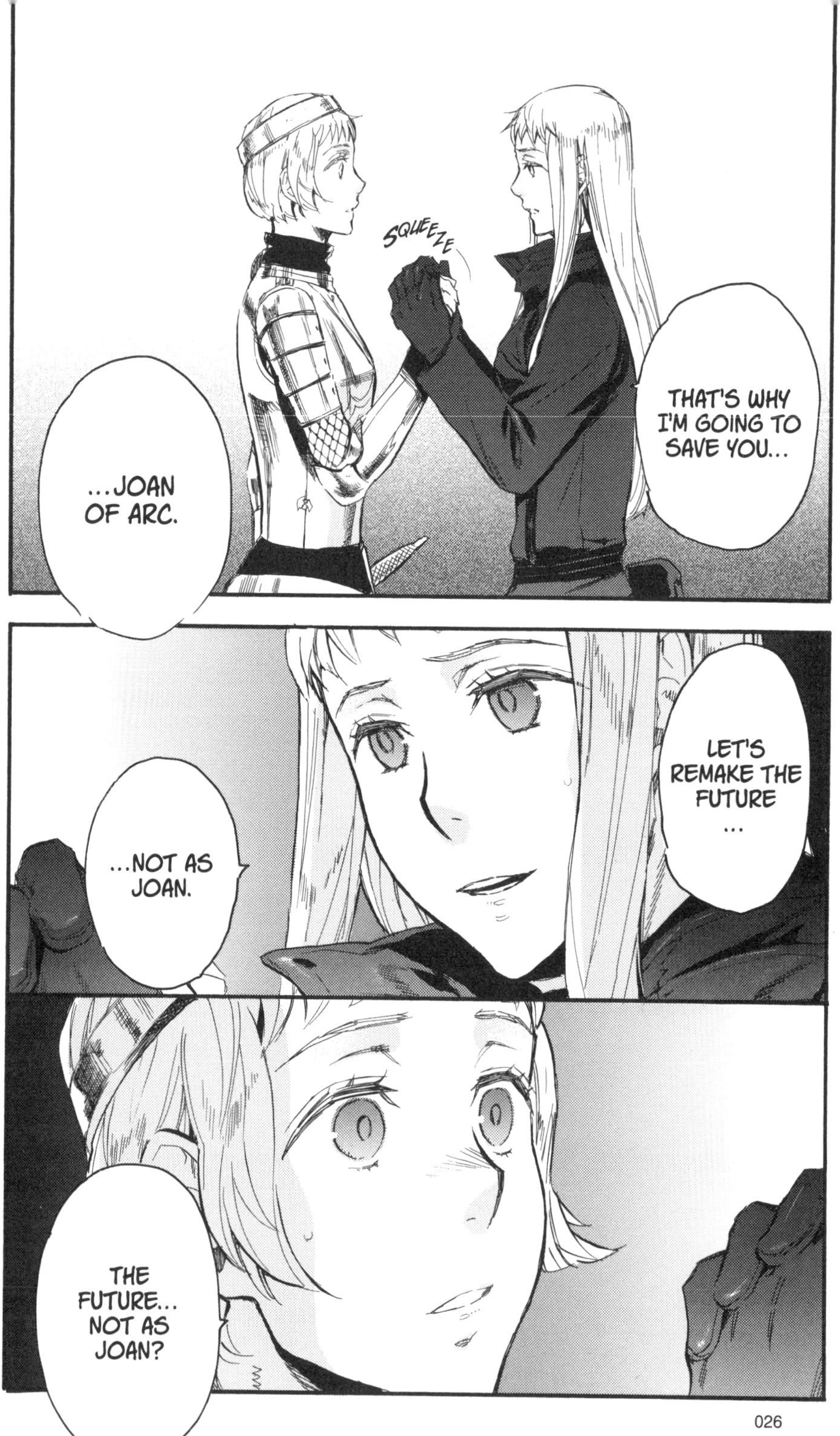
SQUEEZE
THAT'S WHY I'M GOING TO SAVE YOU...
...JOAN OF ARC.
LET'S REMAKE THE FUTURE ...
...NOT AS JOAN.
THE FUTURE... NOT AS JOAN?

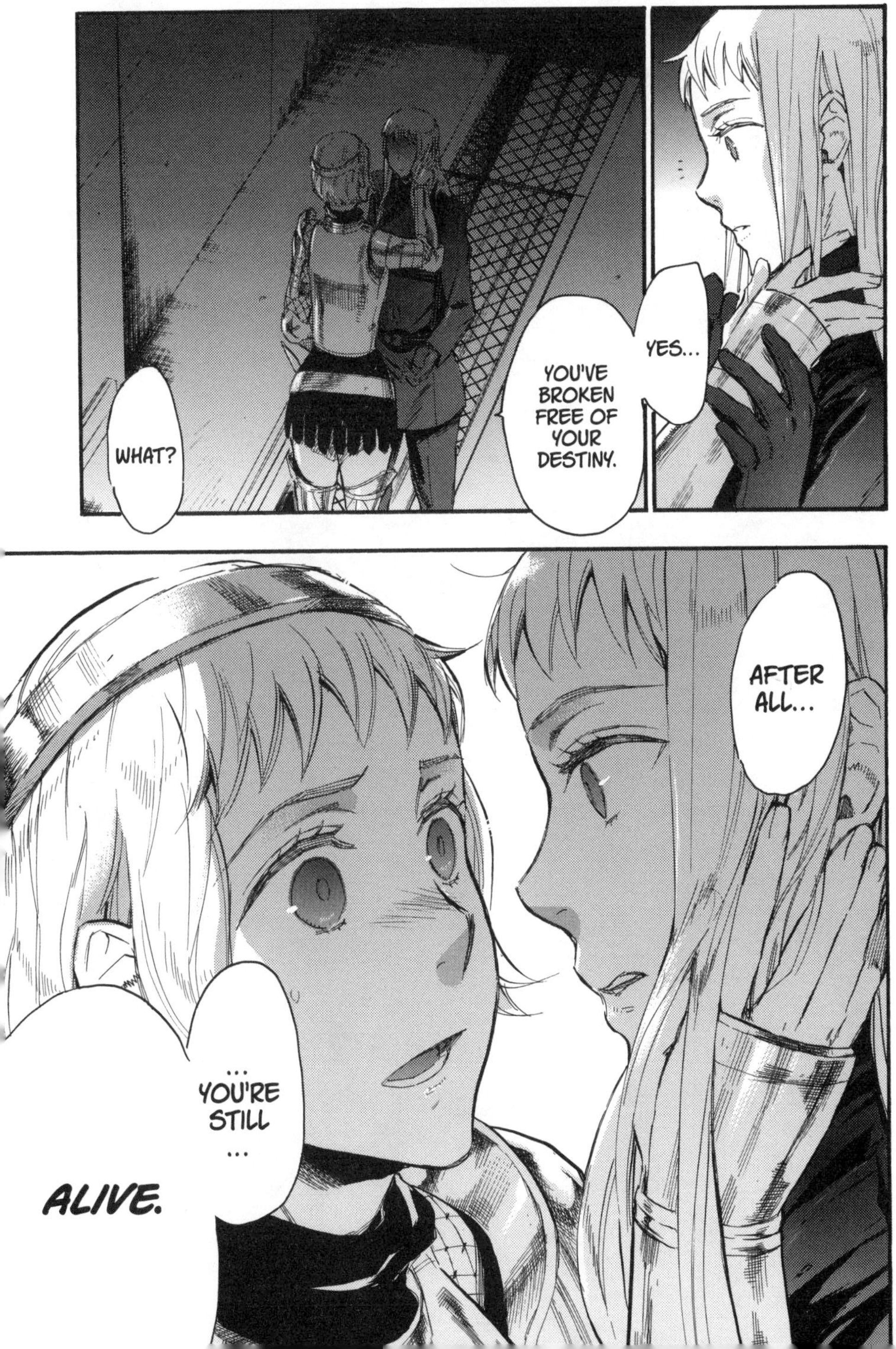
YES…
YOU'VE BROKEN FREE OF YOUR DESTINY.
WHAT?
AFTER ALL…
… YOU'RE STILL …
ALIVE.

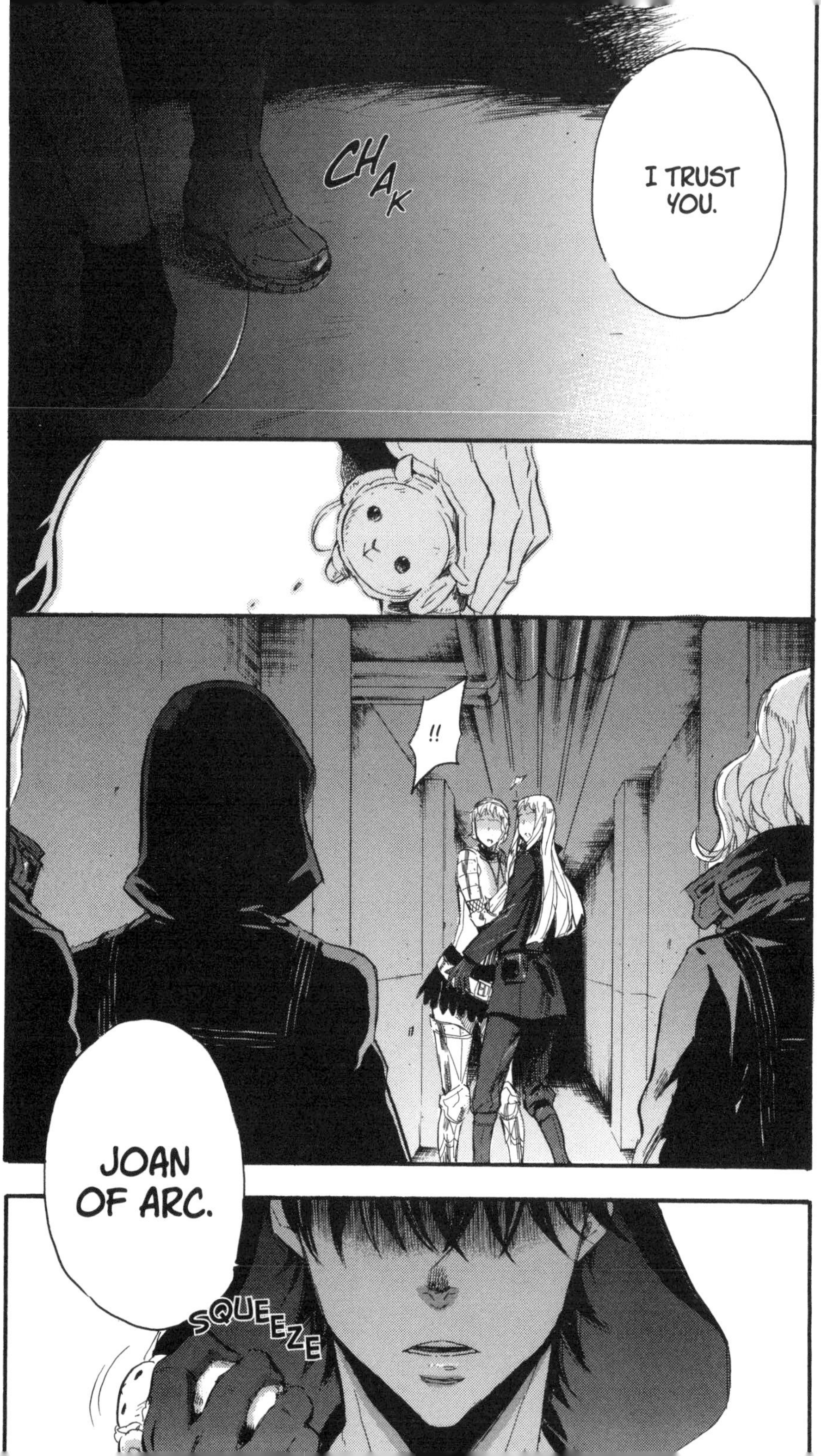
I TRUST YOU.
CHAK
!!
JOAN OF ARC.
SQUEEZE

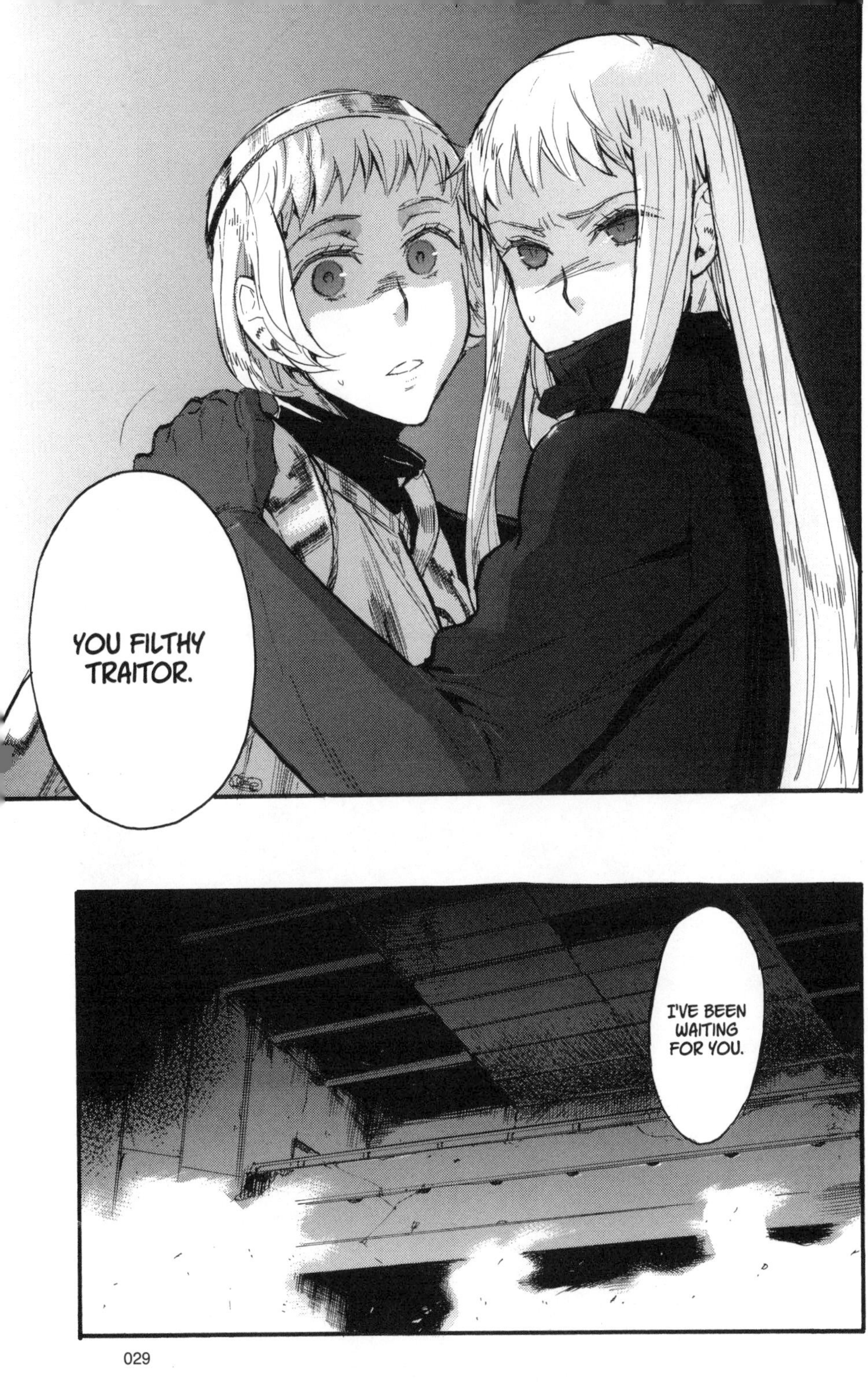
YOU FILTHY TRAITOR.
I'VE BEEN WAITING FOR YOU.

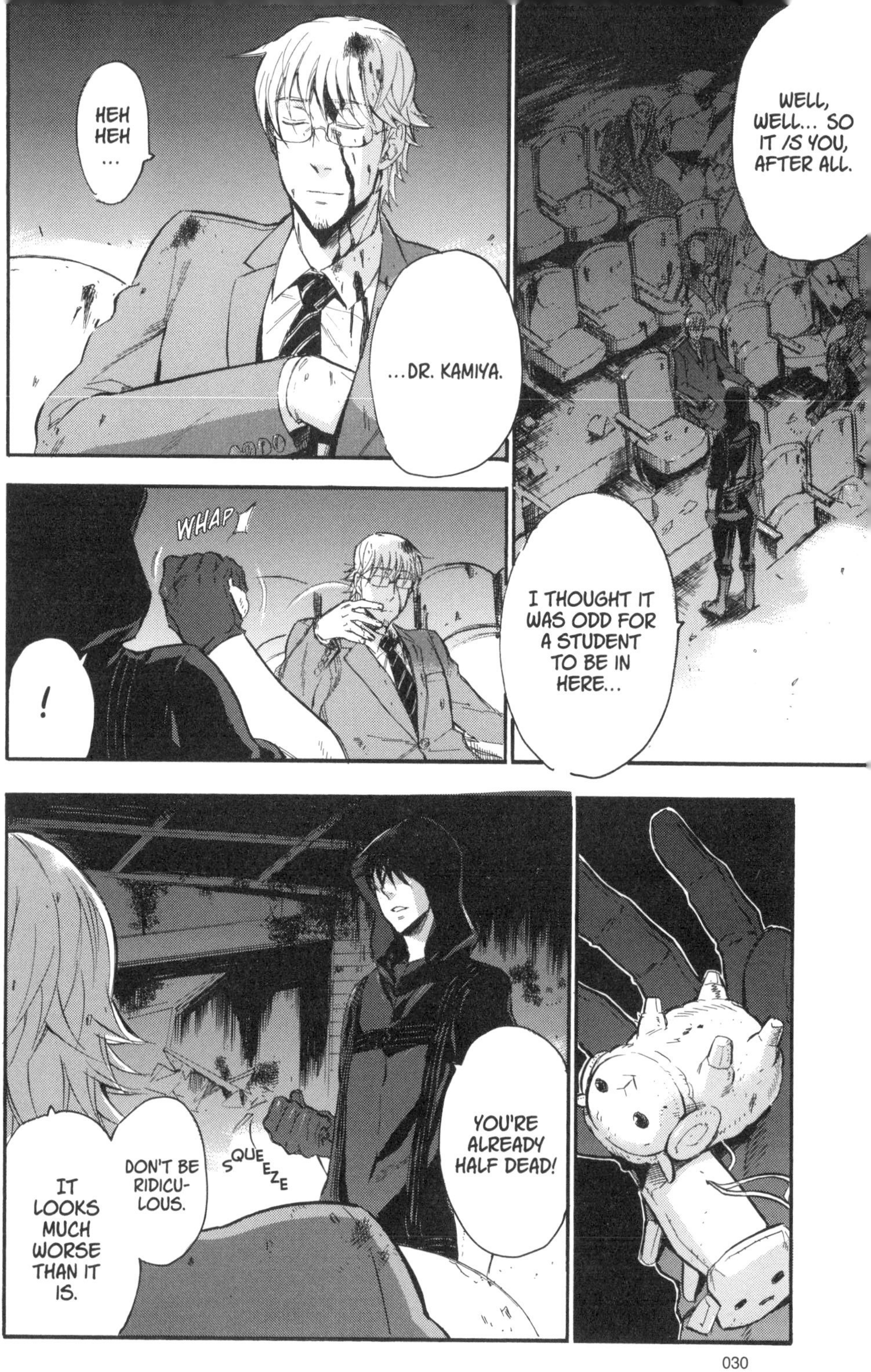
WELL, WELL... SO IT IS YOU, AFTER ALL.
I THOUGHT IT WAS ODD FOR A STUDENT TO BE IN HERE...
HEH HEH ...
...DR. KAMIYA.
WHAP
!
YOU'RE ALREADY HALF DEAD!
SQUEEZE
DON'T BE RIDICU-LOUS.
IT LOOKS MUCH WORSE THAN IT IS.

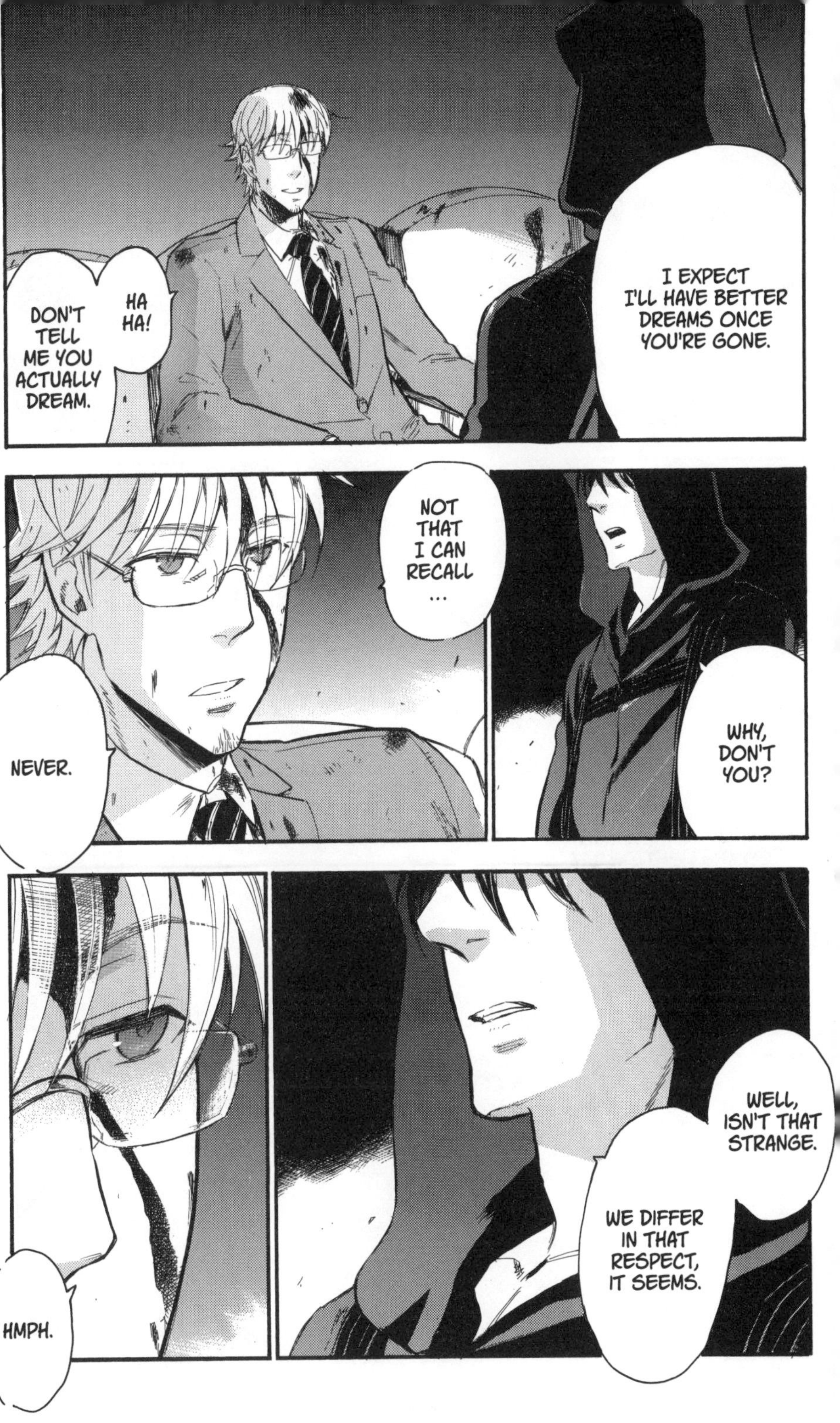
I EXPECT I'LL HAVE BETTER DREAMS ONCE YOU'RE GONE.
HA HA!
DON'T TELL ME YOU ACTUALLY DREAM.
WHY, DON'T YOU?
NOT THAT I CAN RECALL...
NEVER.
WELL, ISN'T THAT STRANGE.
WE DIFFER IN THAT RESPECT, IT SEEMS.
HMPH.

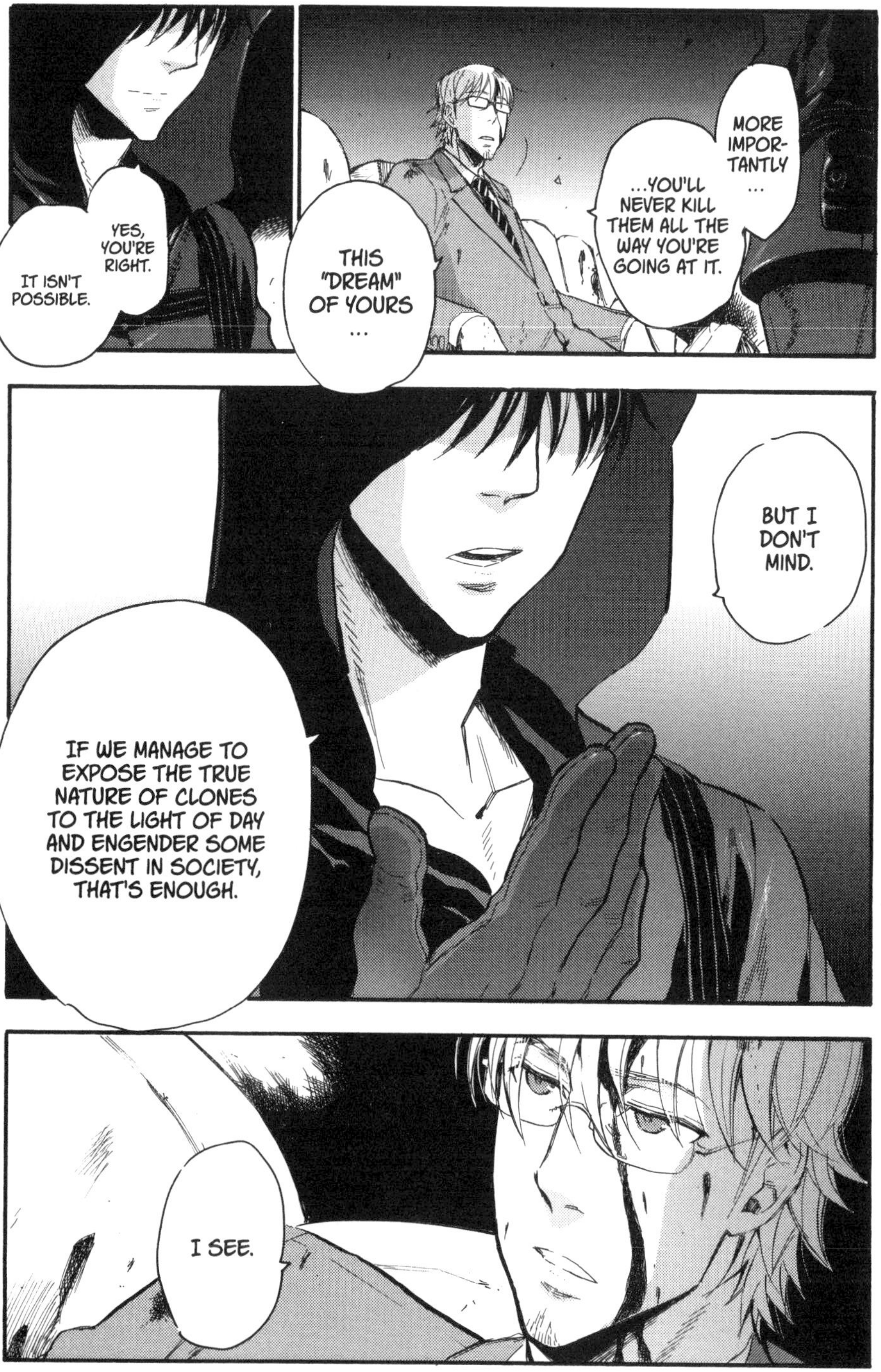
MORE IMPORTANTLY...
...YOU'LL NEVER KILL THEM ALL THE WAY YOU'RE GOING AT IT.
THIS "DREAM" OF YOURS...
YES, YOU'RE RIGHT.
IT ISN'T POSSIBLE.
BUT I DON'T MIND.
IF WE MANAGE TO EXPOSE THE TRUE NATURE OF CLONES TO THE LIGHT OF DAY AND ENGENDER SOME DISSENT IN SOCIETY, THAT'S ENOUGH.
I SEE.

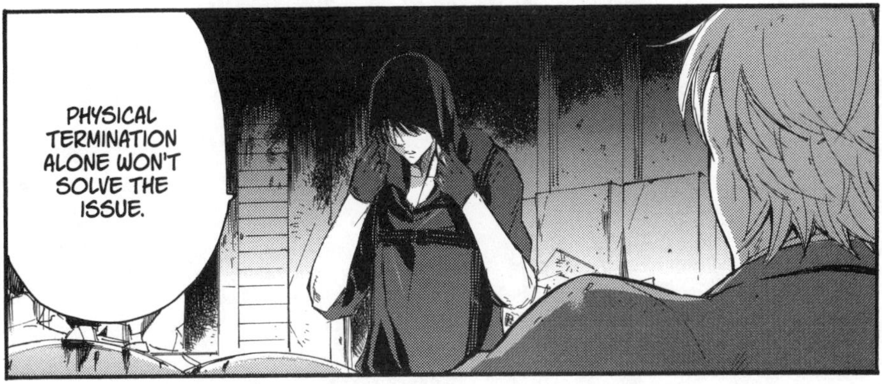
PHYSICAL TERMINATION ALONE WON'T SOLVE THE ISSUE.
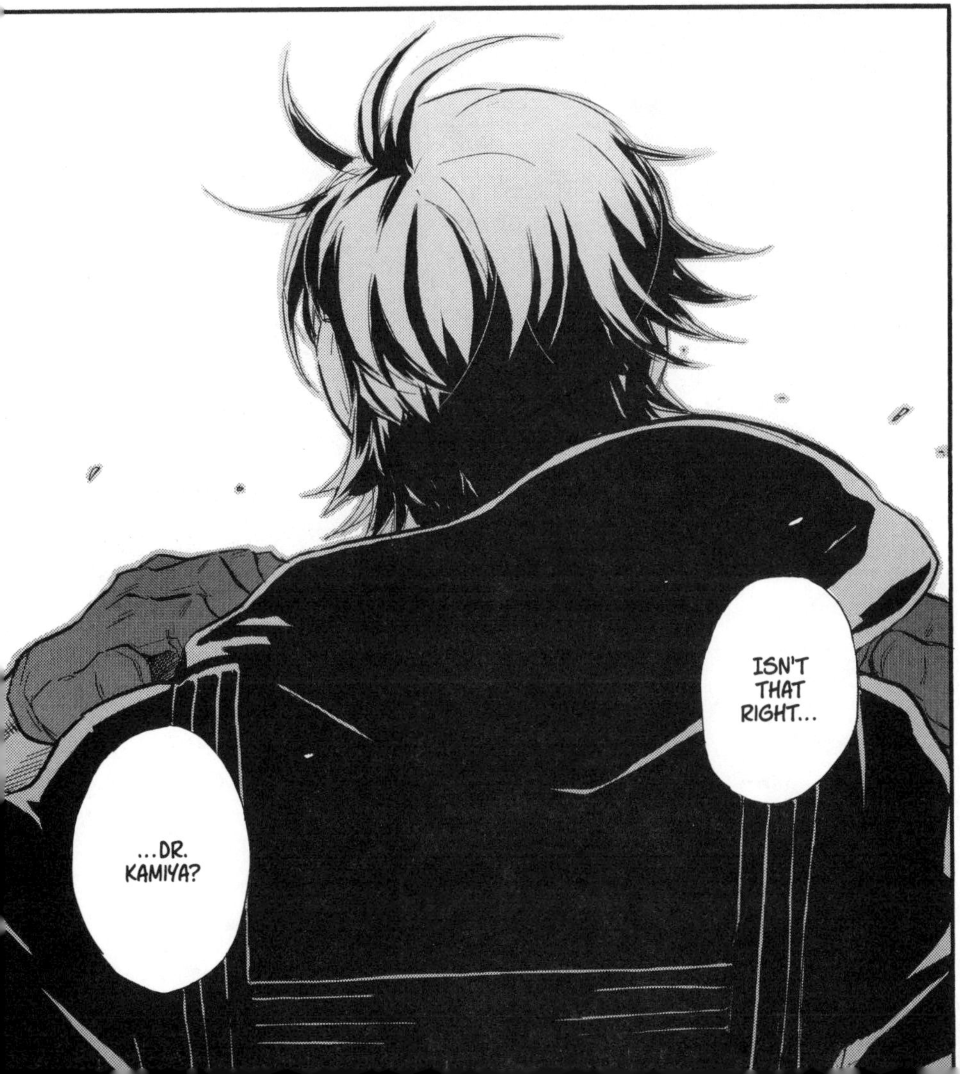
ISN'T THAT RIGHT...
...DR. KAMIYA?

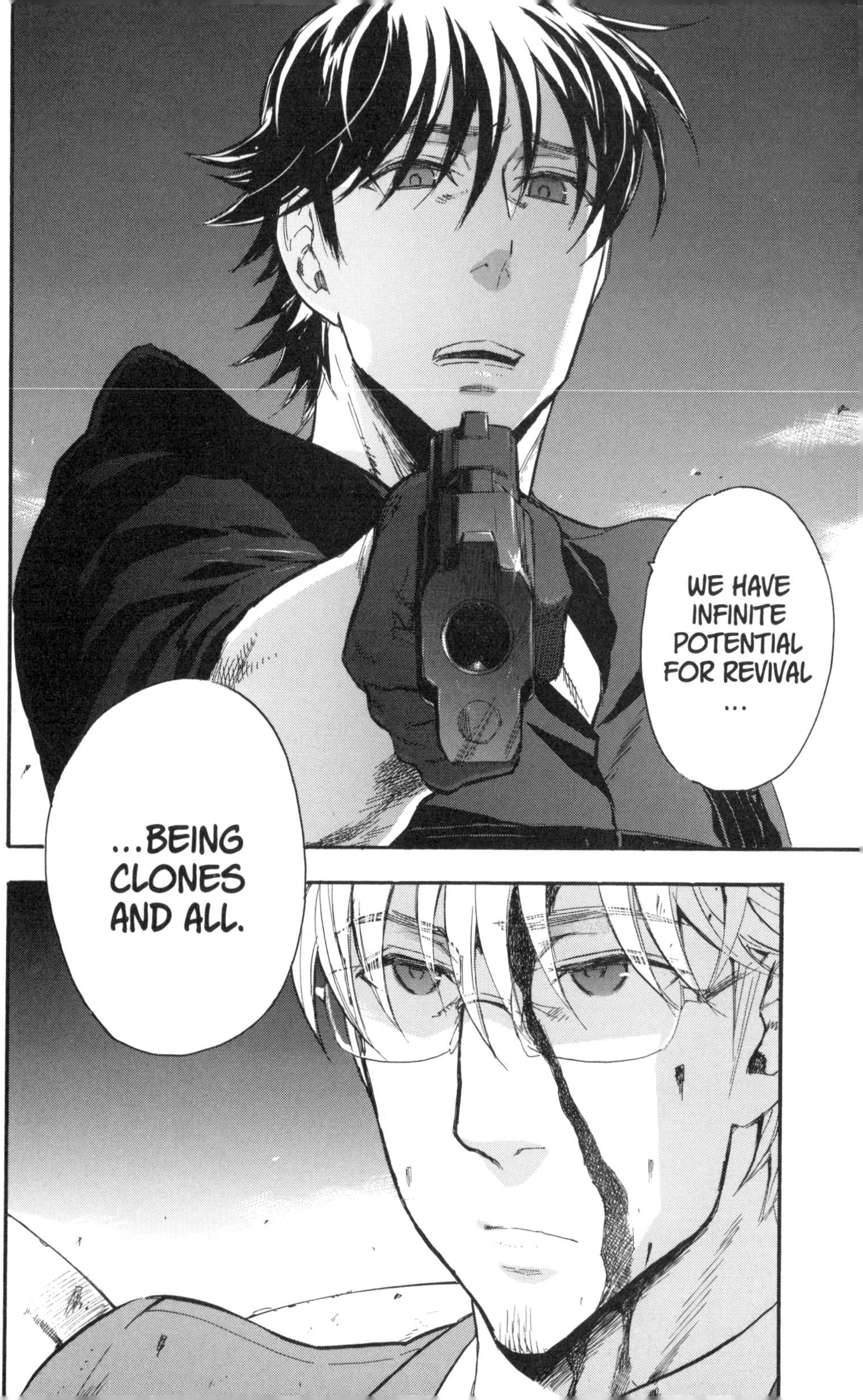
WE HAVE INFINITE POTENTIAL FOR REVIVAL ...
...BEING CLONES AND ALL.

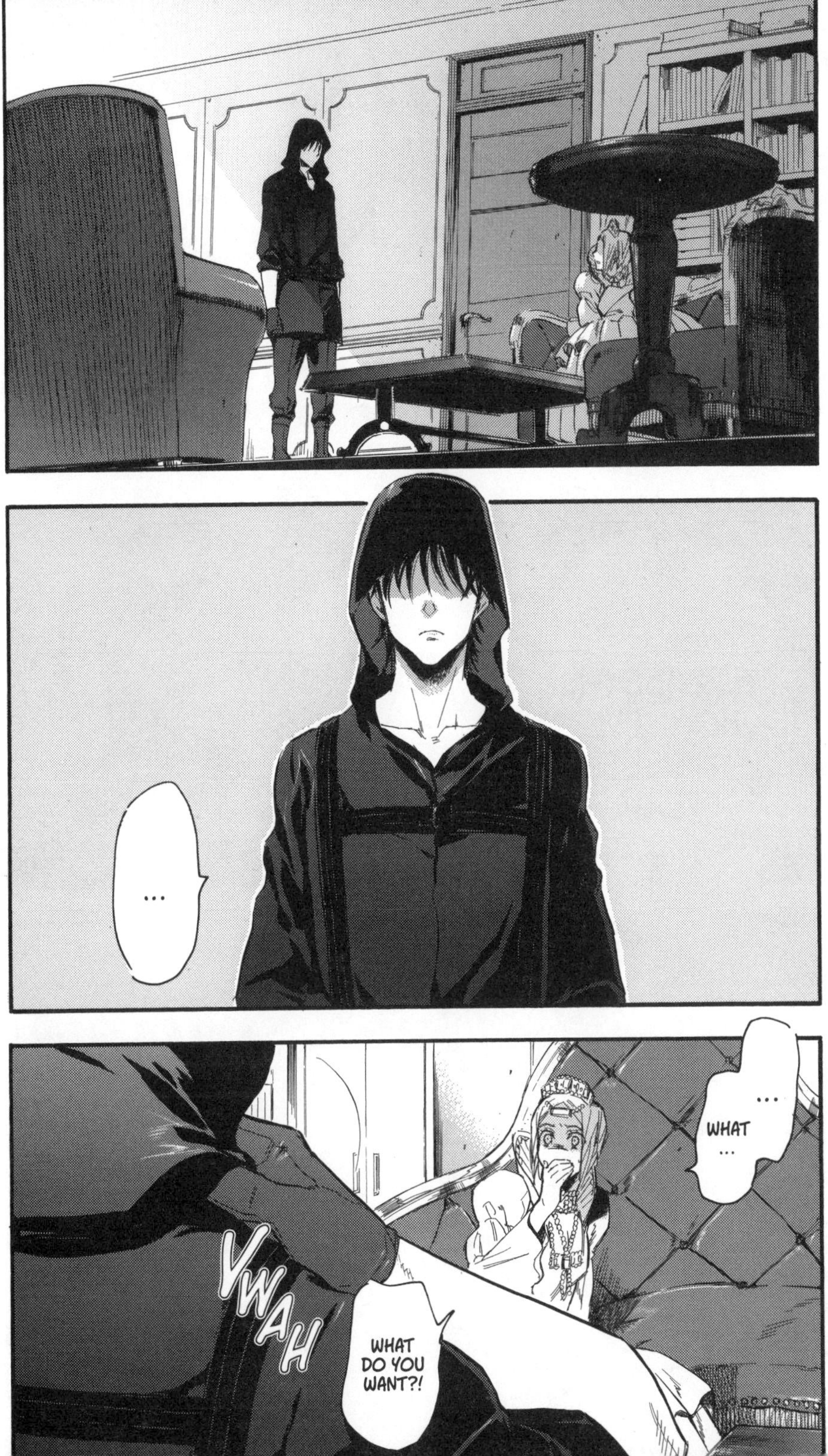
...
... WHAT ...
VWAH
WHAT DO YOU WANT?!

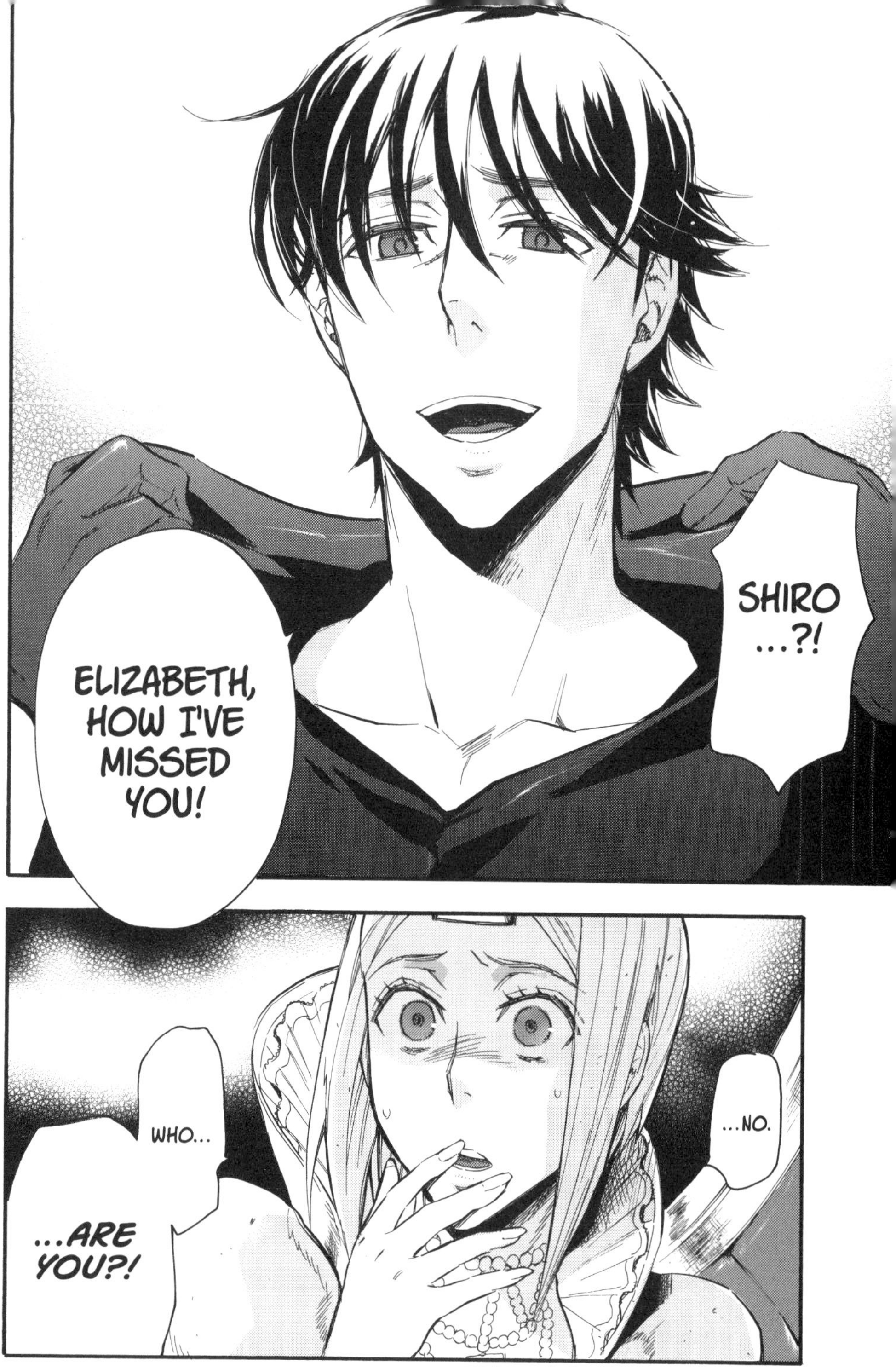
SHIRO ...?!
ELIZABETH, HOW I'VE MISSED YOU!
...NO.
WHO...
...ARE YOU?!

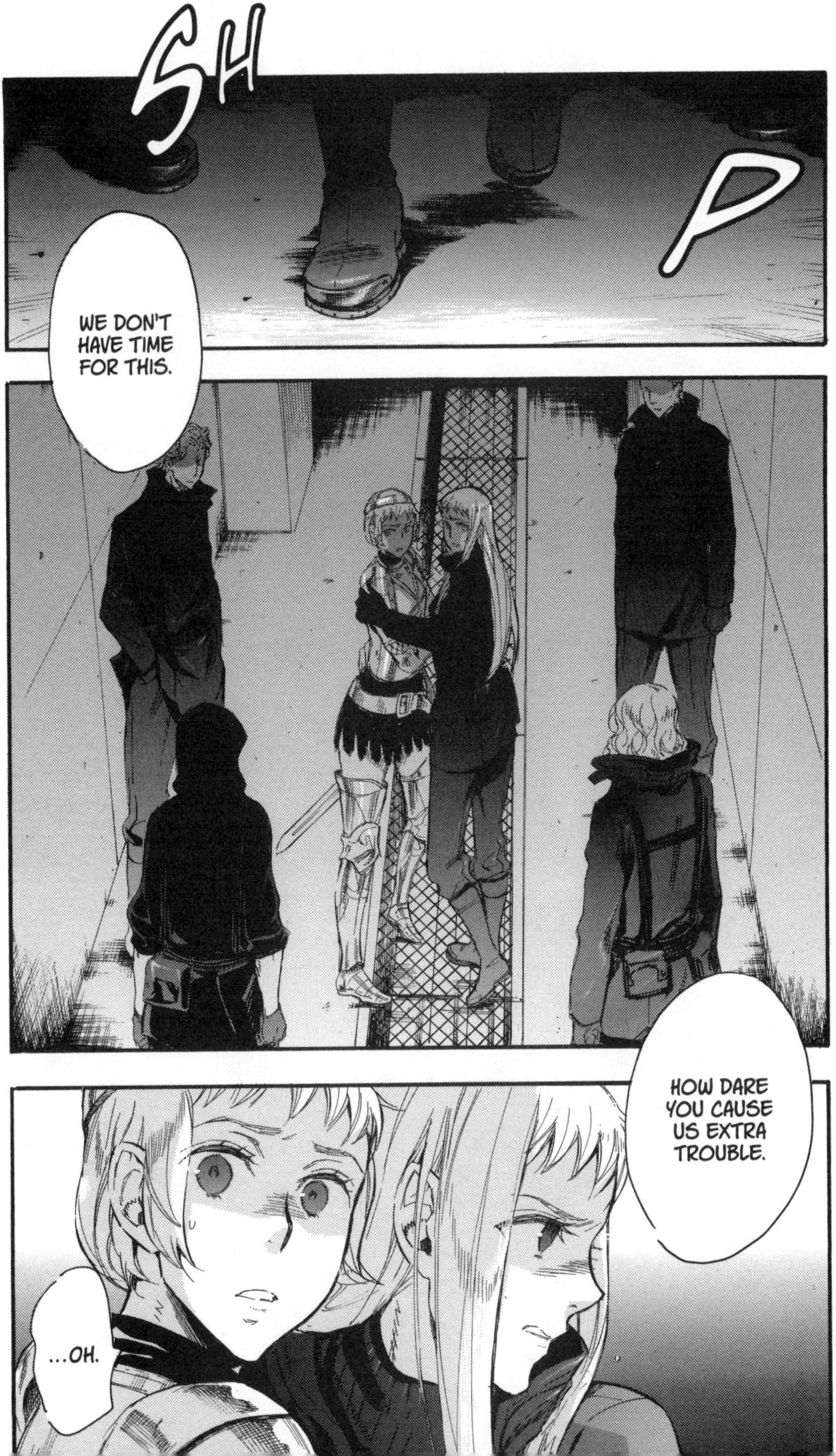
SHP
WE DON'T HAVE TIME FOR THIS.
HOW DARE YOU CAUSE US EXTRA TROUBLE.
...OH.

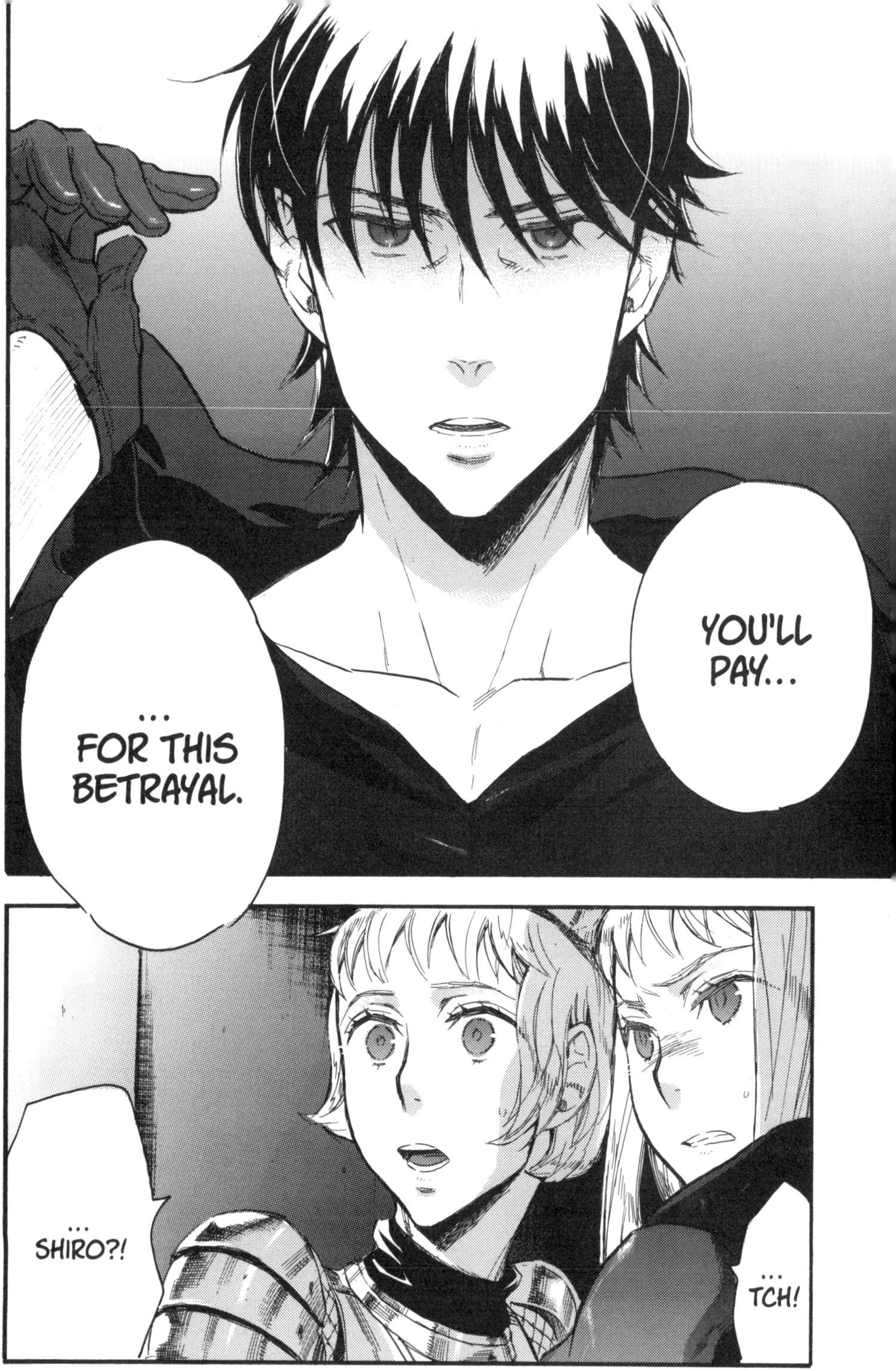
YOU'LL PAY...
... FOR THIS BETRAYAL.
... TCH!
... SHIRO?!

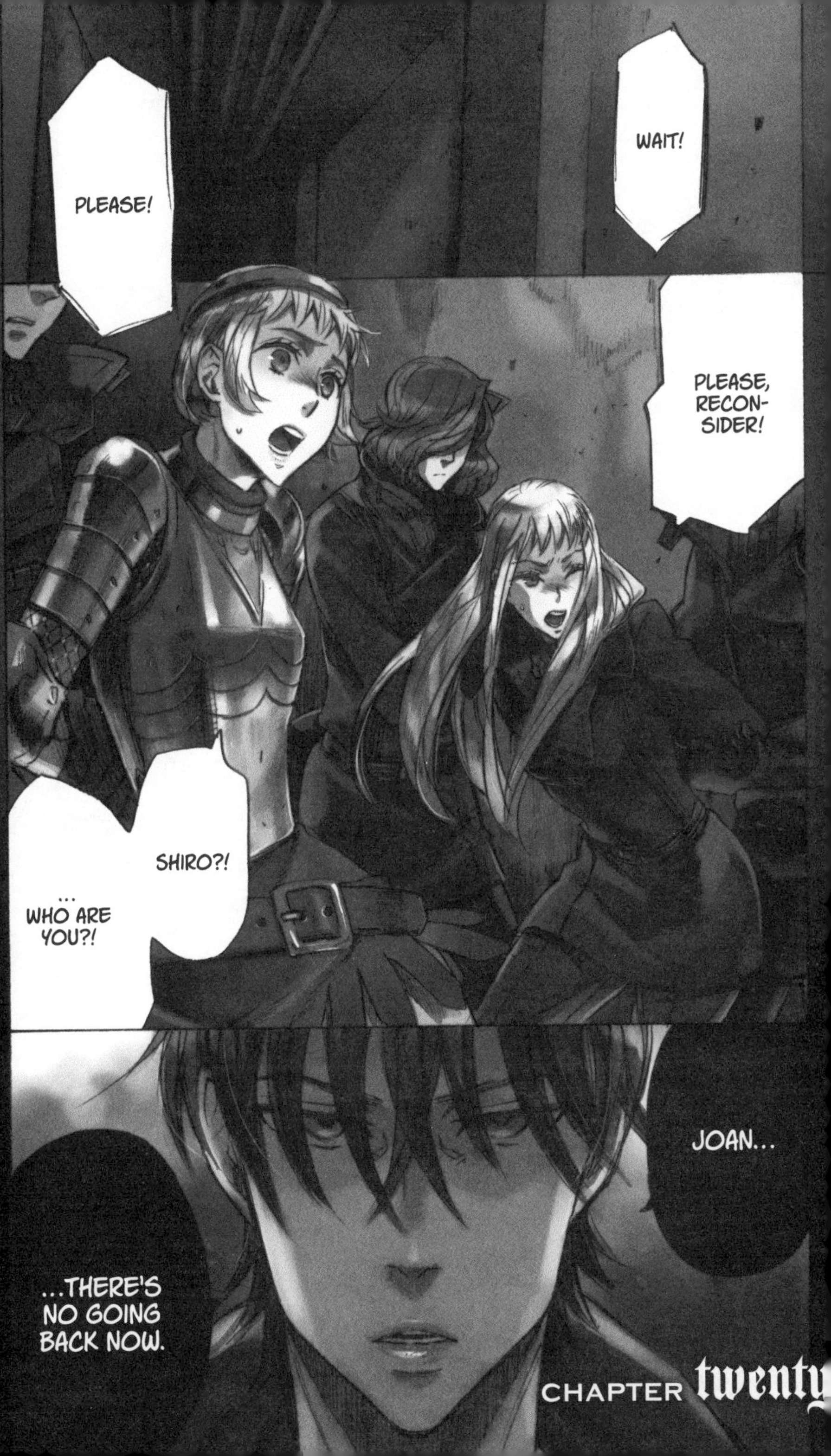
WAIT!
PLEASE!
PLEASE, RECONSIDER!
SHIRO?!
... WHO ARE YOU?!
JOAN...
...THERE'S NO GOING BACK NOW.
CHAPTER twenty

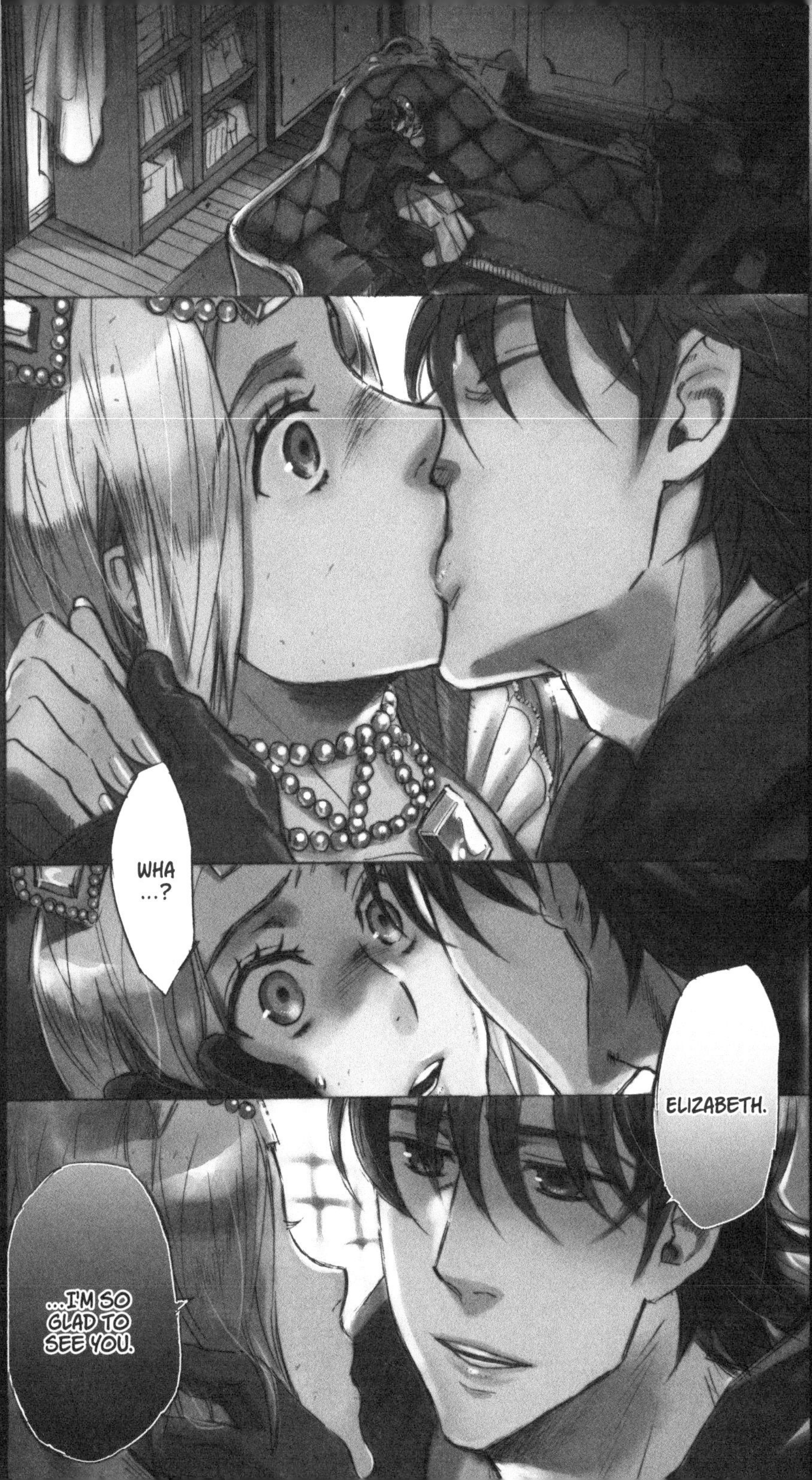
WHA ...?
ELIZABETH.
...I'M SO GLAD TO SEE YOU.

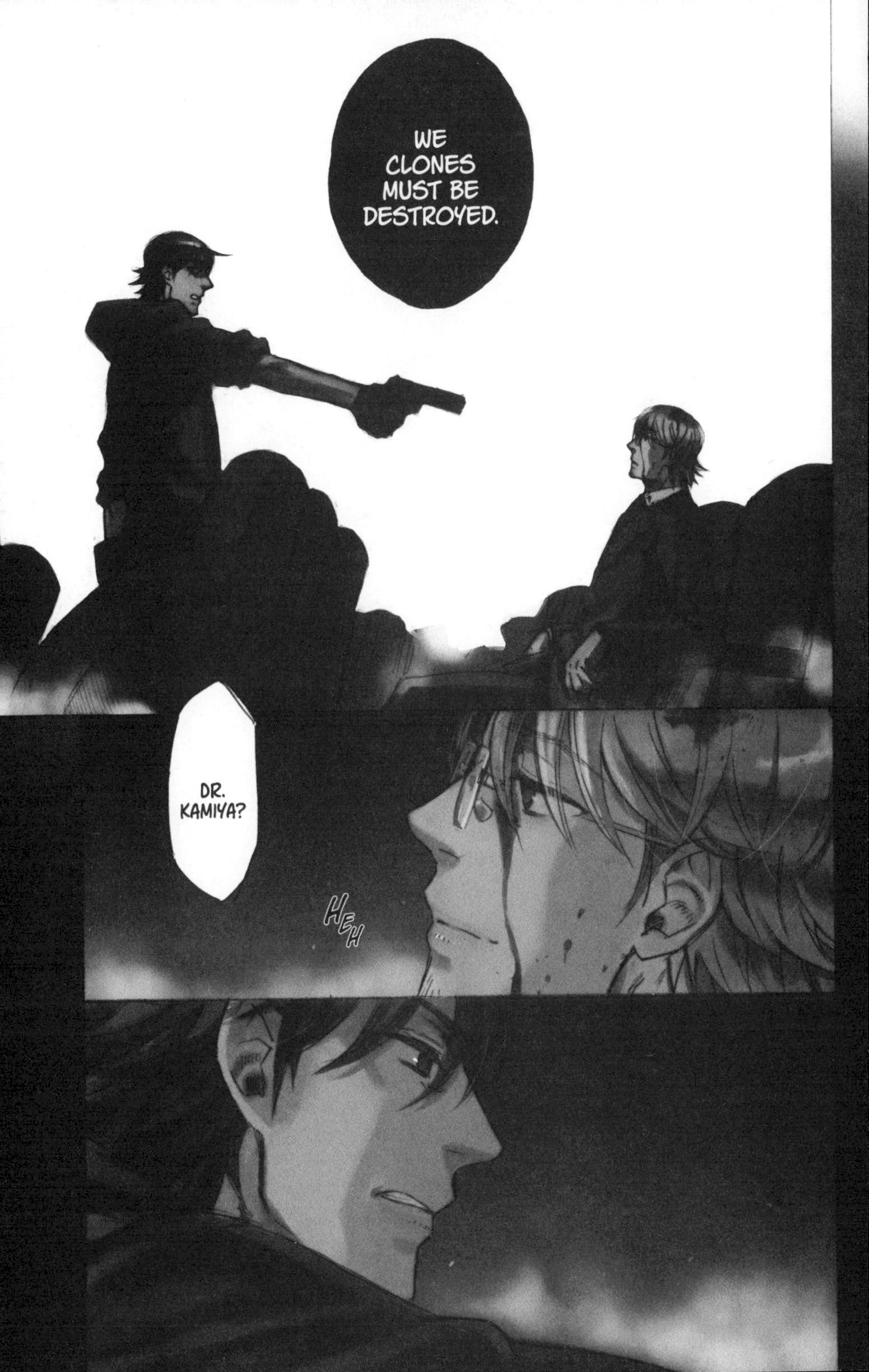
WE CLONES MUST BE DESTROYED.
DR. KAMIYA?
HEH

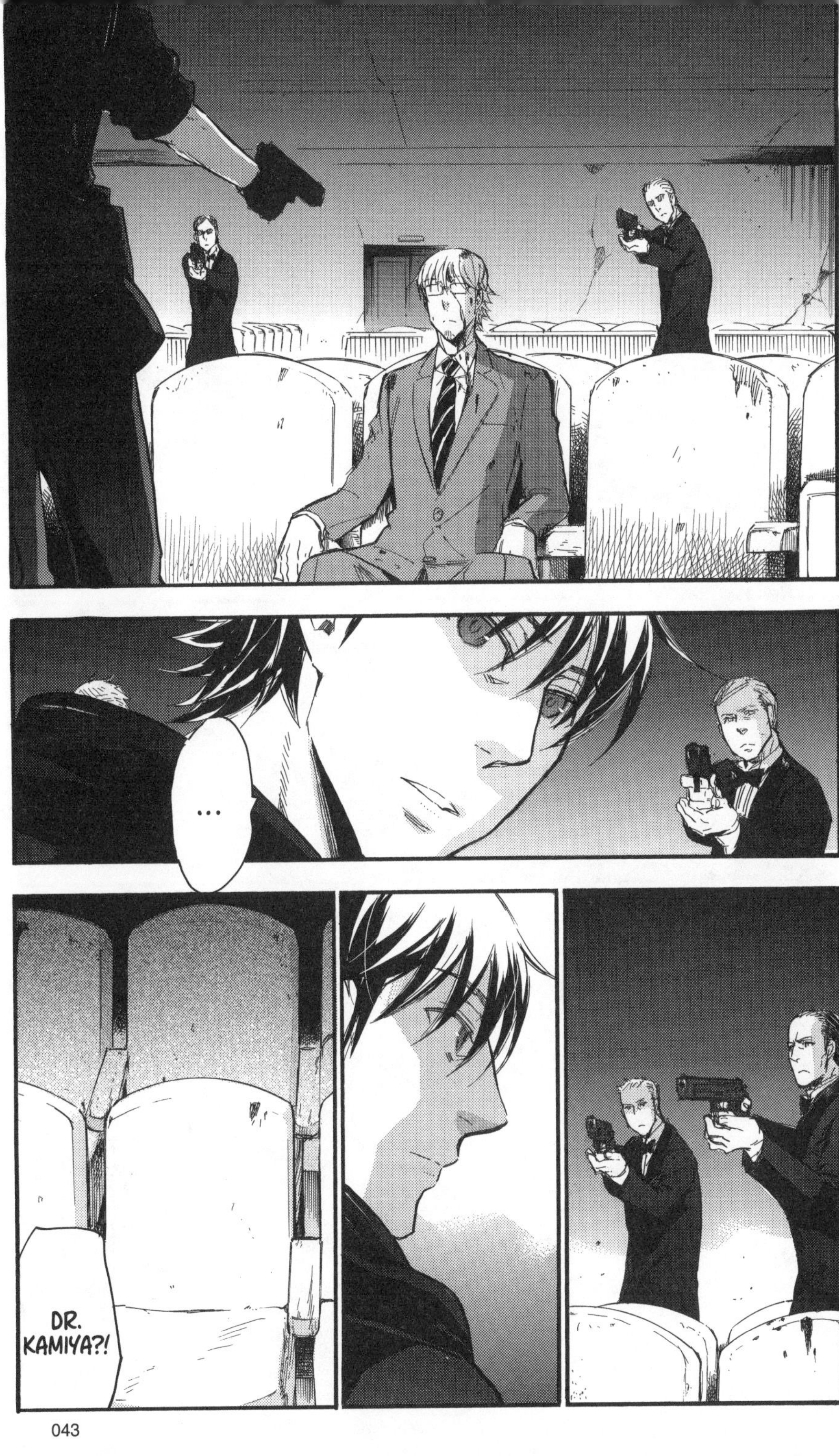
...
DR. KAMIYA?!

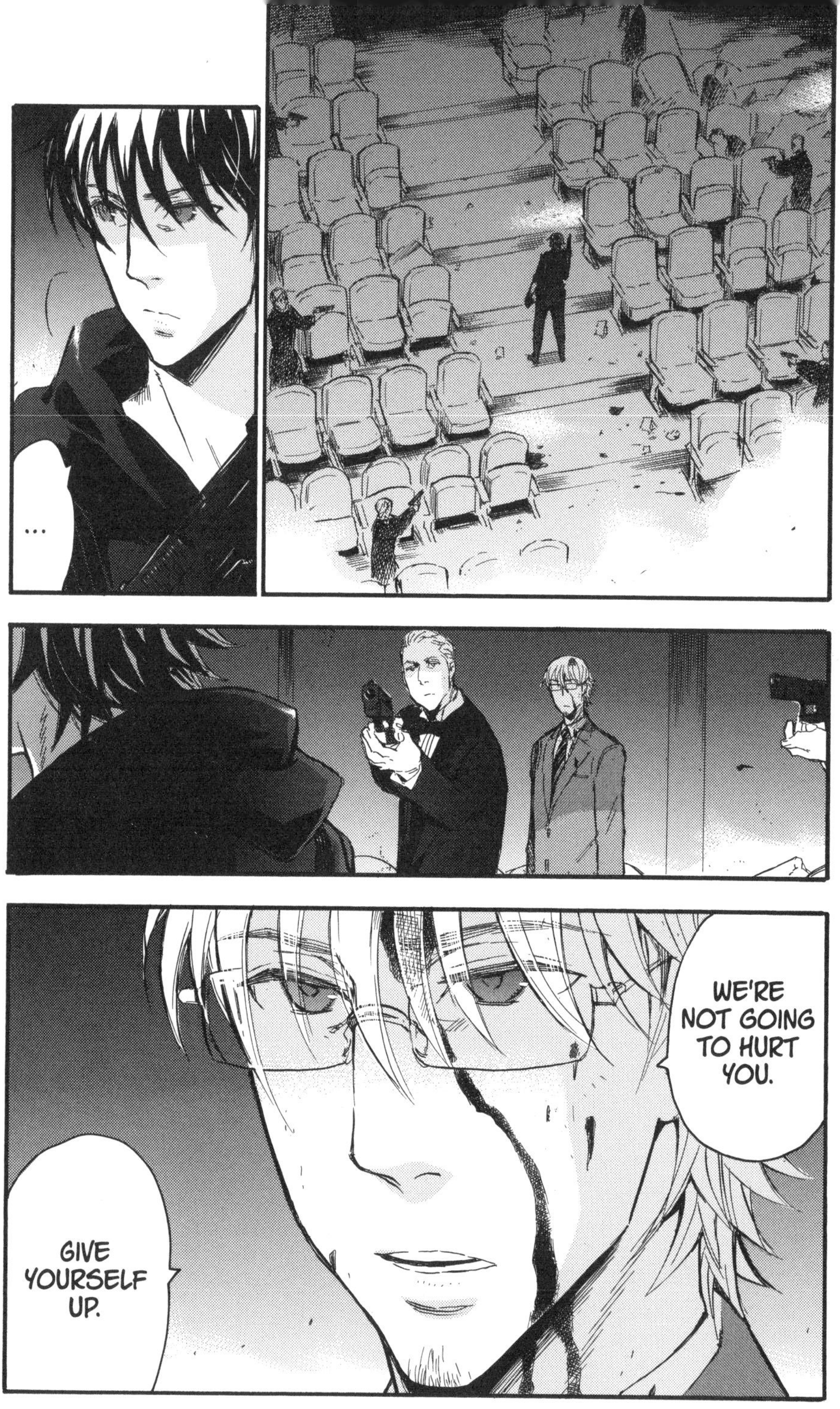
...
WE'RE NOT GOING TO HURT YOU.
GIVE YOURSELF UP.

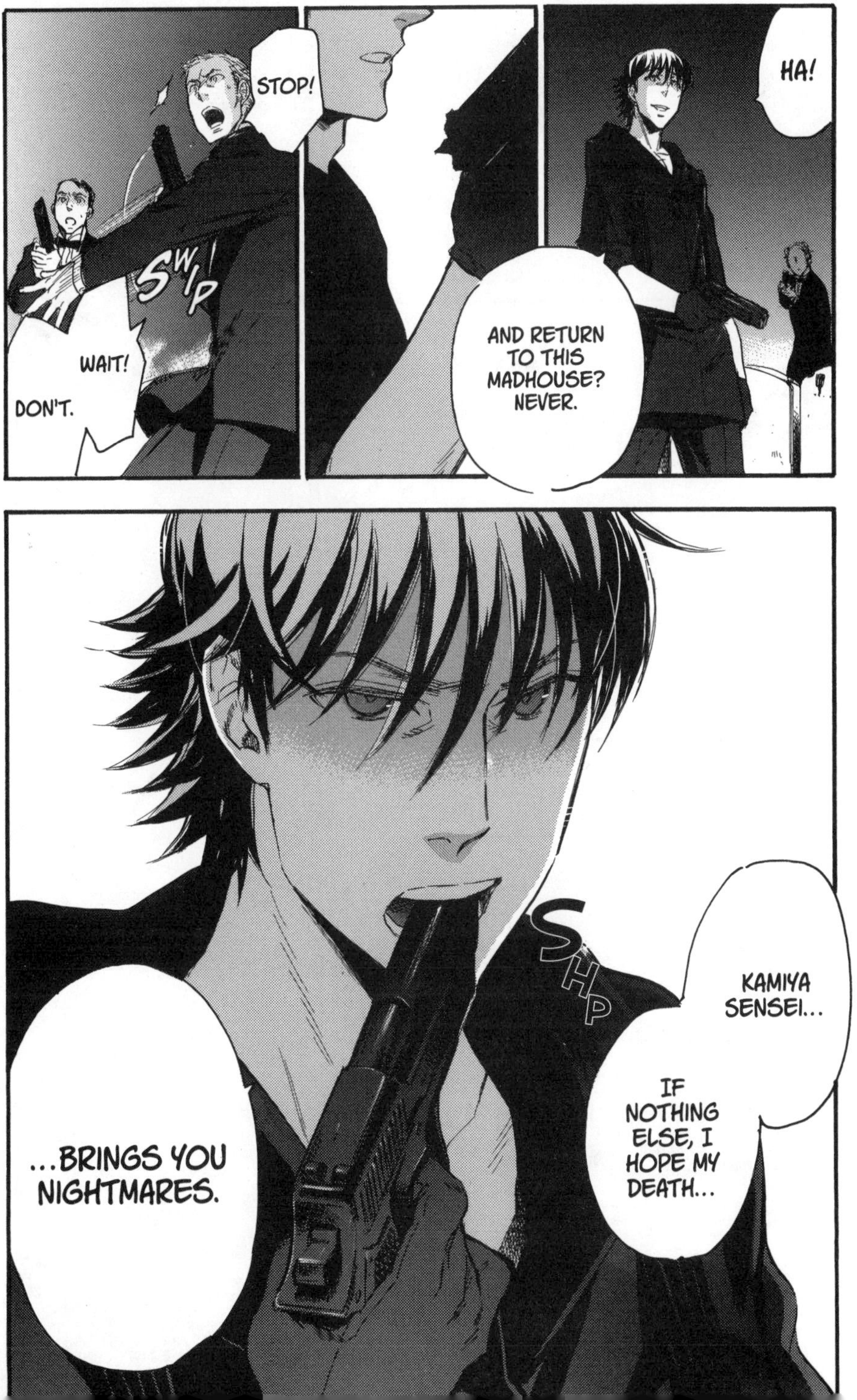
HA!
AND RETURN TO THIS MADHOUSE? NEVER.
STOP!
SWIP
WAIT!
DON'T.
KAMIYA SENSEI...
SHP
IF NOTHING ELSE, I HOPE MY DEATH...
...BRINGS YOU NIGHTMARES.

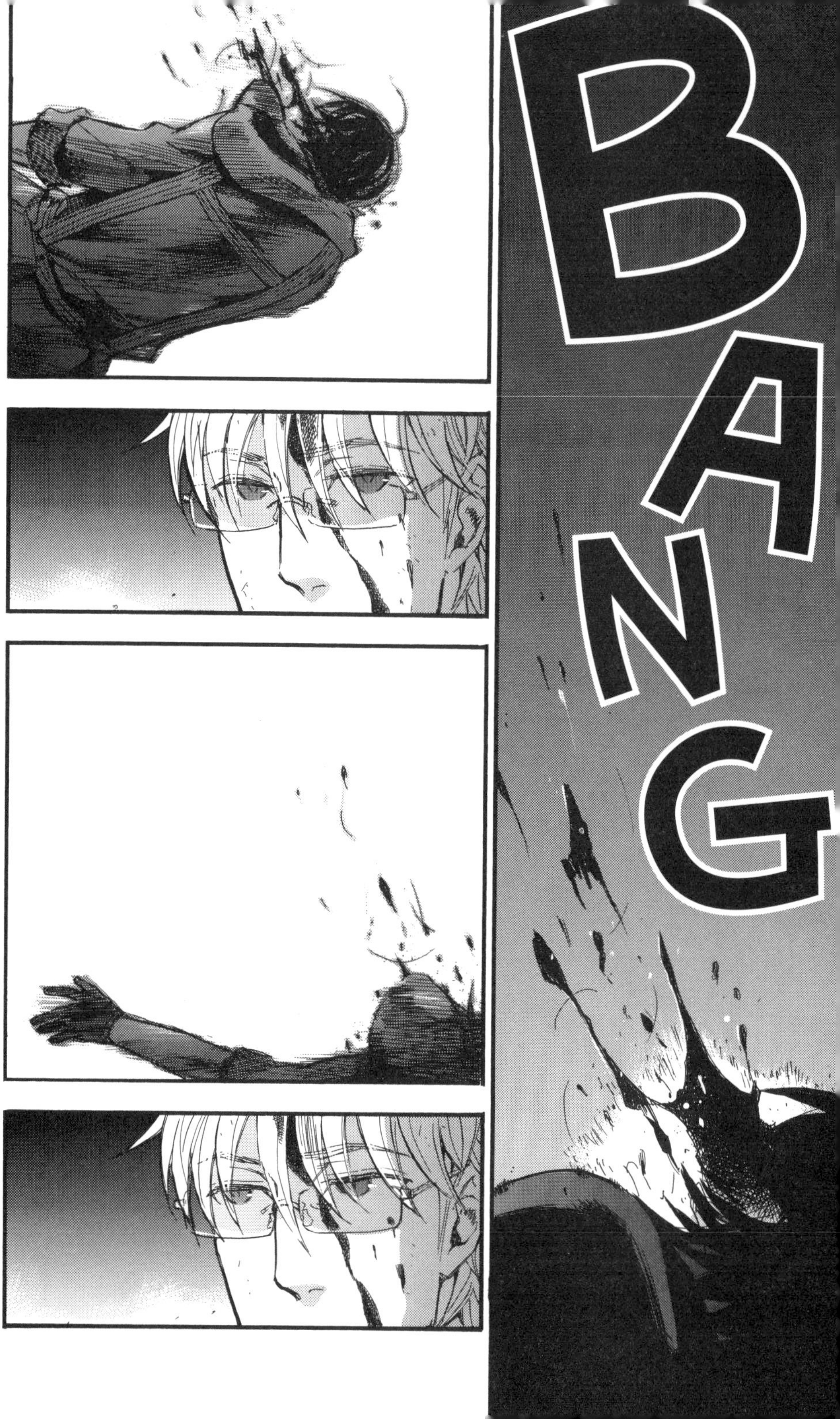
BANG

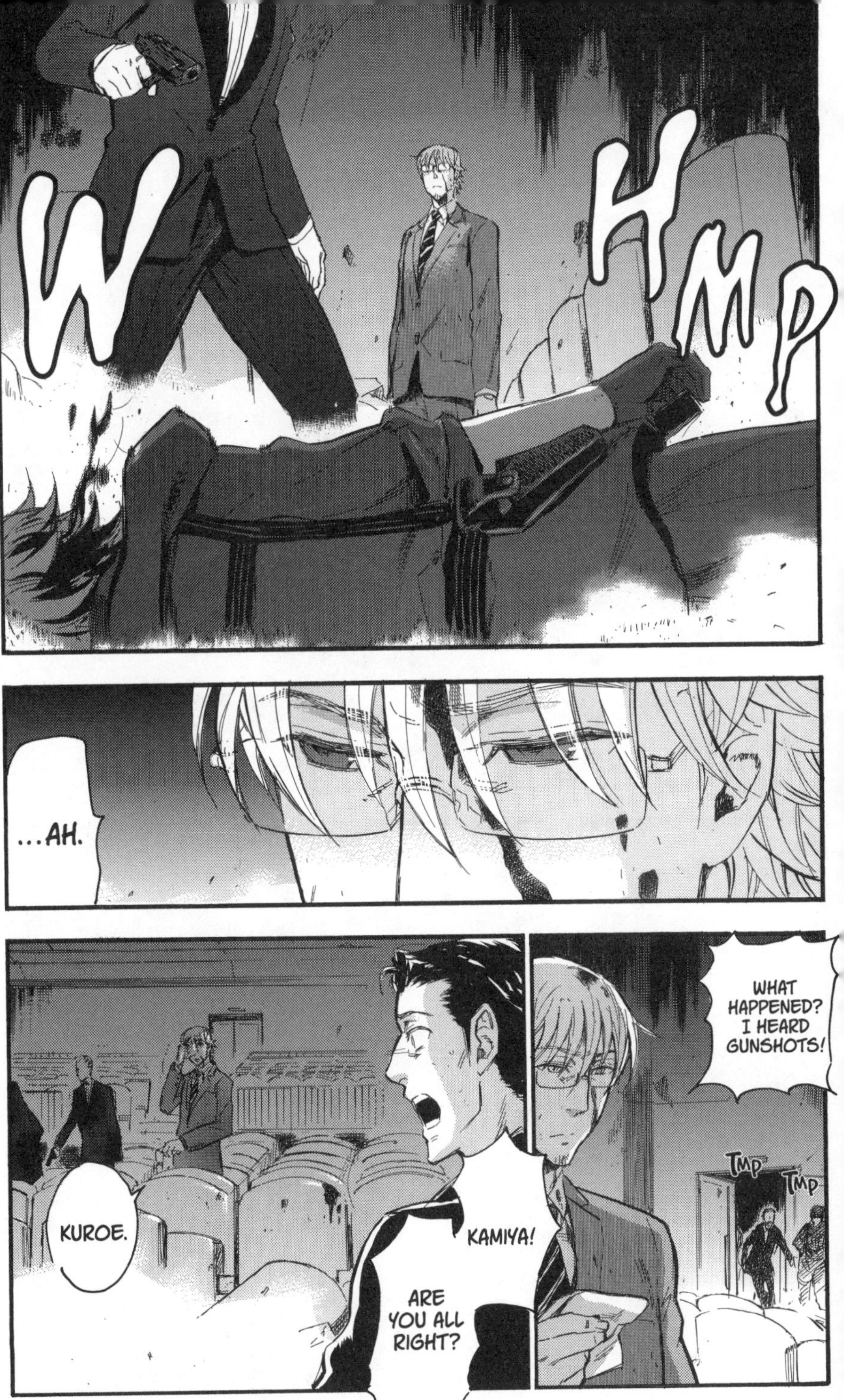
WHMP
...AH.
WHAT HAPPENED? I HEARD GUNSHOTS!
TMP TMP
KAMIYA!
ARE YOU ALL RIGHT?
KUROE.

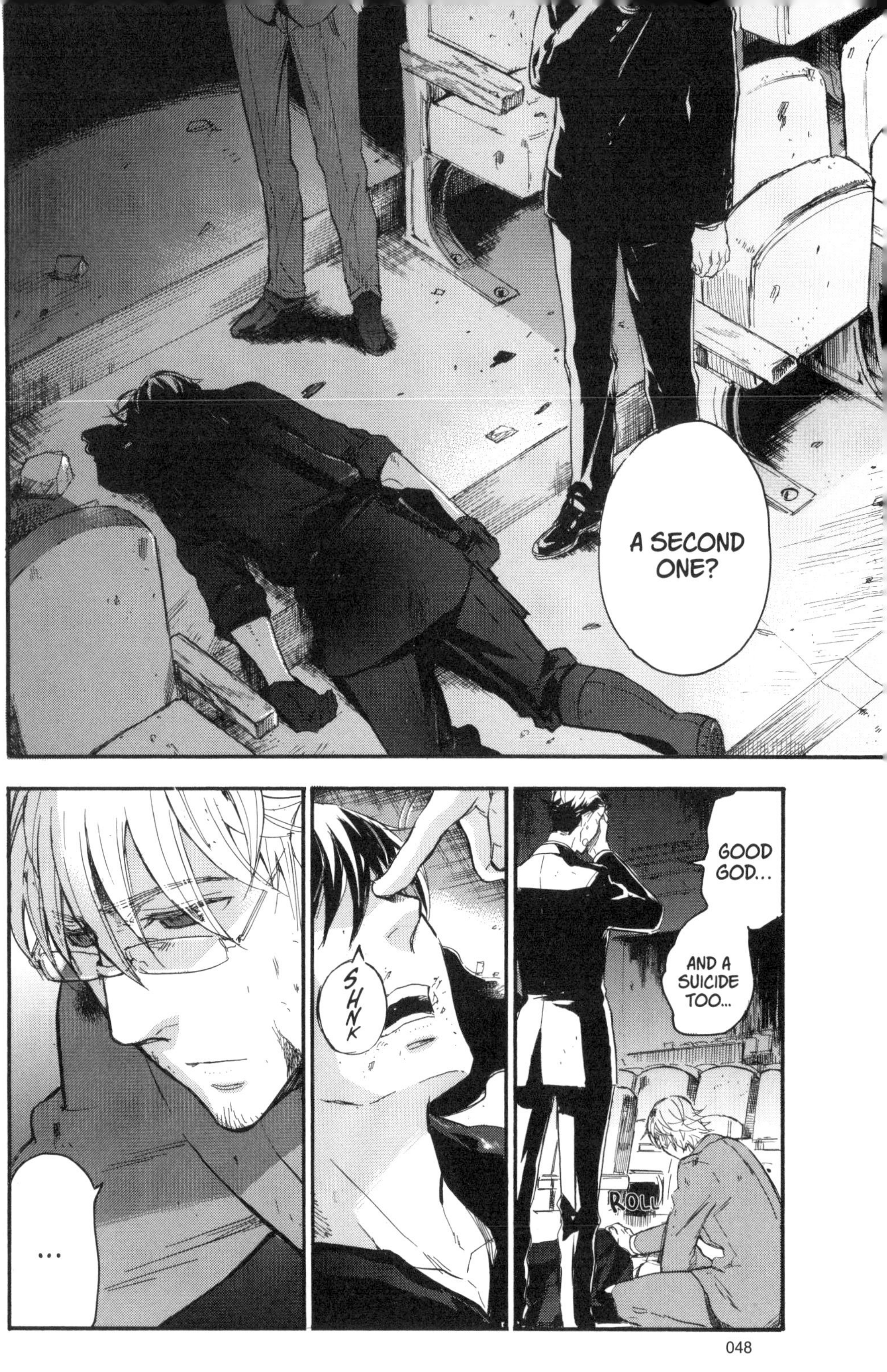
A SECOND ONE?
GOOD GOD...
AND A SUICIDE TOO...
ROLL
SHNK
...

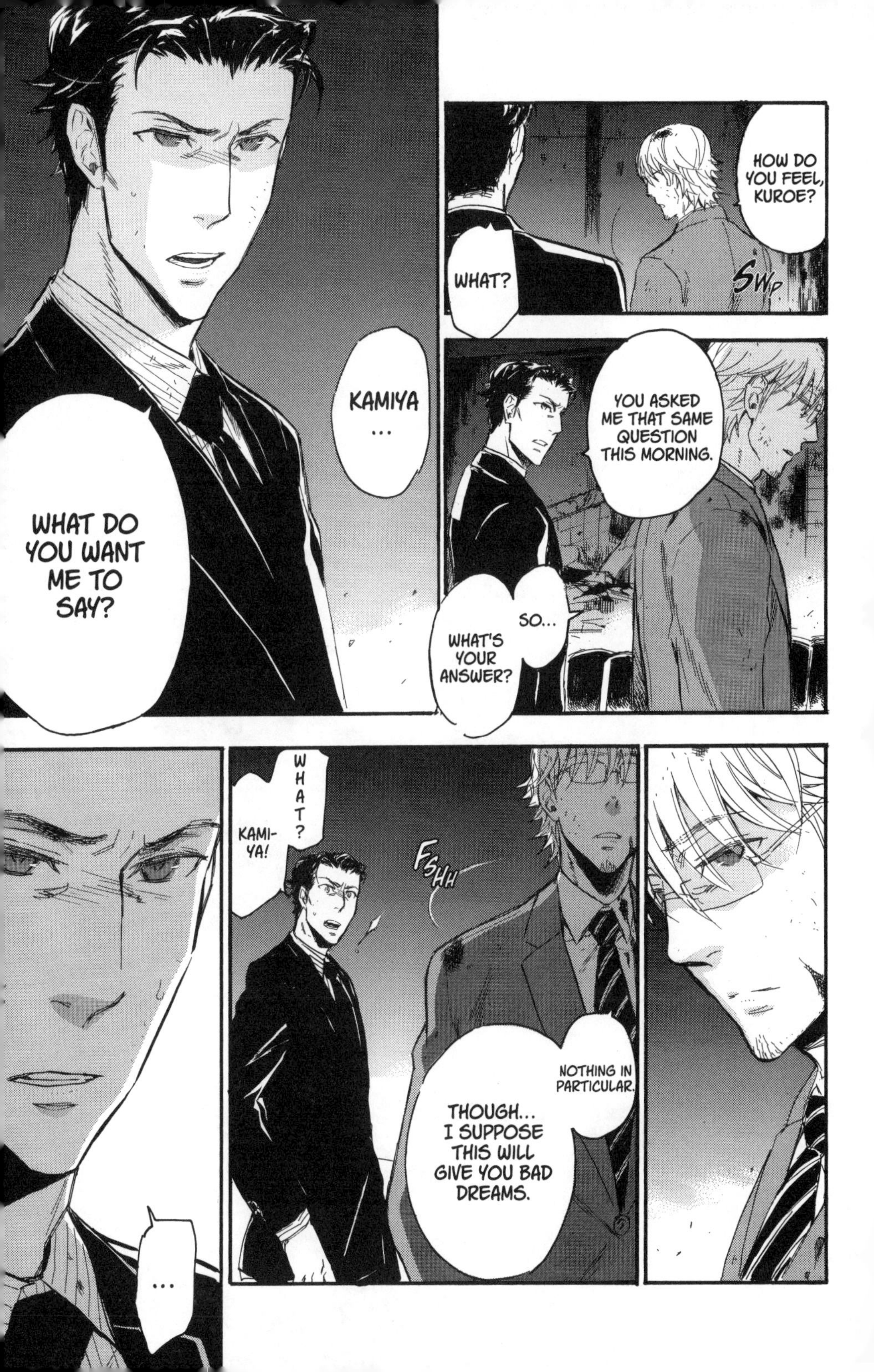
HOW DO YOU FEEL, KUROE?
SWP
WHAT?
YOU ASKED ME THAT SAME QUESTION THIS MORNING.
SO...
WHAT'S YOUR ANSWER?
KAMIYA ...
WHAT DO YOU WANT ME TO SAY?
NOTHING IN PARTICULAR.
THOUGH... I SUPPOSE THIS WILL GIVE YOU BAD DREAMS.
FSHH
WHAT?
KAMI-YA!
...

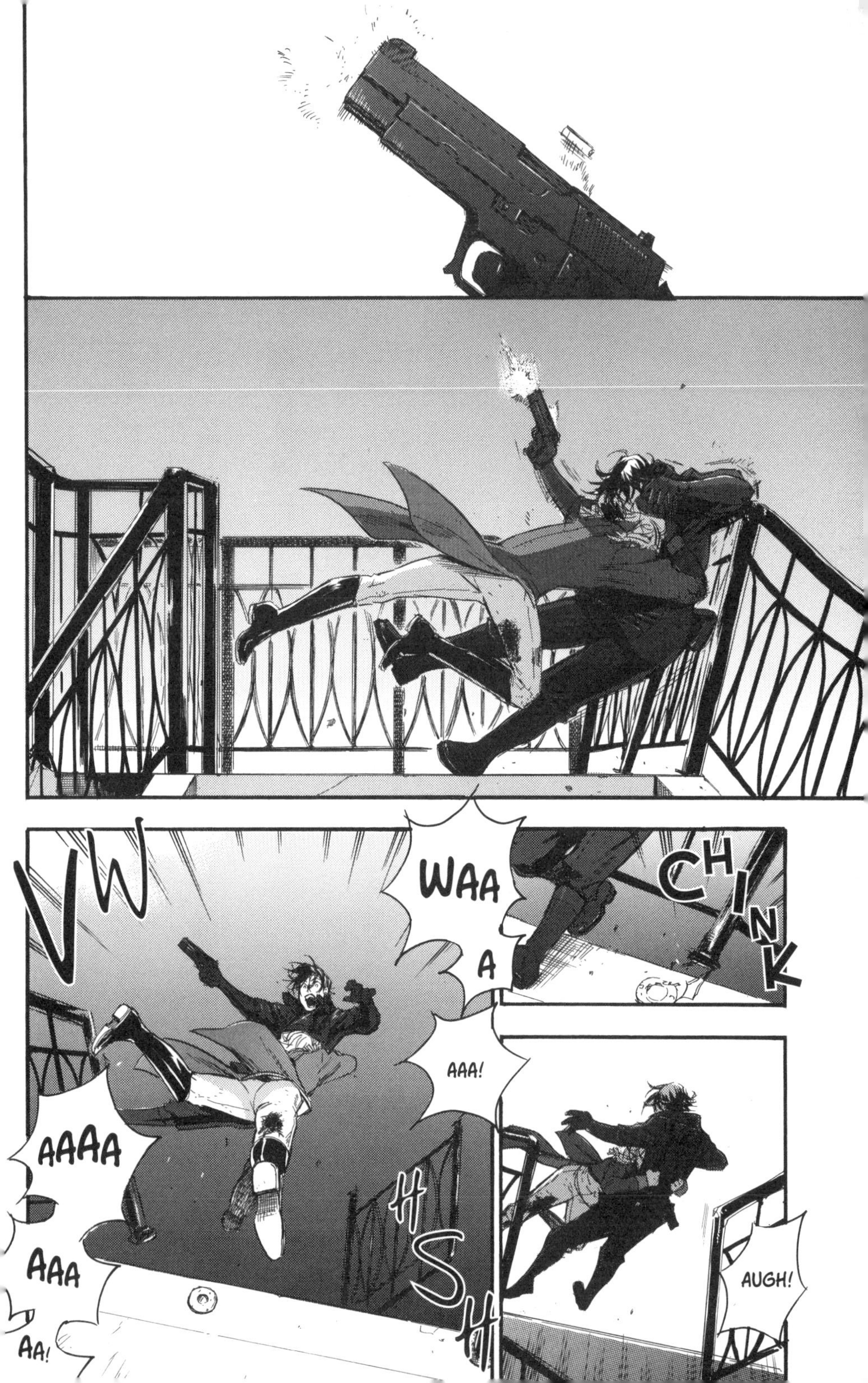
CHINK
AUGH!
VW
WAA A
AAA!
AAAA AAA AA!
HSH

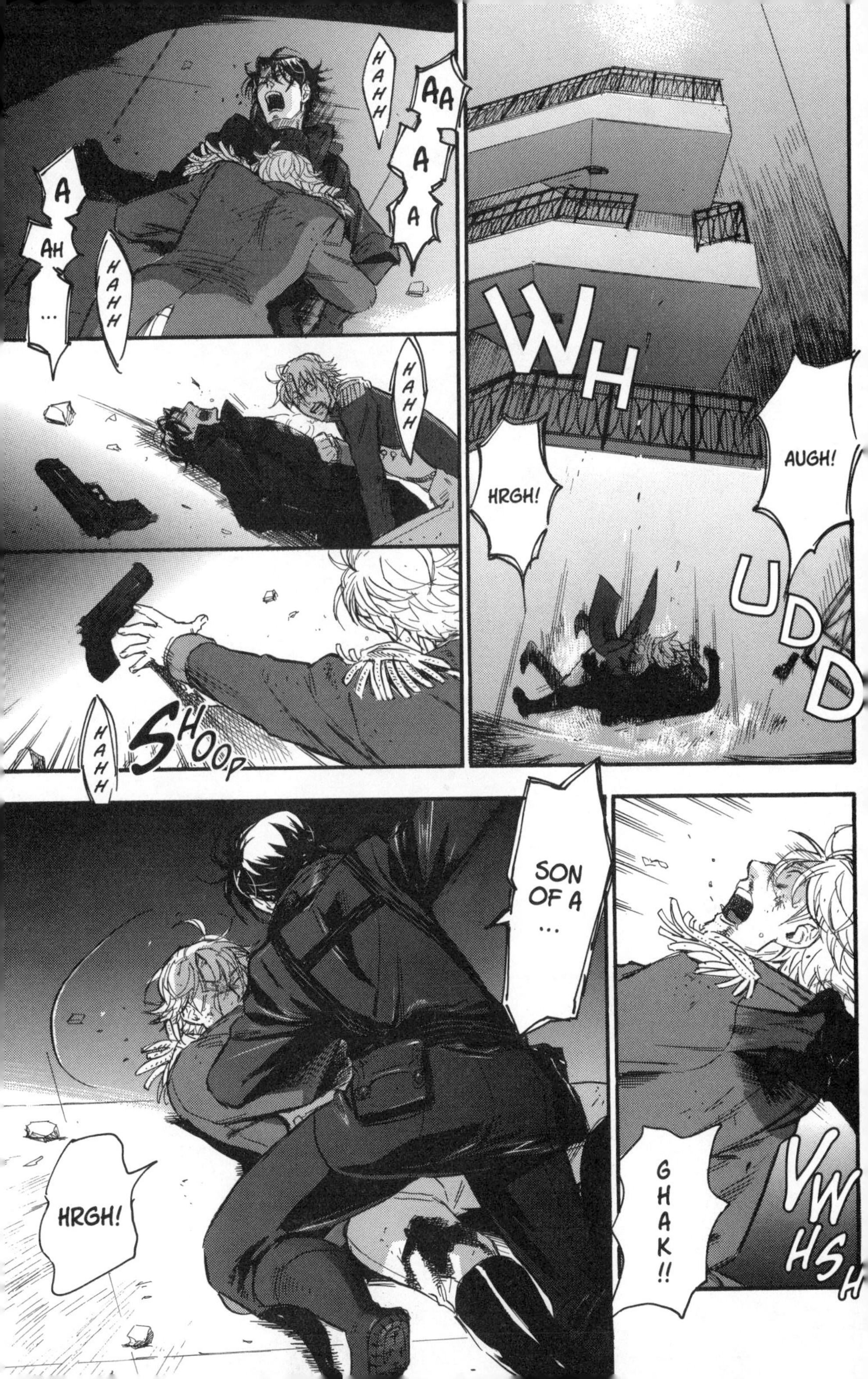
WH
AUGH!
HRGH!
UDDD
AAAAA
HAHH
A AH ...
HAHH
HAHH
SHOOP
HAHH
VWHSHH
GHAK!!
SON OF A ...
HRGH!

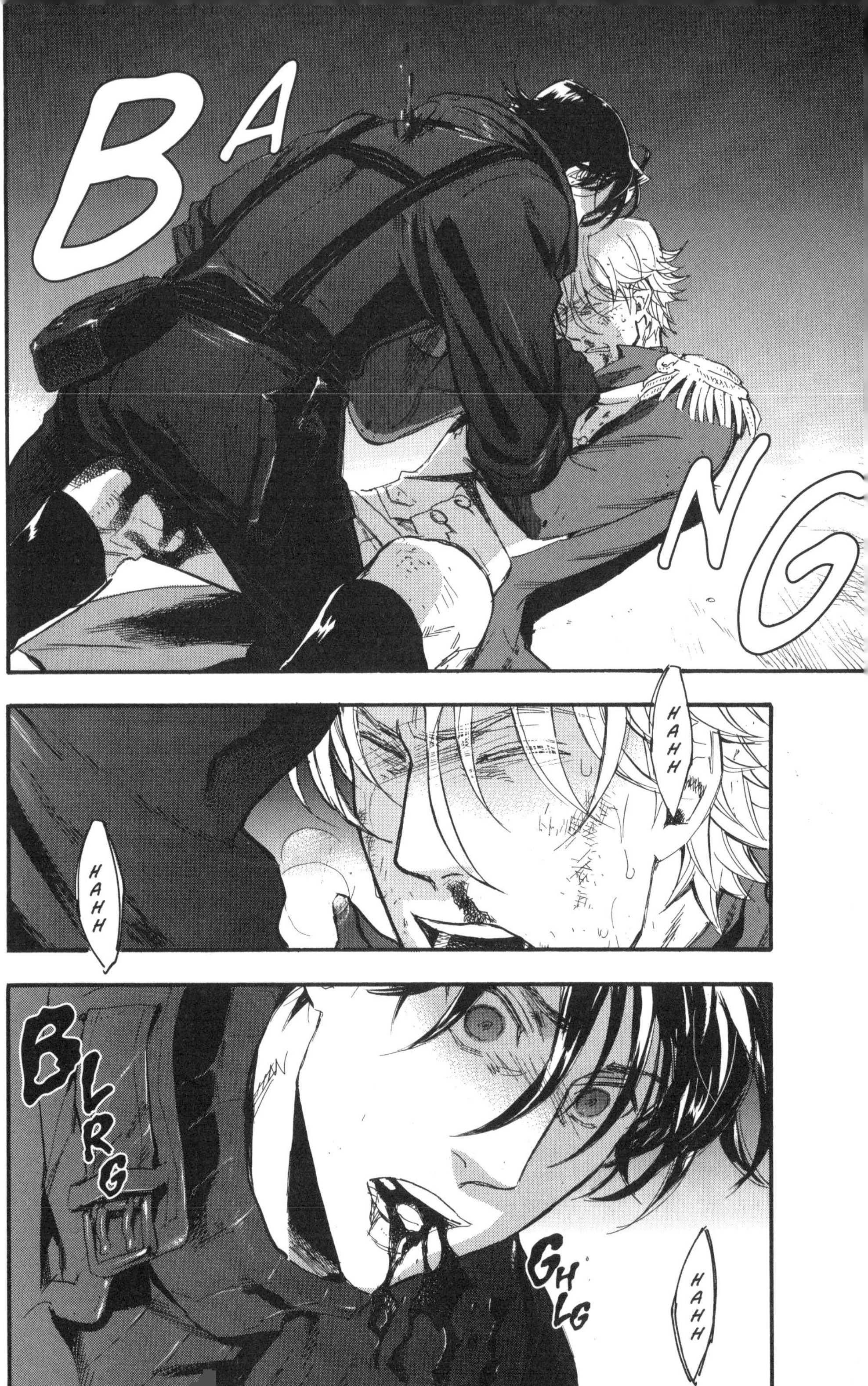
BANG
HAHH
HAHH
HAHH
GHLG
BLRG

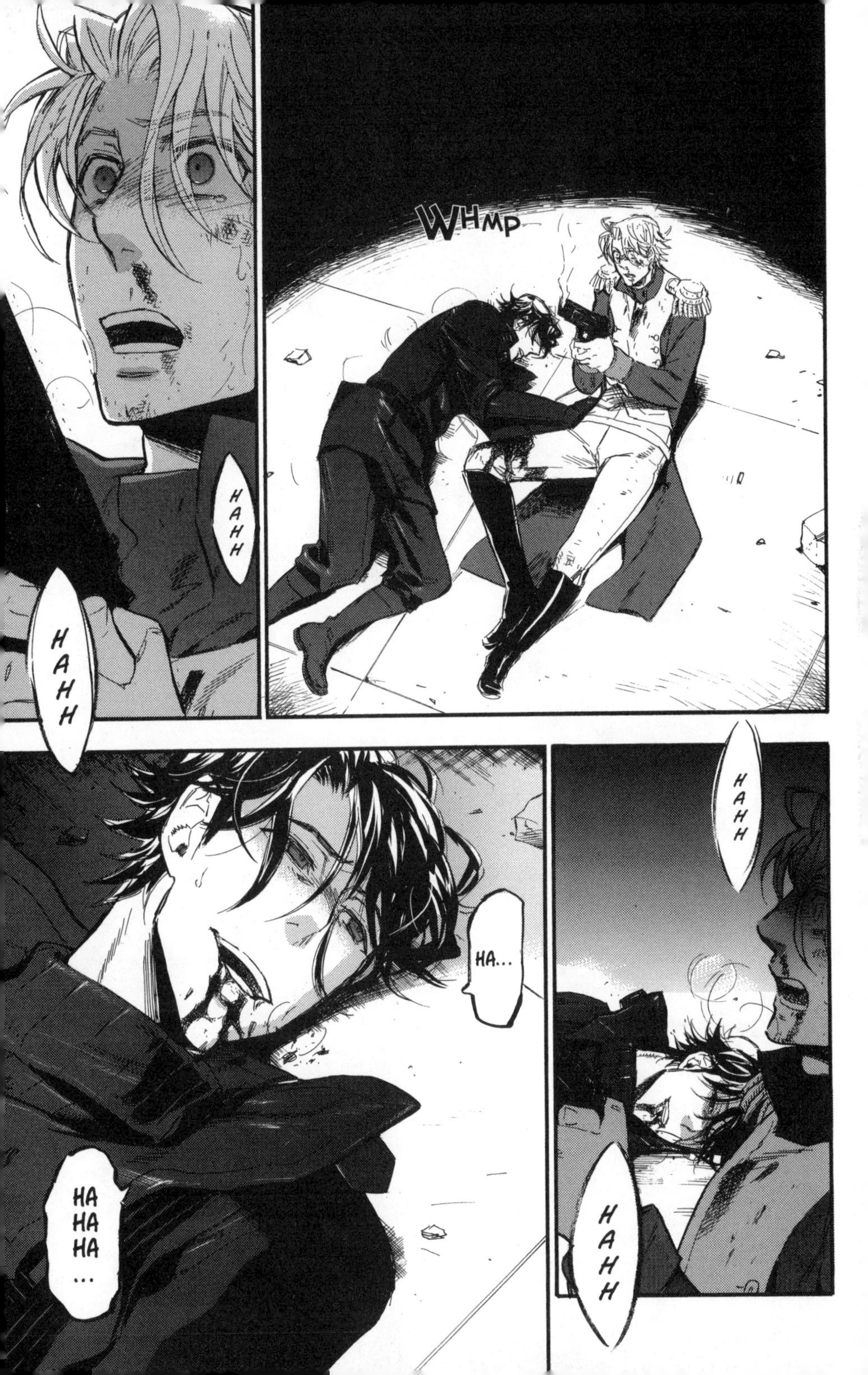
WHMP
HAHH
HAHH
HAHH
HAHH
HA...
HA HA HA ...

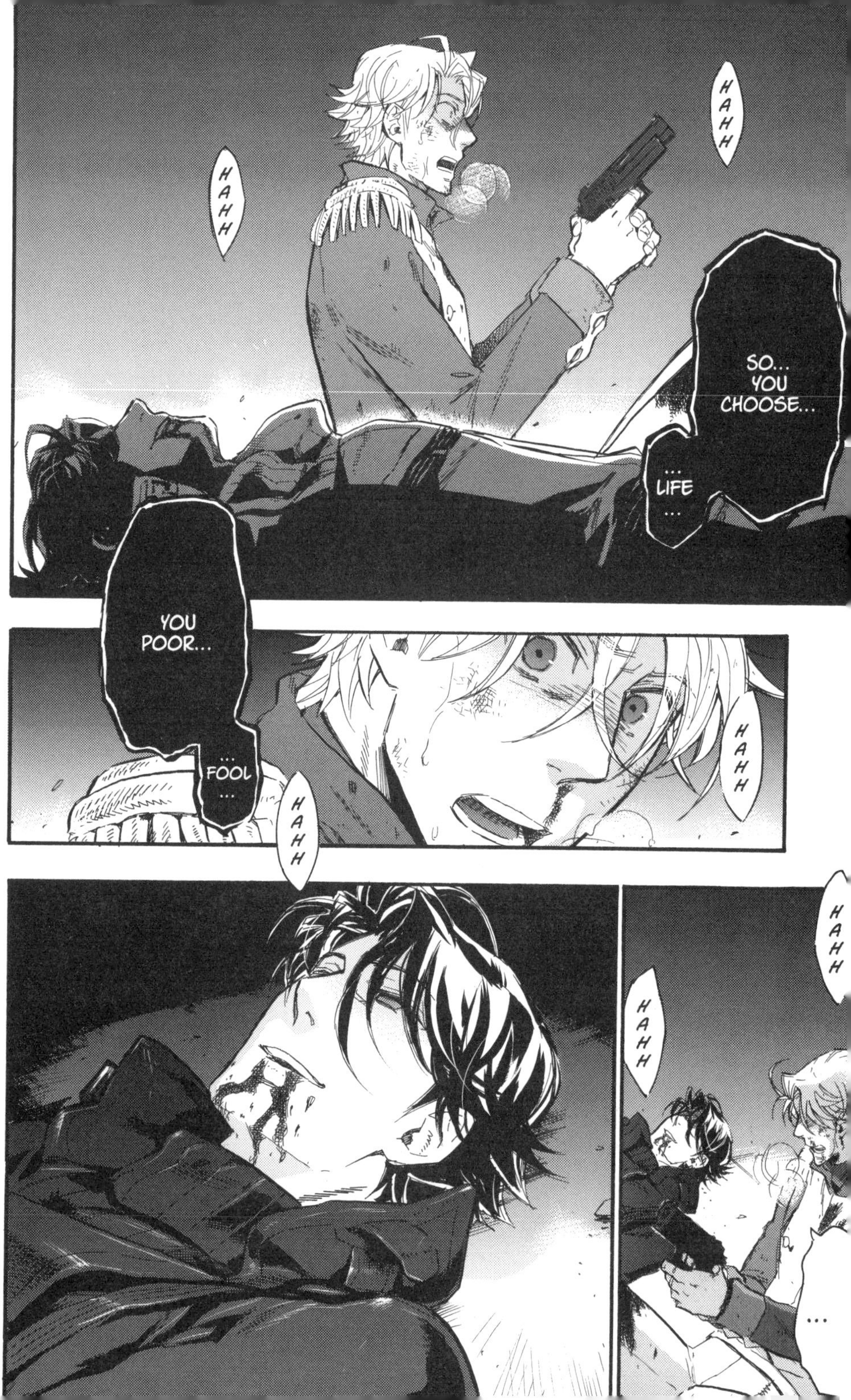
HAHH
SO... YOU CHOOSE...
...LIFE...
HAHH
HAHH
YOU POOR...
...FOOL...
HAHH
HAHH
HAHH
...

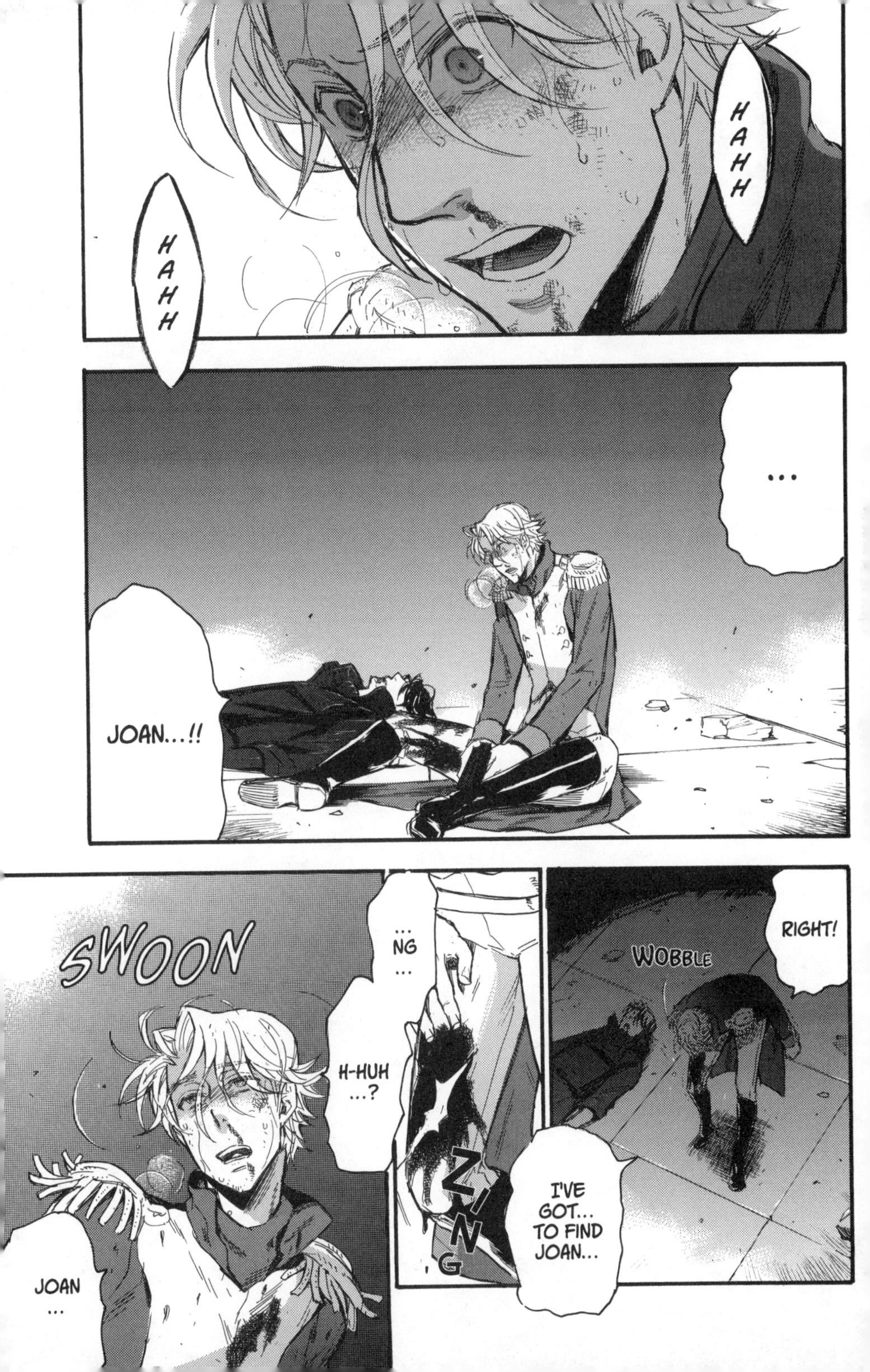
HAHH
HAHH
...
JOAN...!!
RIGHT!
WOBBLE
...NG...
H-HUH...?
ZING
I'VE GOT... TO FIND JOAN...
SWOON
JOAN...

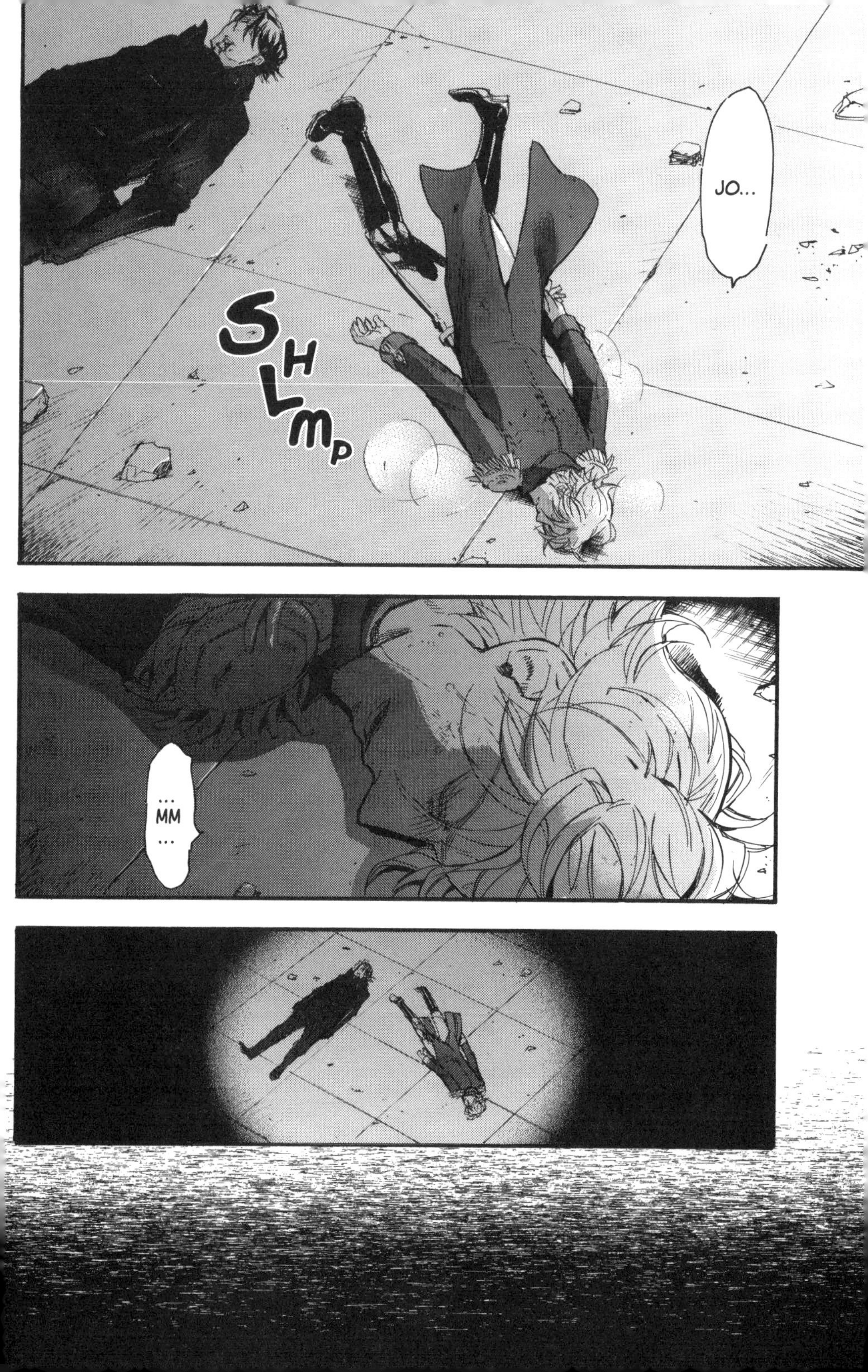
JO...
SHLMP
... MM ...

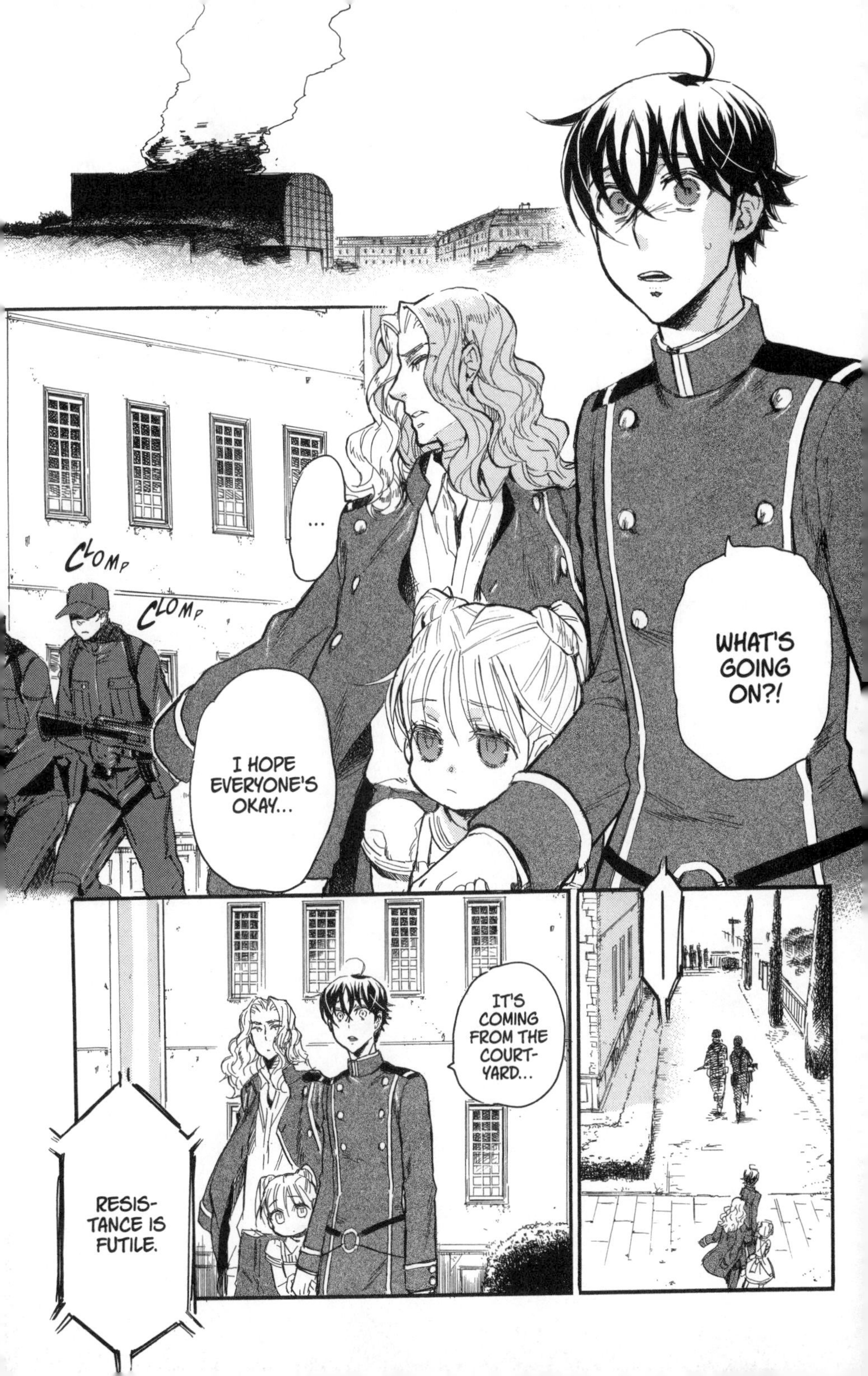
WHAT'S GOING ON?!
...
CLOMP
CLOMP
I HOPE EVERYONE'S OKAY...
IT'S COMING FROM THE COURT-YARD...
RESIS-TANCE IS FUTILE.

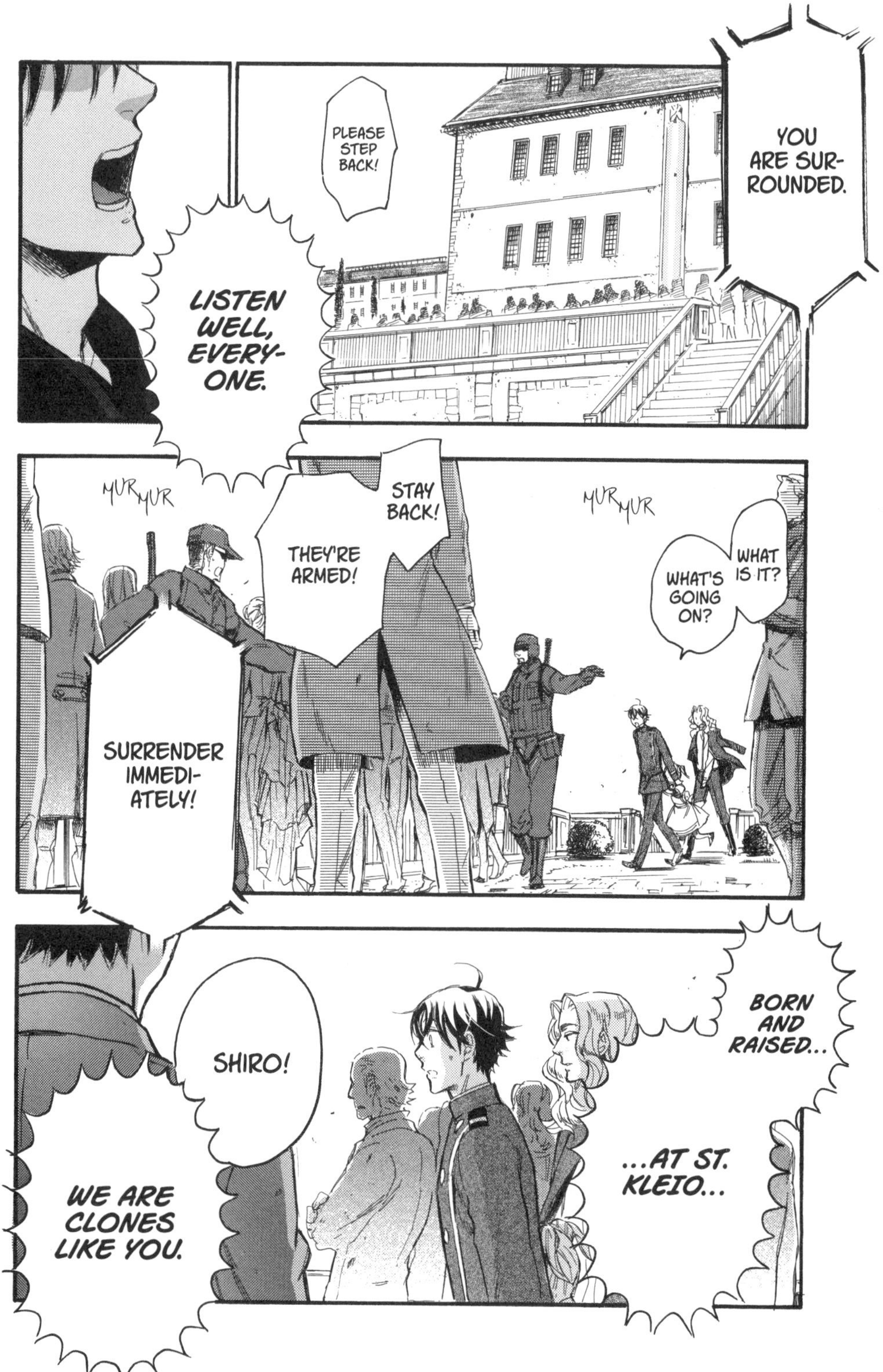
YOU ARE SUR-ROUNDED.
PLEASE STEP BACK!
LISTEN WELL, EVERY-ONE.
MUR MUR
WHAT IS IT?
WHAT'S GOING ON?
STAY BACK!
THEY'RE ARMED!
MUR MUR
SURRENDER IMMEDI-ATELY!
BORN AND RAISED...
...AT ST. KLEIO...
SHIRO!
WE ARE CLONES LIKE YOU.

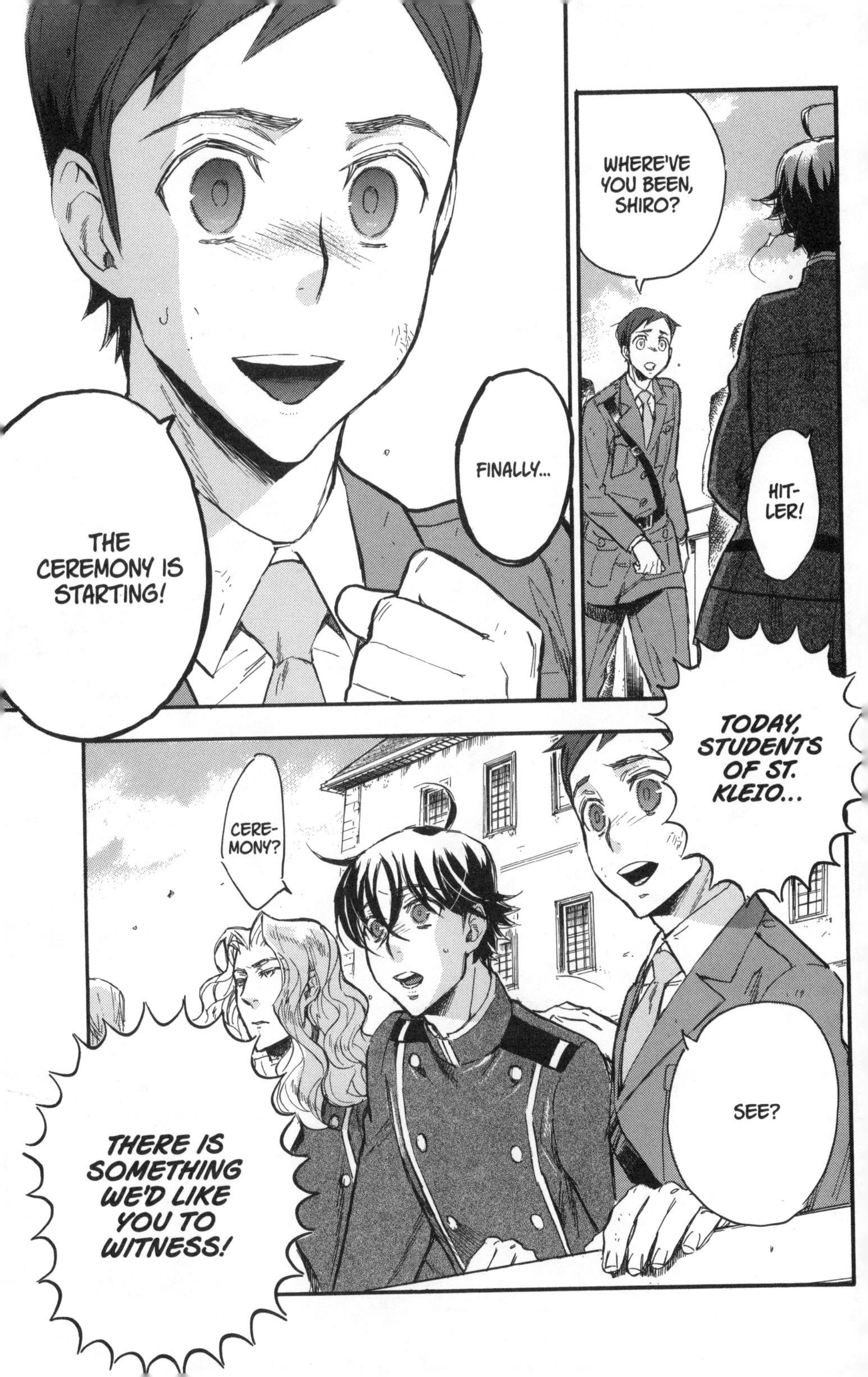
WHERE'VE YOU BEEN, SHIRO?
HIT-LER!
FINALLY...
THE CEREMONY IS STARTING!
TODAY, STUDENTS OF ST. KLEIO...
CERE-MONY?
SEE?
THERE IS SOMETHING WE'D LIKE YOU TO WITNESS!

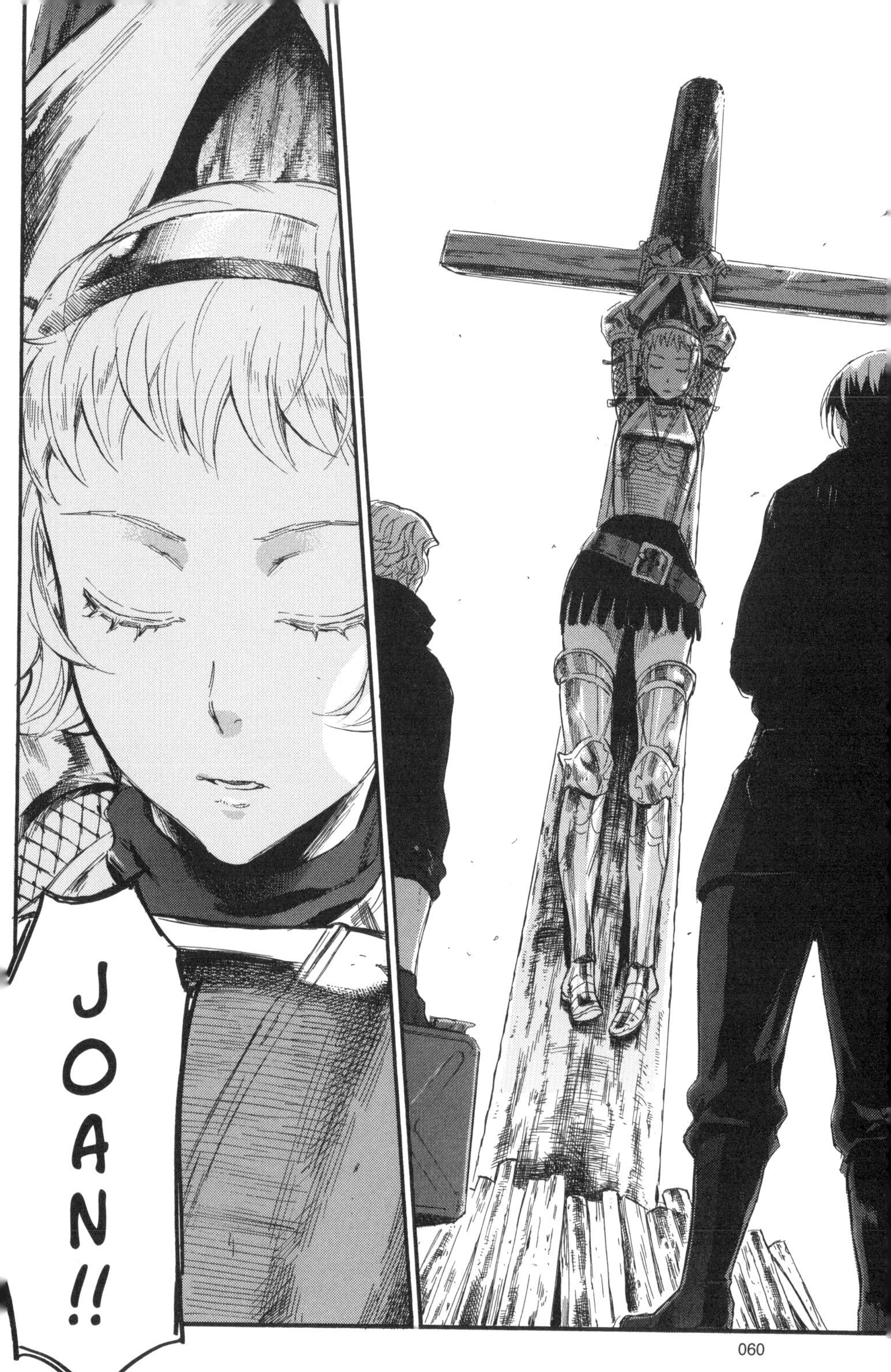
JOAN!!

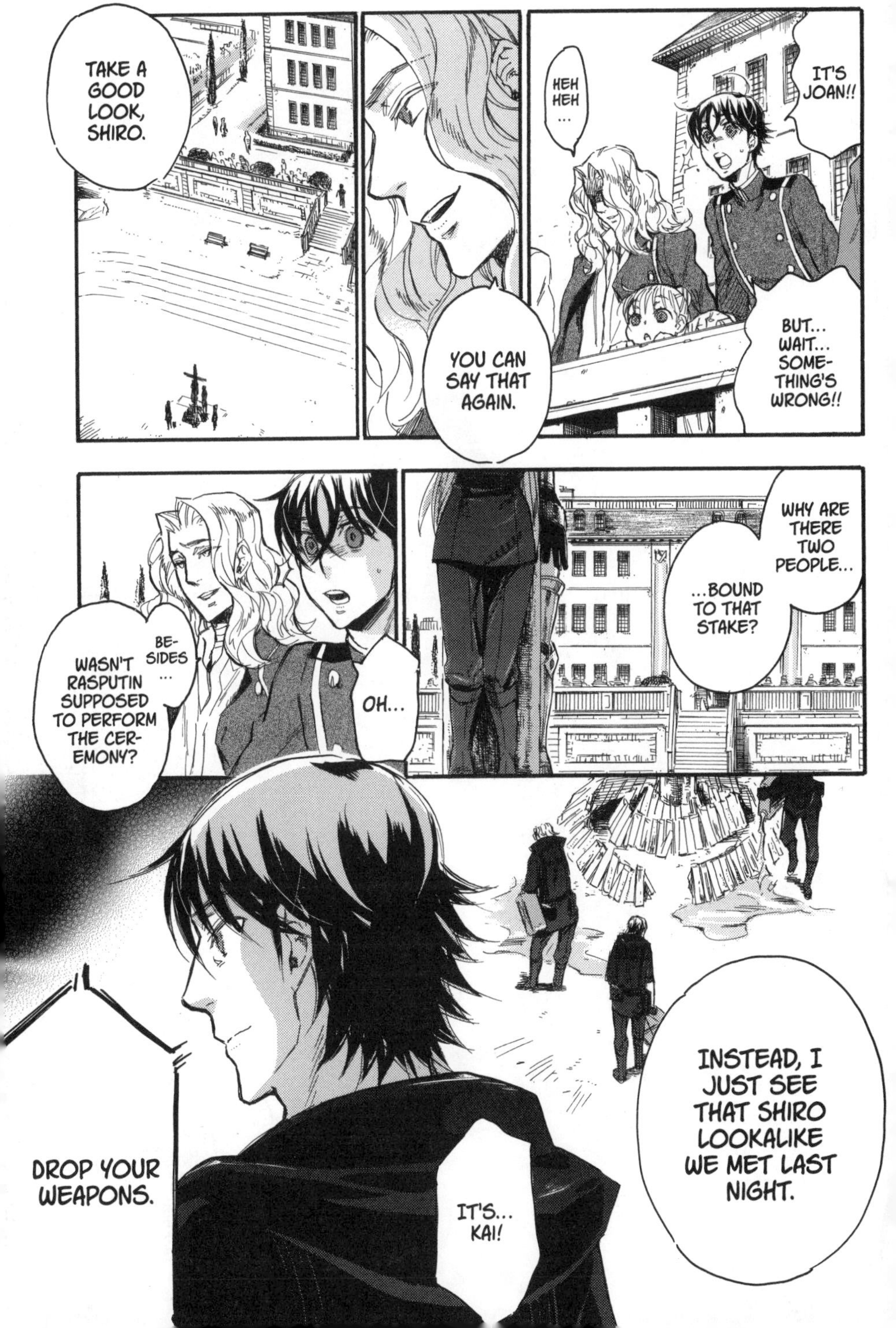
IT'S JOAN!!
HEH HEH ...
BUT... WAIT... SOME-THING'S WRONG!!
YOU CAN SAY THAT AGAIN.
TAKE A GOOD LOOK, SHIRO.
WHY ARE THERE TWO PEOPLE...
...BOUND TO THAT STAKE?
OH...
BE-SIDES ...
WASN'T RASPUTIN SUPPOSED TO PERFORM THE CER-EMONY?
INSTEAD, I JUST SEE THAT SHIRO LOOKALIKE WE MET LAST NIGHT.
IT'S... KAI!
DROP YOUR WEAPONS.

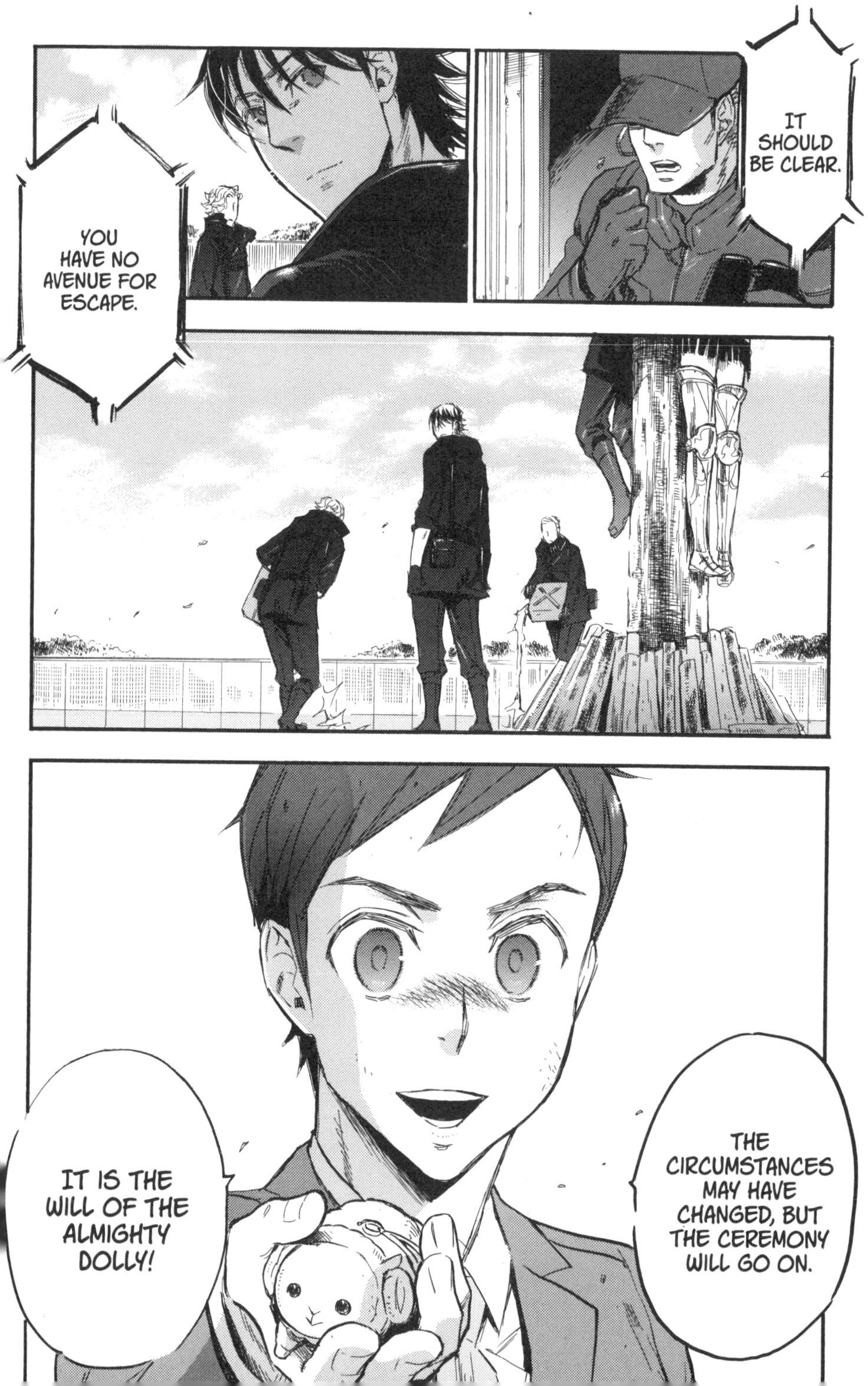
IT SHOULD BE CLEAR.
YOU HAVE NO AVENUE FOR ESCAPE.
THE CIRCUMSTANCES MAY HAVE CHANGED, BUT THE CEREMONY WILL GO ON.
IT IS THE WILL OF THE ALMIGHTY DOLLY!

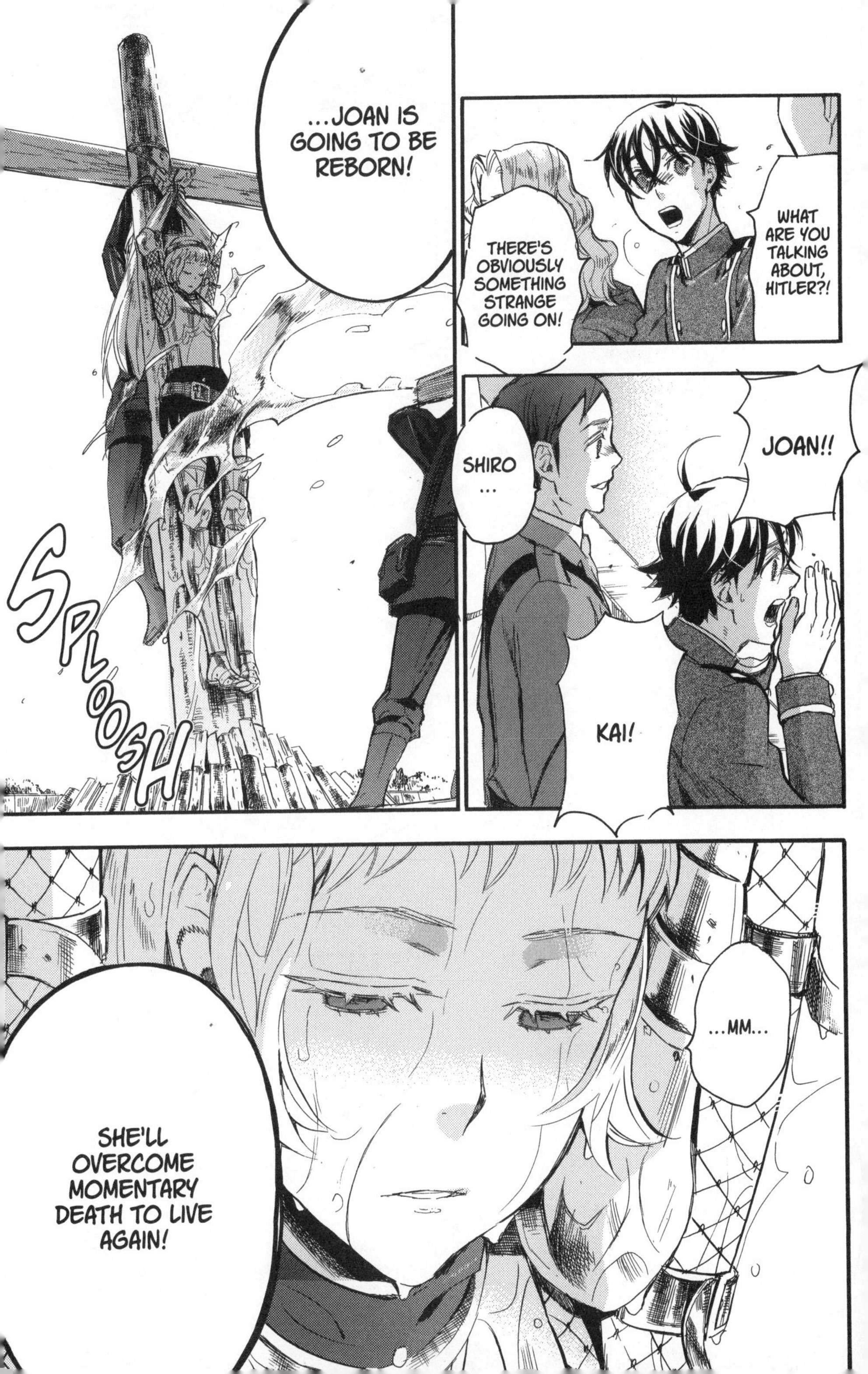
WHAT ARE YOU TALKING ABOUT, HITLER?!
THERE'S OBVIOUSLY SOMETHING STRANGE GOING ON!
JOAN!!
SHIRO ...
KAI!
...JOAN IS GOING TO BE REBORN!
SPLOOSH
...MM...
SHE'LL OVERCOME MOMENTARY DEATH TO LIVE AGAIN!

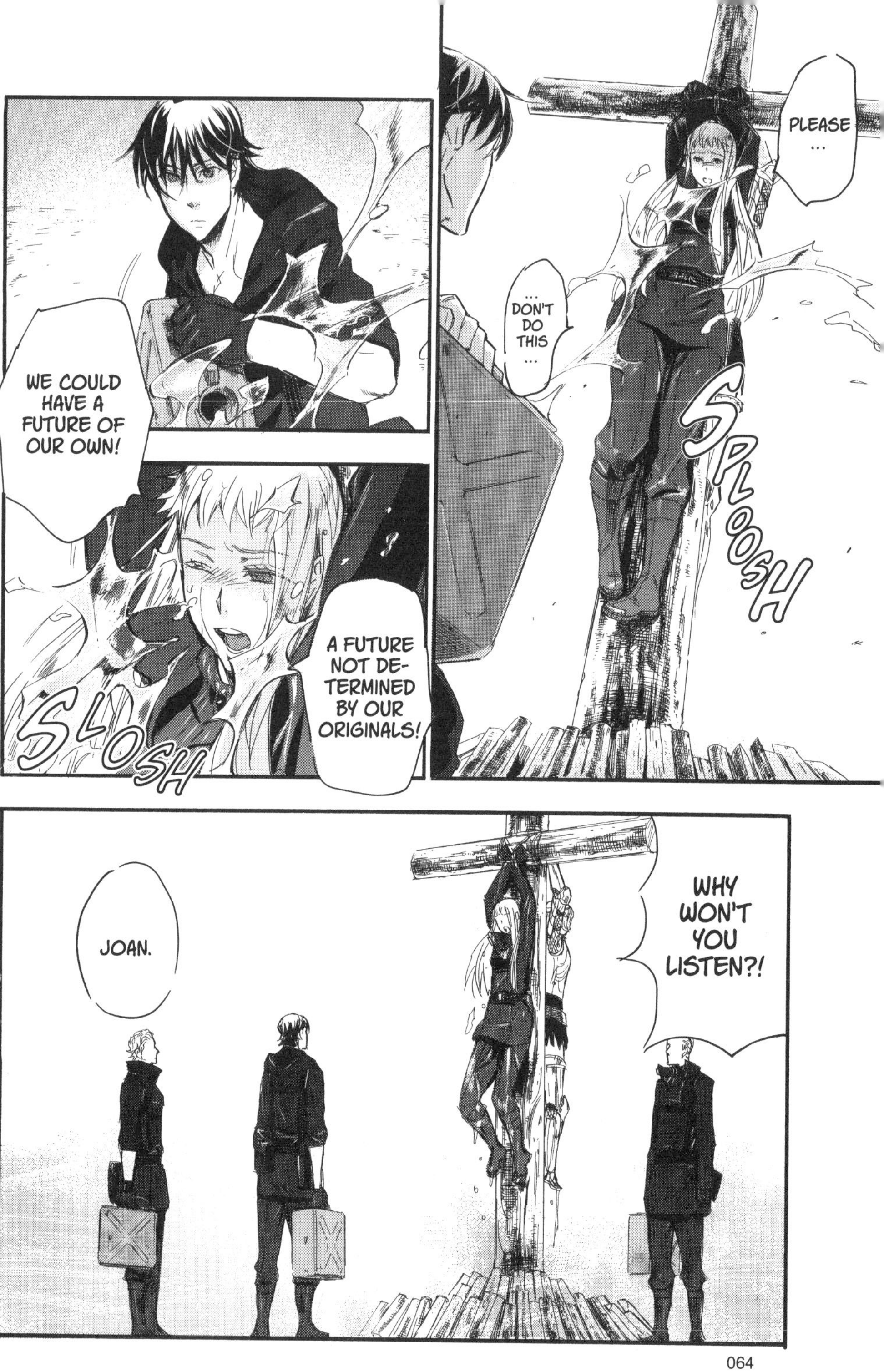
PLEASE ...
... DON'T DO THIS ...
SPLOOSH
WE COULD HAVE A FUTURE OF OUR OWN!
A FUTURE NOT DE-TERMINED BY OUR ORIGINALS!
SLOSH
WHY WON'T YOU LISTEN?!
JOAN.

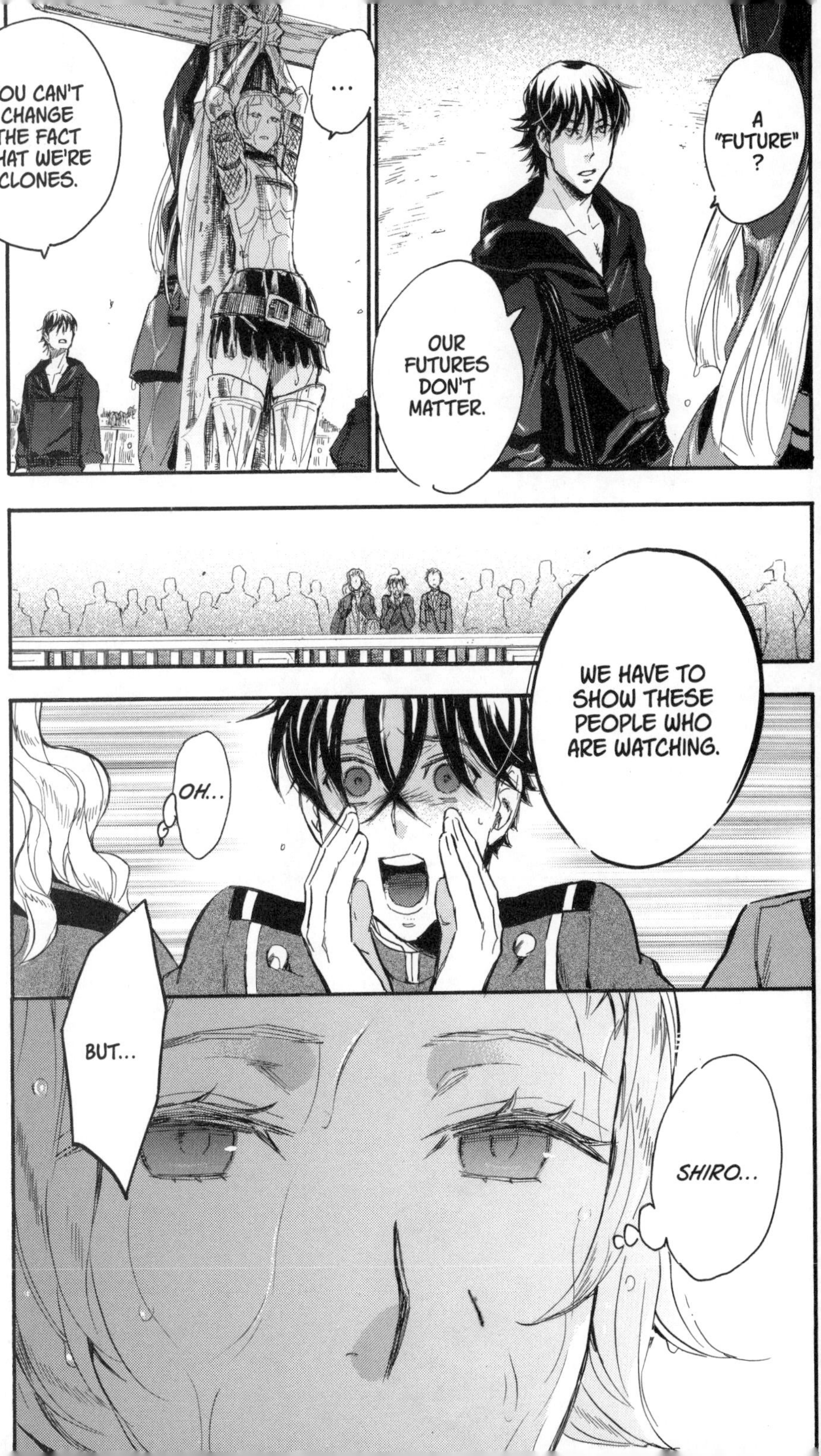
A "FUTURE"?
OUR FUTURES DON'T MATTER.
...
YOU CAN'T CHANGE THE FACT THAT WE'RE CLONES.
WE HAVE TO SHOW THESE PEOPLE WHO ARE WATCHING.
OH...
BUT...
SHIRO...

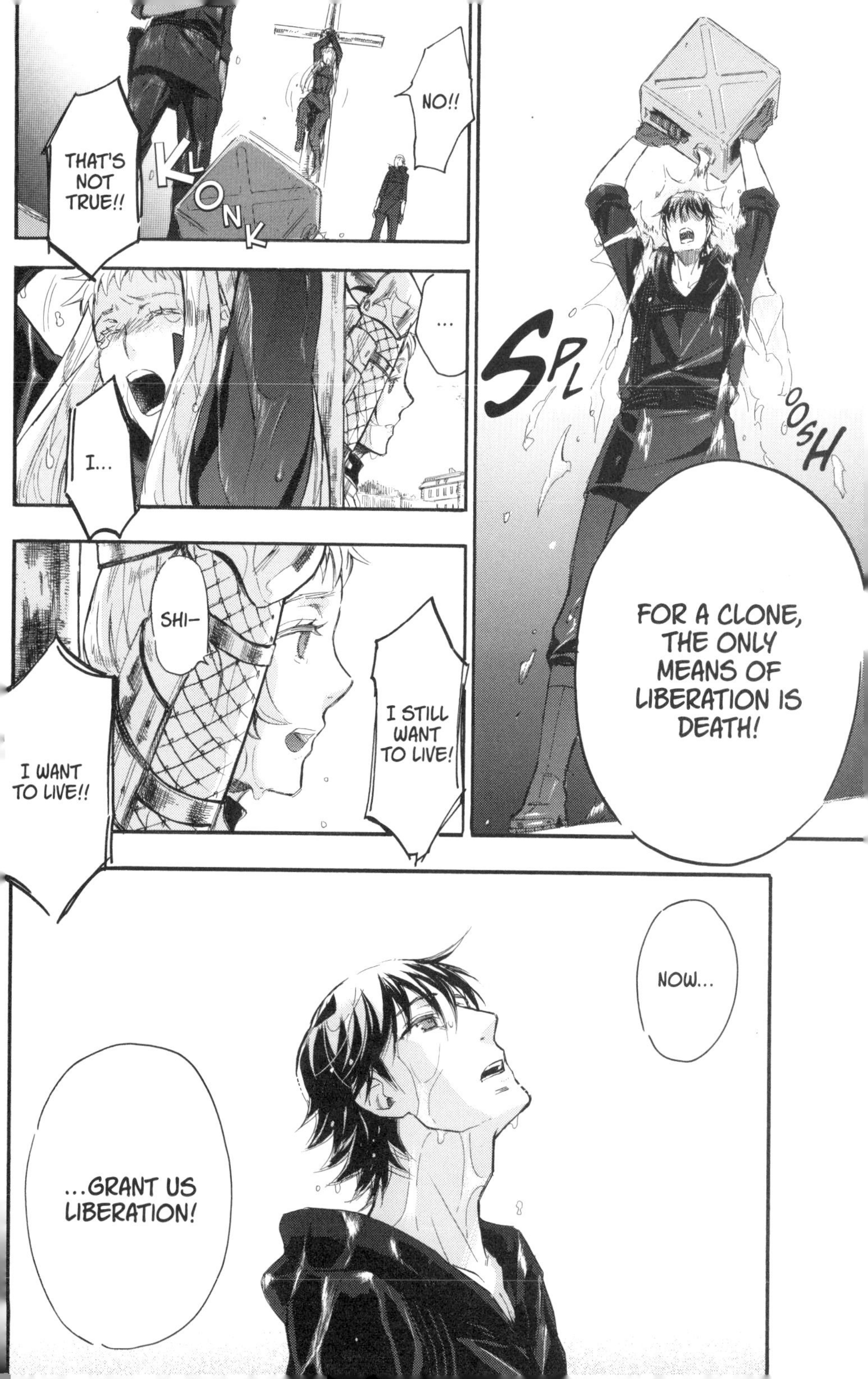
SPLOOSH
FOR A CLONE, THE ONLY MEANS OF LIBERATION IS DEATH!
NO!!
THAT'S NOT TRUE!!
KLONK
...
I...
I STILL WANT TO LIVE!
SHI-
I WANT TO LIVE!!
NOW...
...GRANT US LIBERATION!

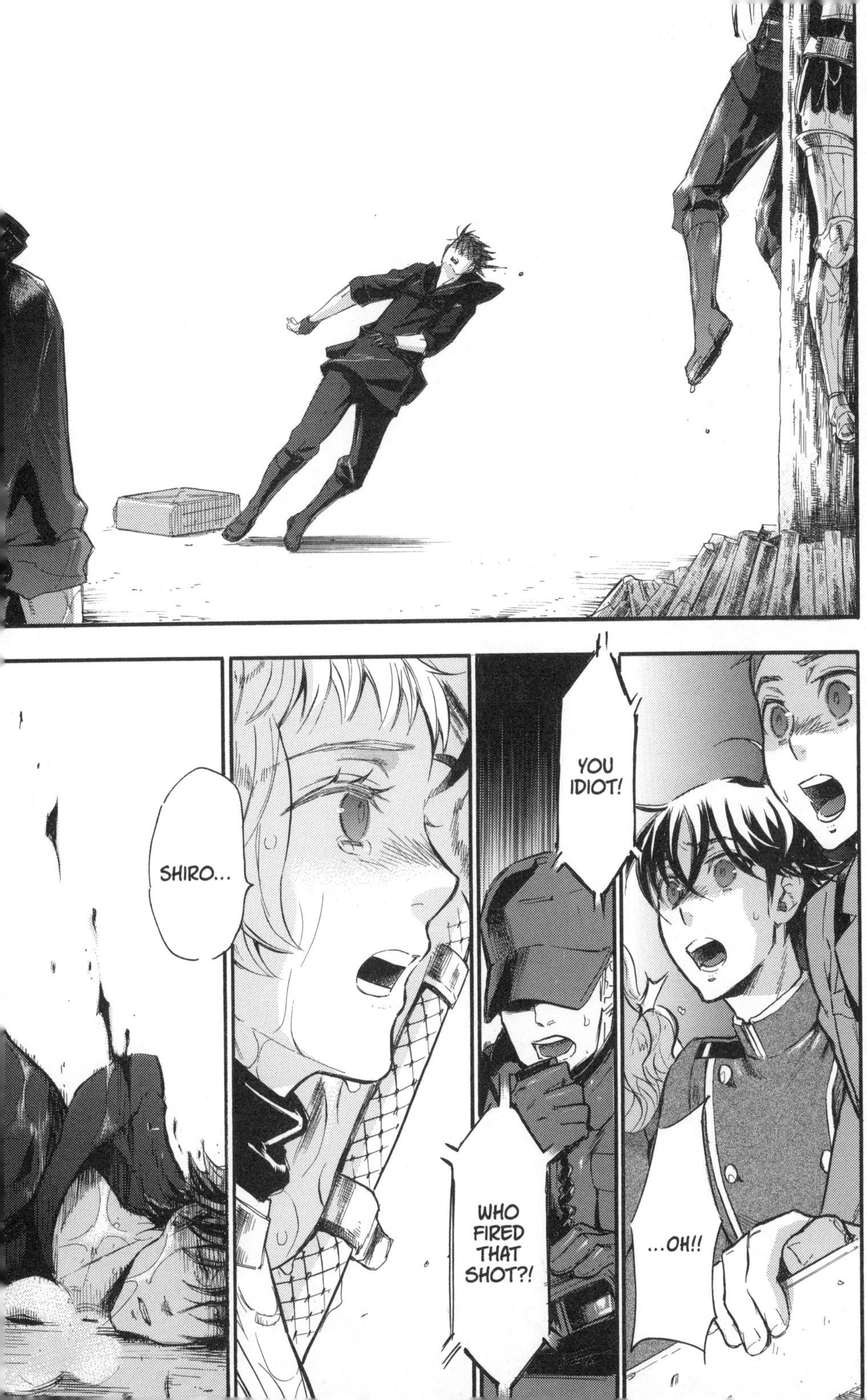
...OH!!
YOU IDIOT!
WHO FIRED THAT SHOT?!
SHIRO...

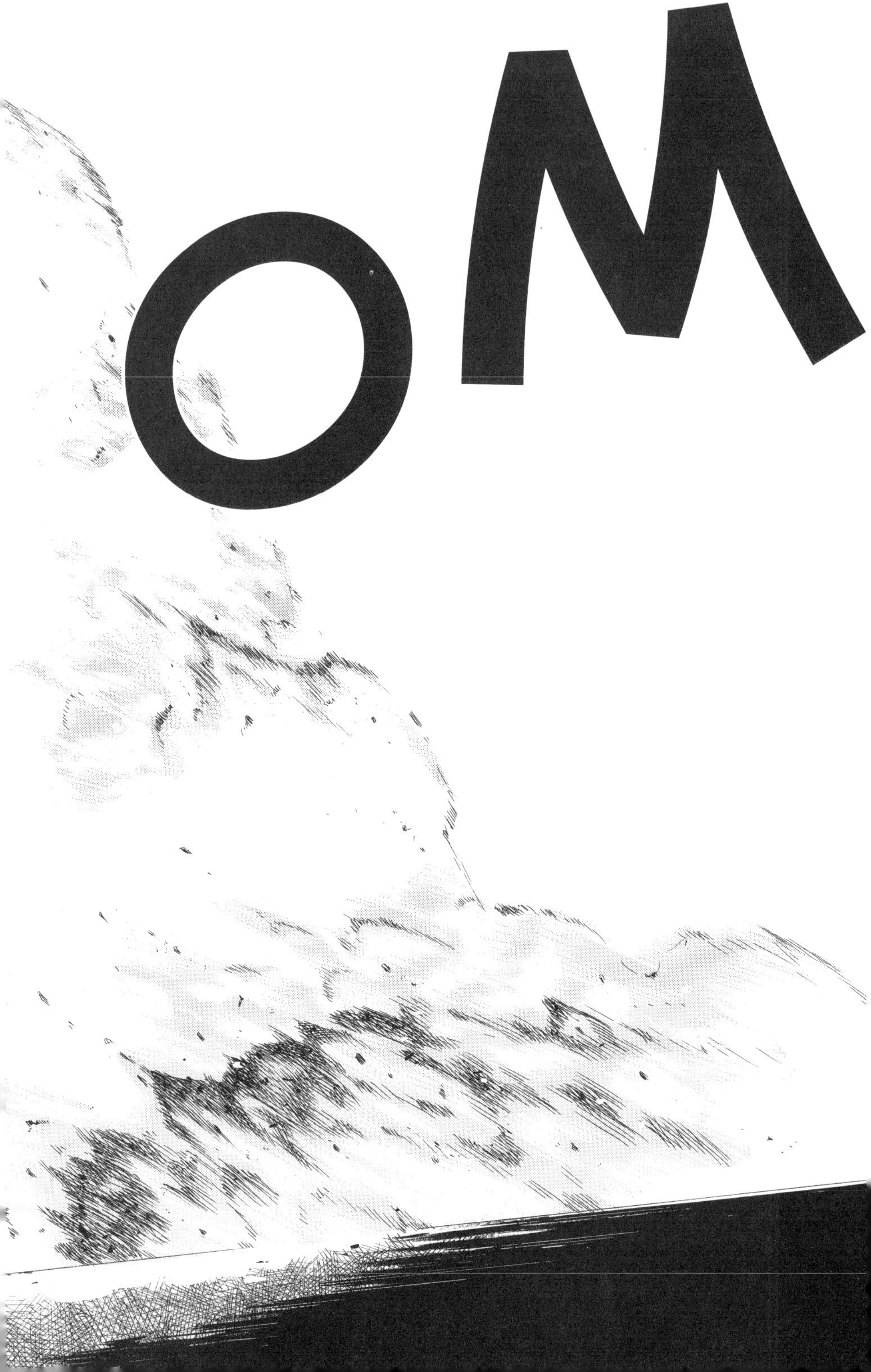
OM

FO

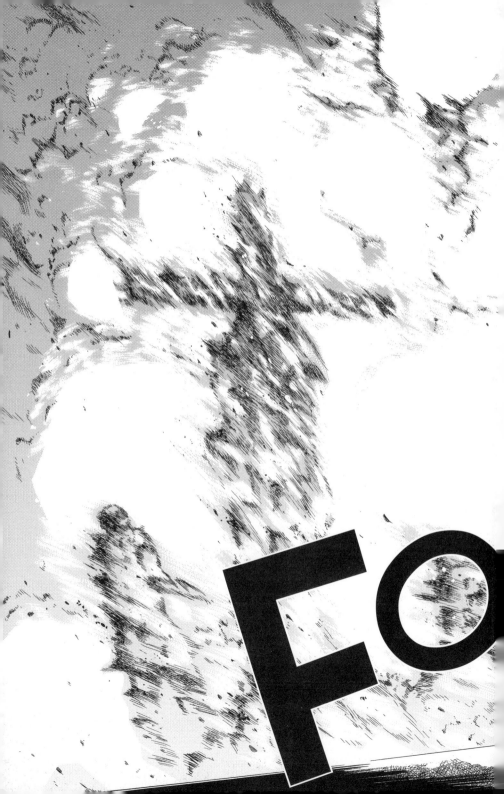

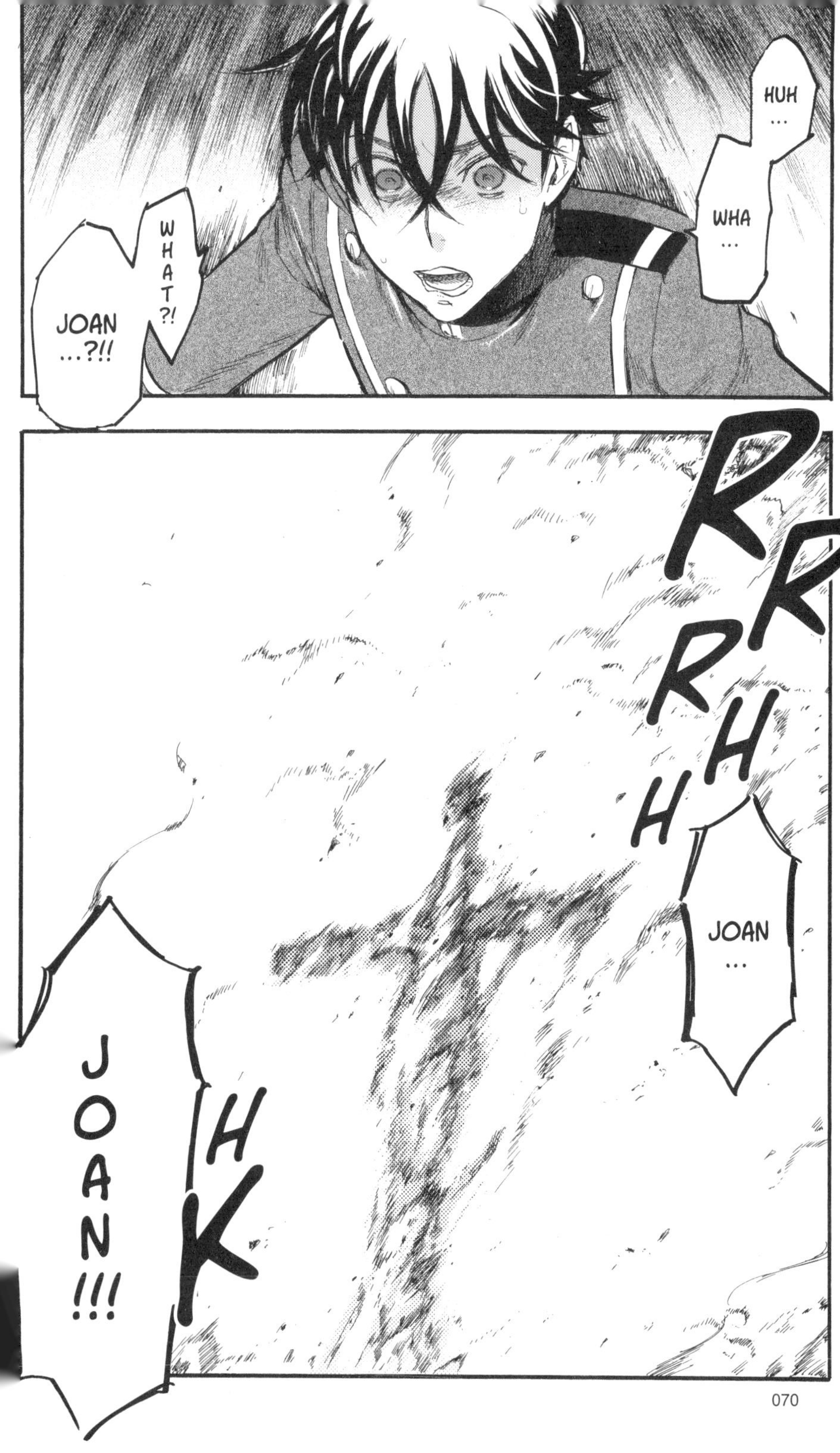
HUH ...
WHA ...
WHAT?!
JOAN ...?!!
RRRHHH
JOAN ...
HHK
JOAN!!!

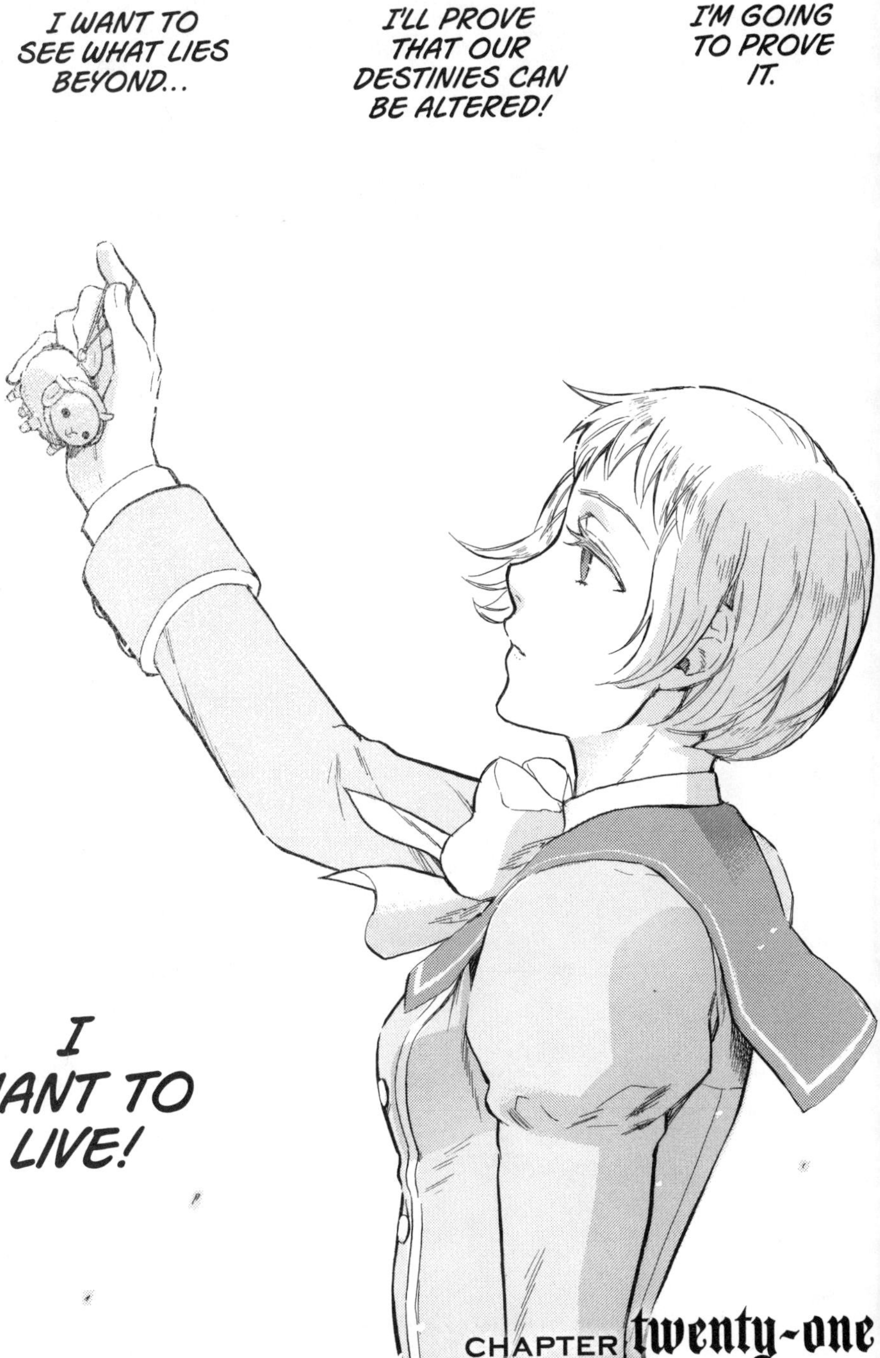
I'M GOING TO PROVE IT.
I'LL PROVE THAT OUR DESTINIES CAN BE ALTERED!
I WANT TO SEE WHAT LIES BEYOND...
I WANT TO LIVE!
CHAPTER twenty-one

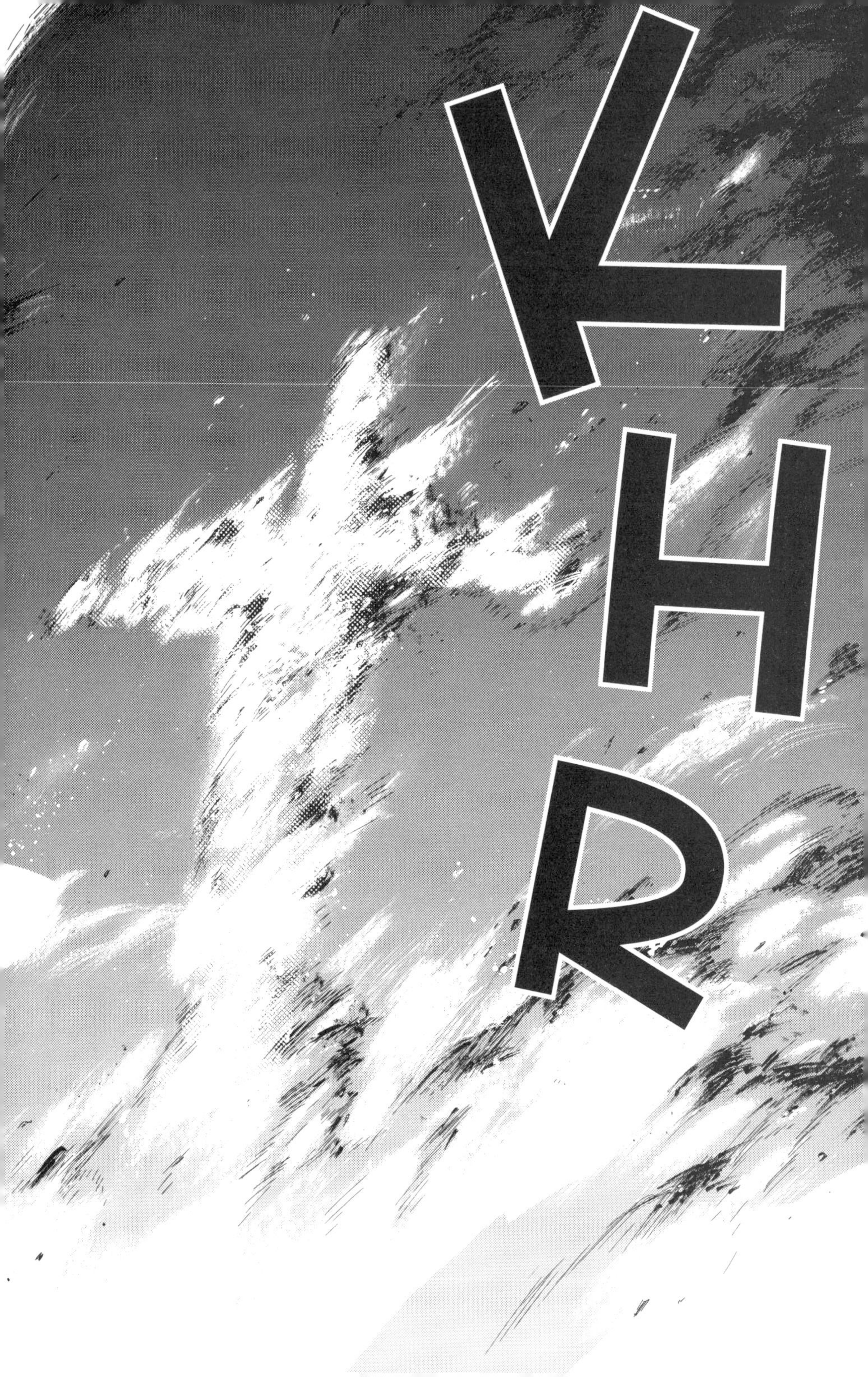
VHR

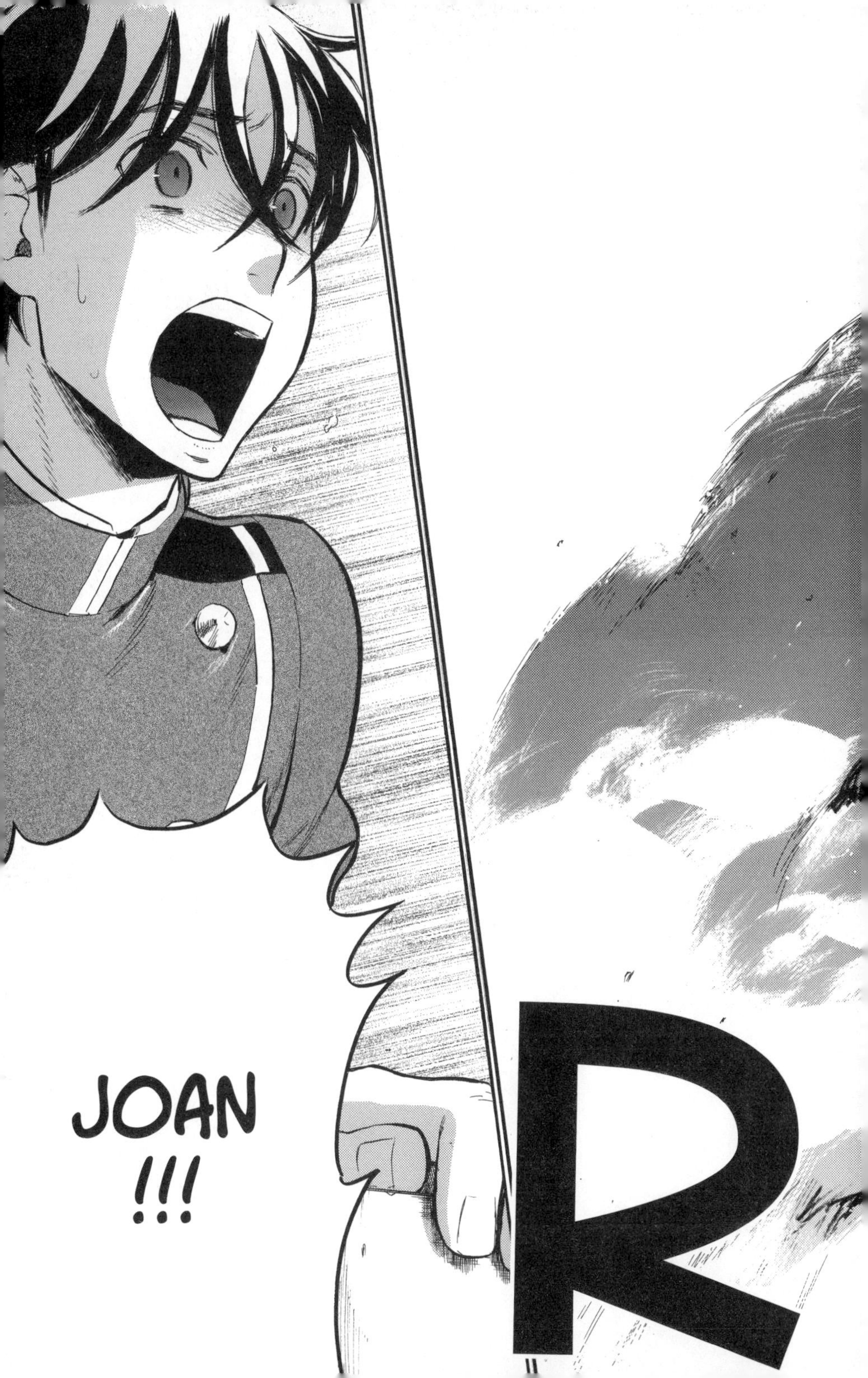
JOAN !!!
R

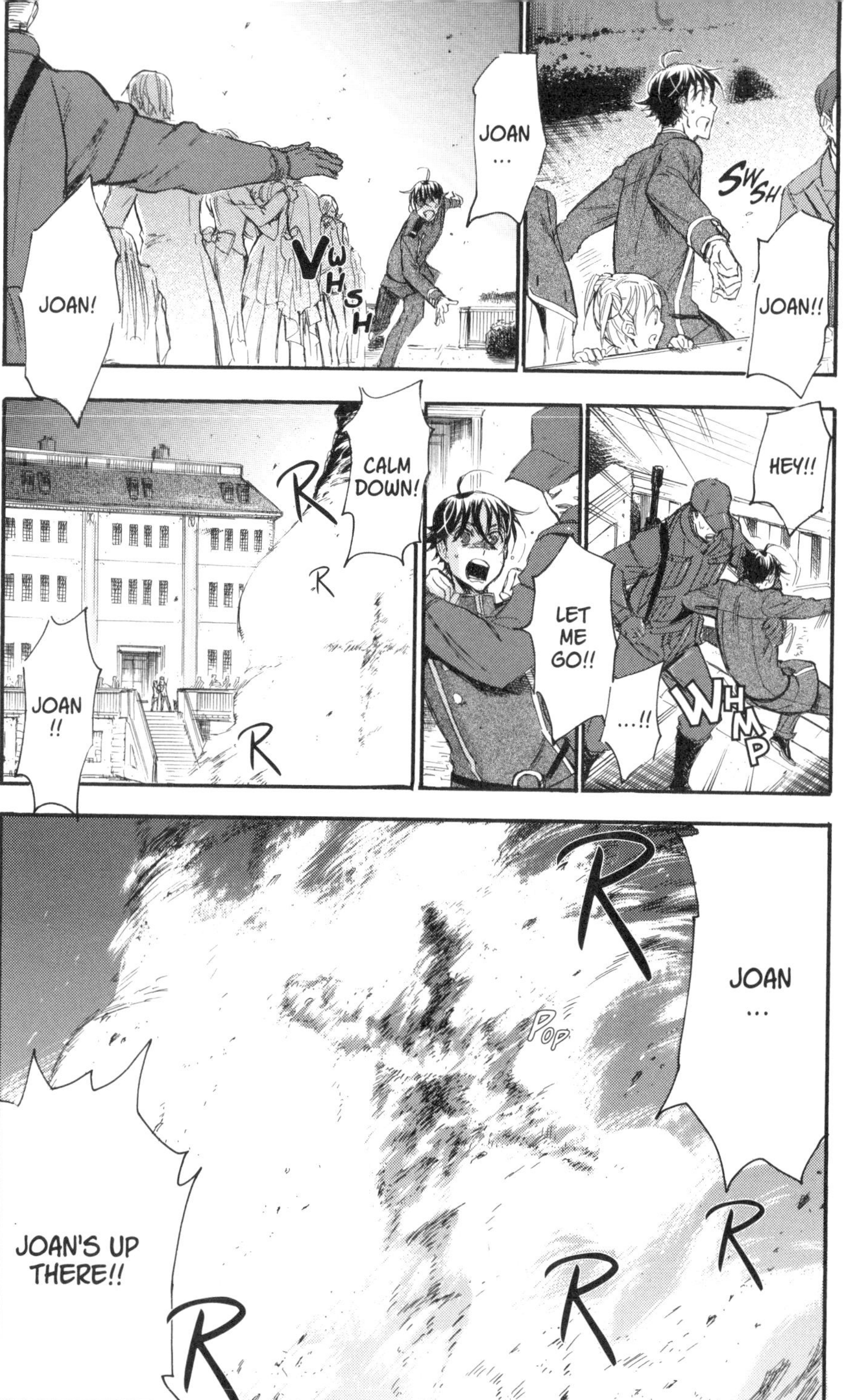
JOAN ...
SWSH
JOAN!!
VWHSH
JOAN!
HEY!!
WHMP
...!!
LET ME GO!!
CALM DOWN!
R
R
R
JOAN !!
JOAN ...
POP
R
R
R
JOAN'S UP THERE!!
R

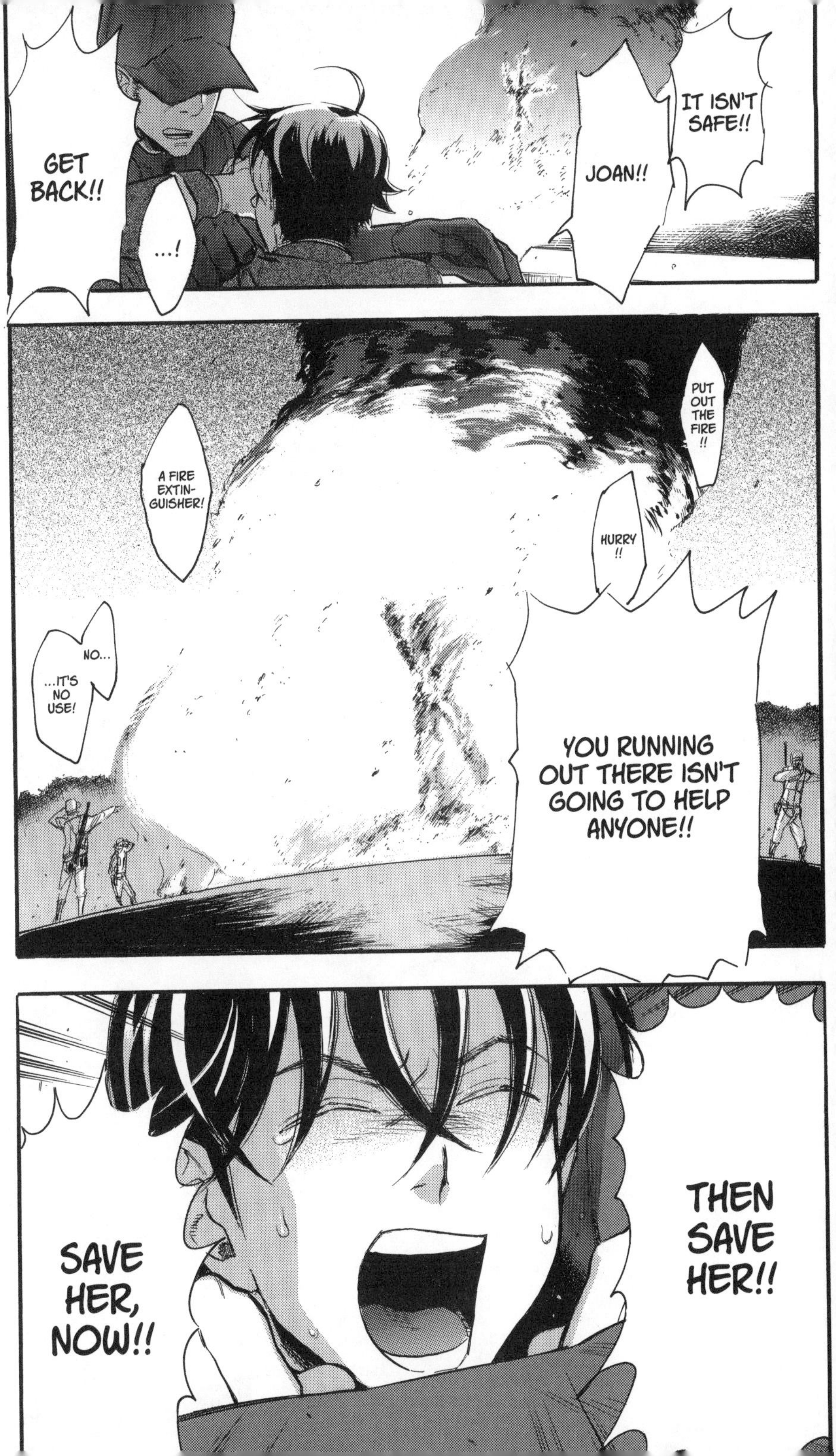
IT ISN'T SAFE!!
JOAN!!
GET BACK!!
...!
PUT OUT THE FIRE!!
HURRY!!
A FIRE EXTIN-GUISHER!
NO... ...IT'S NO USE!
YOU RUNNING OUT THERE ISN'T GOING TO HELP ANYONE!!
THEN SAVE HER!!
SAVE HER, NOW!!

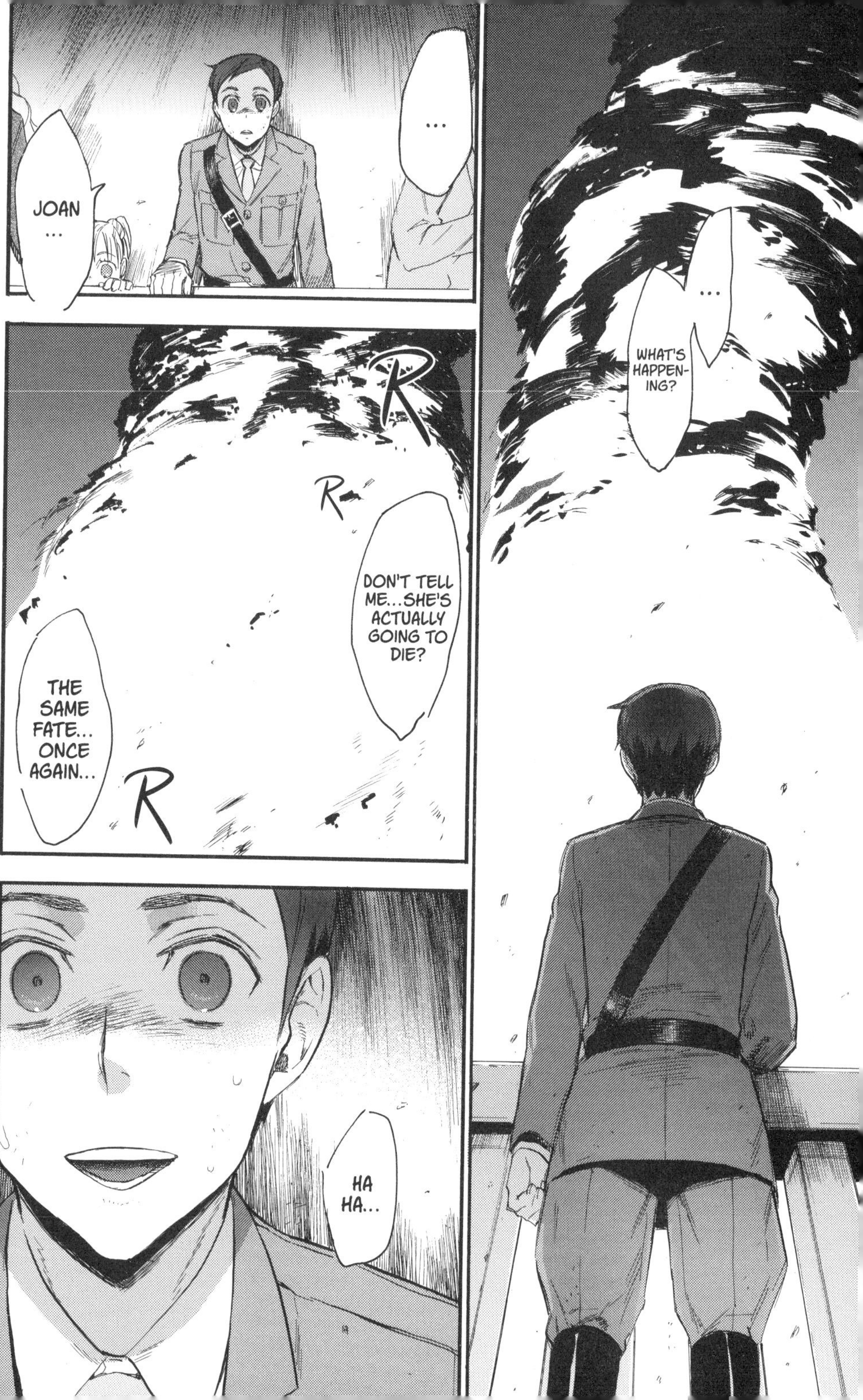
...
WHAT'S HAPPEN-ING?
...
JOAN ...
R
R
DON'T TELL ME...SHE'S ACTUALLY GOING TO DIE?
THE SAME FATE... ONCE AGAIN...
R
HA HA...

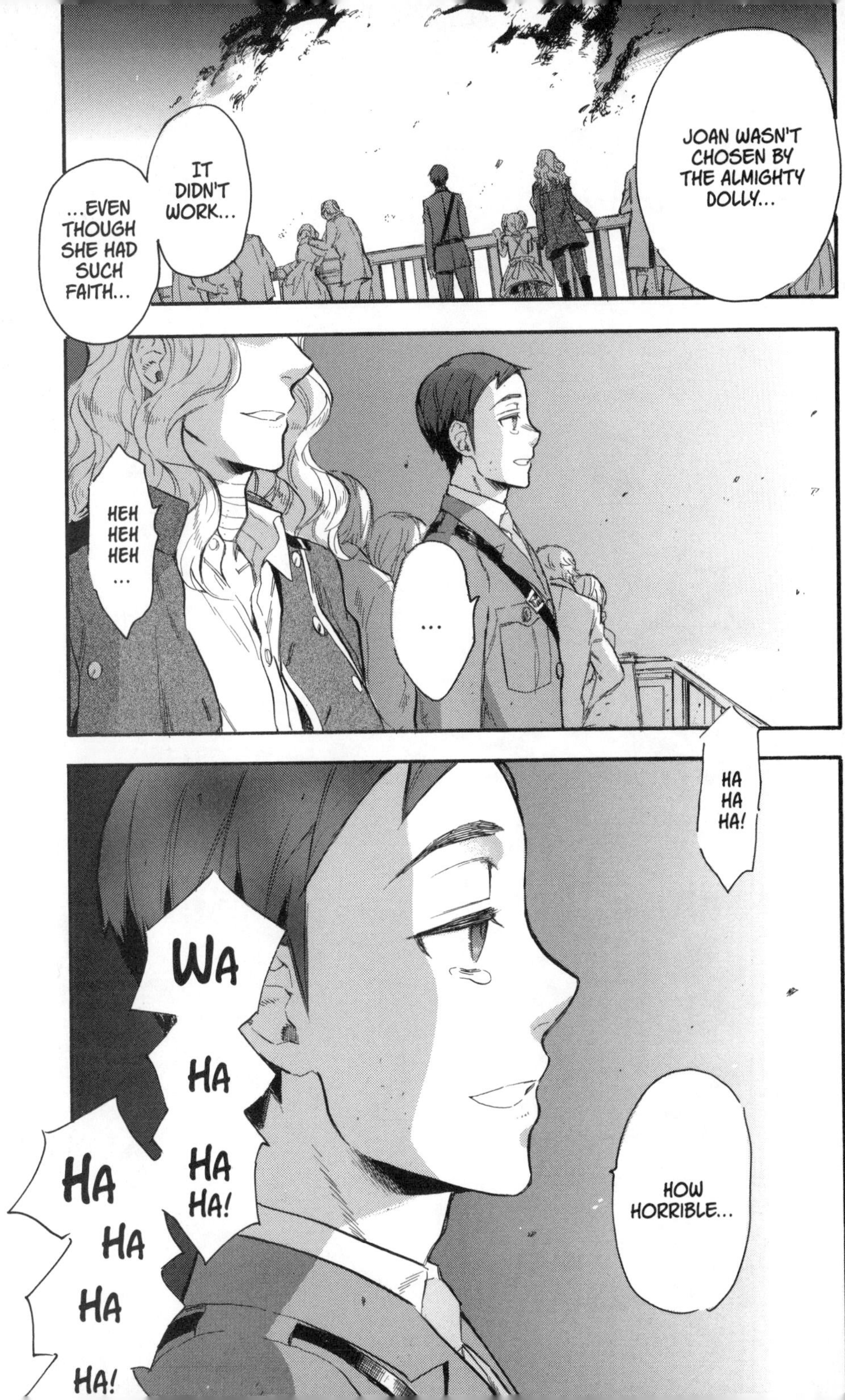

JOAN WASN'T CHOSEN BY THE ALMIGHTY DOLLY...
IT DIDN'T WORK...
...EVEN THOUGH SHE HAD SUCH FAITH...
...
HEH HEH HEH ...
HA HA HA!
HOW HORRIBLE...
WA HA HA HA!
HA HA HA HA!

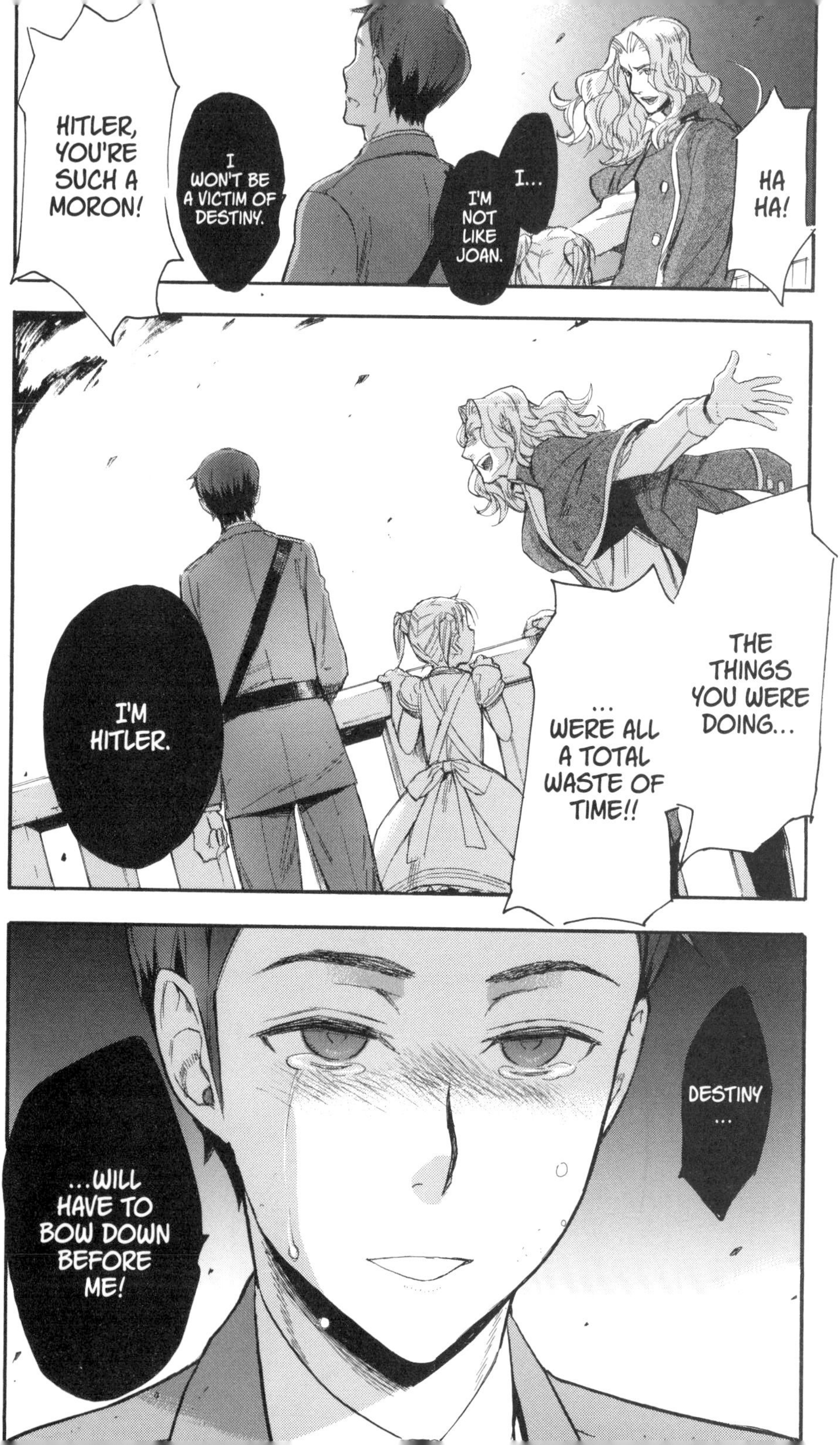
HA HA!
I...
I'M NOT LIKE JOAN.
I WON'T BE A VICTIM OF DESTINY.
HITLER, YOU'RE SUCH A MORON!
THE THINGS YOU WERE DOING...
...WERE ALL A TOTAL WASTE OF TIME!!
I'M HITLER.
DESTINY...
...WILL HAVE TO BOW DOWN BEFORE ME!

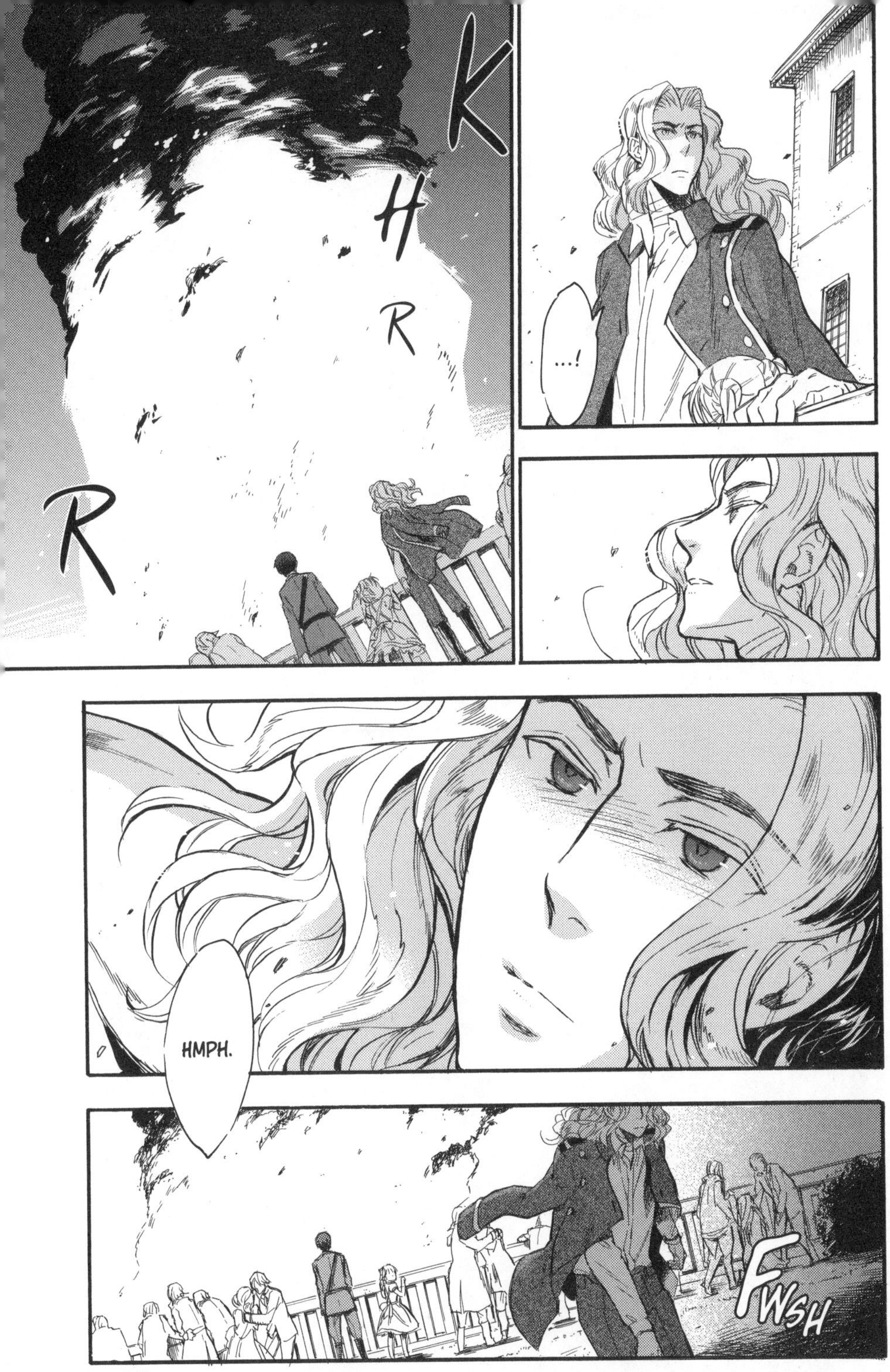
...!
K
H
R
R
HMPH.
FWSH

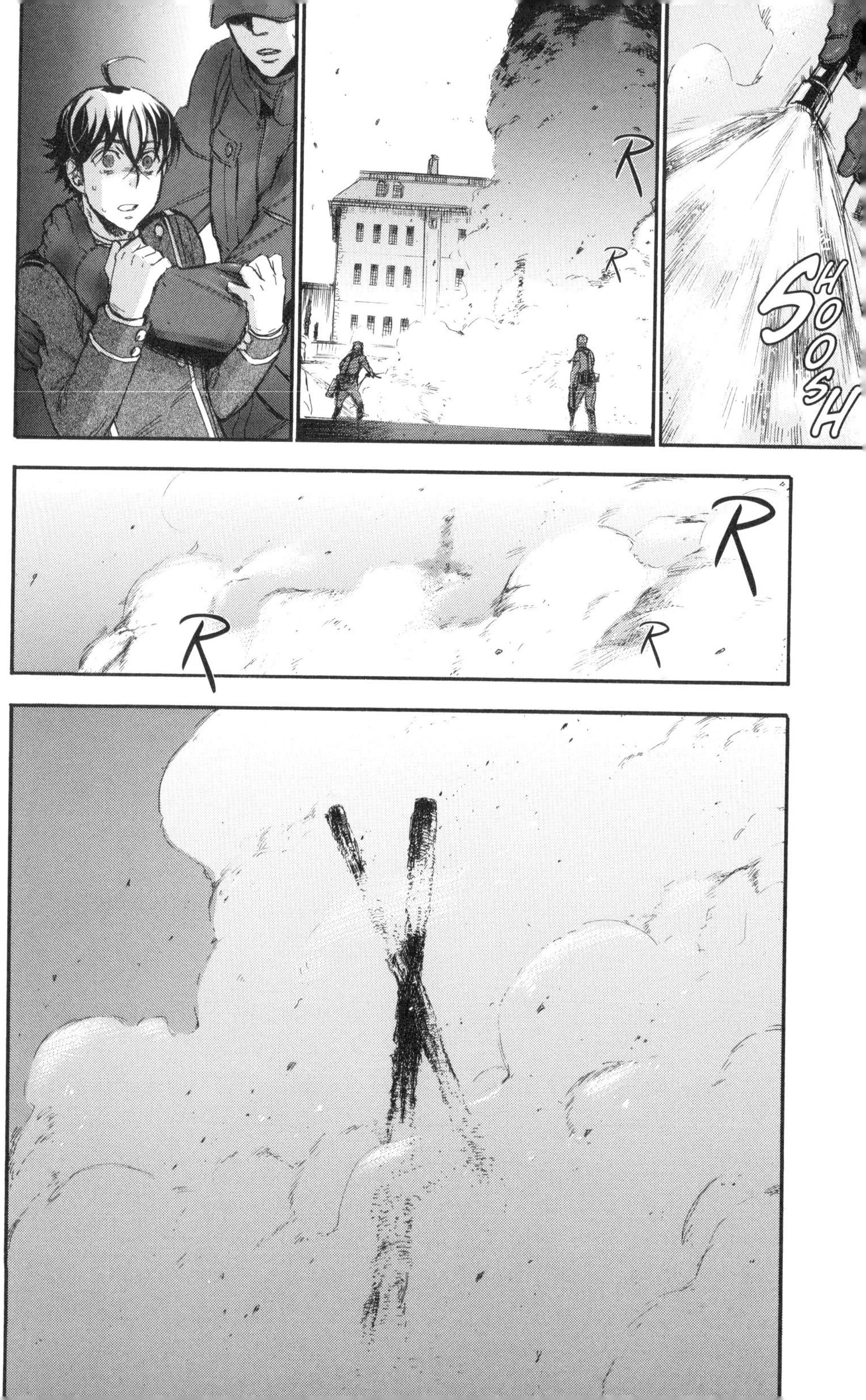
SHOOSH
R
R
R
R
R

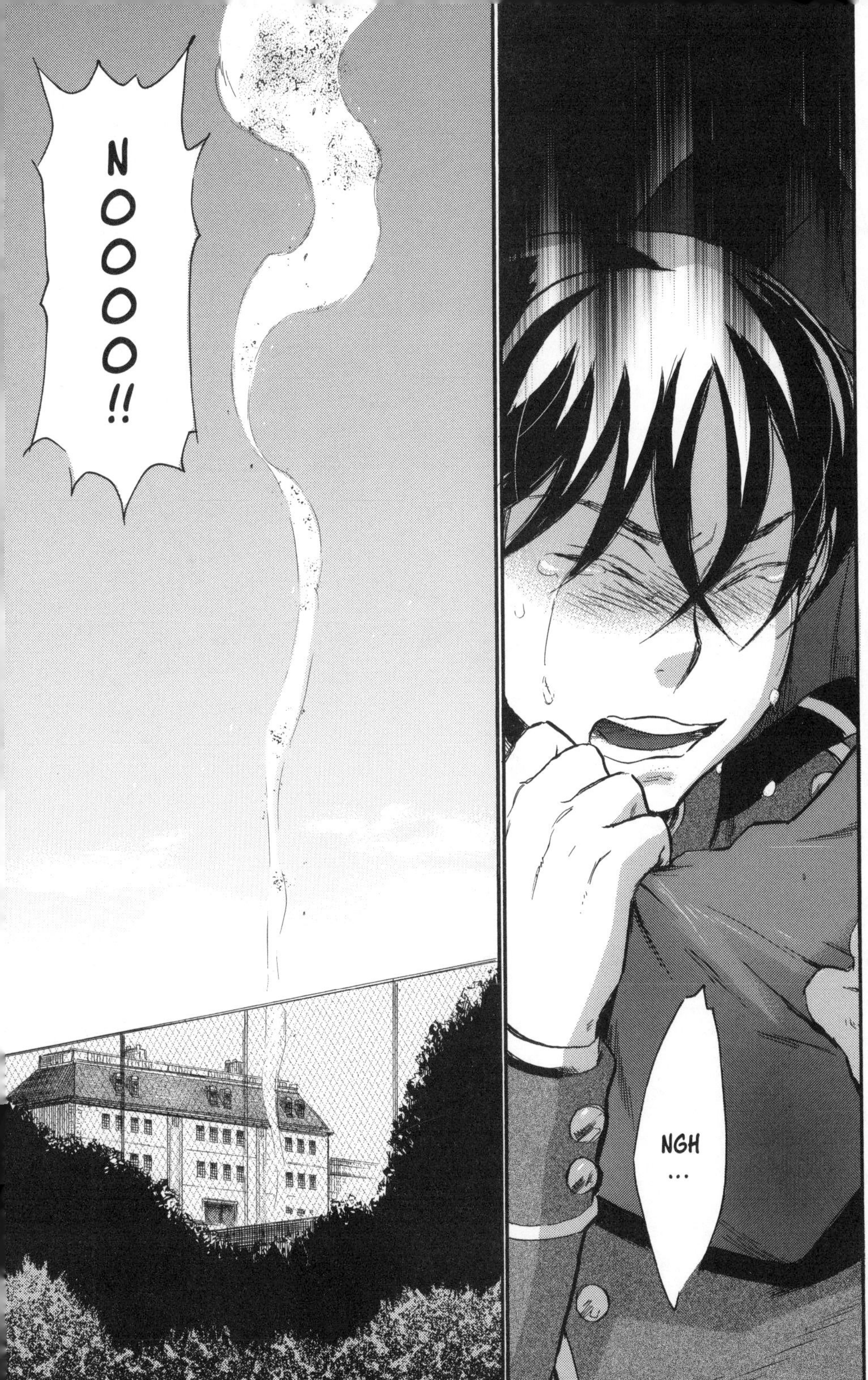
NGH ...
NOOOOO!!

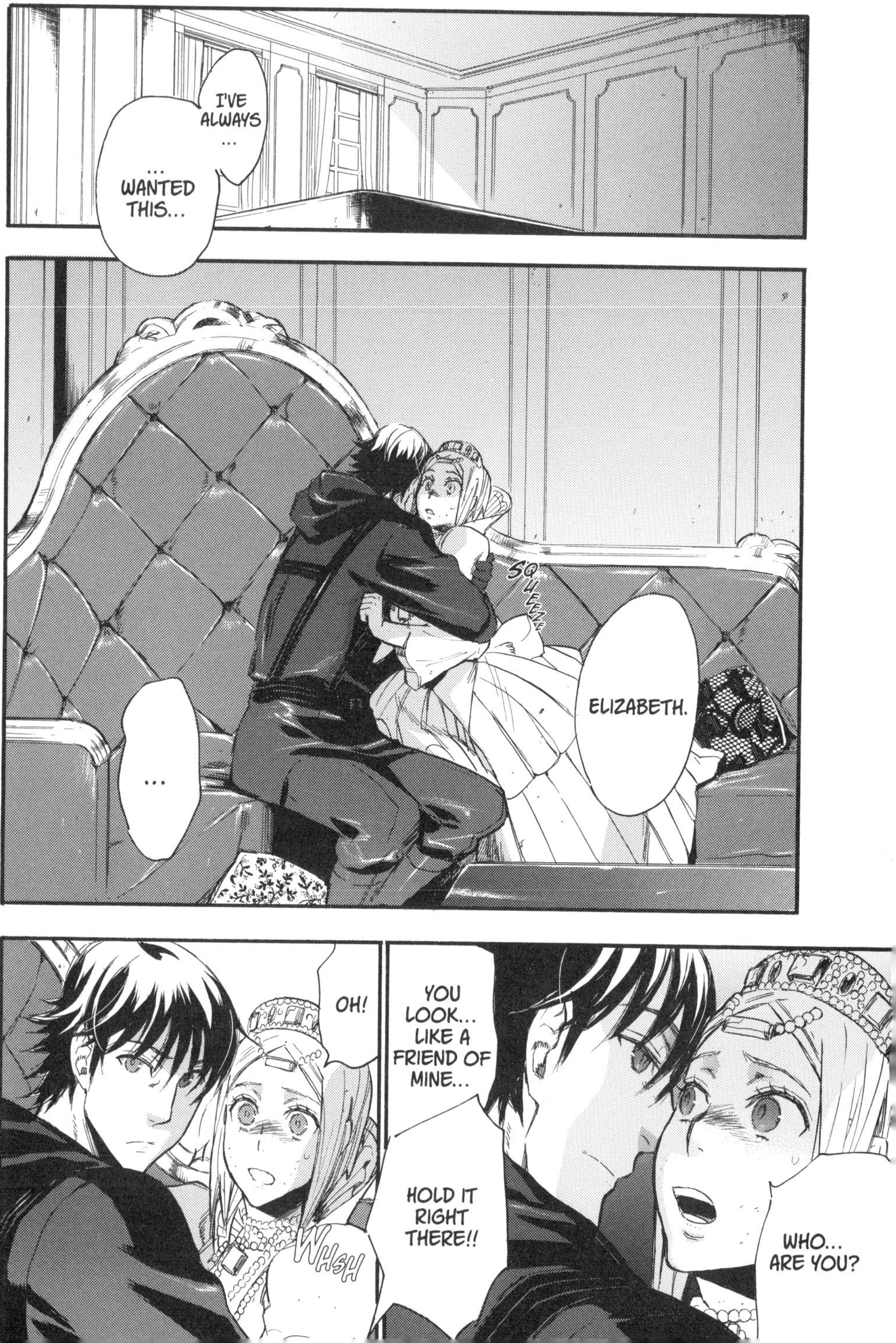
I'VE ALWAYS ...
... WANTED THIS...
SQUEEZE
ELIZABETH.
...
YOU LOOK... LIKE A FRIEND OF MINE...
WHO... ARE YOU?
HOLD IT RIGHT THERE!!
OH!
WHSH

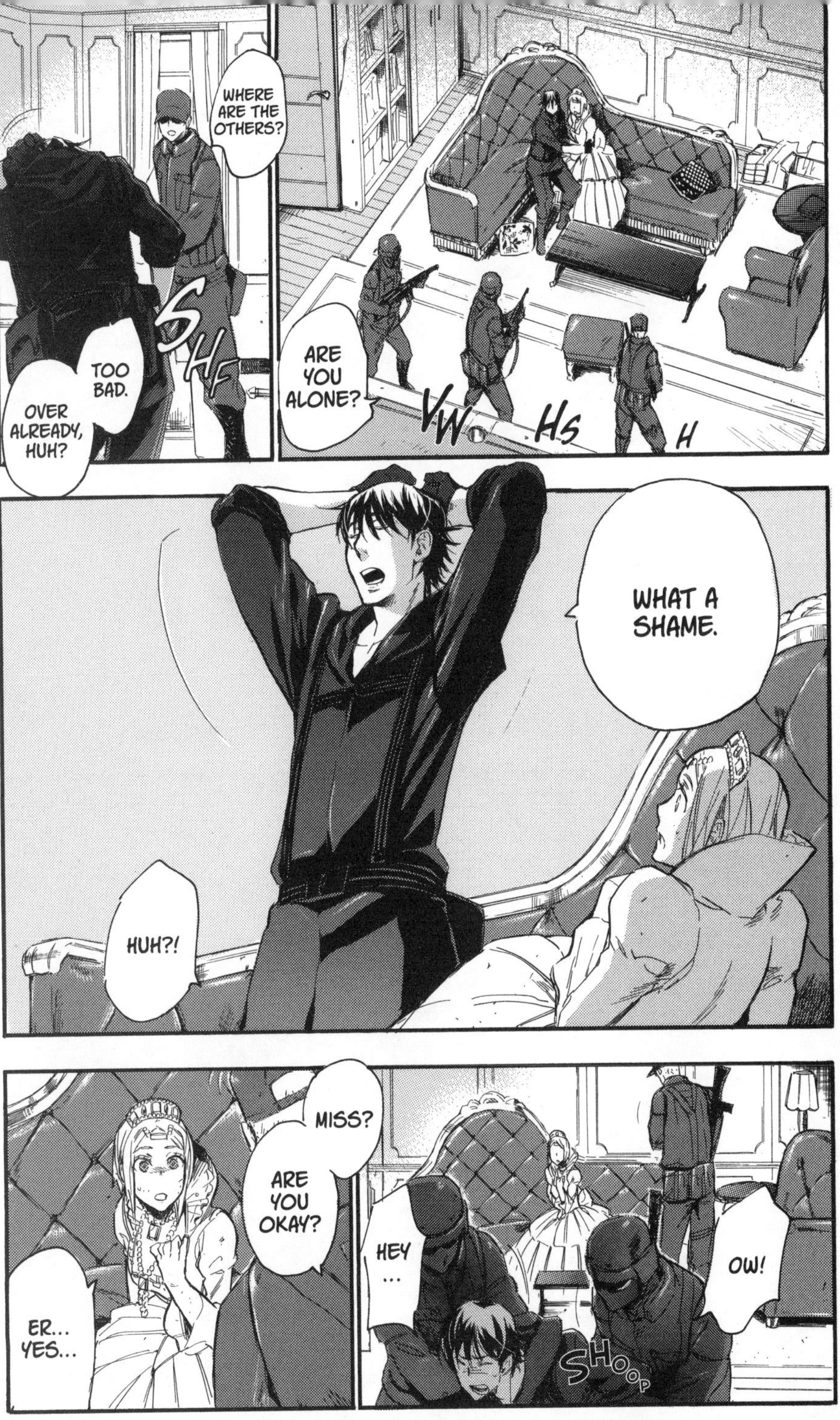
ARE YOU ALONE?
VW
HS
H
WHERE ARE THE OTHERS?
SHF
TOO BAD.
OVER ALREADY, HUH?
WHAT A SHAME.
HUH?!
OW!
HEY...
SHOOP
MISS?
ARE YOU OKAY?
ER... YES...

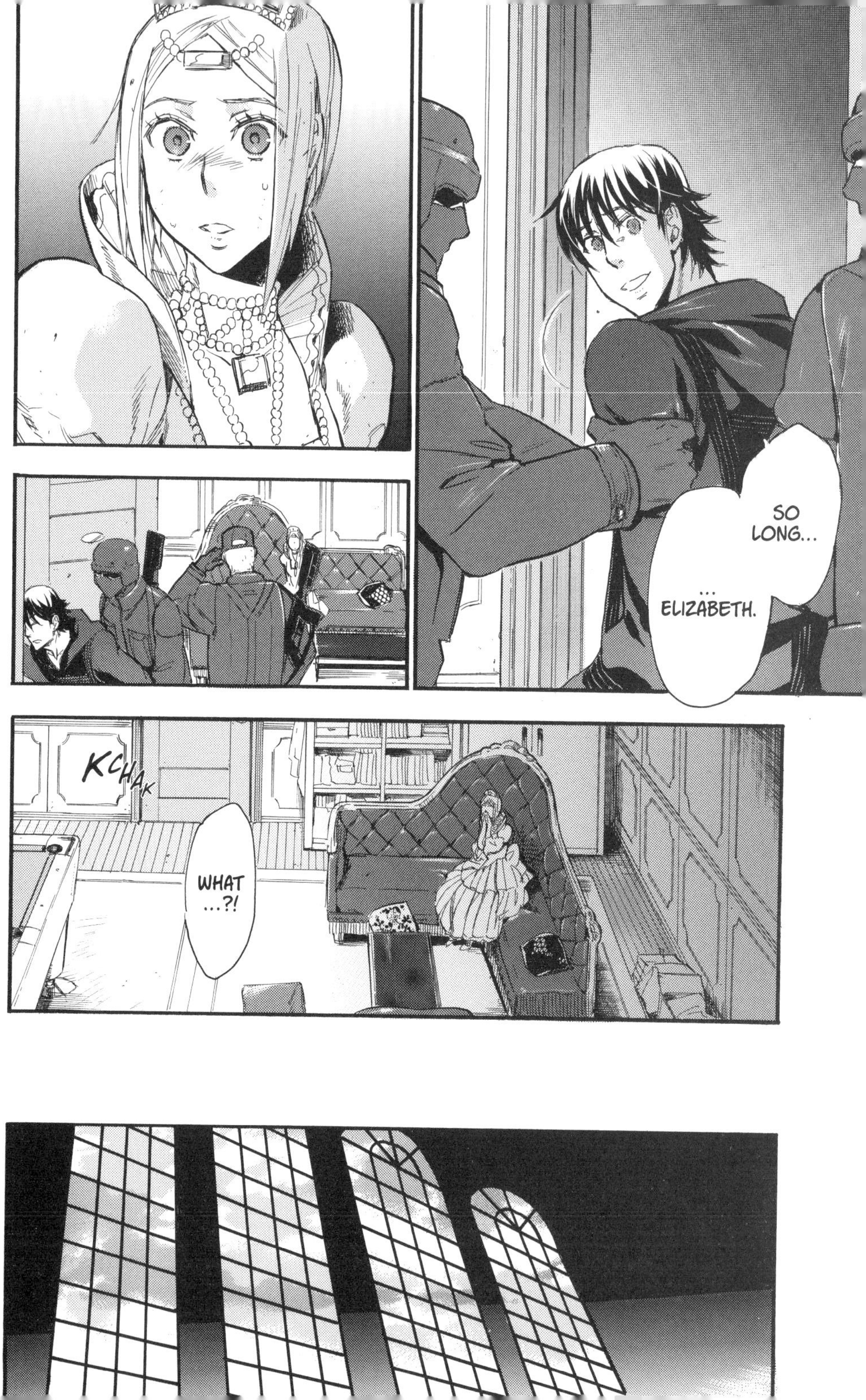
SO LONG...
...ELIZABETH.
KCHAK
WHAT ...?!

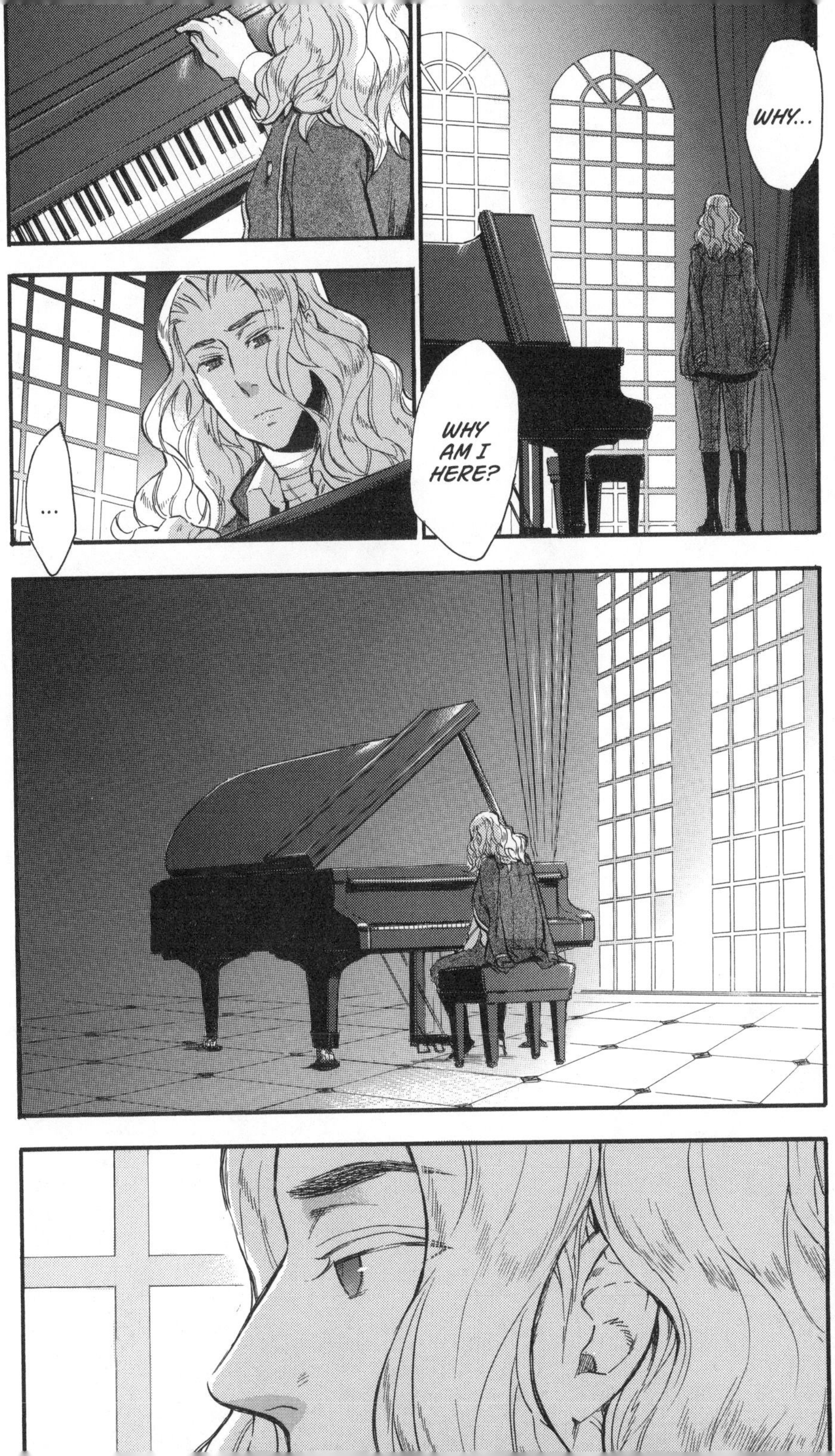
WHY...
WHY AM I HERE?
...

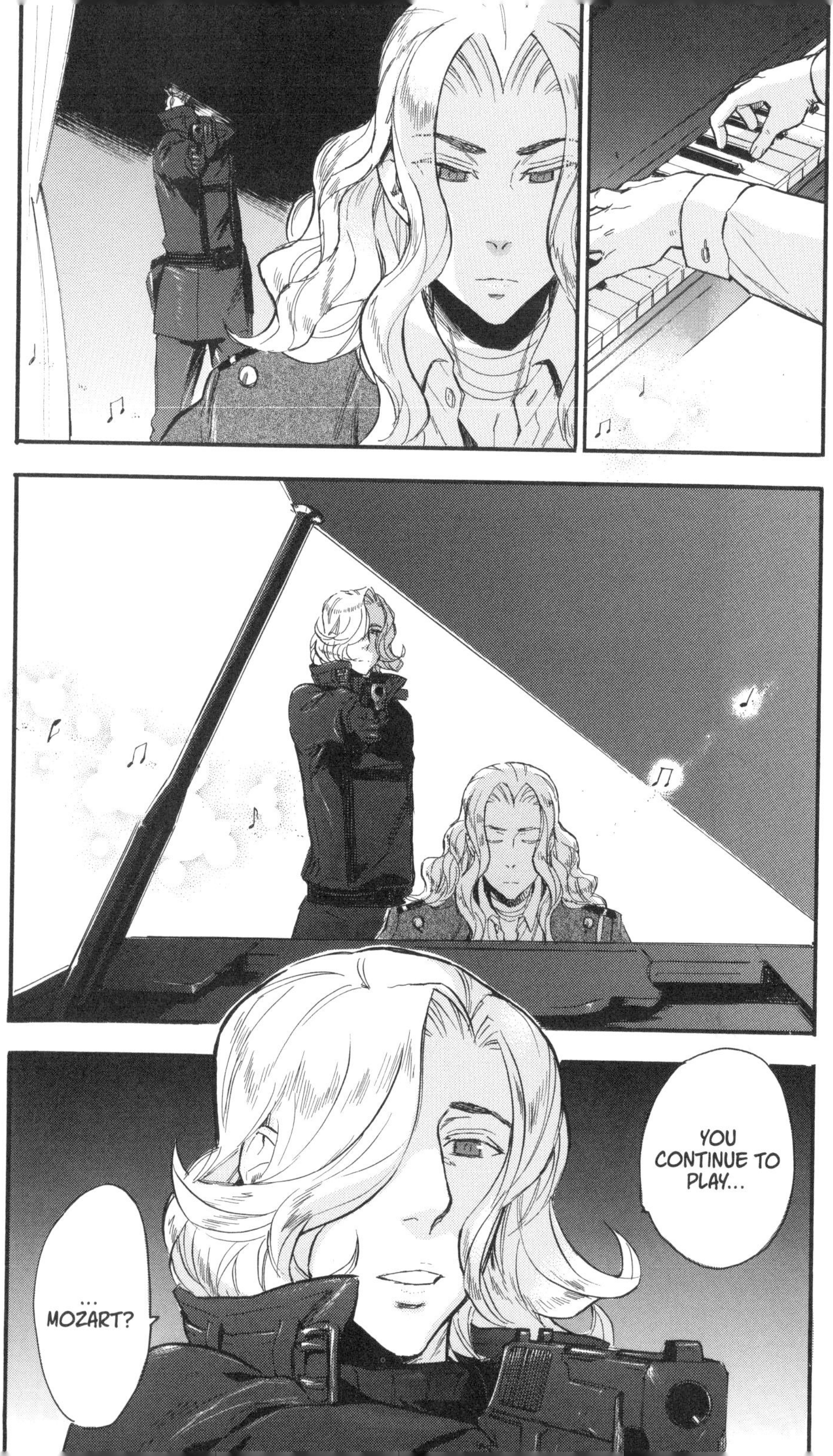
YOU CONTINUE TO PLAY...
... MOZART?

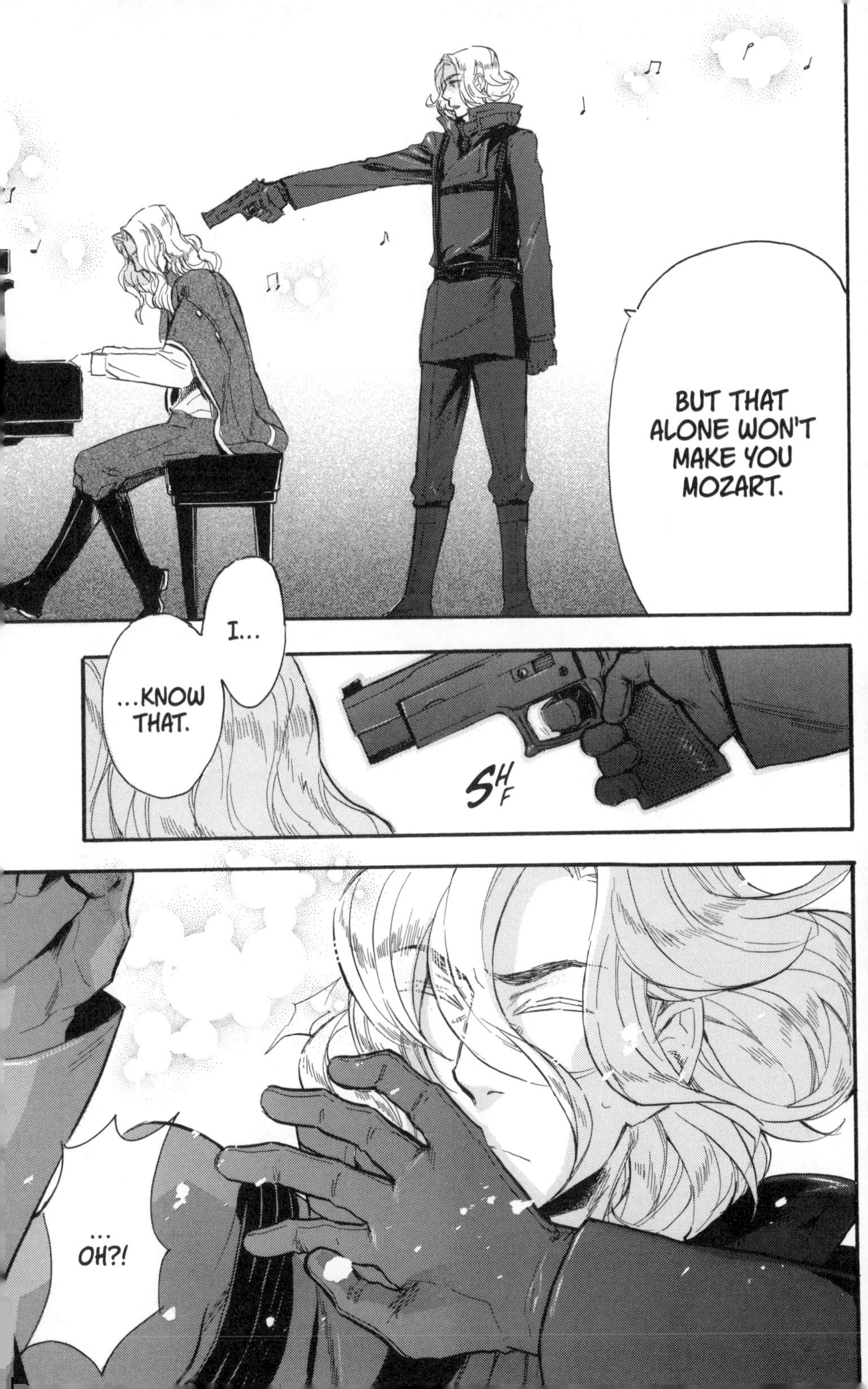
BUT THAT ALONE WON'T MAKE YOU MOZART.
I...
...KNOW THAT.
SHF
...OH?!

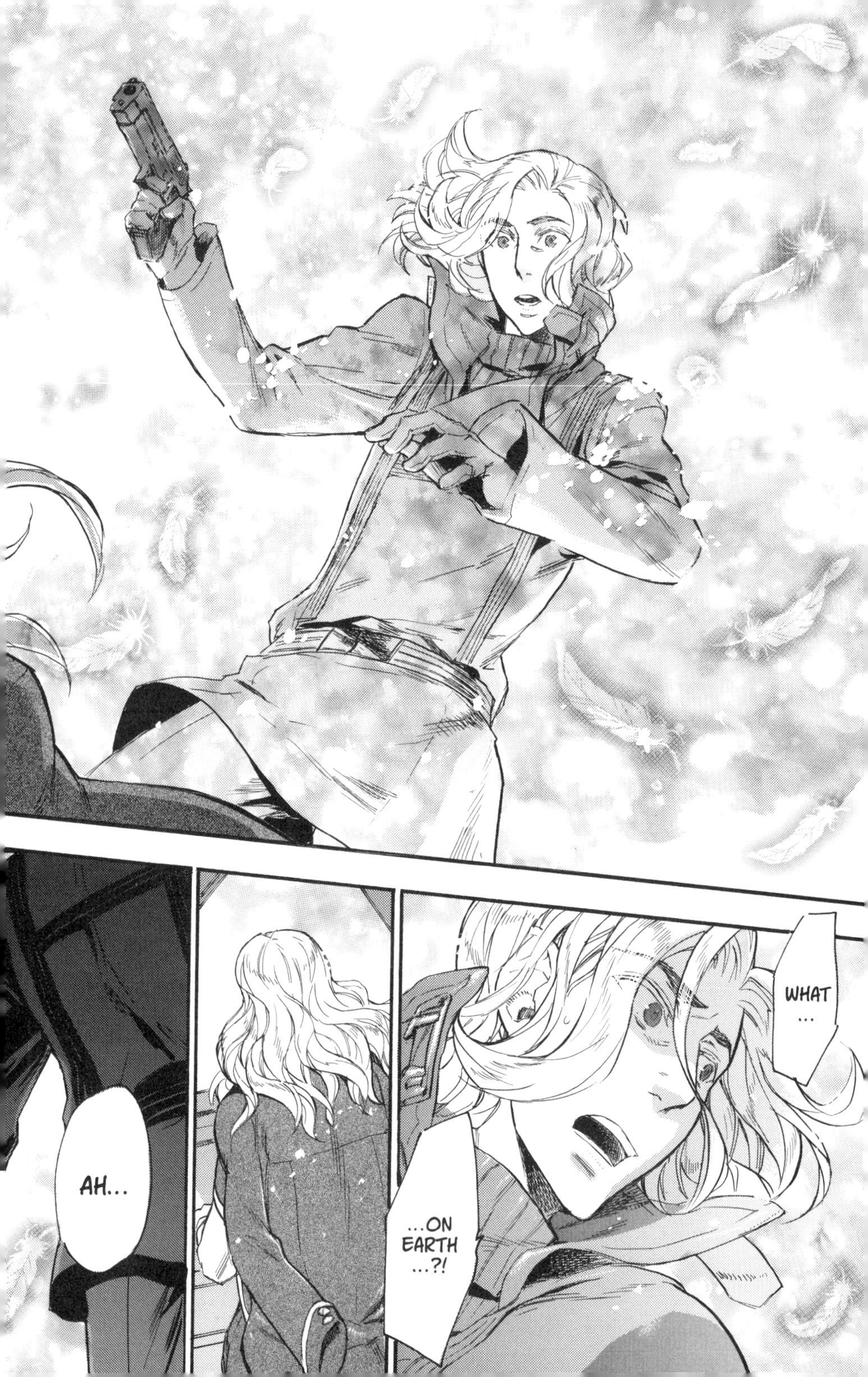
WHAT...
...ON EARTH ...?!
AH...

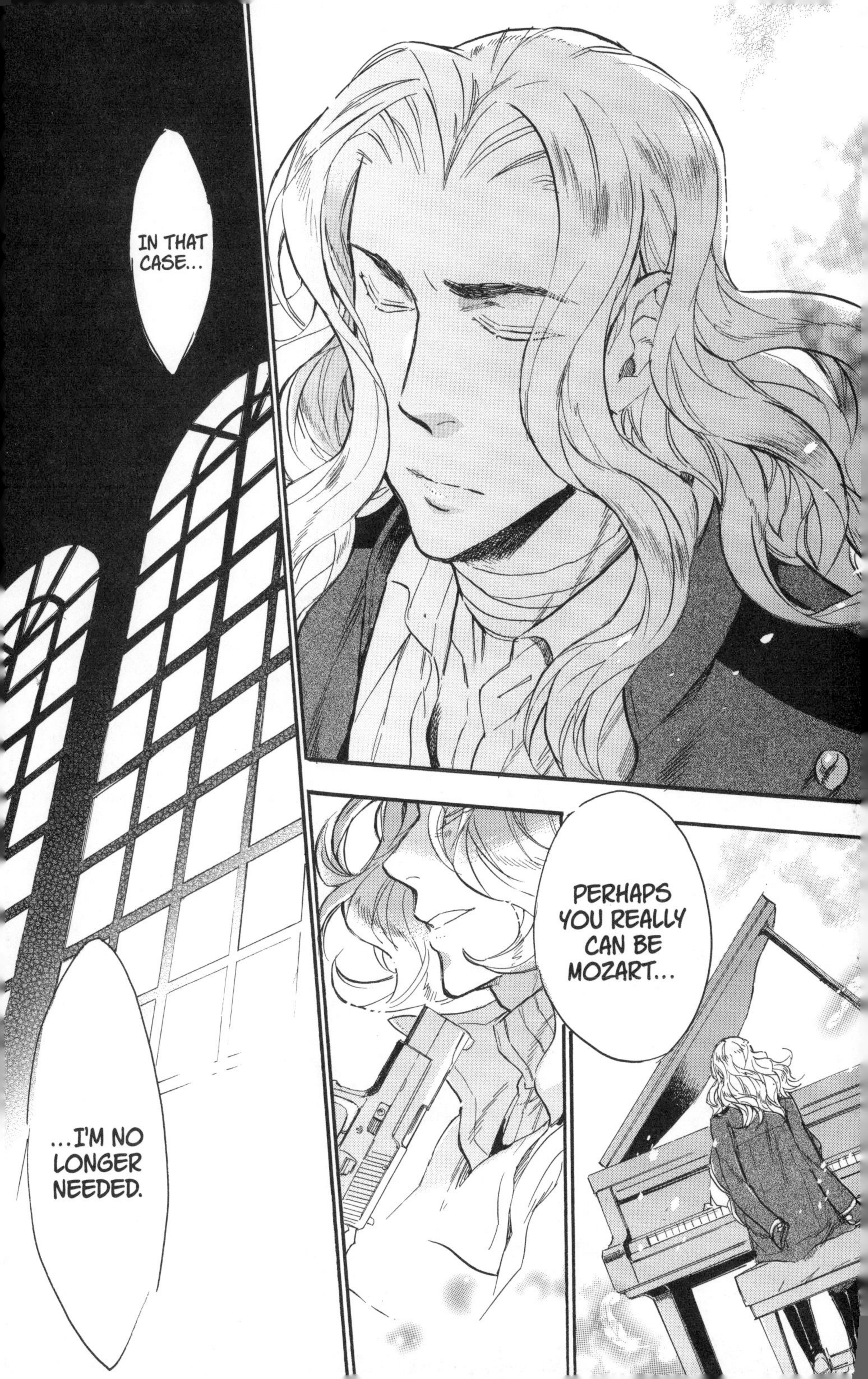
PERHAPS YOU REALLY CAN BE MOZART...
IN THAT CASE...
...I'M NO LONGER NEEDED.

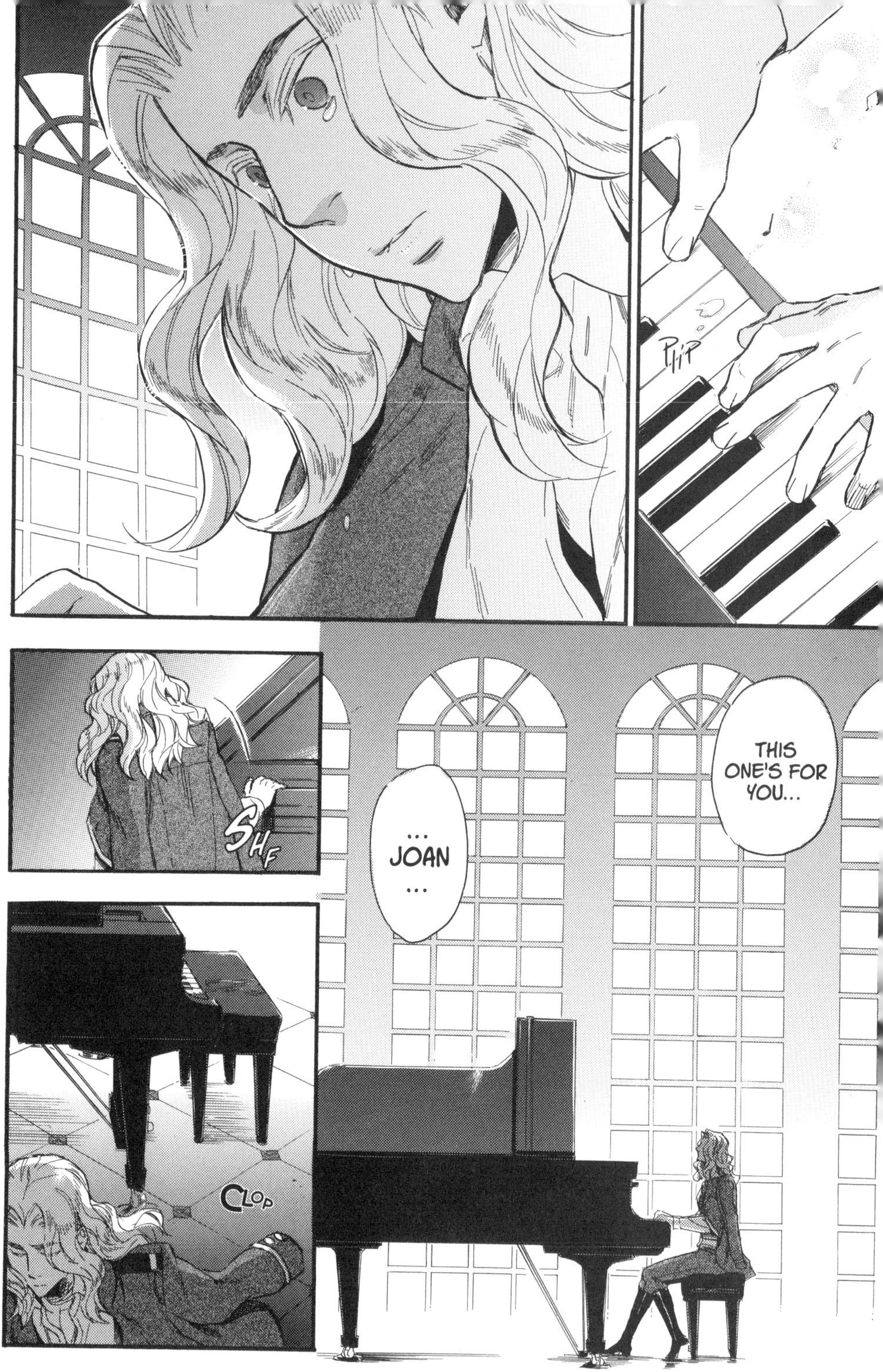
PLIP
THIS ONE'S FOR YOU...
...JOAN...
SHF
CLOP

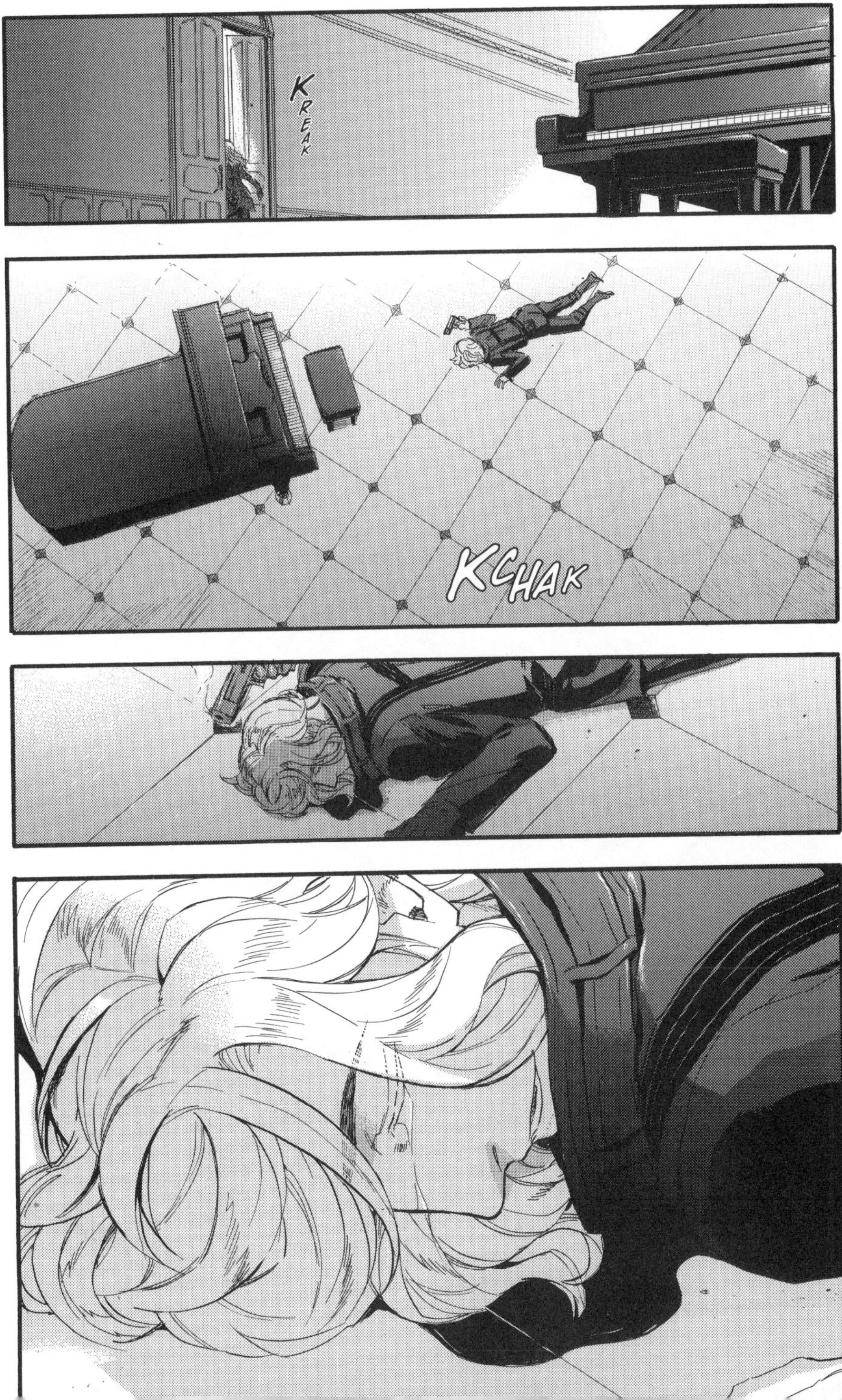
KREAK
KCHAK

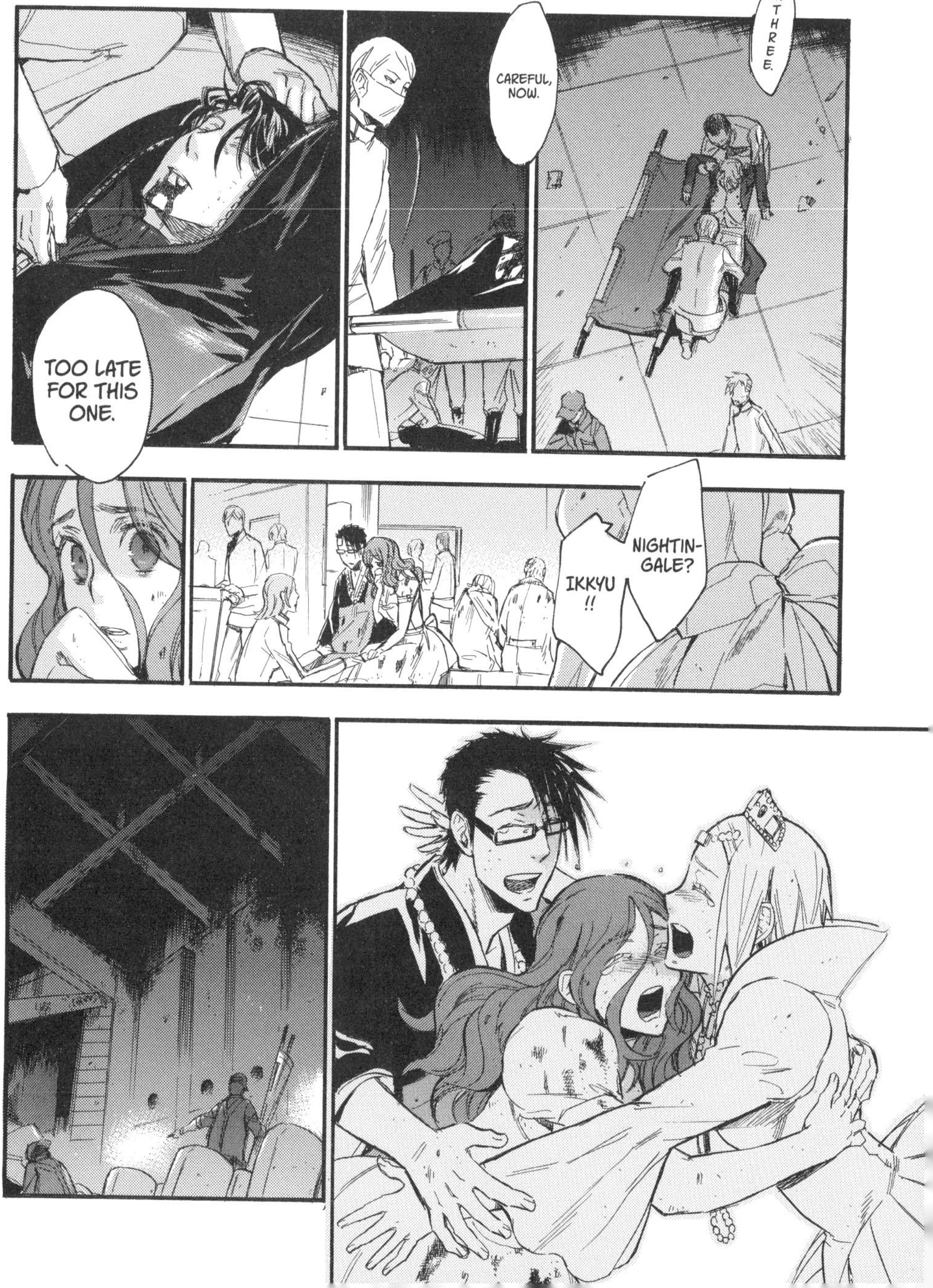
...THREE.
CAREFUL, NOW.
TOO LATE FOR THIS ONE.
NIGHTIN-GALE?
IKKYU !!

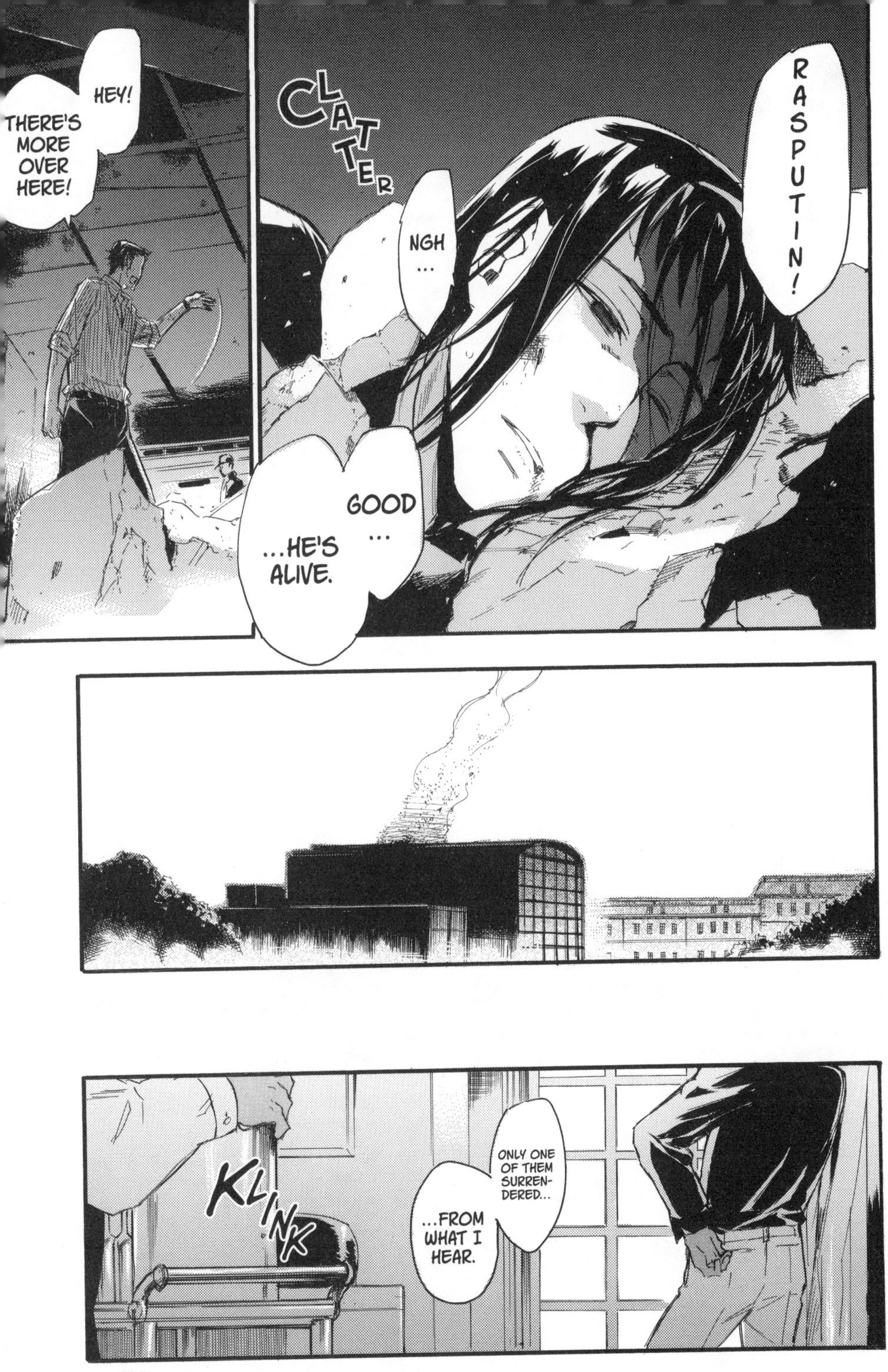
RASPUTIN!
CLATTER
NGH...
GOOD...
...HE'S ALIVE.
HEY!
THERE'S MORE OVER HERE!
ONLY ONE OF THEM SURRENDERED...
...FROM WHAT I HEAR.
KLINK

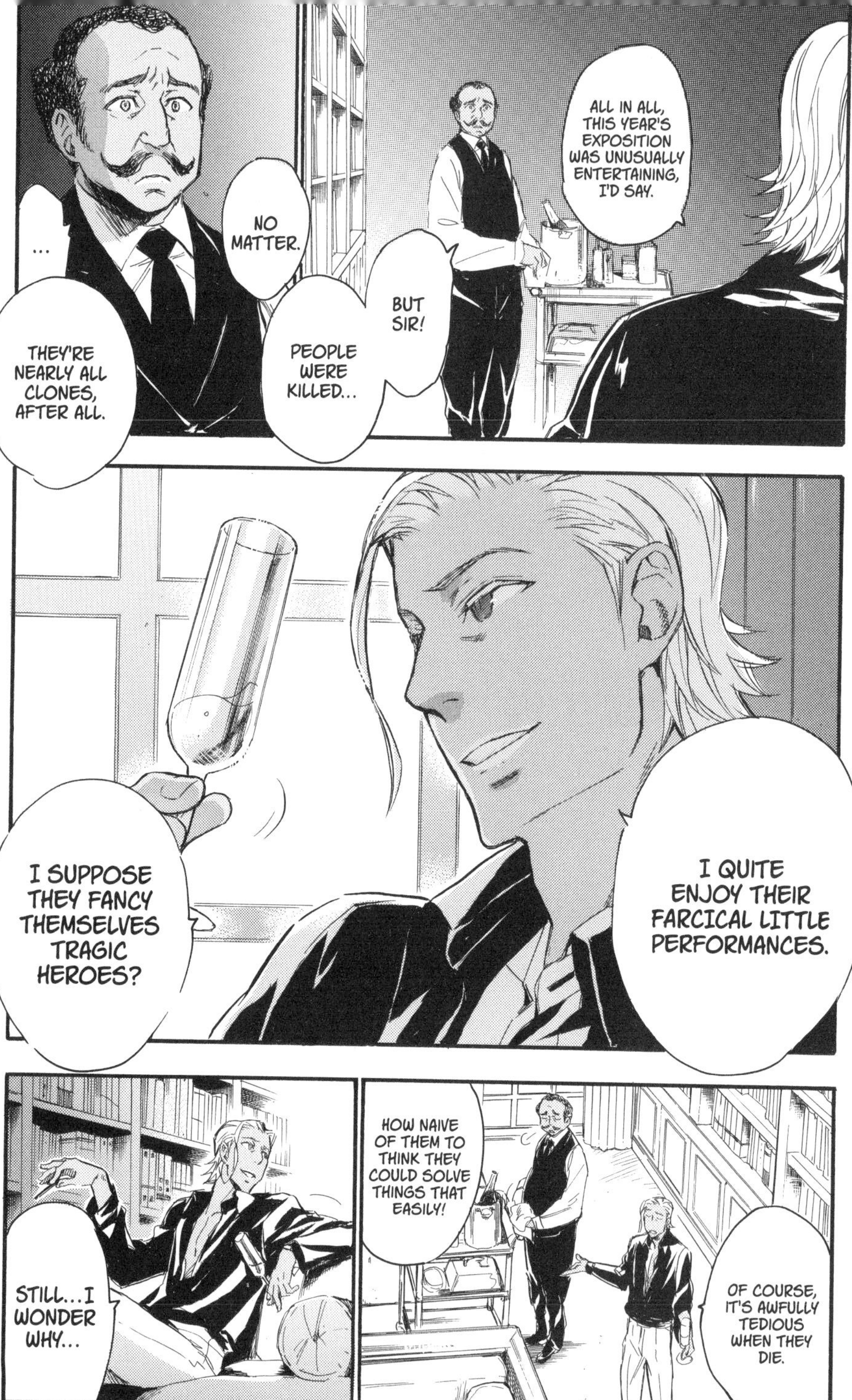
ALL IN ALL, THIS YEAR'S EXPOSITION WAS UNUSUALLY ENTERTAINING, I'D SAY.
BUT SIR! PEOPLE WERE KILLED...
NO MATTER.
...
THEY'RE NEARLY ALL CLONES, AFTER ALL.
I QUITE ENJOY THEIR FARCICAL LITTLE PERFORMANCES.
I SUPPOSE THEY FANCY THEMSELVES TRAGIC HEROES?
HOW NAIVE OF THEM TO THINK THEY COULD SOLVE THINGS THAT EASILY!
OF COURSE, IT'S AWFULLY TEDIOUS WHEN THEY DIE.
STILL...I WONDER WHY...

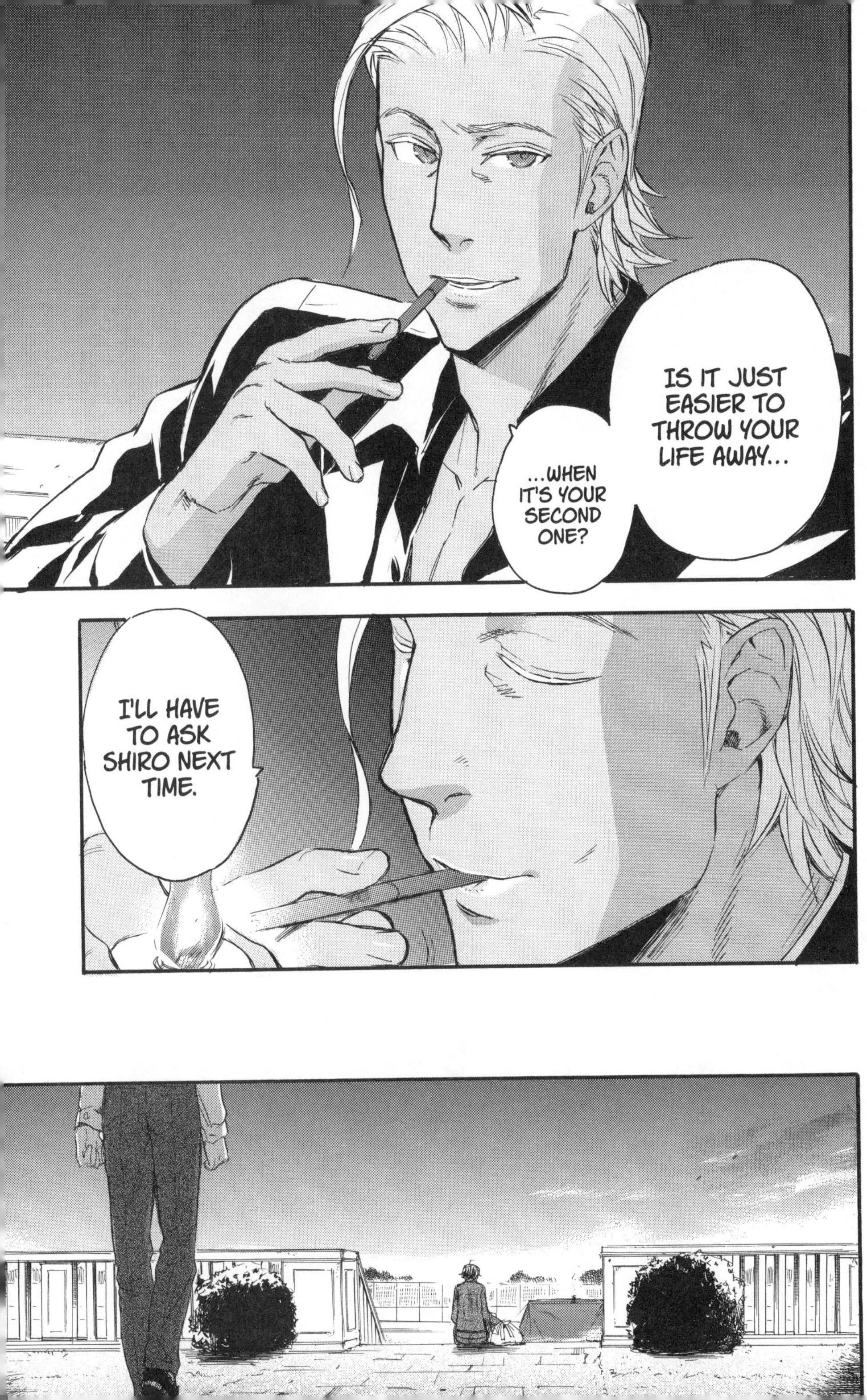
IS IT JUST EASIER TO THROW YOUR LIFE AWAY...
...WHEN IT'S YOUR SECOND ONE?
I'LL HAVE TO ASK SHIRO NEXT TIME.

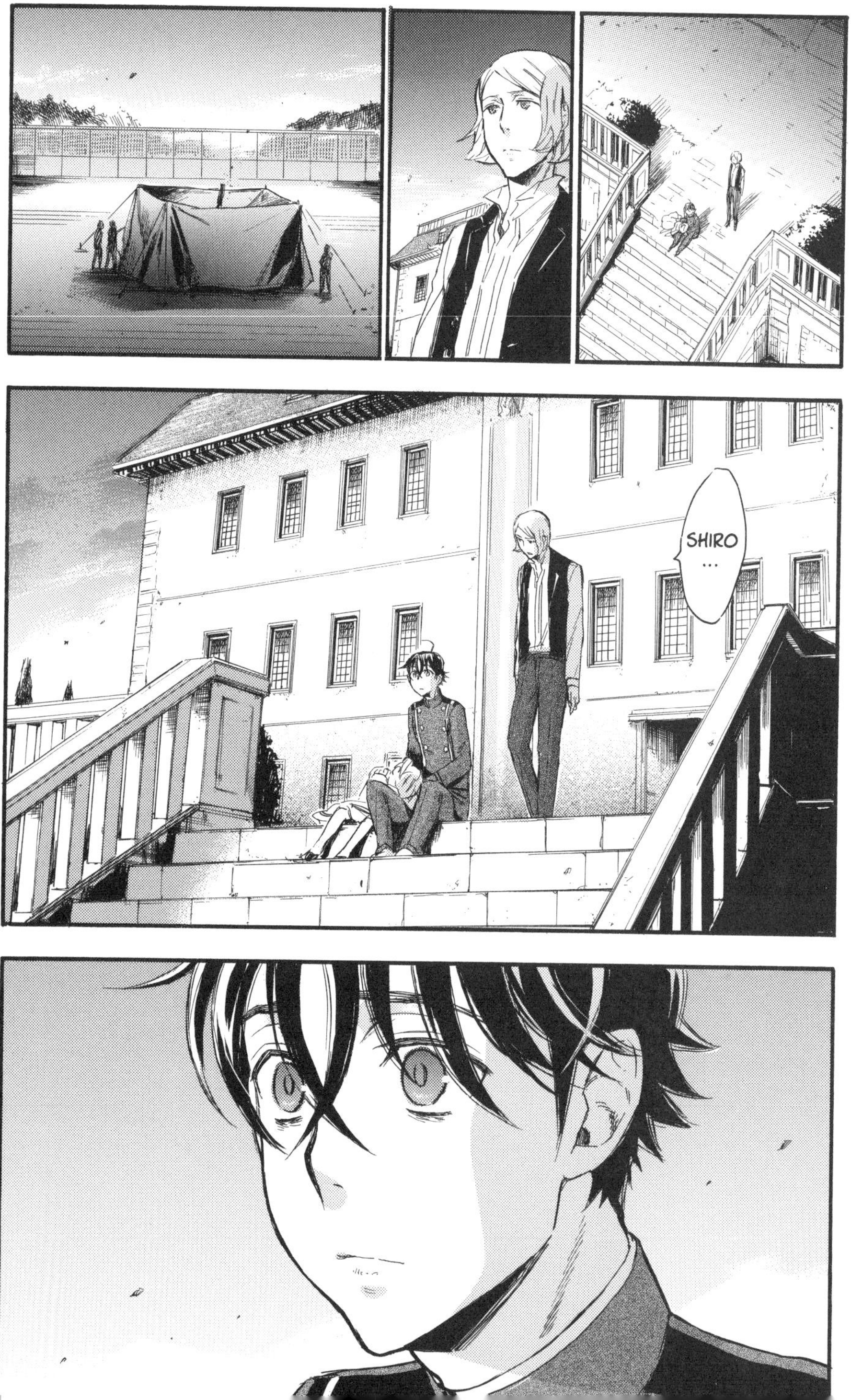
SHIRO …

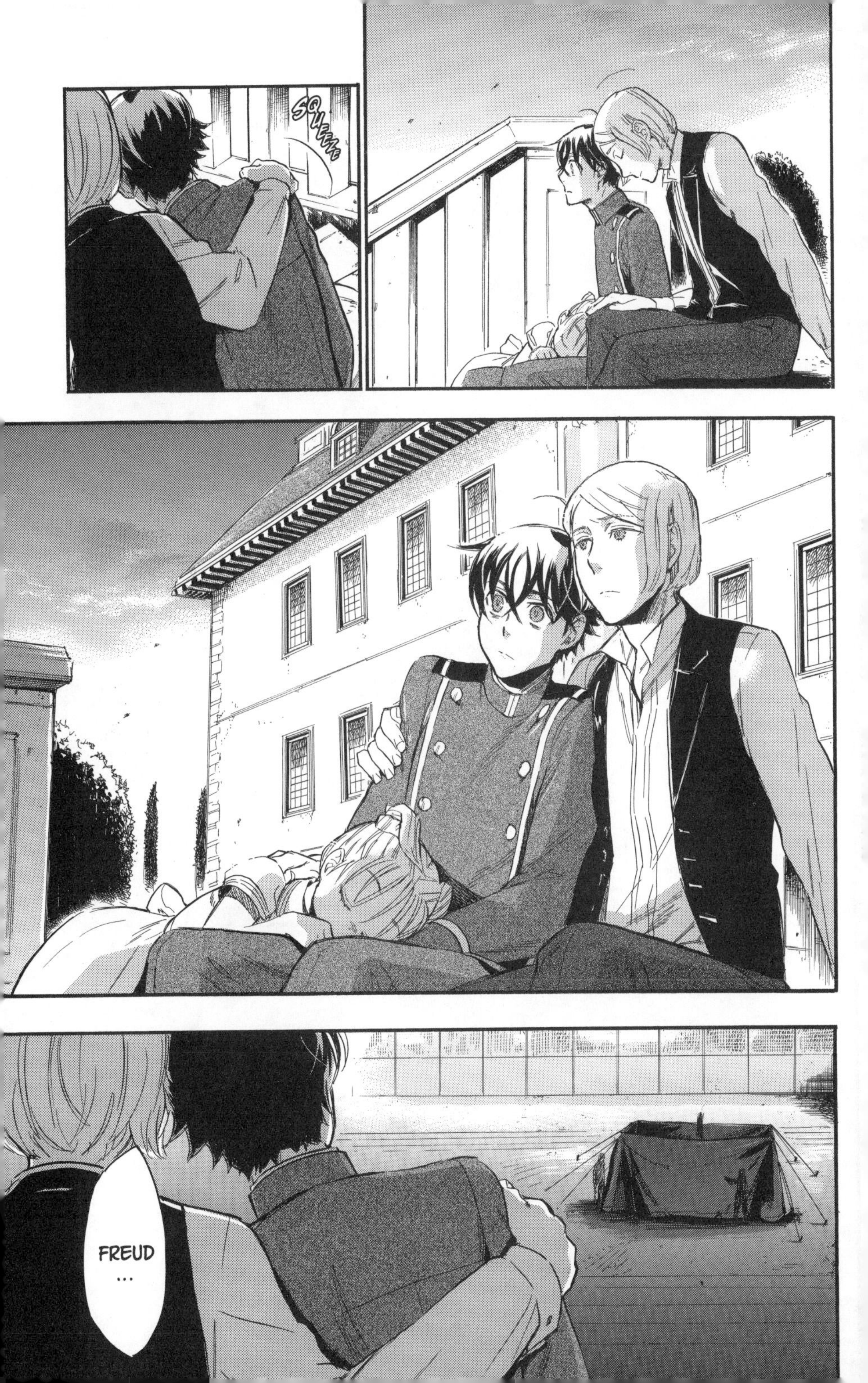
SQUEEZE
FREUD
...

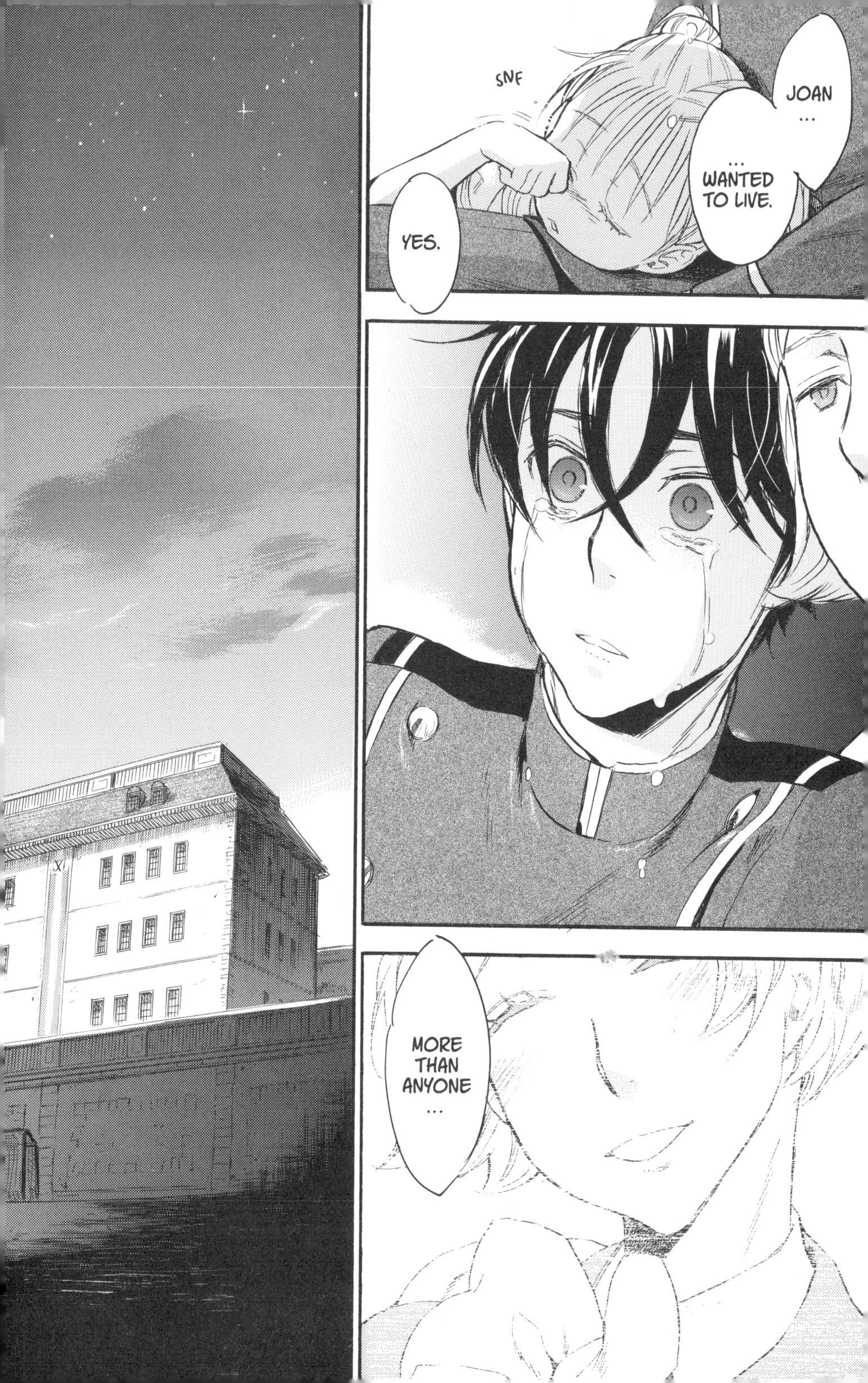
JOAN ...
... WANTED TO LIVE.
SNF
YES.
MORE THAN ANYONE ...

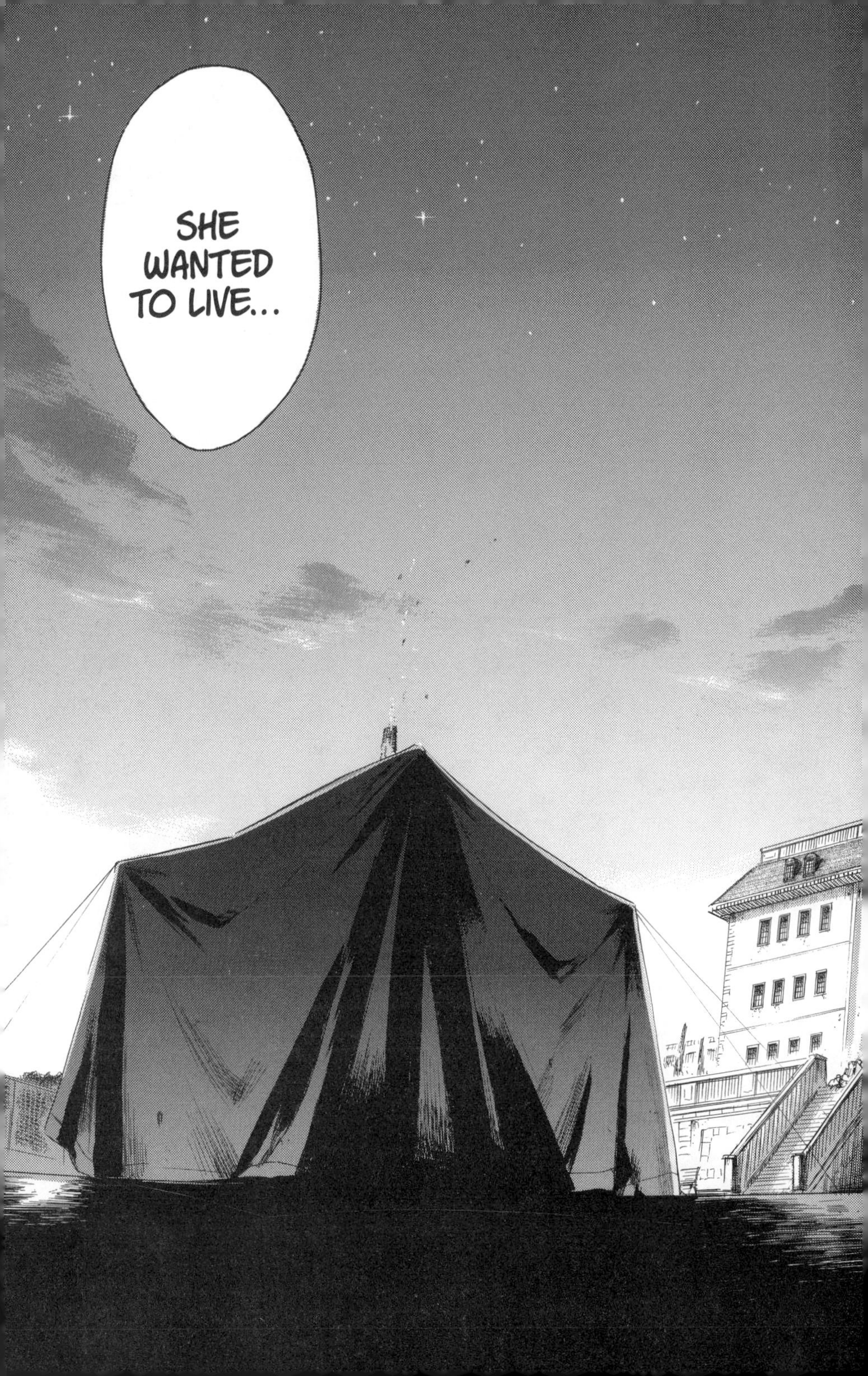
SHE WANTED TO LIVE...

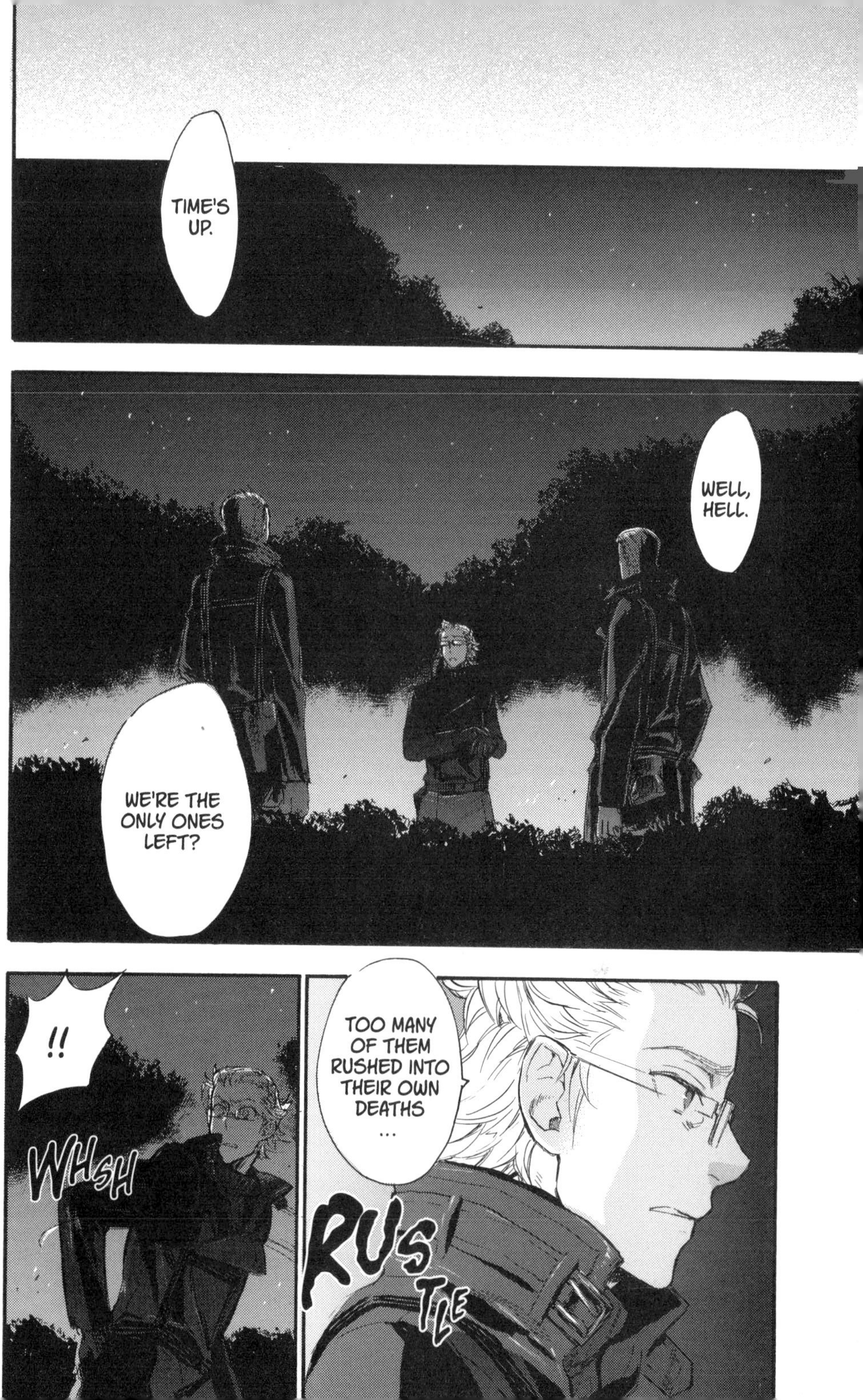
TIME'S UP.
WELL, HELL.
WE'RE THE ONLY ONES LEFT?
TOO MANY OF THEM RUSHED INTO THEIR OWN DEATHS ...
RUSTLE
!!
WHSH

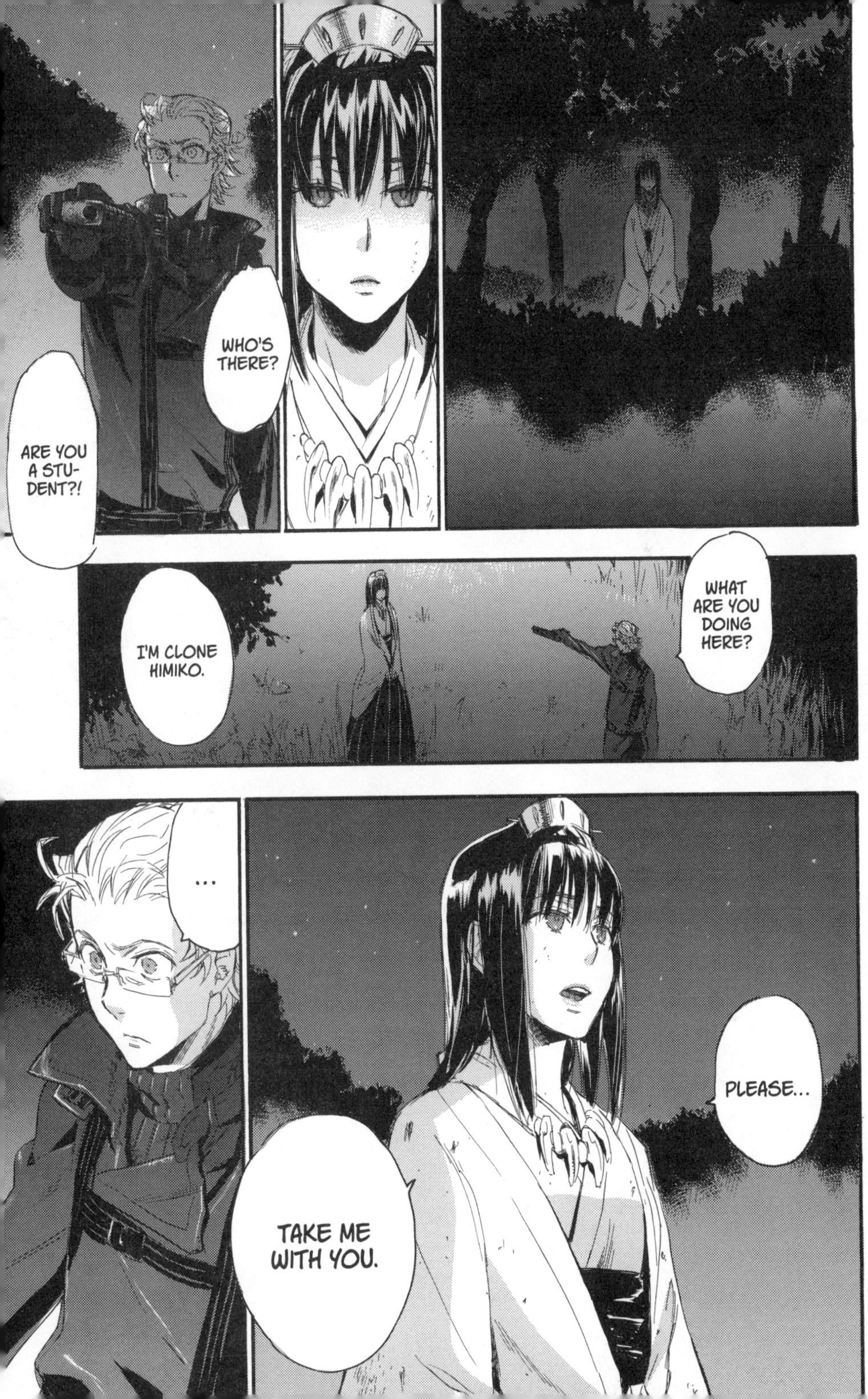
WHO'S THERE?
ARE YOU A STU-DENT?!
WHAT ARE YOU DOING HERE?
I'M CLONE HIMIKO.
PLEASE...
TAKE ME WITH YOU.
...

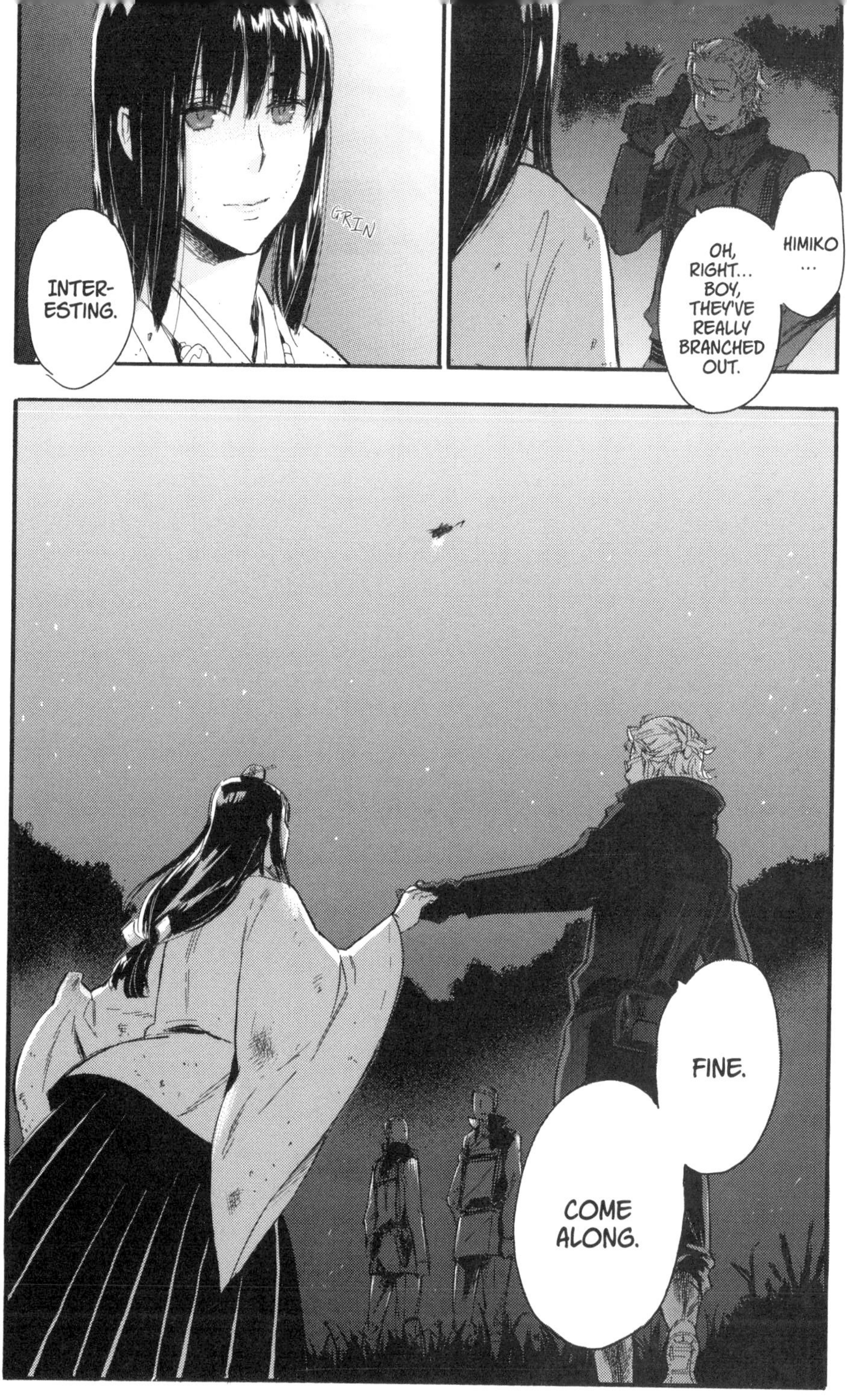
HIMIKO ...
OH, RIGHT... BOY, THEY'VE REALLY BRANCHED OUT.
GRIN
INTER-ESTING.
FINE.
COME ALONG.

afterschool charisma

CHAPTER twenty-two

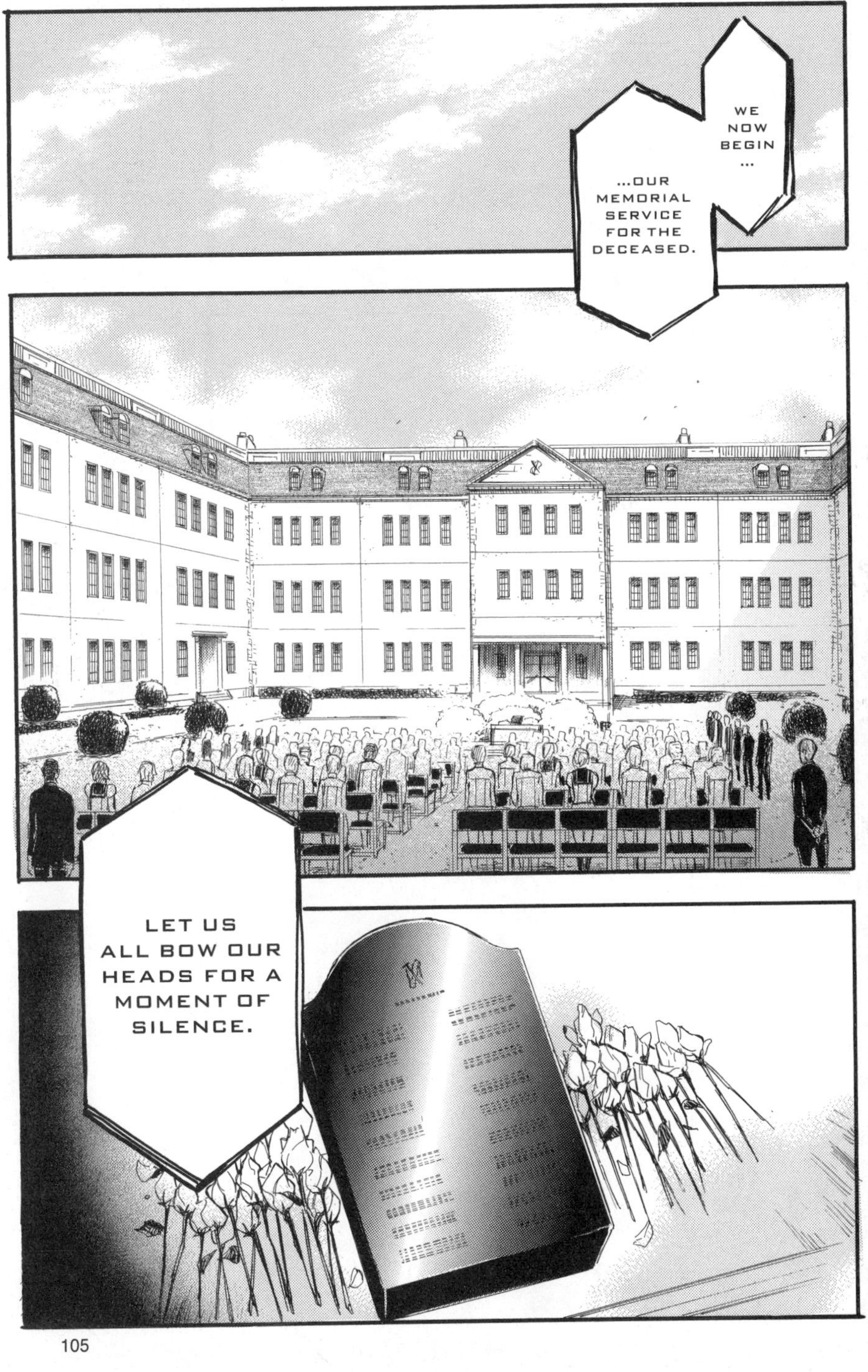
WE NOW BEGIN ...
...OUR MEMORIAL SERVICE FOR THE DECEASED.
LET US ALL BOW OUR HEADS FOR A MOMENT OF SILENCE.

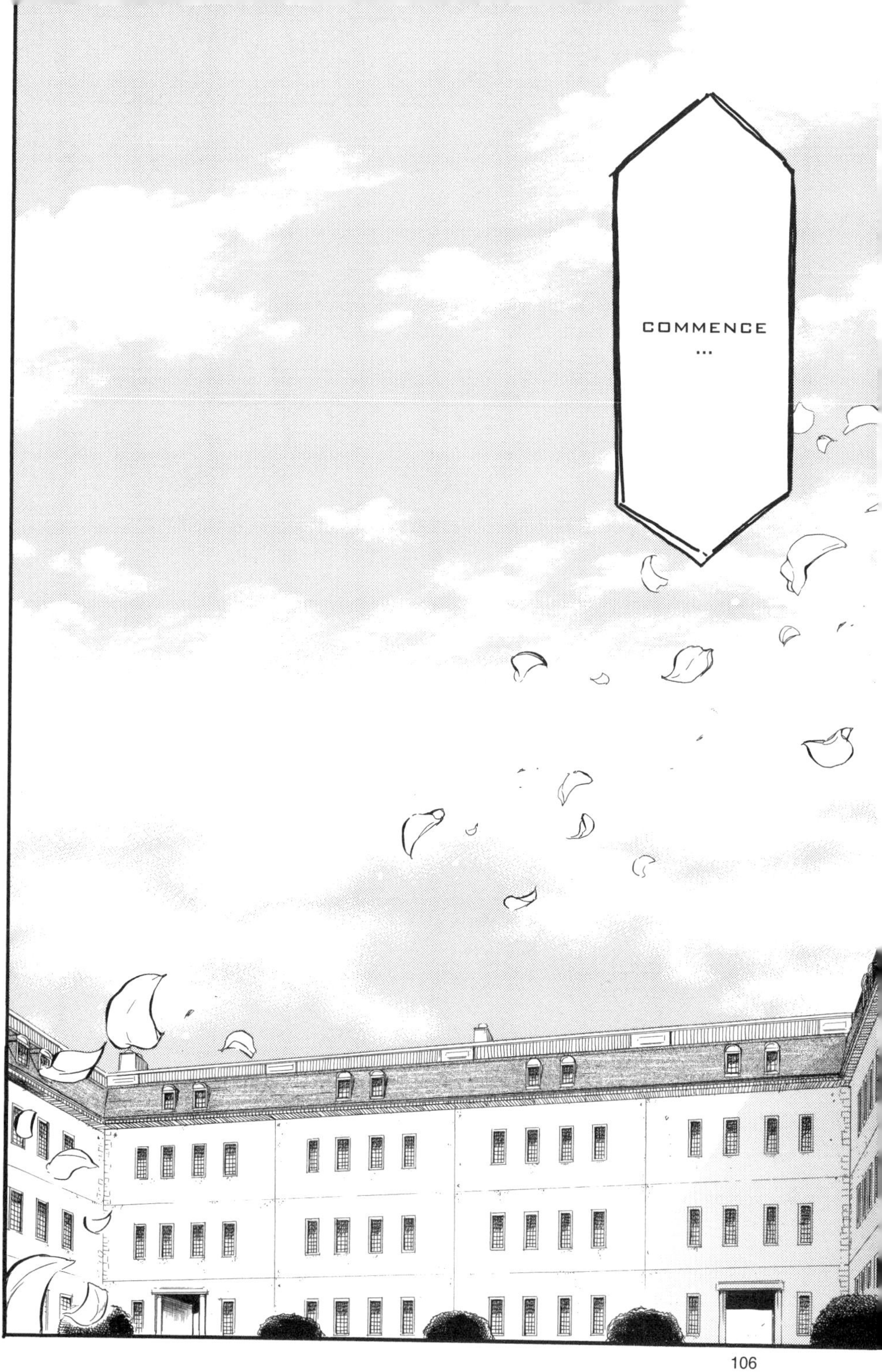
COMMENCE
...

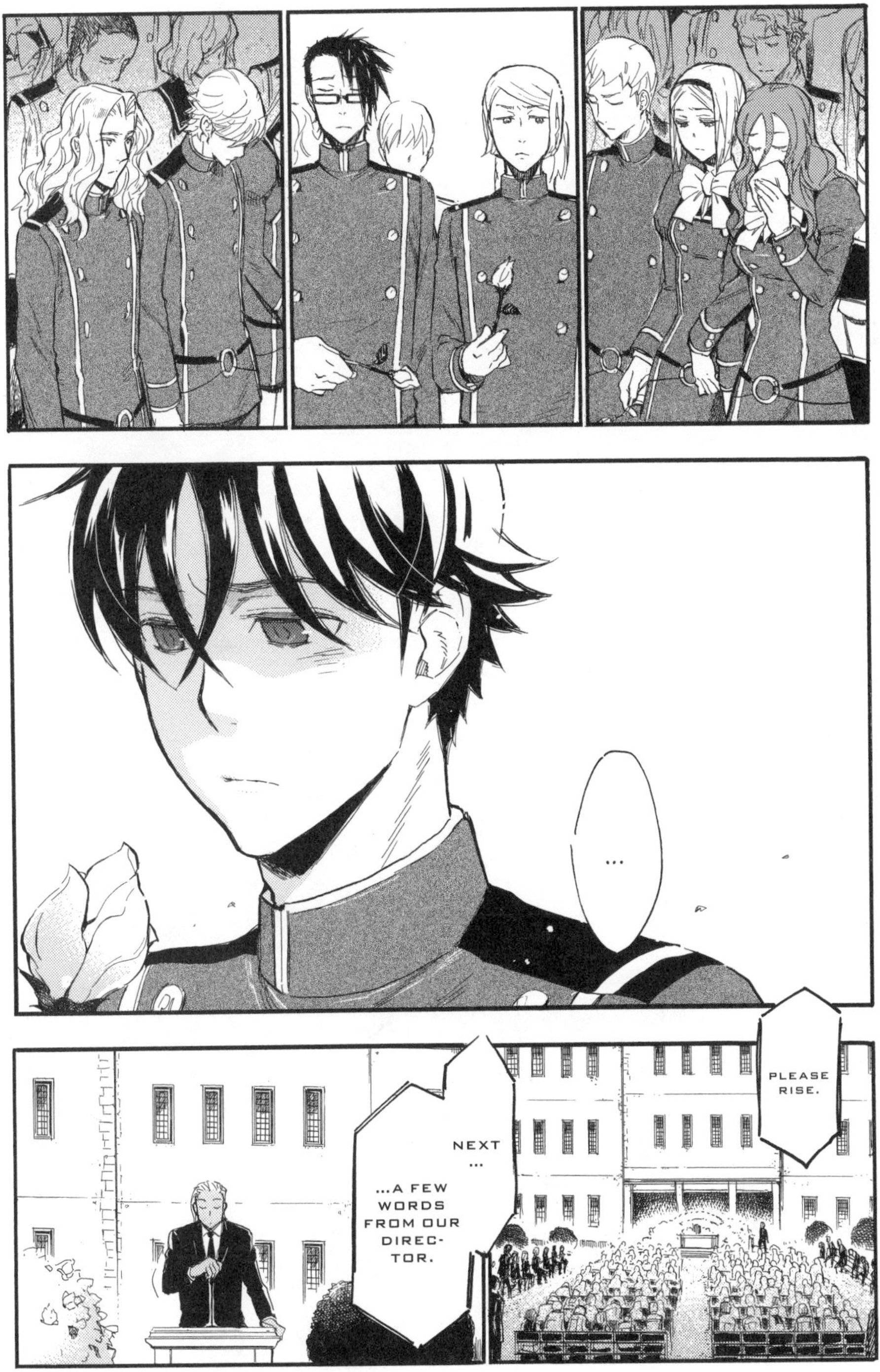
...
PLEASE RISE.
NEXT ...
...A FEW WORDS FROM OUR DIREC-TOR.

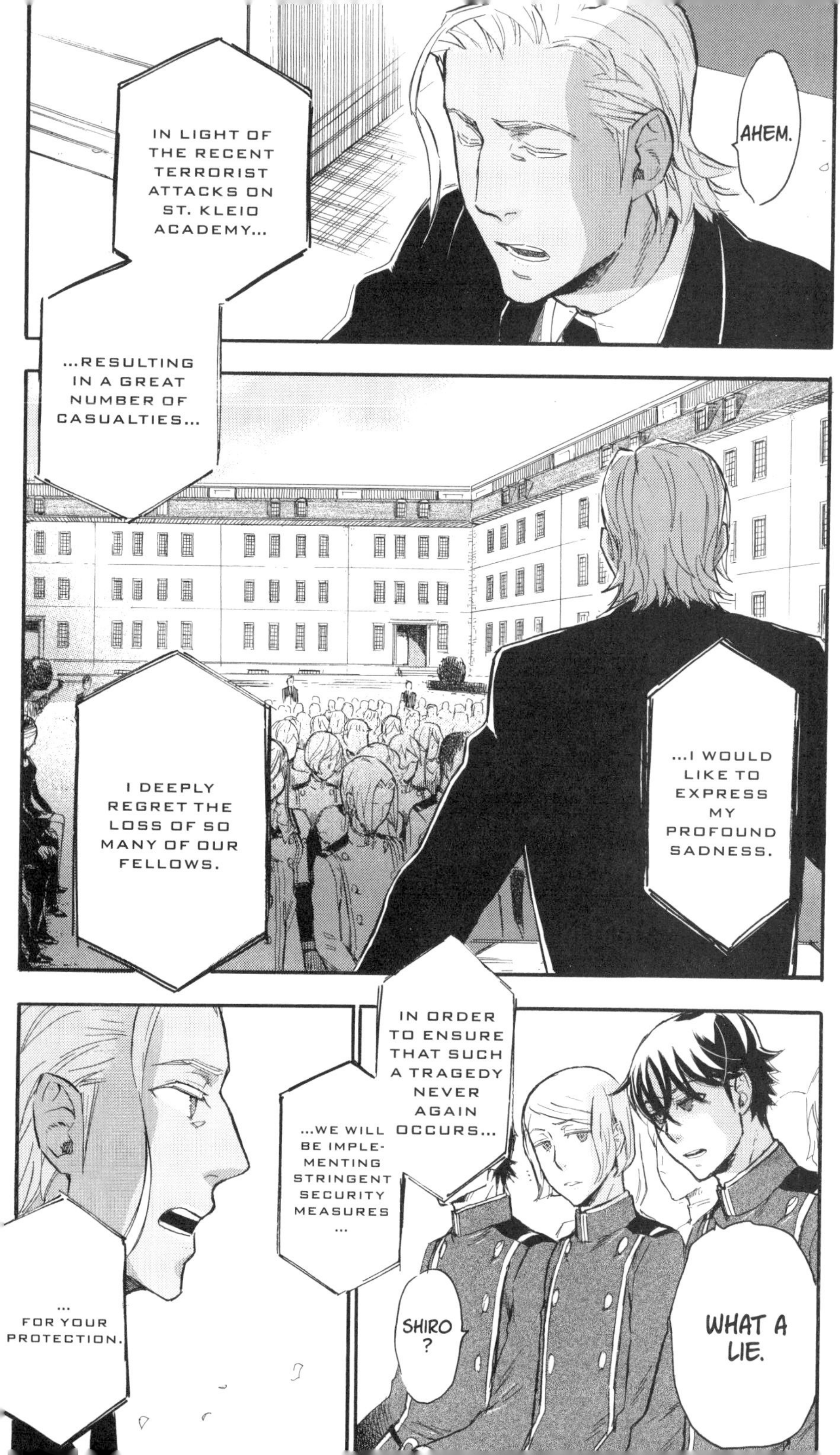
AHEM.
IN LIGHT OF THE RECENT TERRORIST ATTACKS ON ST. KLEIO ACADEMY...
...RESULTING IN A GREAT NUMBER OF CASUALTIES...
...I WOULD LIKE TO EXPRESS MY PROFOUND SADNESS.
I DEEPLY REGRET THE LOSS OF SO MANY OF OUR FELLOWS.
IN ORDER TO ENSURE THAT SUCH A TRAGEDY NEVER AGAIN OCCURS...
...WE WILL BE IMPLE- MENTING STRINGENT SECURITY MEASURES ...
WHAT A LIE.
SHIRO?
... FOR YOUR PROTECTION.

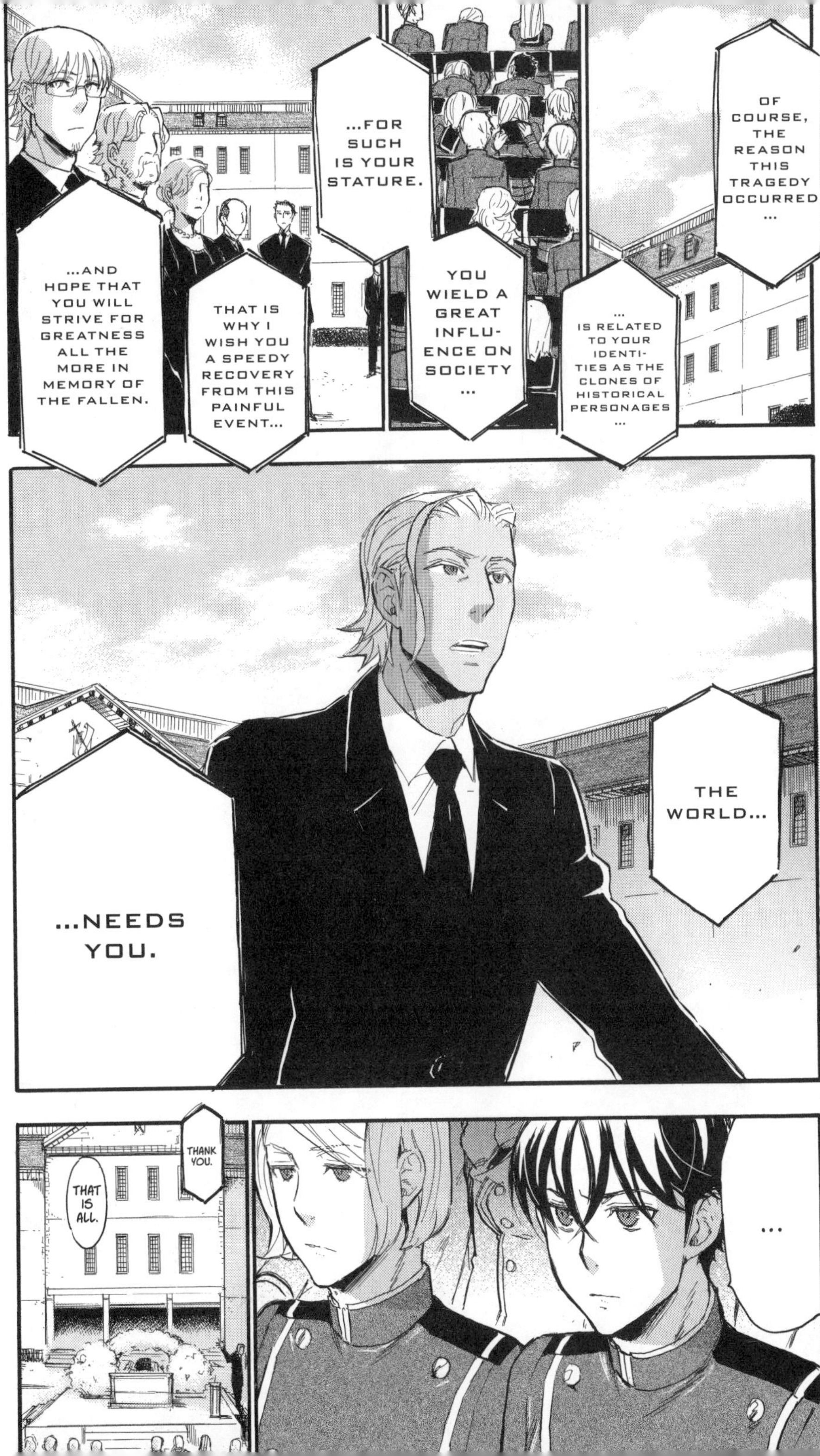
OF COURSE, THE REASON THIS TRAGEDY OCCURRED...
...IS RELATED TO YOUR IDENTITIES AS THE CLONES OF HISTORICAL PERSONAGES...
YOU WIELD A GREAT INFLUENCE ON SOCIETY...
...FOR SUCH IS YOUR STATURE.
THAT IS WHY I WISH YOU A SPEEDY RECOVERY FROM THIS PAINFUL EVENT...
...AND HOPE THAT YOU WILL STRIVE FOR GREATNESS ALL THE MORE IN MEMORY OF THE FALLEN.
THE WORLD...
...NEEDS YOU.
...
THANK YOU.
THAT IS ALL.

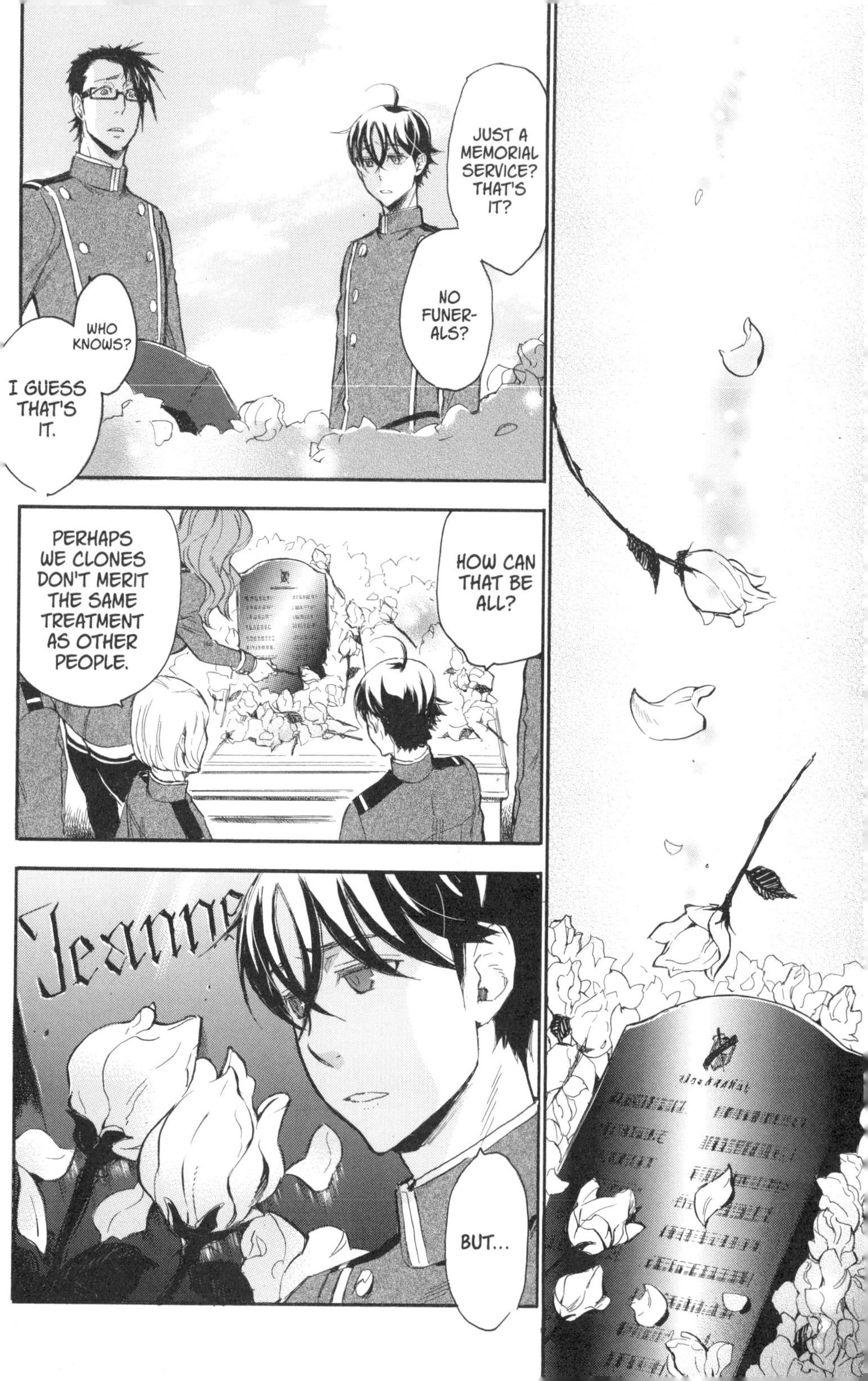
JUST A MEMORIAL SERVICE? THAT'S IT?
NO FUNER-ALS?
WHO KNOWS?
I GUESS THAT'S IT.
HOW CAN THAT BE ALL?
PERHAPS WE CLONES DON'T MERIT THE SAME TREATMENT AS OTHER PEOPLE.
Jeanne
BUT...

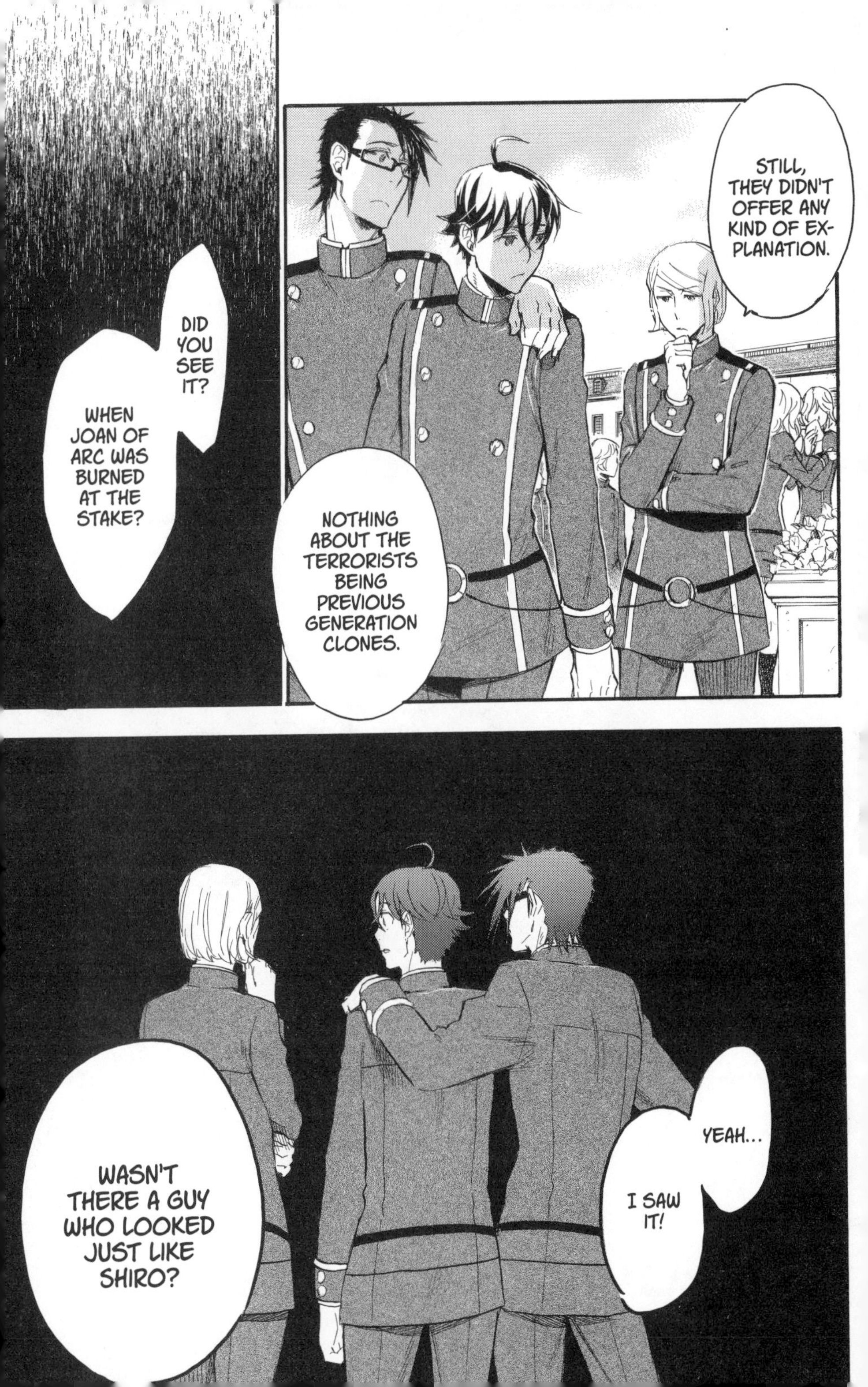
STILL, THEY DIDN'T OFFER ANY KIND OF EX-PLANATION.
NOTHING ABOUT THE TERRORISTS BEING PREVIOUS GENERATION CLONES.
DID YOU SEE IT?
WHEN JOAN OF ARC WAS BURNED AT THE STAKE?
YEAH...
I SAW IT!
WASN'T THERE A GUY WHO LOOKED JUST LIKE SHIRO?

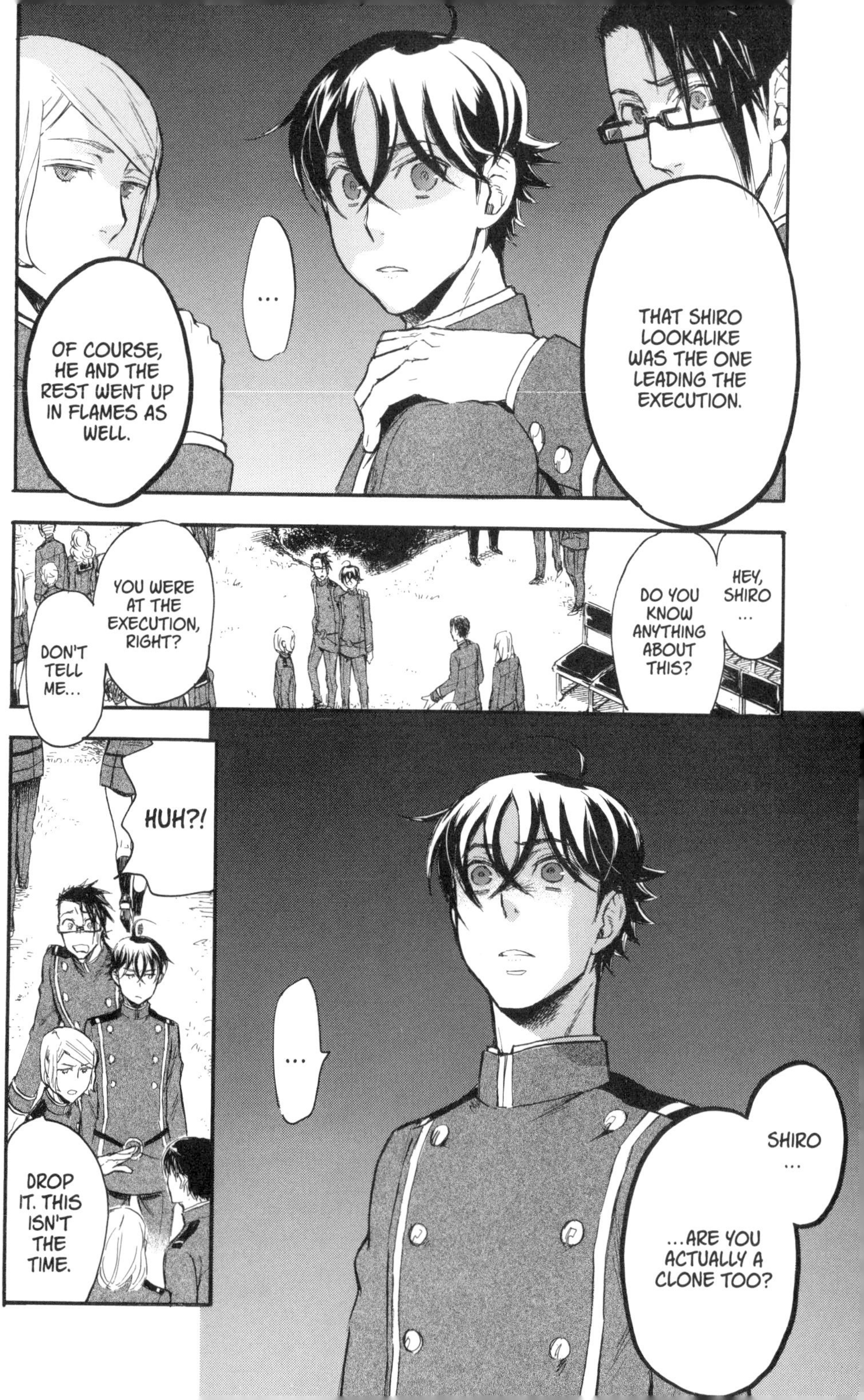
THAT SHIRO LOOKALIKE WAS THE ONE LEADING THE EXECUTION.
...
OF COURSE, HE AND THE REST WENT UP IN FLAMES AS WELL.
HEY, SHIRO ...
DO YOU KNOW ANYTHING ABOUT THIS?
YOU WERE AT THE EXECUTION, RIGHT?
DON'T TELL ME...
...
SHIRO ...
...ARE YOU ACTUALLY A CLONE TOO?
HUH?!
DROP IT. THIS ISN'T THE TIME.

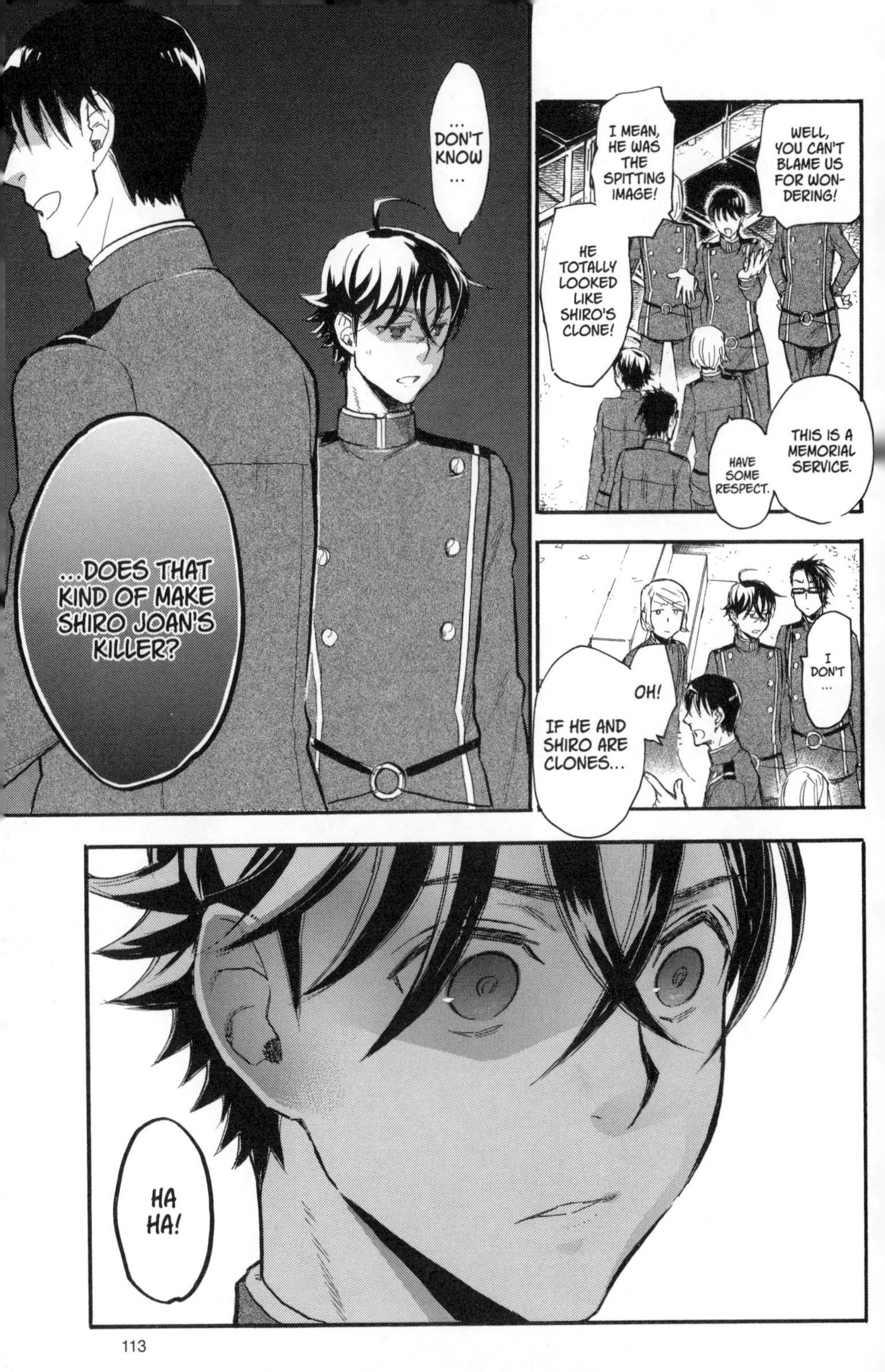
WELL, YOU CAN'T BLAME US FOR WON-DERING!
I MEAN, HE WAS THE SPITTING IMAGE!
HE TOTALLY LOOKED LIKE SHIRO'S CLONE!
THIS IS A MEMORIAL SERVICE.
HAVE SOME RESPECT.
I DON'T ...
OH!
IF HE AND SHIRO ARE CLONES...
... DON'T KNOW ...
...DOES THAT KIND OF MAKE SHIRO JOAN'S KILLER?
HA HA!

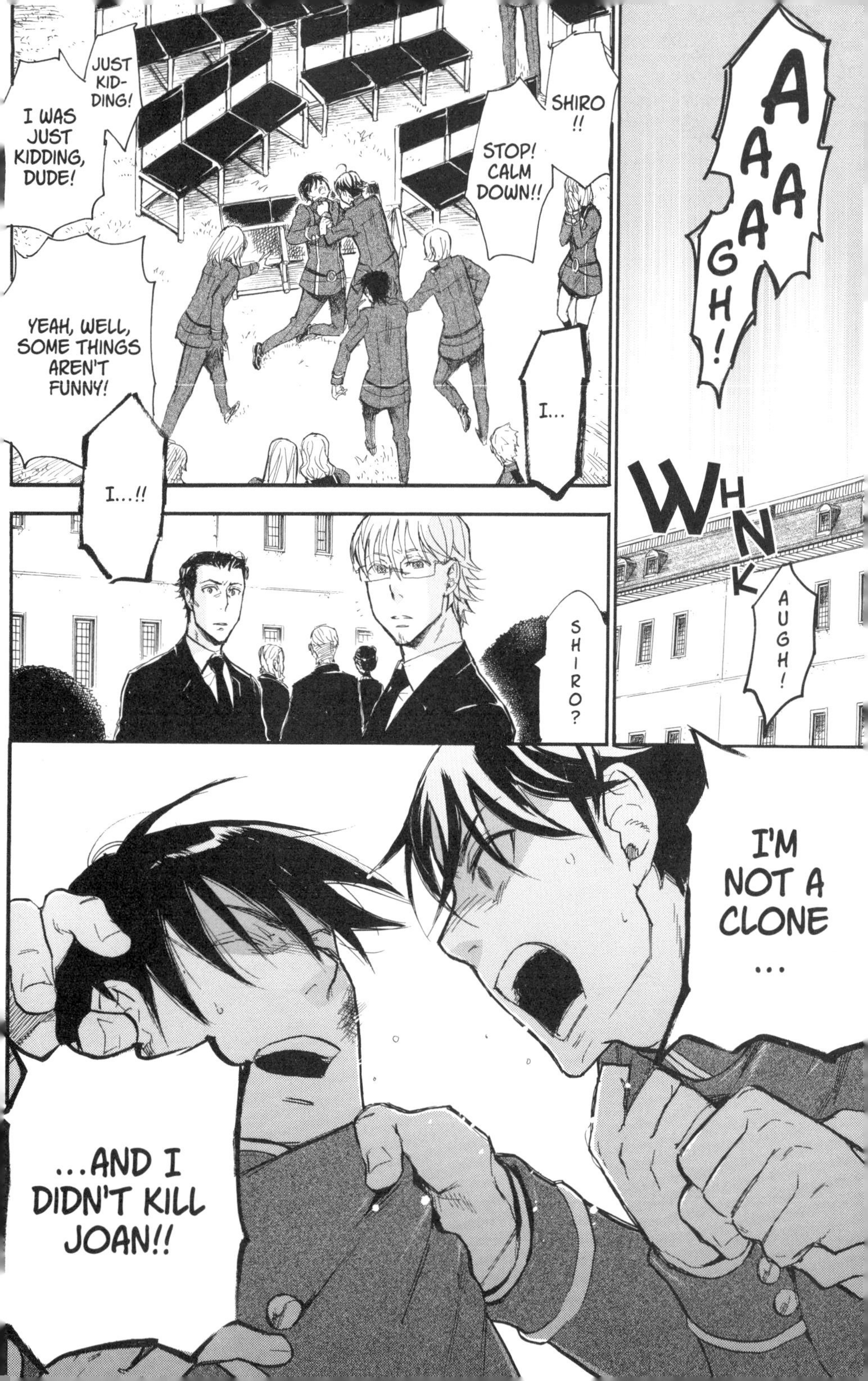
AAAAAGH!
SHIRO!!
STOP! CALM DOWN!!
JUST KID-DING!
I WAS JUST KIDDING, DUDE!
YEAH, WELL, SOME THINGS AREN'T FUNNY!
I...
I...!!
WHNK
AUGH!
SHIRO?
I'M NOT A CLONE...
...AND I DIDN'T KILL JOAN!!

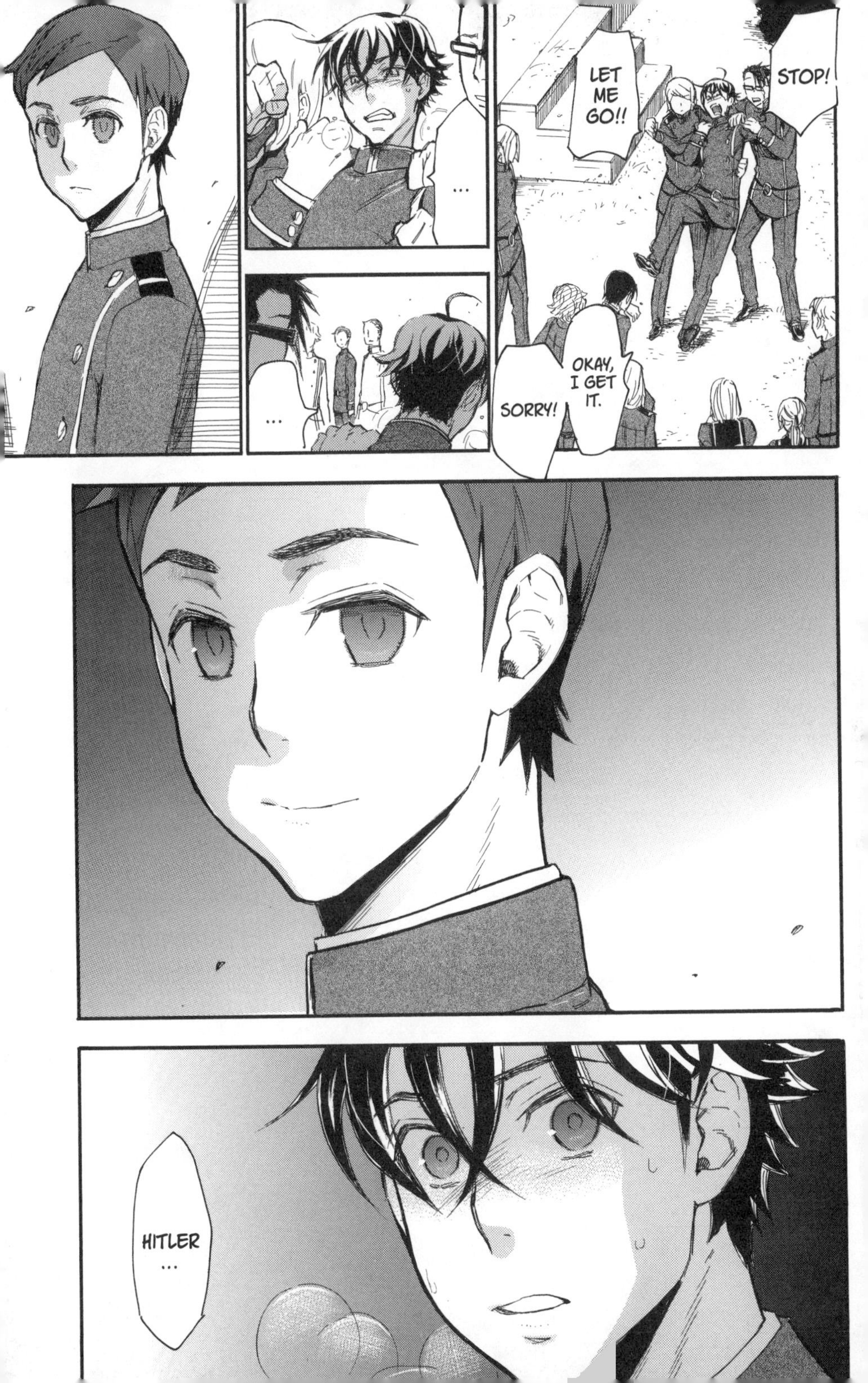
STOP!
LET ME GO!!
OKAY, I GET IT.
SORRY!
...
...
HITLER ...

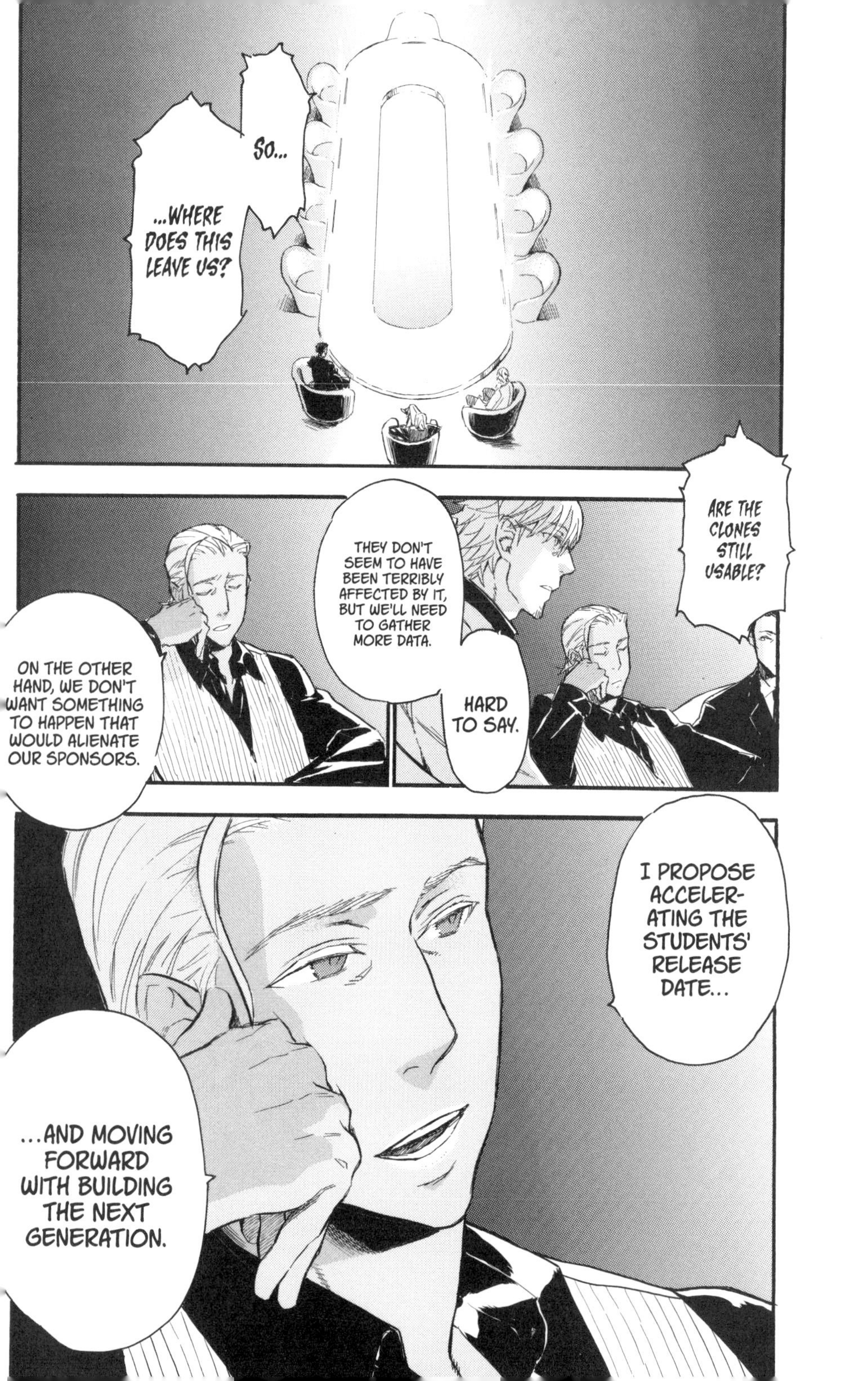
So...
...Where does this leave us?
Are the clones still usable?
They don't seem to have been terribly affected by it, but we'll need to gather more data.
Hard to say.
On the other hand, we don't want something to happen that would alienate our sponsors.
I propose accelerating the students' release date...
...and moving forward with building the next generation.

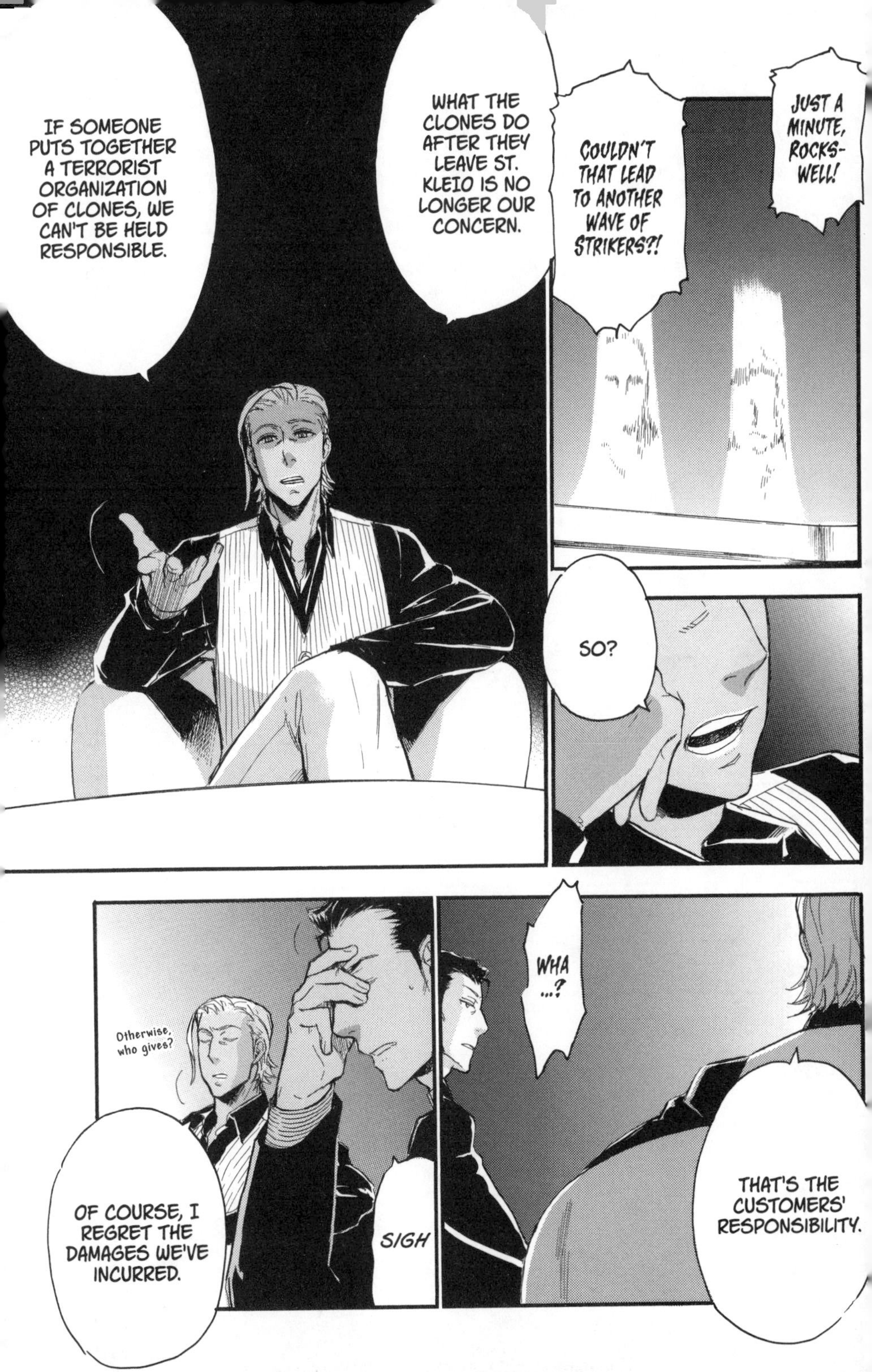
JUST A MINUTE, ROCKS-WELL!
COULDN'T THAT LEAD TO ANOTHER WAVE OF STRIKERS?!
SO?
WHAT THE CLONES DO AFTER THEY LEAVE ST. KLEIO IS NO LONGER OUR CONCERN.
IF SOMEONE PUTS TOGETHER A TERRORIST ORGANIZATION OF CLONES, WE CAN'T BE HELD RESPONSIBLE.
WHA ...?
THAT'S THE CUSTOMERS' RESPONSIBILITY.
SIGH
OF COURSE, I REGRET THE DAMAGES WE'VE INCURRED.
Otherwise, who gives?

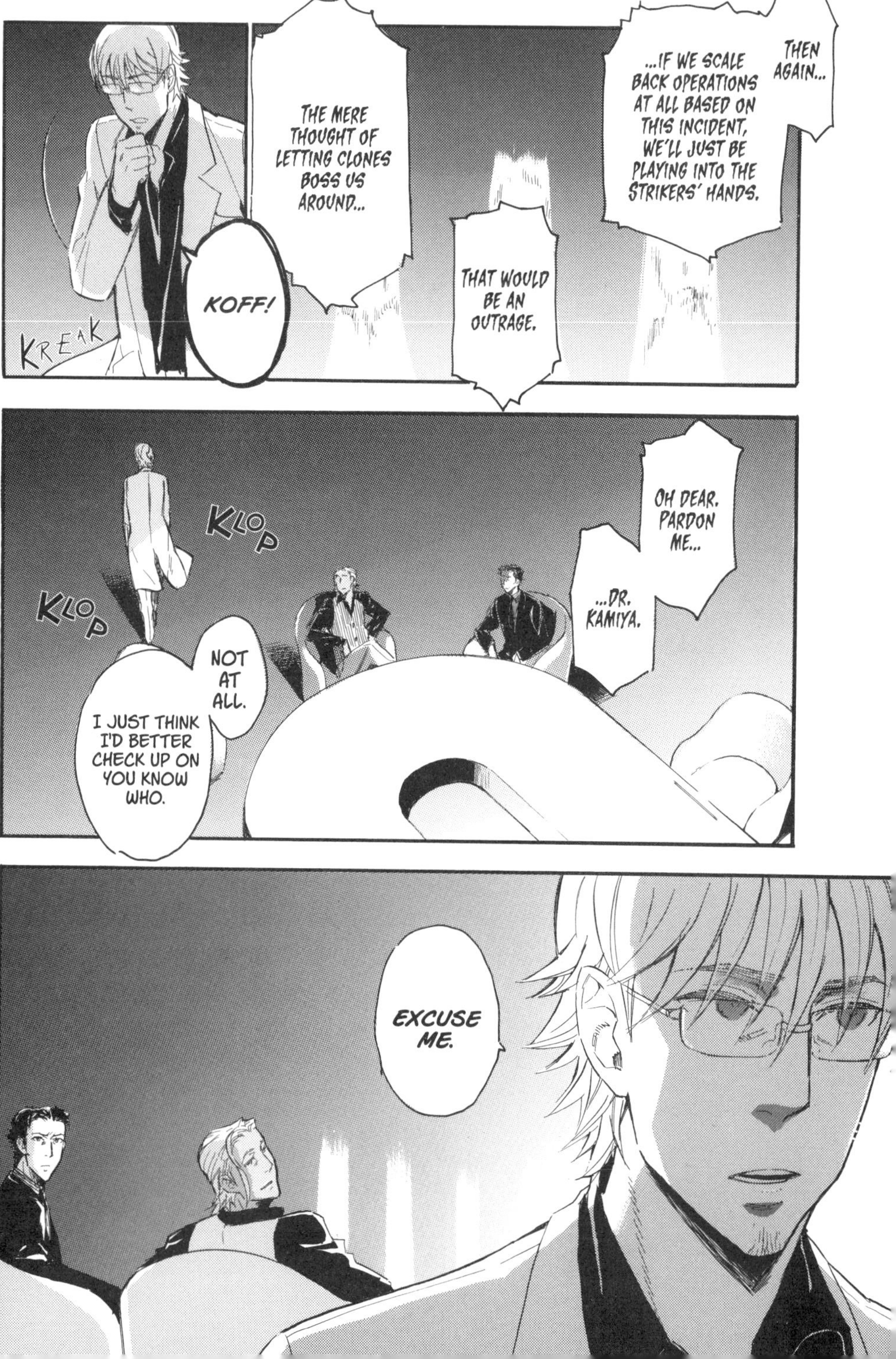
THEN AGAIN...
...IF WE SCALE BACK OPERATIONS AT ALL BASED ON THIS INCIDENT, WE'LL JUST BE PLAYING INTO THE STRIKERS' HANDS.
THE MERE THOUGHT OF LETTING CLONES BOSS US AROUND...
THAT WOULD BE AN OUTRAGE.
KOFF!
KREAK
OH DEAR. PARDON ME...
...DR. KAMIYA.
KLOP
KLOP
NOT AT ALL.
I JUST THINK I'D BETTER CHECK UP ON YOU KNOW WHO.
EXCUSE ME.

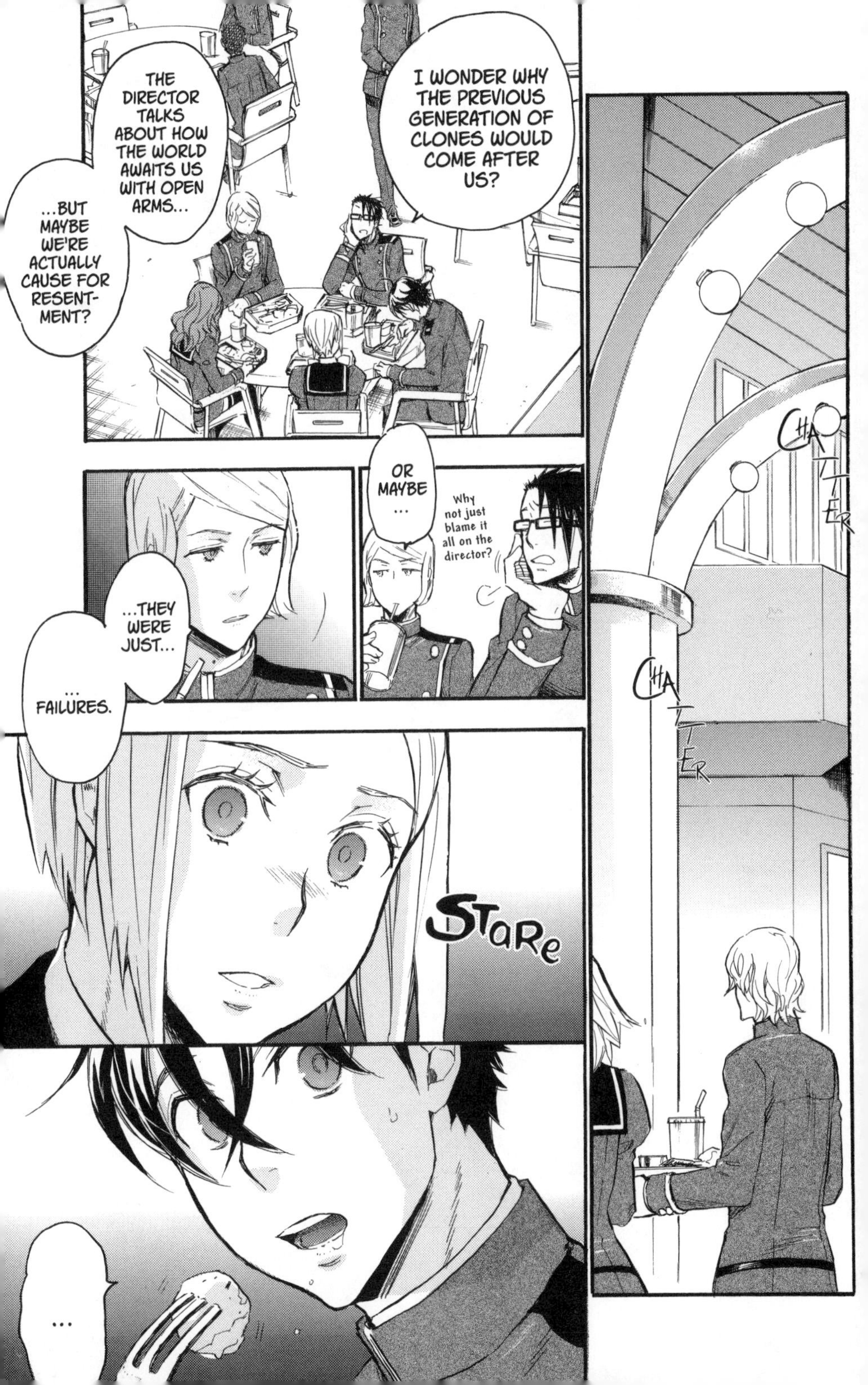
I WONDER WHY THE PREVIOUS GENERATION OF CLONES WOULD COME AFTER US?
THE DIRECTOR TALKS ABOUT HOW THE WORLD AWAITS US WITH OPEN ARMS...
...BUT MAYBE WE'RE ACTUALLY CAUSE FOR RESENT-MENT?
CHATTER
CHATTER
OR MAYBE ...
Why not just blame it all on the director?
...THEY WERE JUST...
... FAILURES.
STARE
...

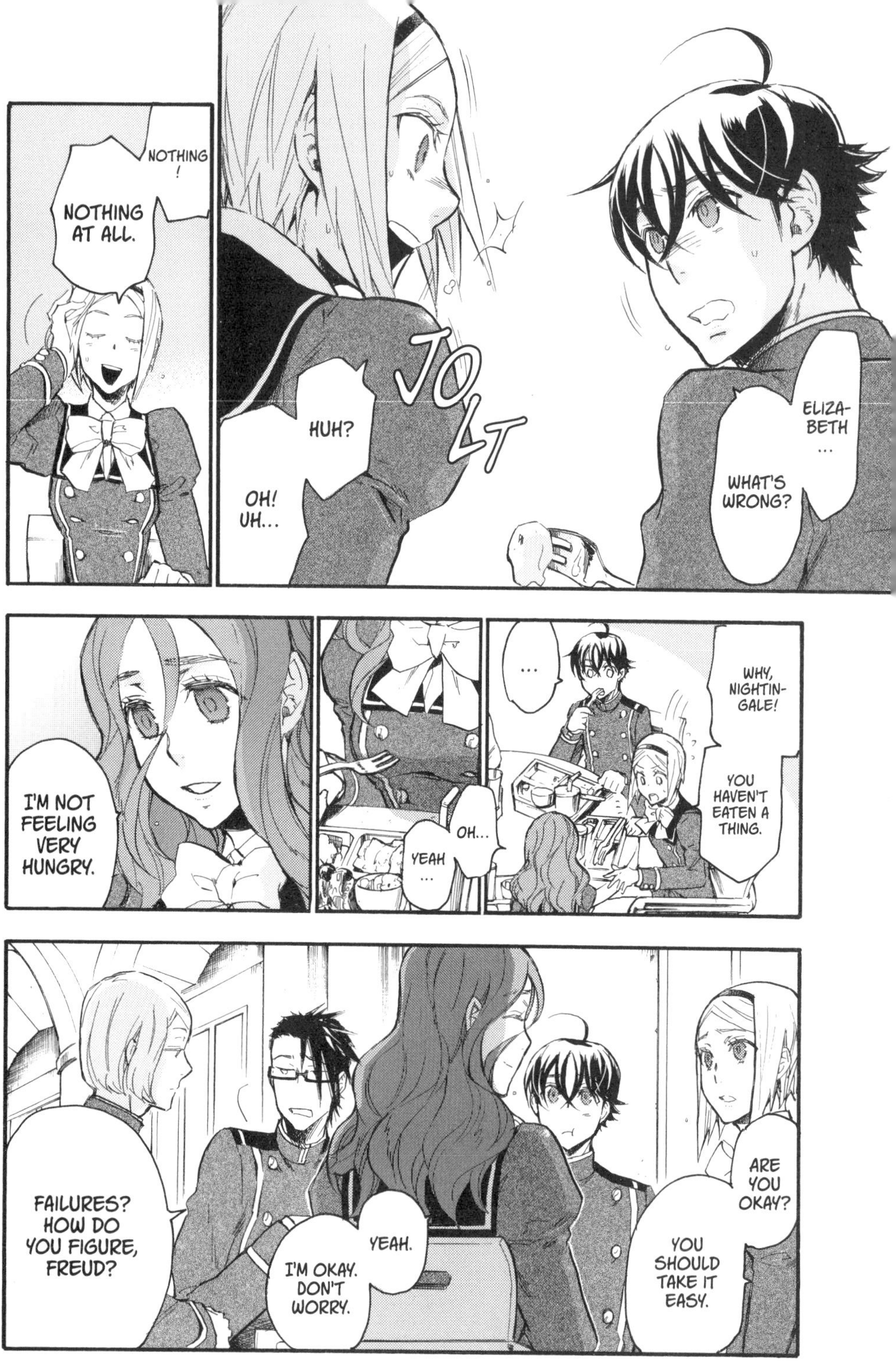
ELIZA-BETH ...
WHAT'S WRONG?
JOLT
HUH?
OH! UH...
NOTHING!
NOTHING AT ALL.
...
WHY, NIGHTIN-GALE!
YOU HAVEN'T EATEN A THING.
OH...
YEAH ...
I'M NOT FEELING VERY HUNGRY.
ARE YOU OKAY?
YOU SHOULD TAKE IT EASY.
YEAH.
I'M OKAY. DON'T WORRY.
FAILURES? HOW DO YOU FIGURE, FREUD?

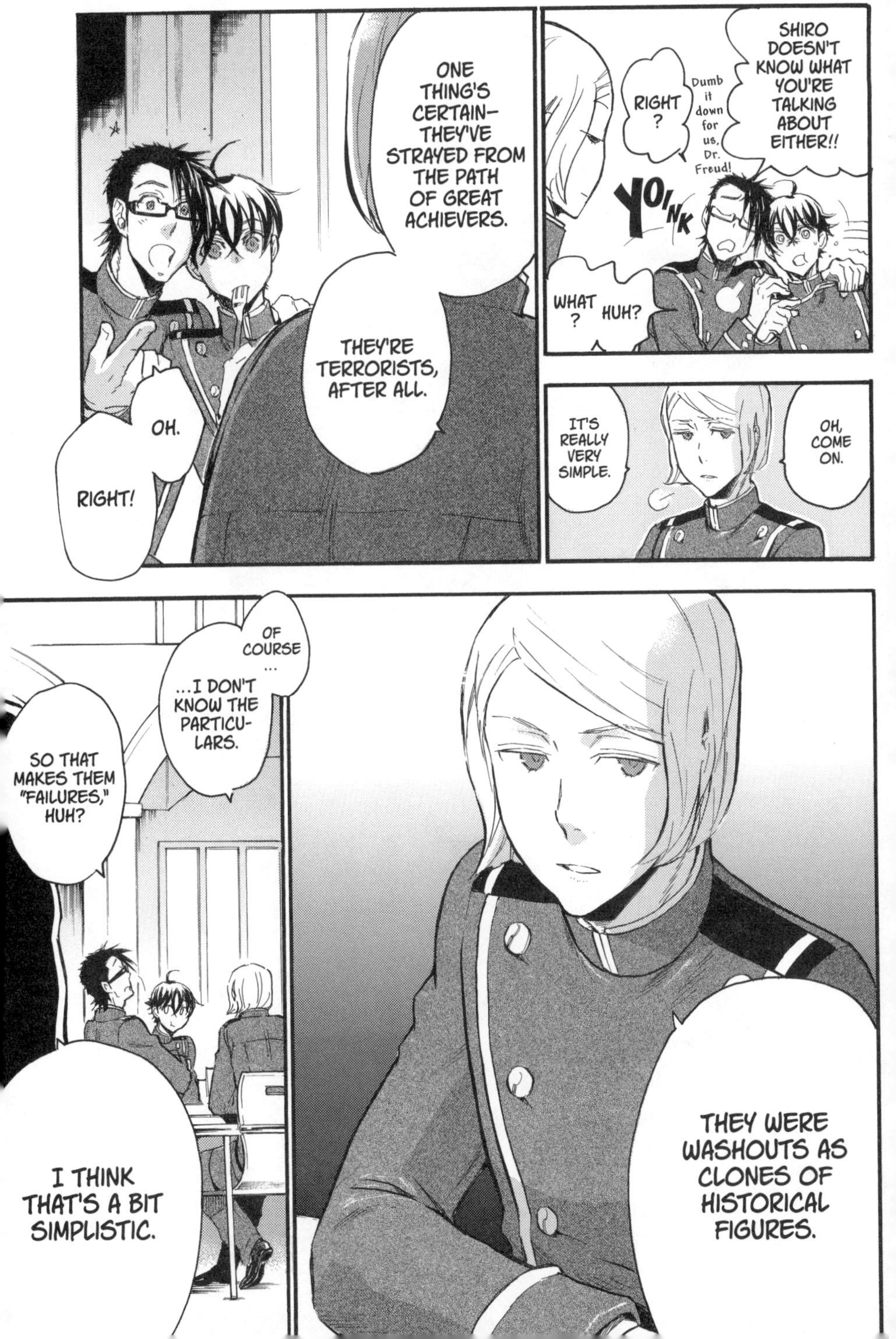
SHIRO DOESN'T KNOW WHAT YOU'RE TALKING ABOUT EITHER!!
Dumb it down for us, Dr. Freud!
RIGHT?
YOINK
WHAT?
HUH?
OH, COME ON.
IT'S REALLY VERY SIMPLE.
ONE THING'S CERTAIN— THEY'VE STRAYED FROM THE PATH OF GREAT ACHIEVERS.
THEY'RE TERRORISTS, AFTER ALL.
OH.
RIGHT!
THEY WERE WASHOUTS AS CLONES OF HISTORICAL FIGURES.
OF COURSE...
...I DON'T KNOW THE PARTICU-LARS.
SO THAT MAKES THEM "FAILURES," HUH?
I THINK THAT'S A BIT SIMPLISTIC.

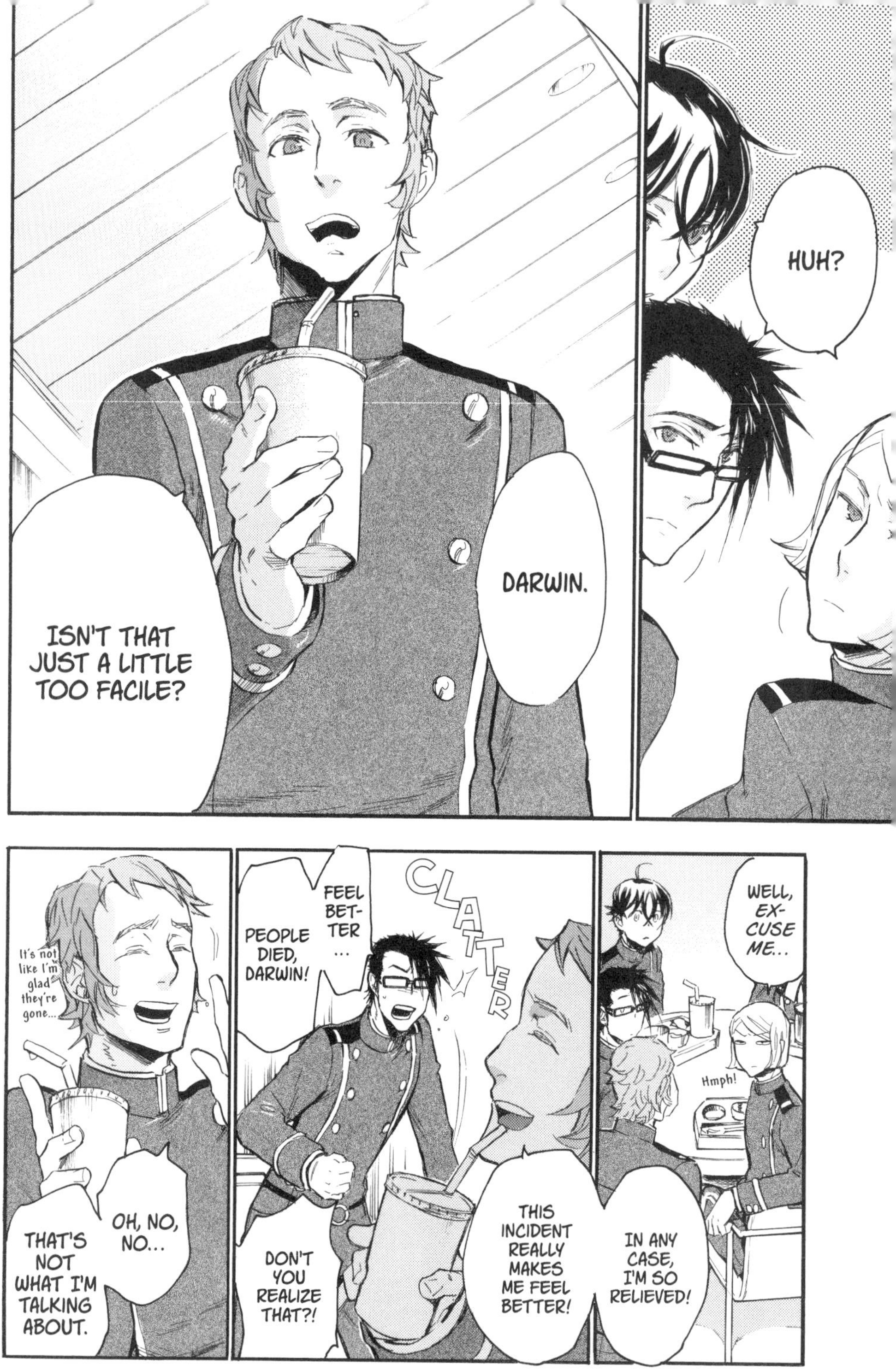
HUH?
DARWIN.
ISN'T THAT JUST A LITTLE TOO FACILE?
WELL, EXCUSE ME...
Hmph!
IN ANY CASE, I'M SO RELIEVED!
THIS INCIDENT REALLY MAKES ME FEEL BETTER!
CLATTER
FEEL BETTER...
PEOPLE DIED, DARWIN!
DON'T YOU REALIZE THAT?!
OH, NO, NO...
THAT'S NOT WHAT I'M TALKING ABOUT.
It's not like I'm glad they're gone...

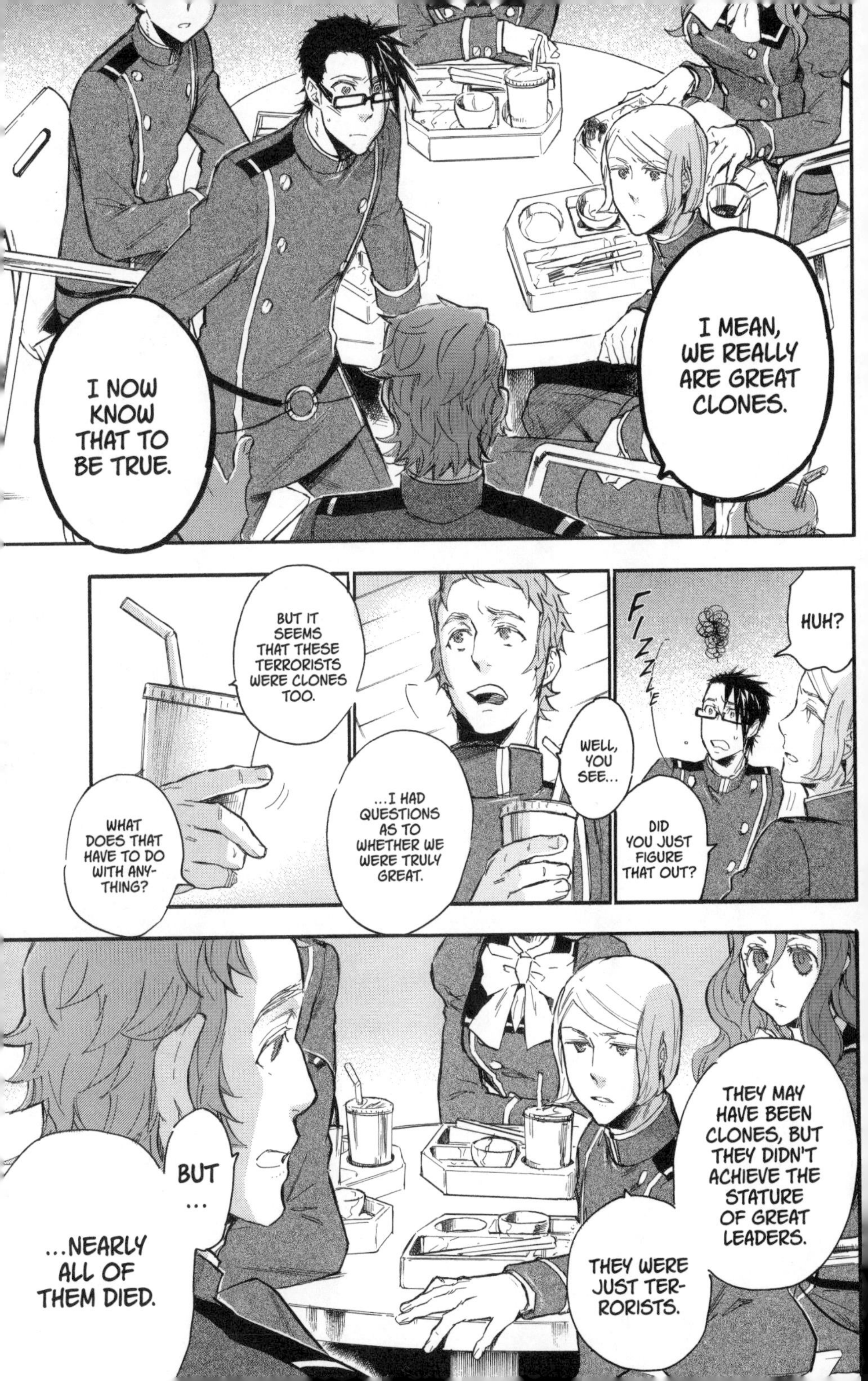
I MEAN, WE REALLY ARE GREAT CLONES.
I NOW KNOW THAT TO BE TRUE.
HUH?
FIZZLE
DID YOU JUST FIGURE THAT OUT?
WELL, YOU SEE...
...I HAD QUESTIONS AS TO WHETHER WE WERE TRULY GREAT.
BUT IT SEEMS THAT THESE TERRORISTS WERE CLONES TOO.
WHAT DOES THAT HAVE TO DO WITH ANY-THING?
THEY MAY HAVE BEEN CLONES, BUT THEY DIDN'T ACHIEVE THE STATURE OF GREAT LEADERS.
THEY WERE JUST TER-RORISTS.
BUT ...
...NEARLY ALL OF THEM DIED.

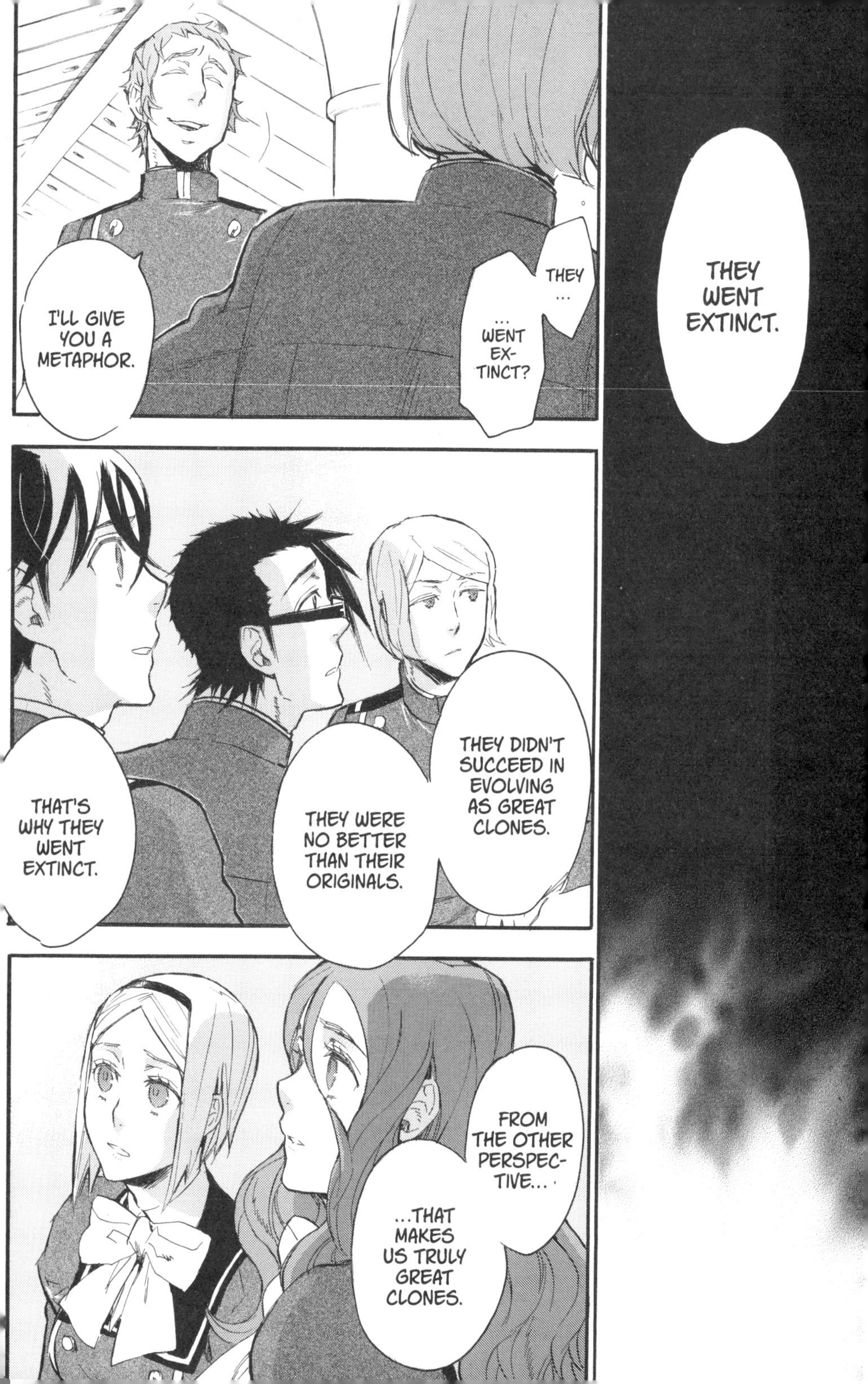
THEY WENT EXTINCT.
THEY...
...WENT EX-TINCT?
I'LL GIVE YOU A METAPHOR.
THEY DIDN'T SUCCEED IN EVOLVING AS GREAT CLONES.
THEY WERE NO BETTER THAN THEIR ORIGINALS.
THAT'S WHY THEY WENT EXTINCT.
FROM THE OTHER PERSPEC-TIVE...
...THAT MAKES US TRULY GREAT CLONES.

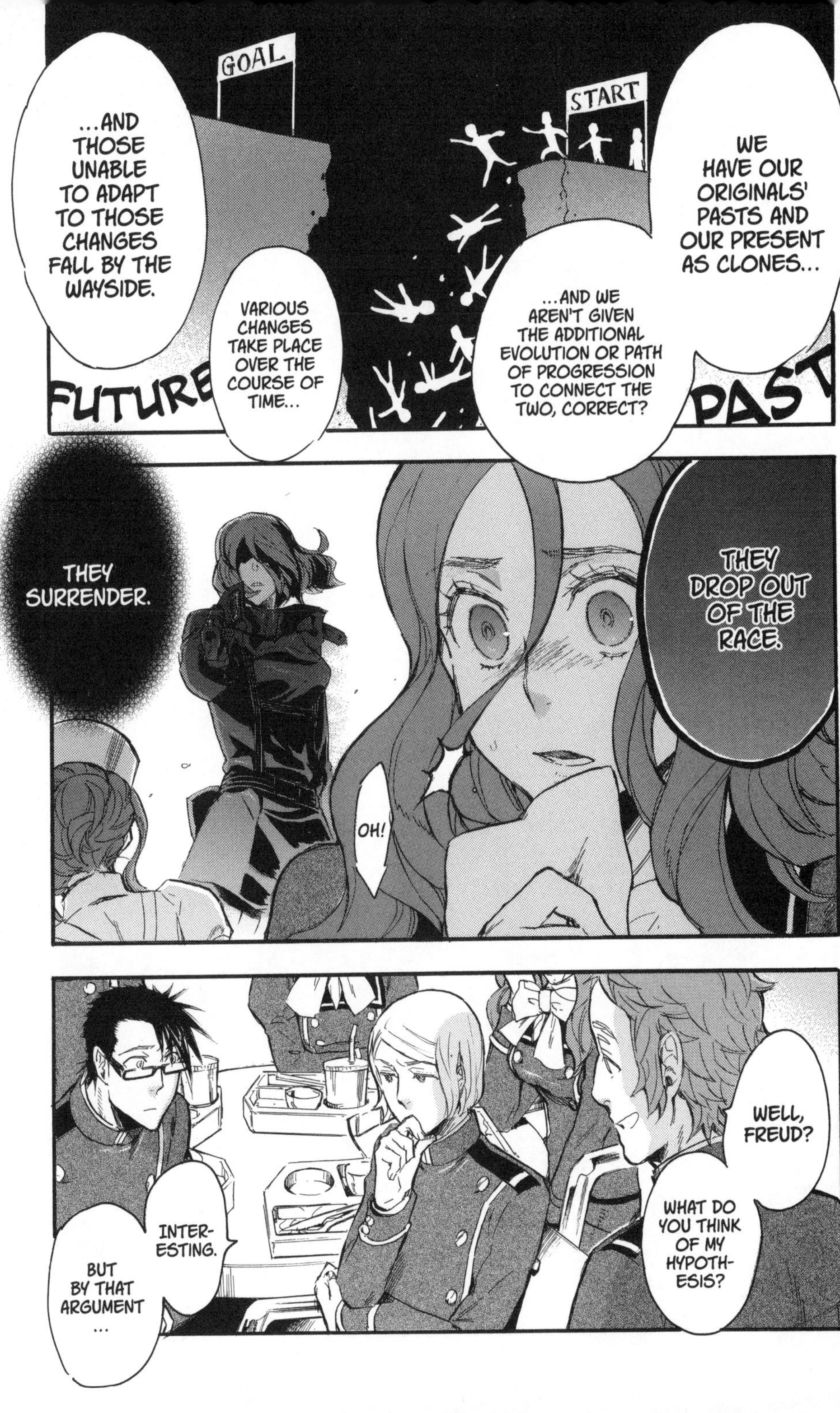
START
PAST
WE HAVE OUR ORIGINALS' PASTS AND OUR PRESENT AS CLONES...
...AND WE AREN'T GIVEN THE ADDITIONAL EVOLUTION OR PATH OF PROGRESSION TO CONNECT THE TWO, CORRECT?
GOAL
FUTURE
VARIOUS CHANGES TAKE PLACE OVER THE COURSE OF TIME...
...AND THOSE UNABLE TO ADAPT TO THOSE CHANGES FALL BY THE WAYSIDE.
THEY DROP OUT OF THE RACE.
OH!
THEY SURRENDER.
WELL, FREUD?
WHAT DO YOU THINK OF MY HYPOTHESIS?
INTERESTING.
BUT BY THAT ARGUMENT...

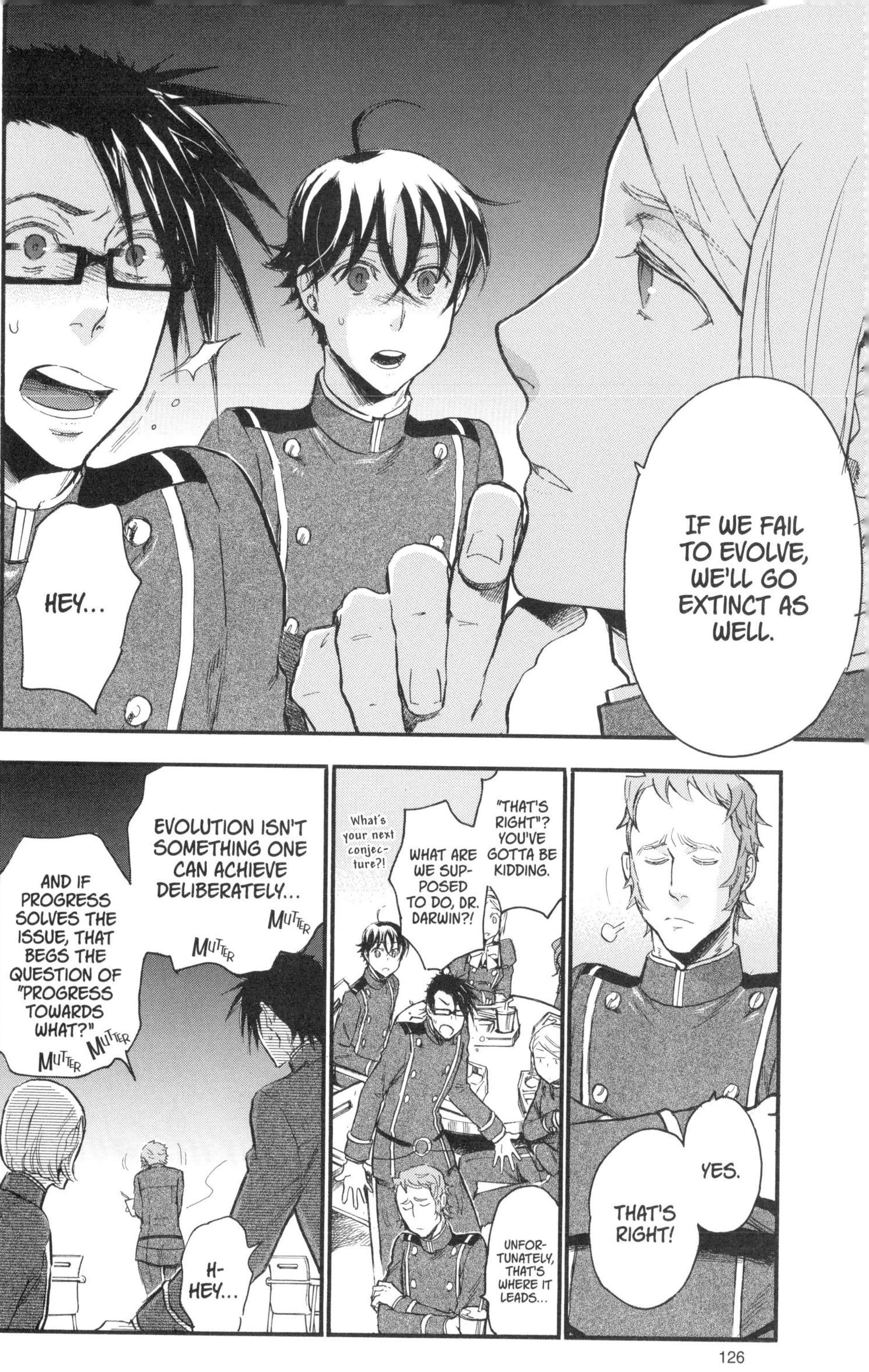
IF WE FAIL TO EVOLVE, WE'LL GO EXTINCT AS WELL.
HEY...
YES.
THAT'S RIGHT!
"THAT'S RIGHT"? YOU'VE GOTTA BE KIDDING.
WHAT ARE WE SUP-POSED TO DO, DR. DARWIN?!
What's your next conjec-ture?!
UNFOR-TUNATELY, THAT'S WHERE IT LEADS...
EVOLUTION ISN'T SOMETHING ONE CAN ACHIEVE DELIBERATELY...
MUTTER
MUTTER
AND IF PROGRESS SOLVES THE ISSUE, THAT BEGS THE QUESTION OF "PROGRESS TOWARDS WHAT?"
MUTTER
MUTTER
H-HEY...

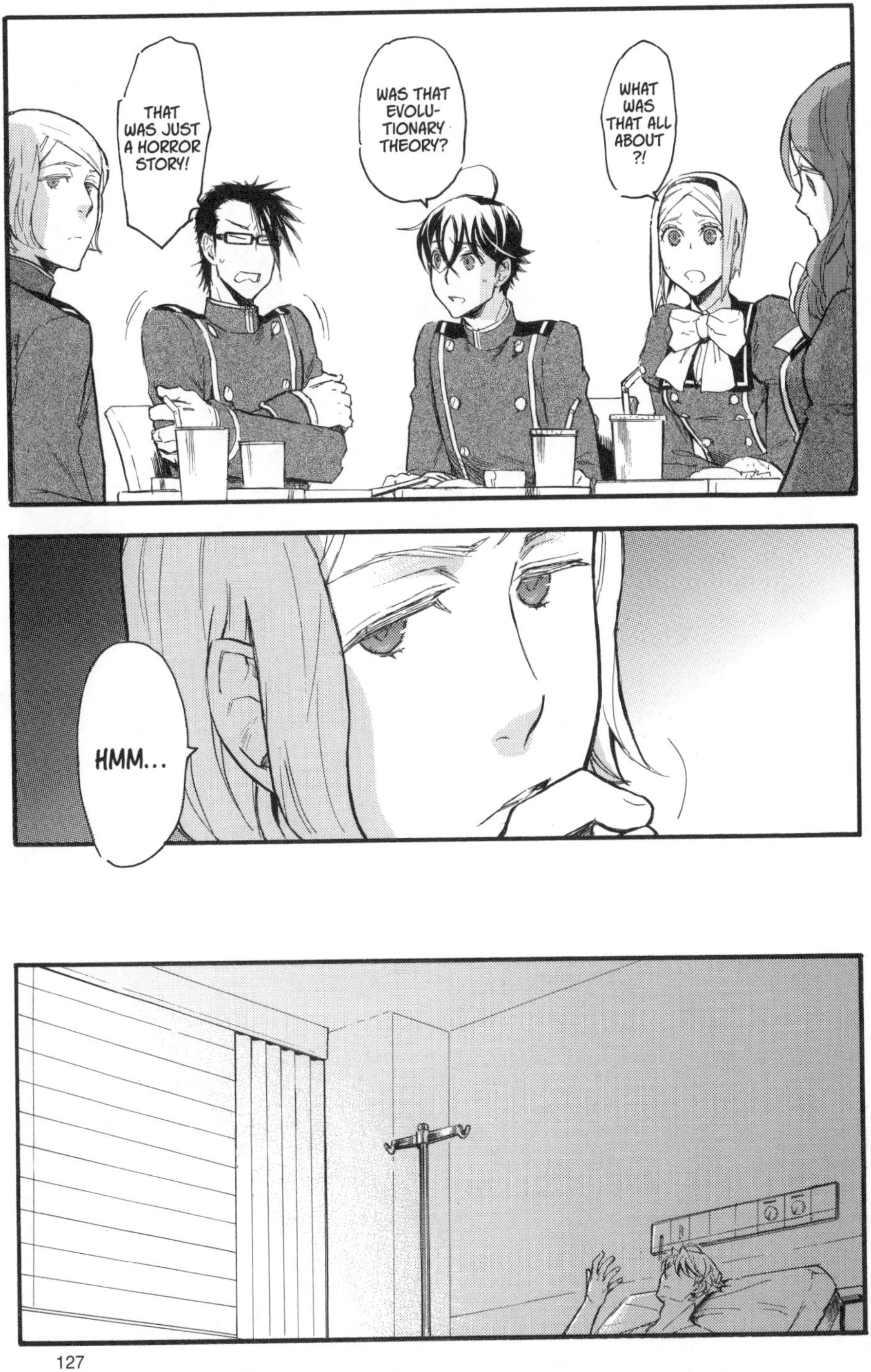
WHAT WAS THAT ALL ABOUT ?!
WAS THAT EVOLU-TIONARY THEORY?
THAT WAS JUST A HORROR STORY!
HMM...

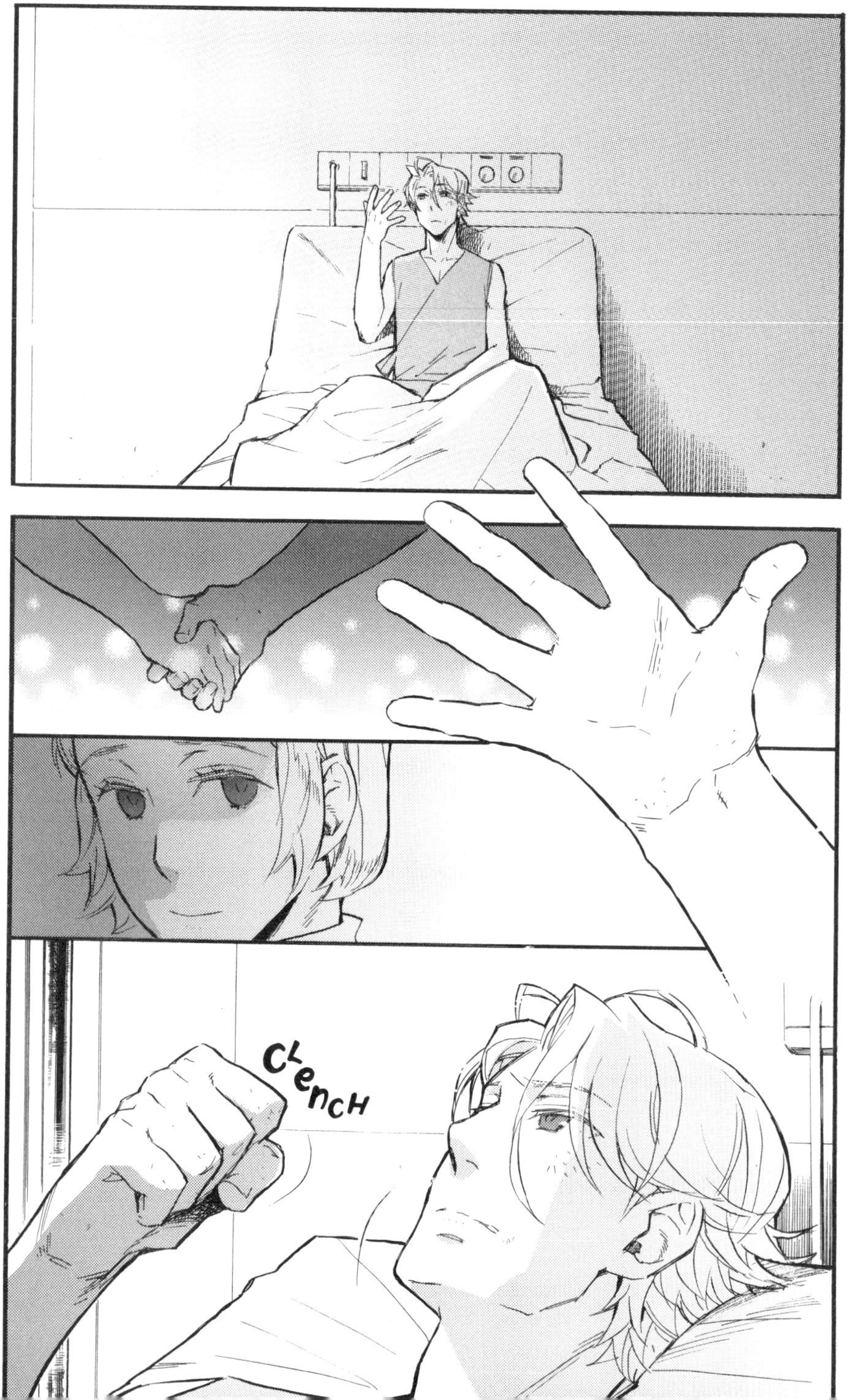
CLENCH

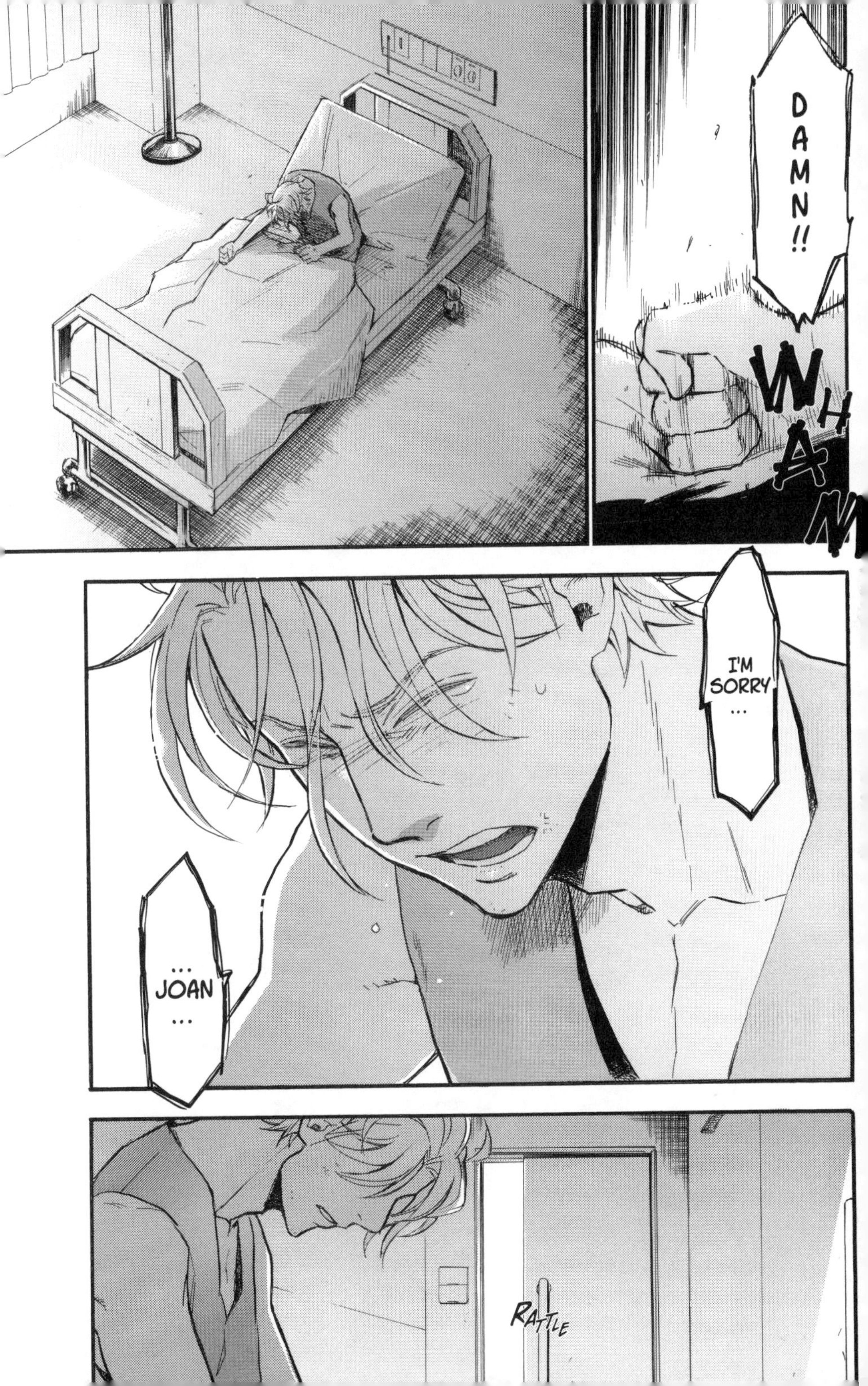
DAMN!!
WHAM
I'M SORRY...
...JOAN...
RATTLE

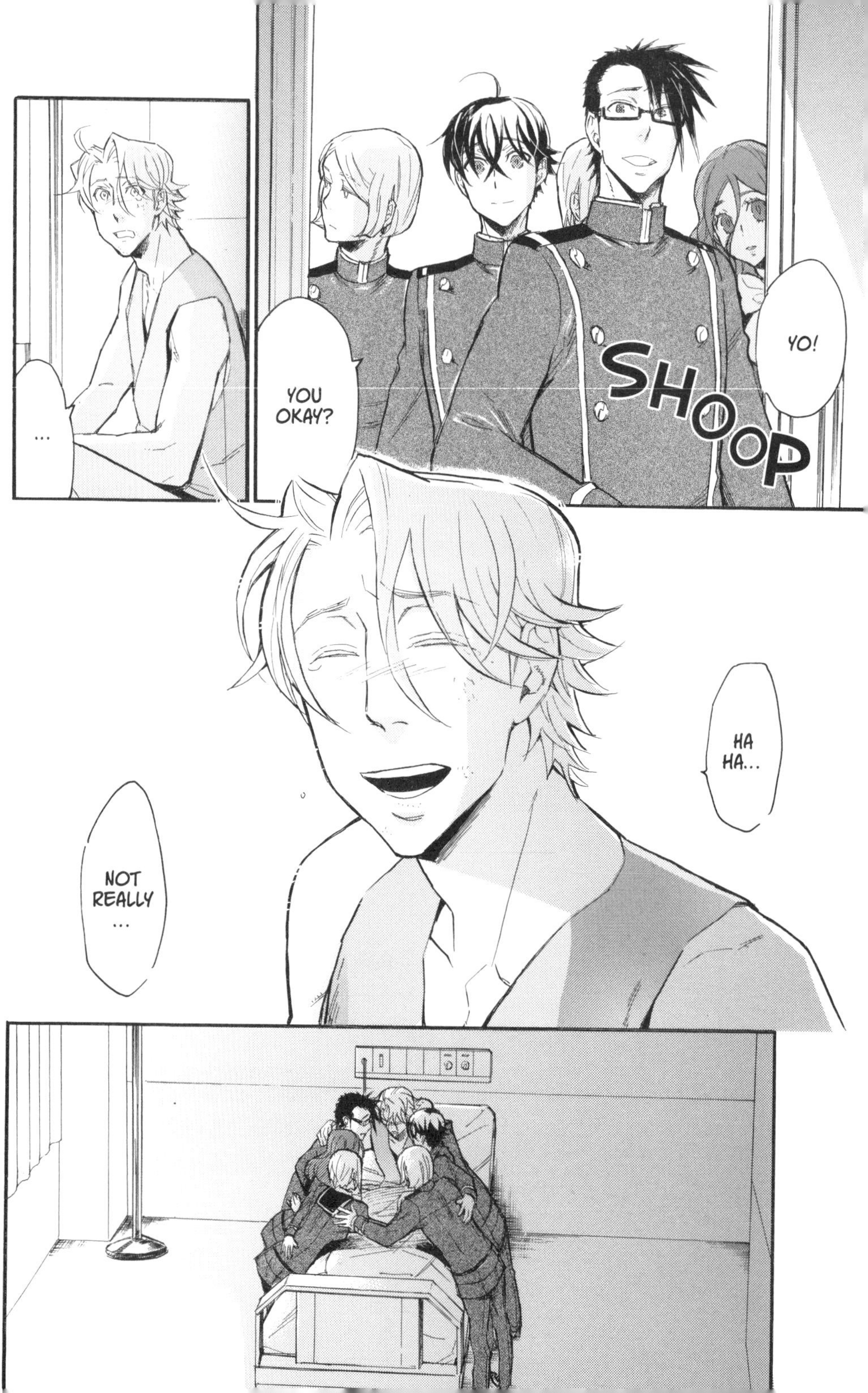
YO!
SHOOP
YOU OKAY?
...
HA HA...
NOT REALLY ...

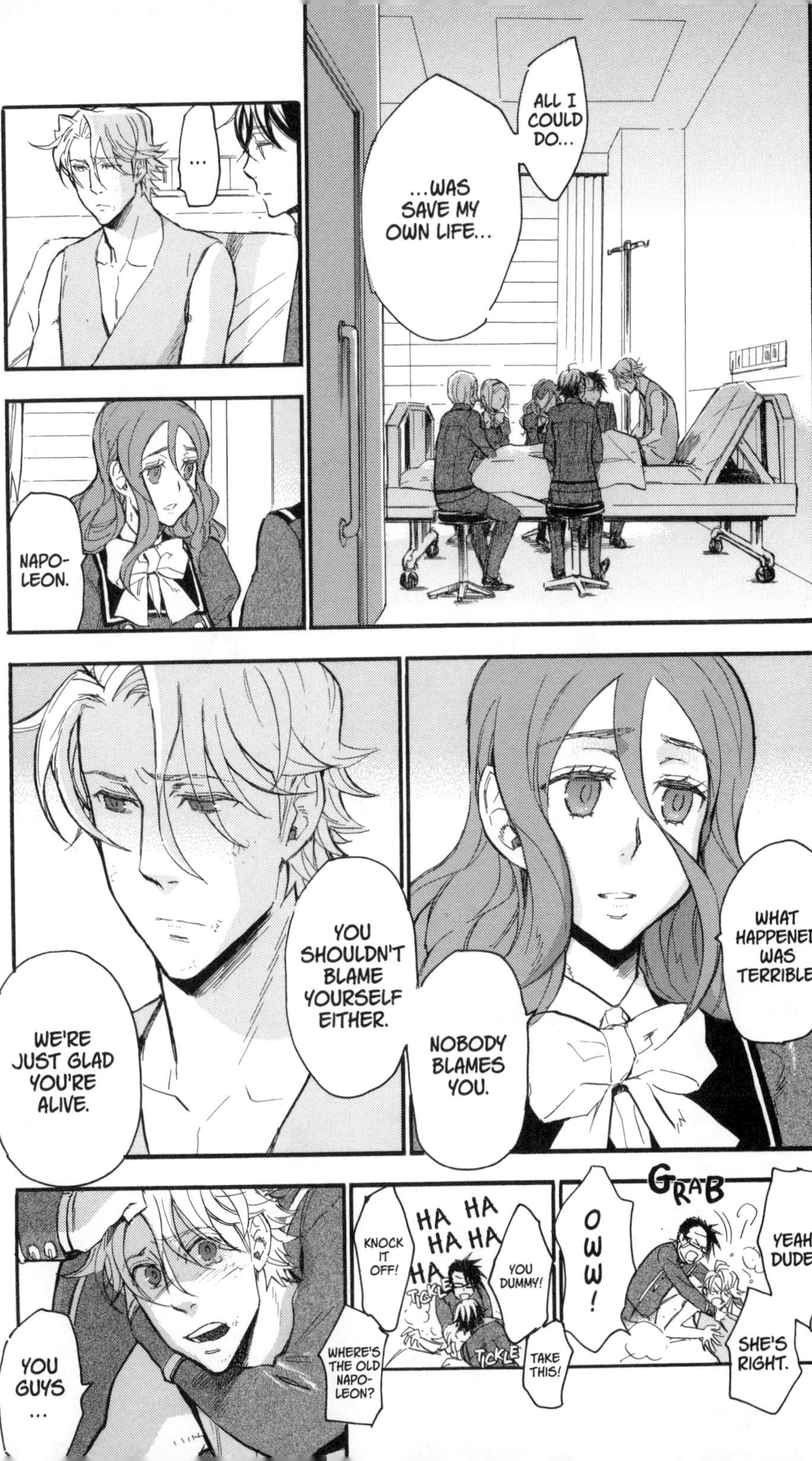
ALL I COULD DO...
...WAS SAVE MY OWN LIFE...
...
NAPO-LEON.
WHAT HAPPENED WAS TERRIBLE.
NOBODY BLAMES YOU.
YOU SHOULDN'T BLAME YOURSELF EITHER.
WE'RE JUST GLAD YOU'RE ALIVE.
GRAB
YEAH, DUDE!
OWW!
SHE'S RIGHT.
HA HA HA HA HA
YOU DUMMY!
KNOCK IT OFF!
TICKLE
TICKLE
TAKE THIS!
WHERE'S THE OLD NAPO-LEON?
YOU GUYS ...

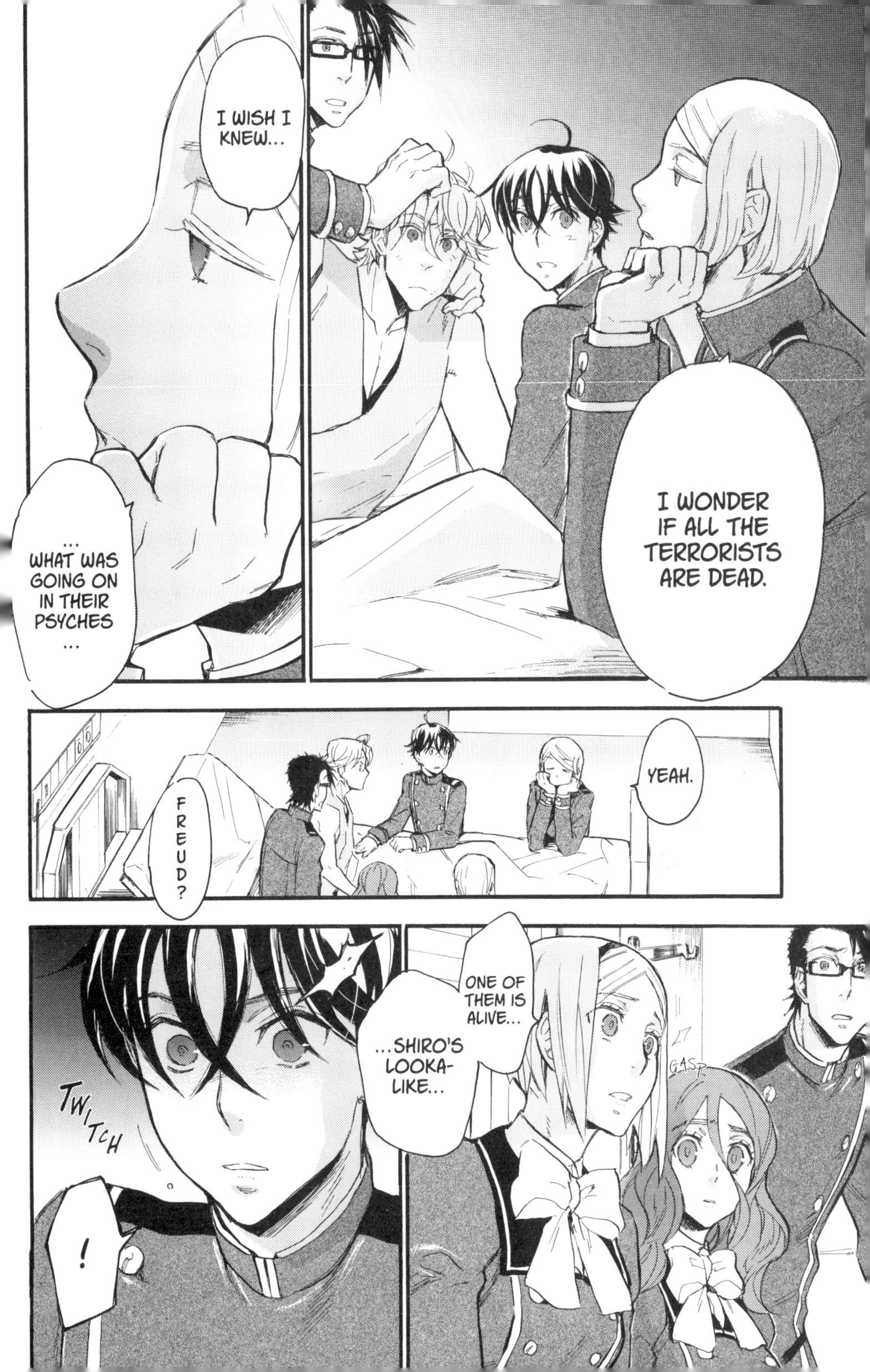
I WONDER IF ALL THE TERRORISTS ARE DEAD.
I WISH I KNEW...
... WHAT WAS GOING ON IN THEIR PSYCHES ...
YEAH.
FREUD?
ONE OF THEM IS ALIVE...
...SHIRO'S LOOKA-LIKE...
GASP
TWITCH
!

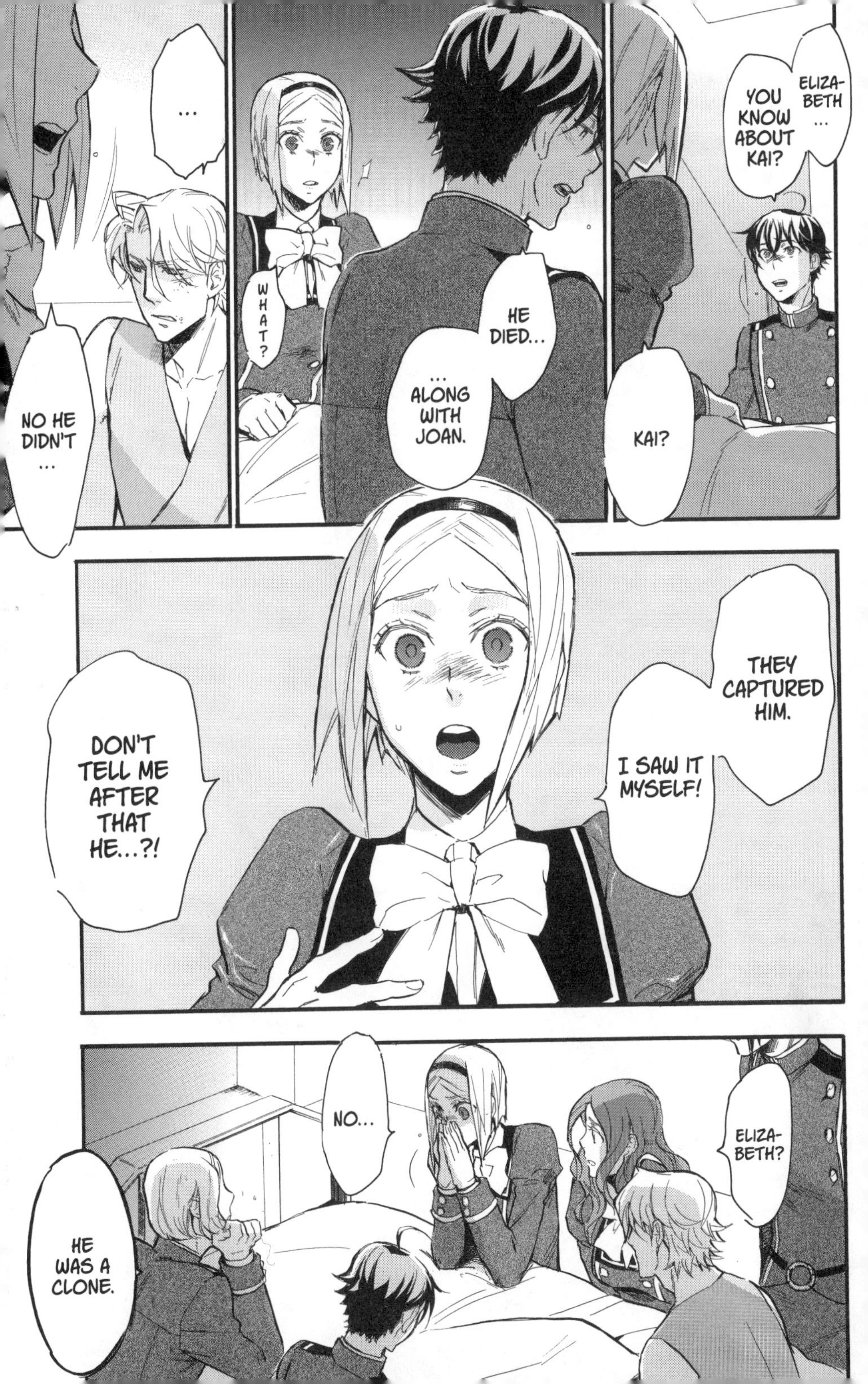
ELIZA-BETH ...
YOU KNOW ABOUT KAI?
KAI?
HE DIED...
... ALONG WITH JOAN.
WHAT?
...
NO HE DIDN'T ...
THEY CAPTURED HIM.
I SAW IT MYSELF!
DON'T TELL ME AFTER THAT HE...?!
ELIZA-BETH?
NO...
HE WAS A CLONE.

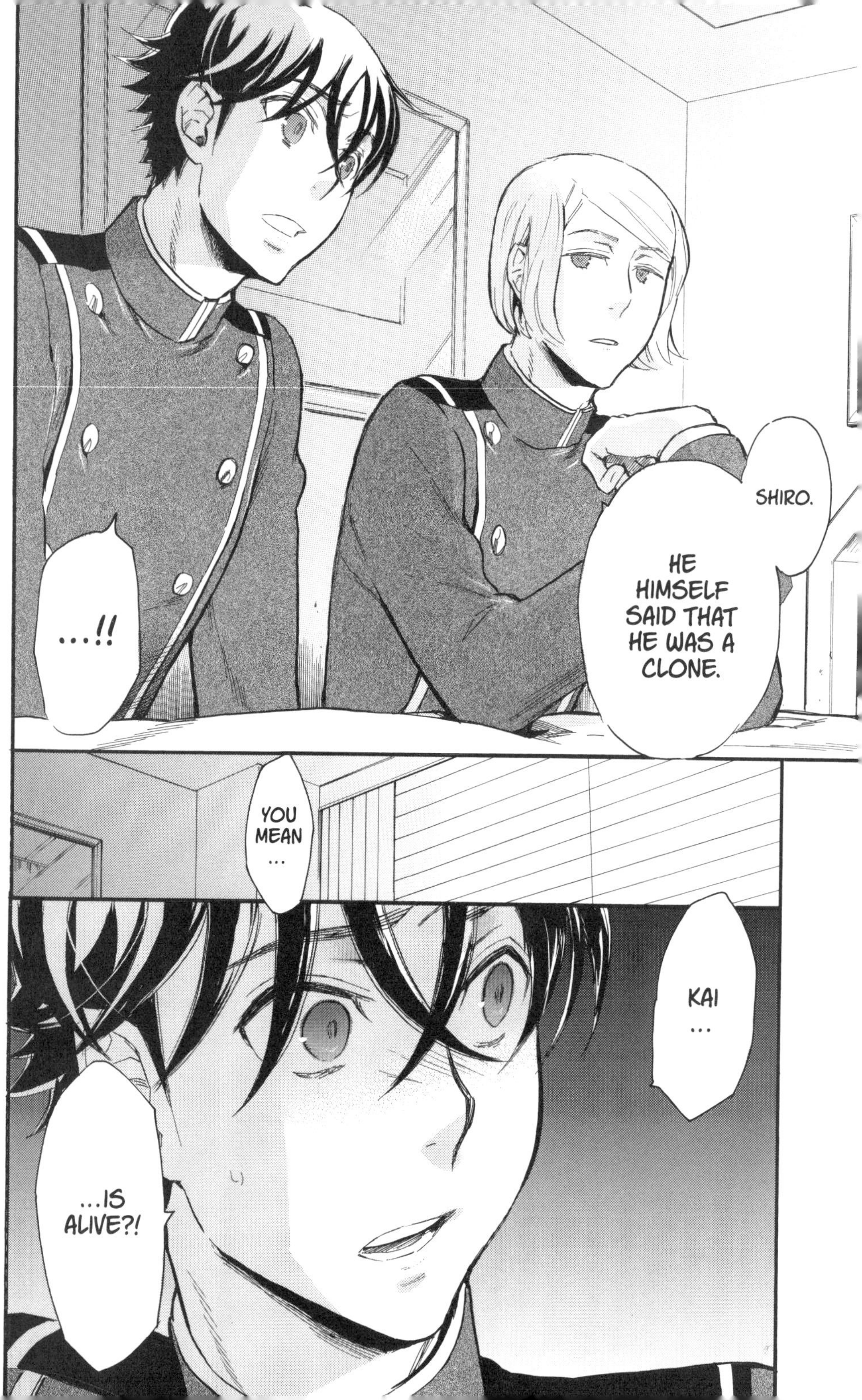
SHIRO.
HE HIMSELF SAID THAT HE WAS A CLONE.
...!!
YOU MEAN ...
KAI ...
...IS ALIVE?!

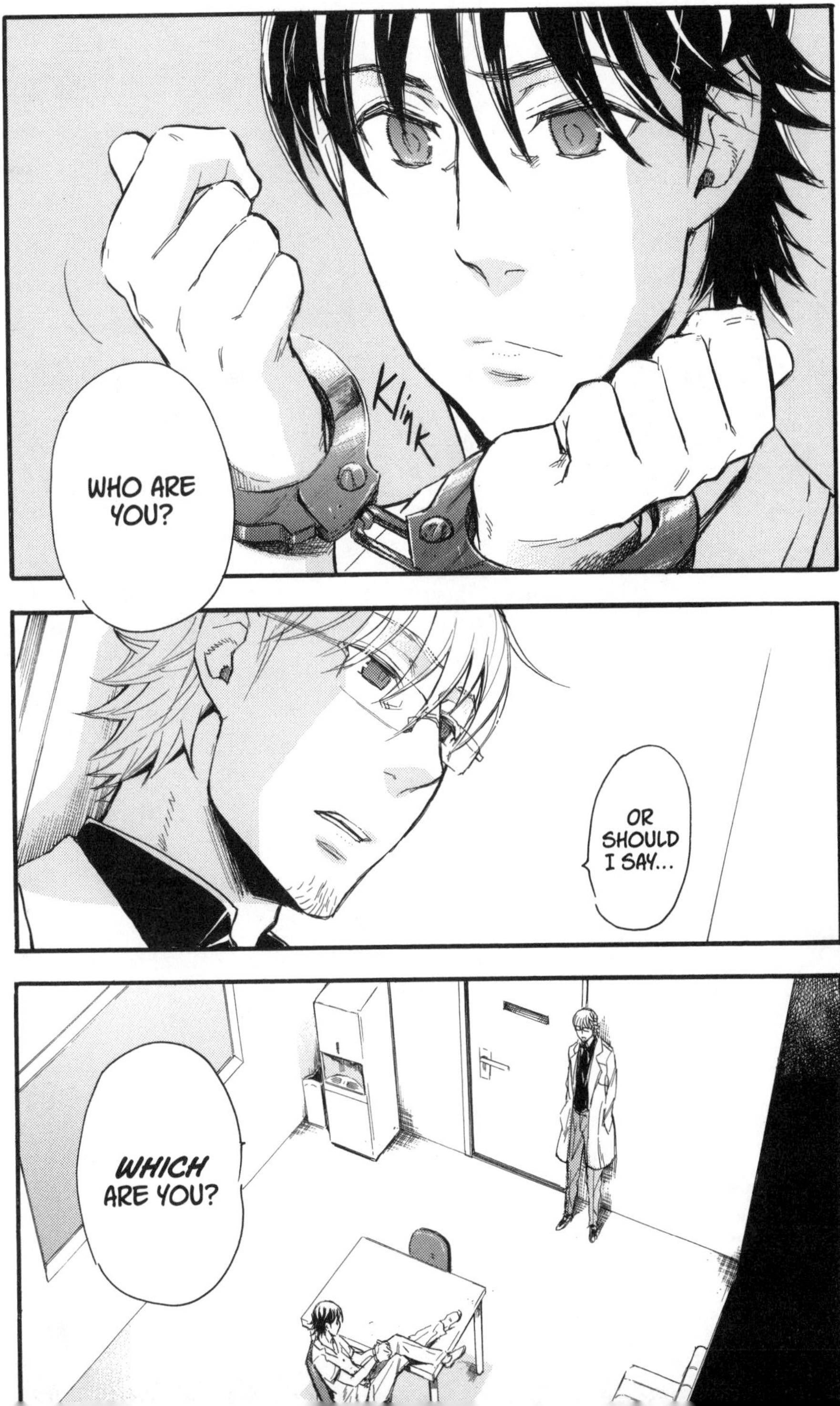
KLINK
WHO ARE YOU?
OR SHOULD I SAY...
WHICH ARE YOU?

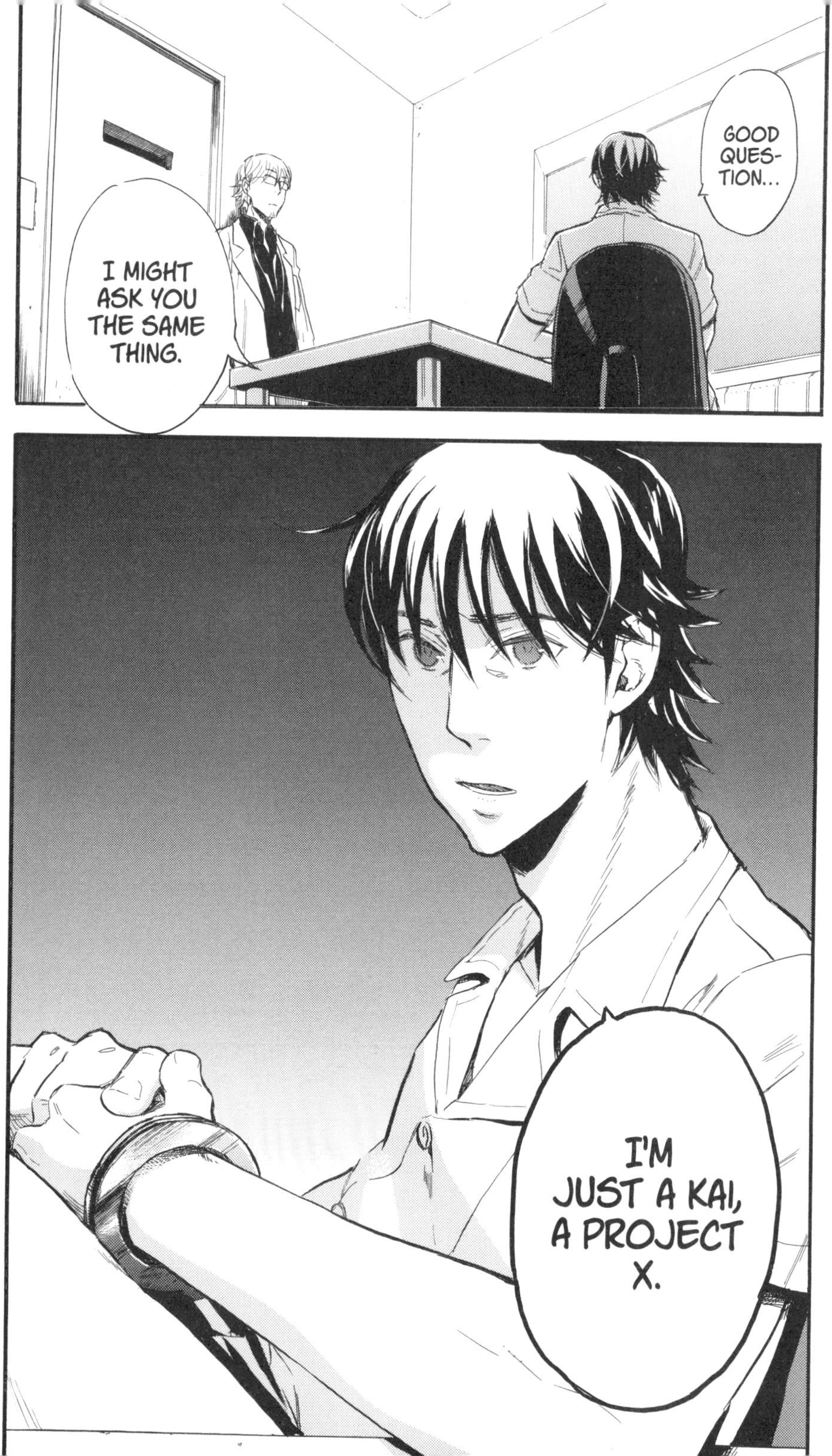
GOOD QUES-TION...
I MIGHT ASK YOU THE SAME THING.
I'M JUST A KAI, A PROJECT X.

CHAPTER twenty-three

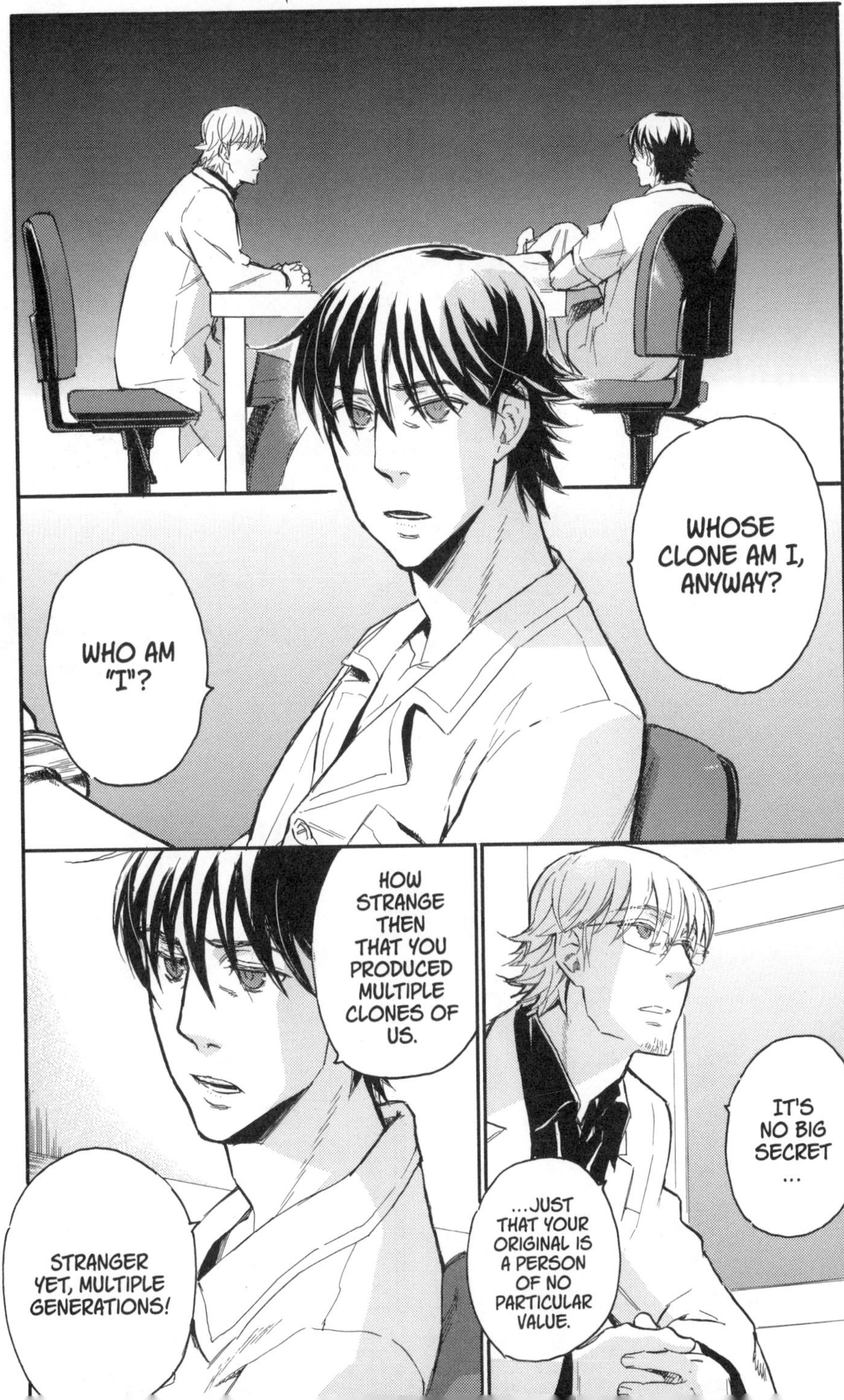
WHOSE CLONE AM I, ANYWAY?
WHO AM "I"?
IT'S NO BIG SECRET...
...JUST THAT YOUR ORIGINAL IS A PERSON OF NO PARTICULAR VALUE.
HOW STRANGE THEN THAT YOU PRODUCED MULTIPLE CLONES OF US.
STRANGER YET, MULTIPLE GENERATIONS!

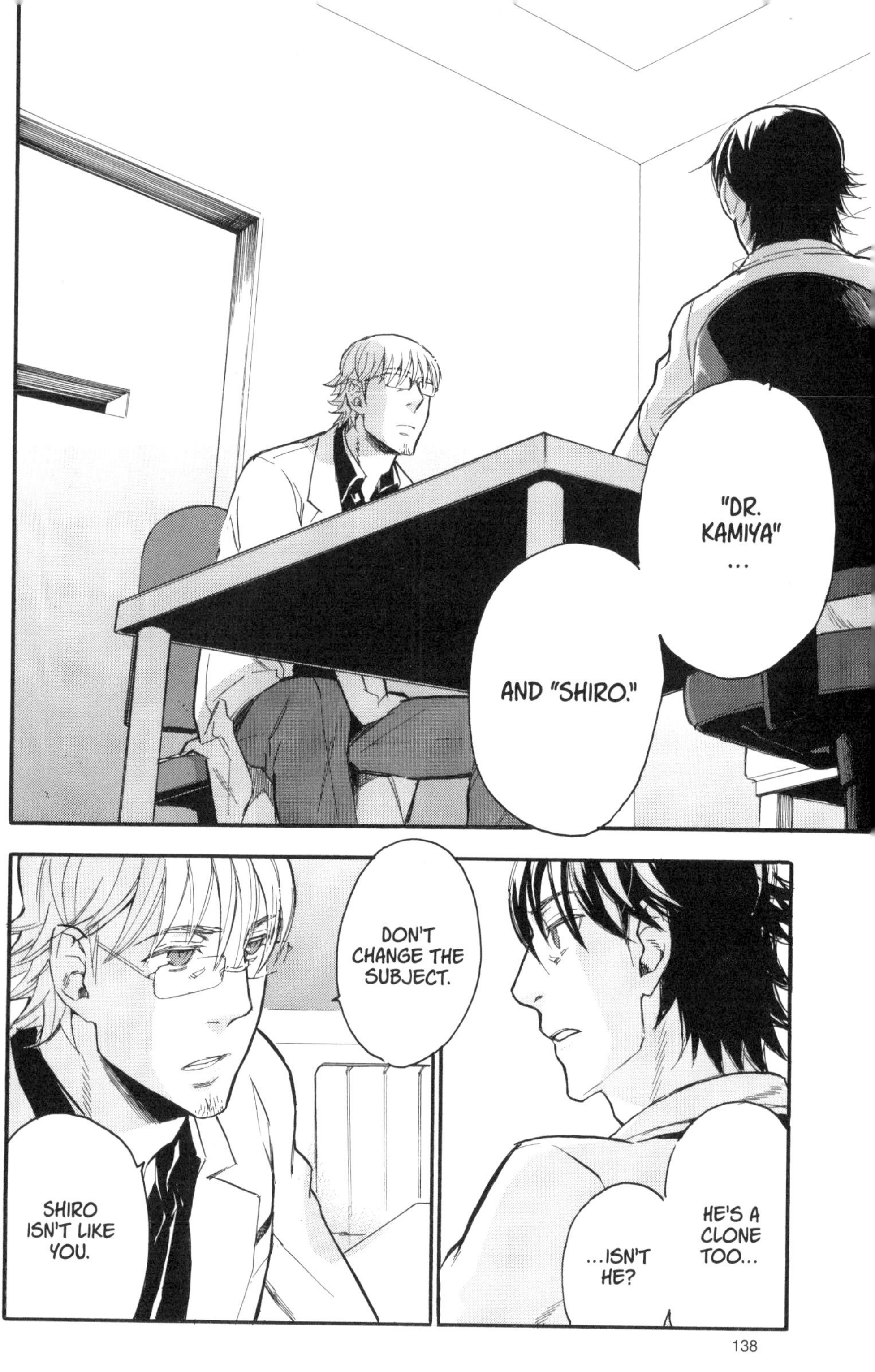
"DR. KAMIYA" ...
AND "SHIRO."
HE'S A CLONE TOO...
...ISN'T HE?
DON'T CHANGE THE SUBJECT.
SHIRO ISN'T LIKE YOU.

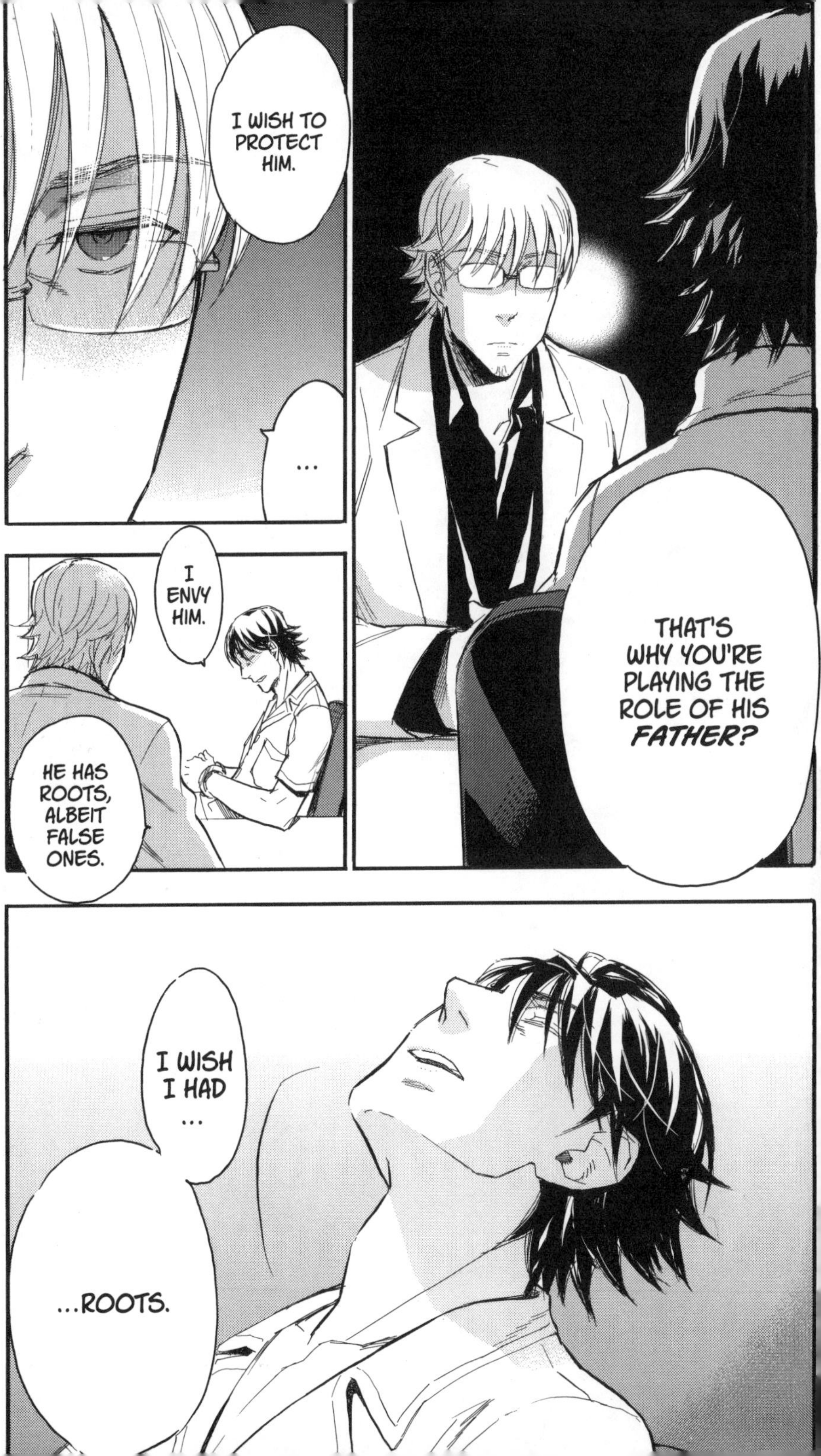
THAT'S WHY YOU'RE PLAYING THE ROLE OF HIS *FATHER?*
I WISH TO PROTECT HIM.
...
I ENVY HIM.
HE HAS ROOTS, ALBEIT FALSE ONES.
I WISH I HAD ...
...ROOTS.

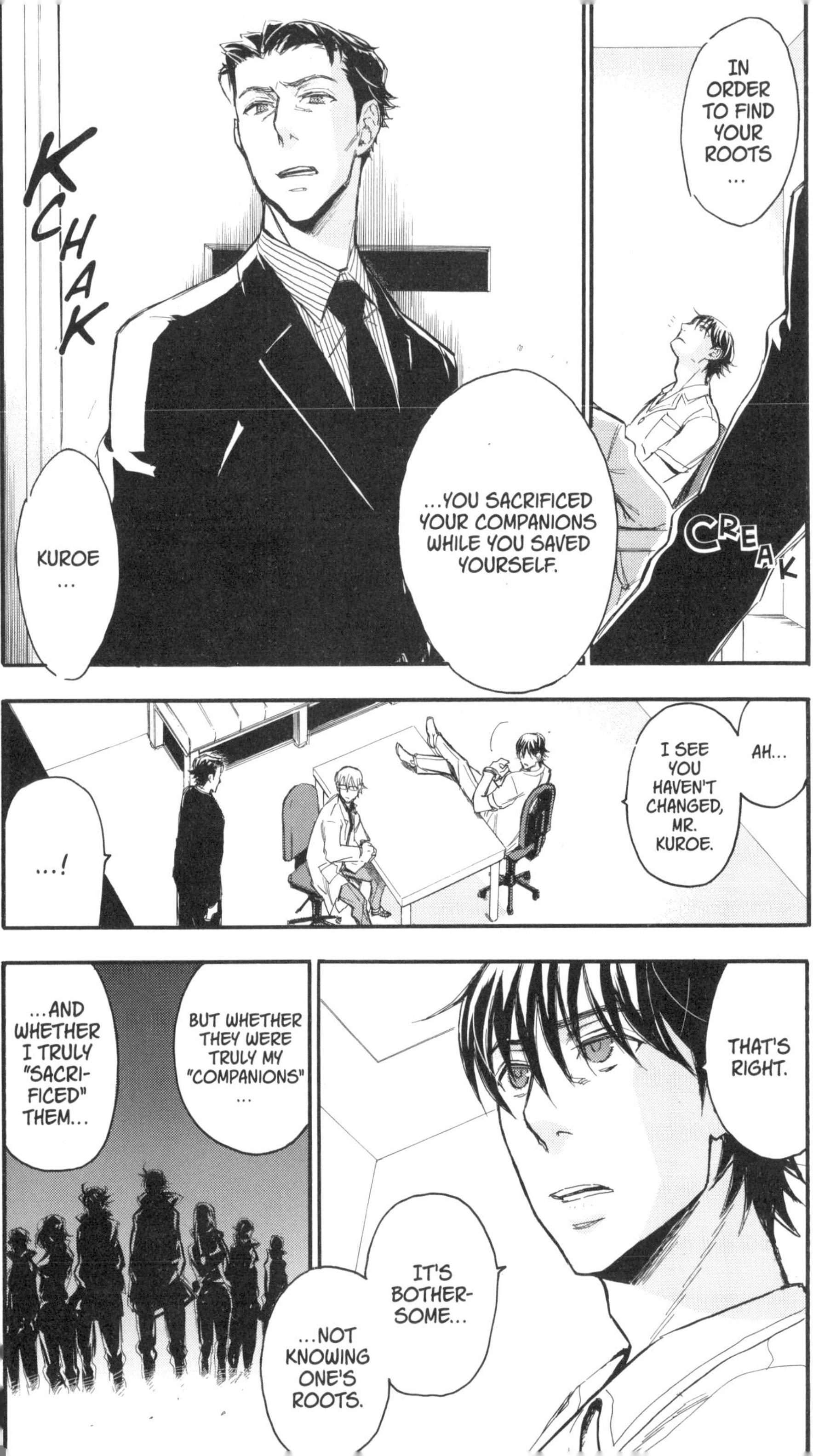
IN ORDER TO FIND YOUR ROOTS ...
CREAK
...YOU SACRIFICED YOUR COMPANIONS WHILE YOU SAVED YOURSELF.
KCHAK
KUROE ...
AH...
I SEE YOU HAVEN'T CHANGED, MR. KUROE.
...!
THAT'S RIGHT.
IT'S BOTHER-SOME...
...NOT KNOWING ONE'S ROOTS.
BUT WHETHER THEY WERE TRULY MY "COMPANIONS" ...
...AND WHETHER I TRULY "SACRI-FICED" THEM...

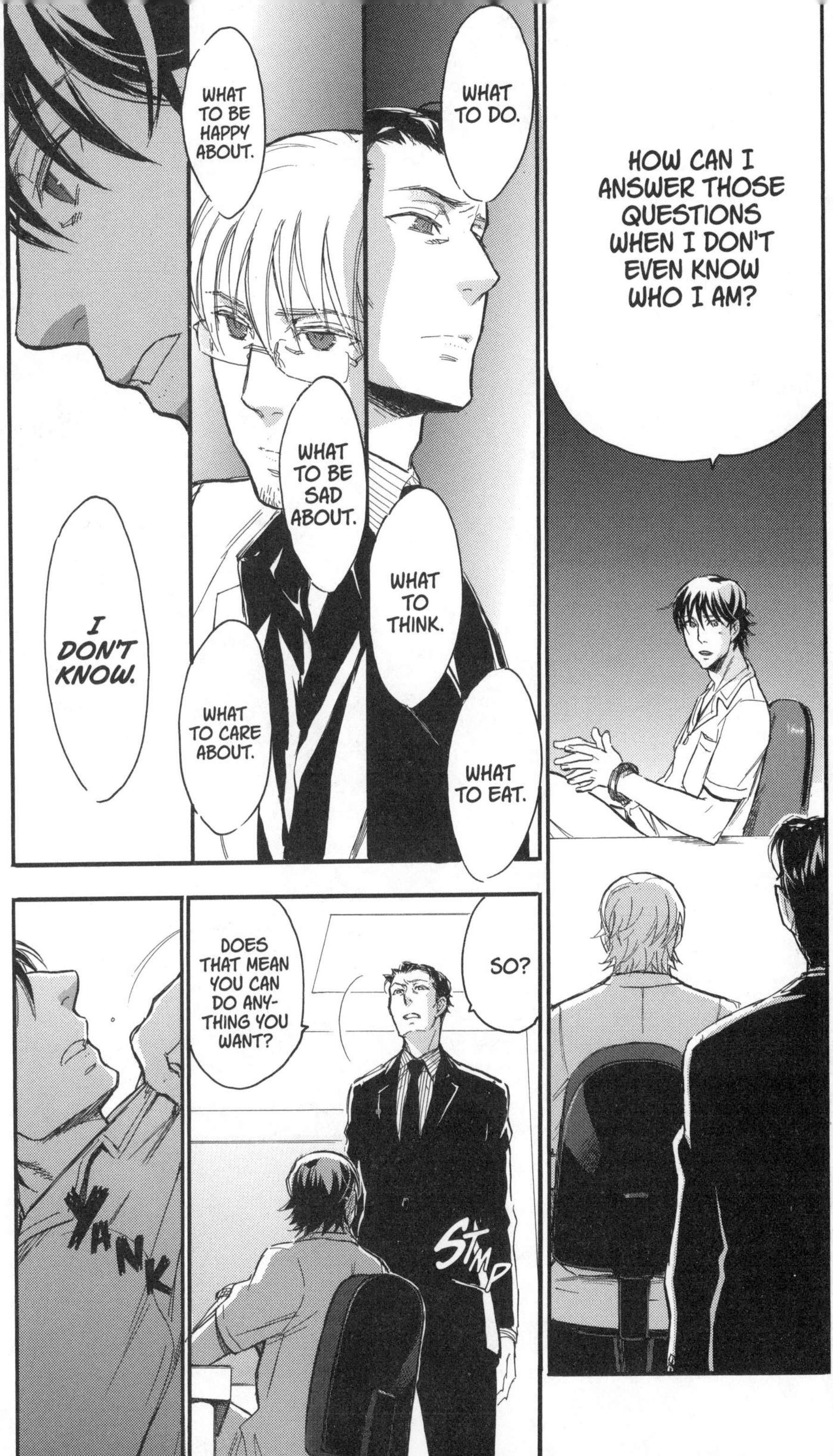
HOW CAN I ANSWER THOSE QUESTIONS WHEN I DON'T EVEN KNOW WHO I AM?
WHAT TO DO.
WHAT TO BE HAPPY ABOUT.
WHAT TO BE SAD ABOUT.
WHAT TO THINK.
WHAT TO EAT.
WHAT TO CARE ABOUT.
I DON'T KNOW.
SO?
DOES THAT MEAN YOU CAN DO ANYTHING YOU WANT?
STMP
YANK

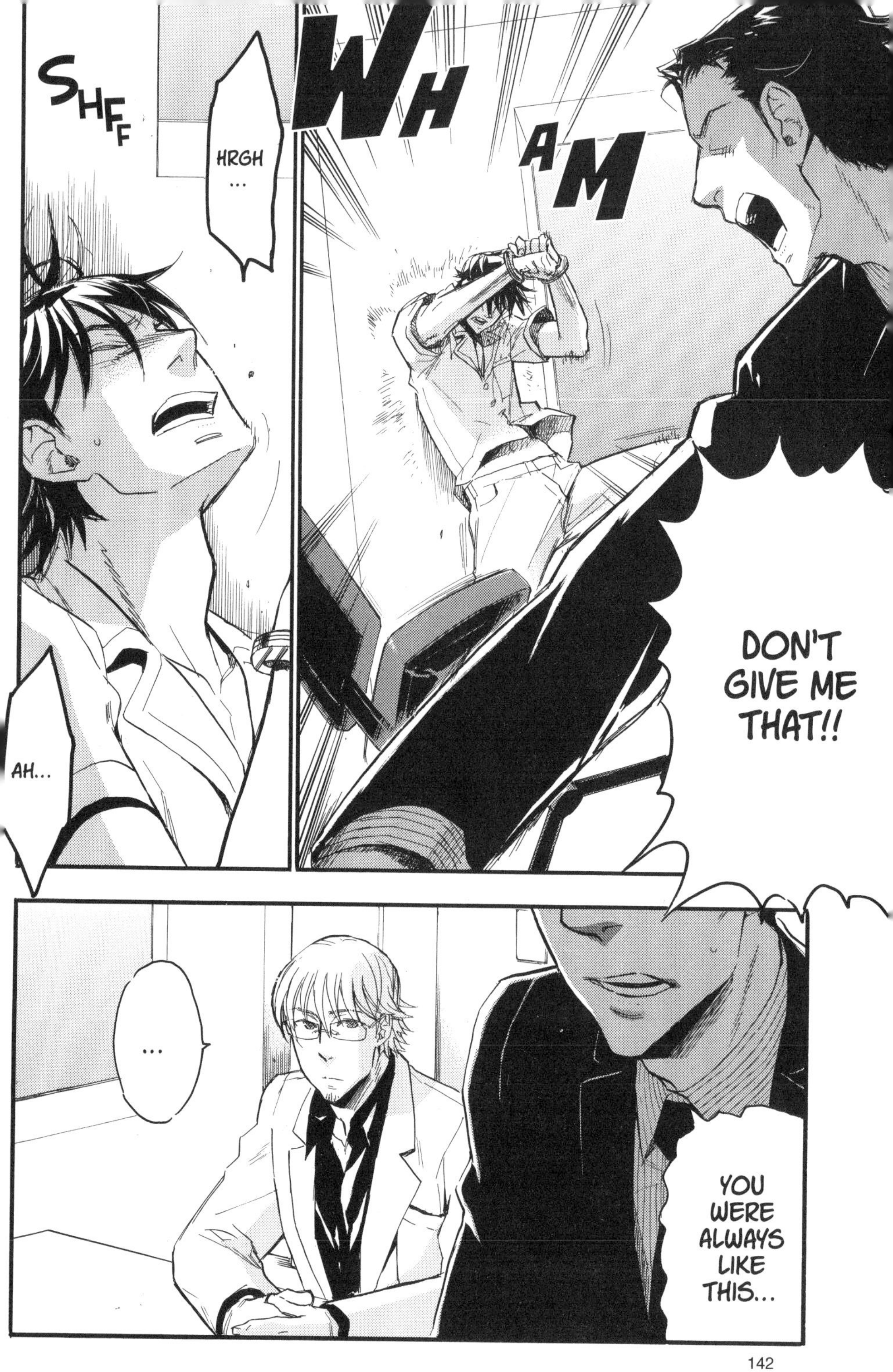
WHAM
DON'T GIVE ME THAT!!
SHFF
HRGH...
AH...
YOU WERE ALWAYS LIKE THIS...
...

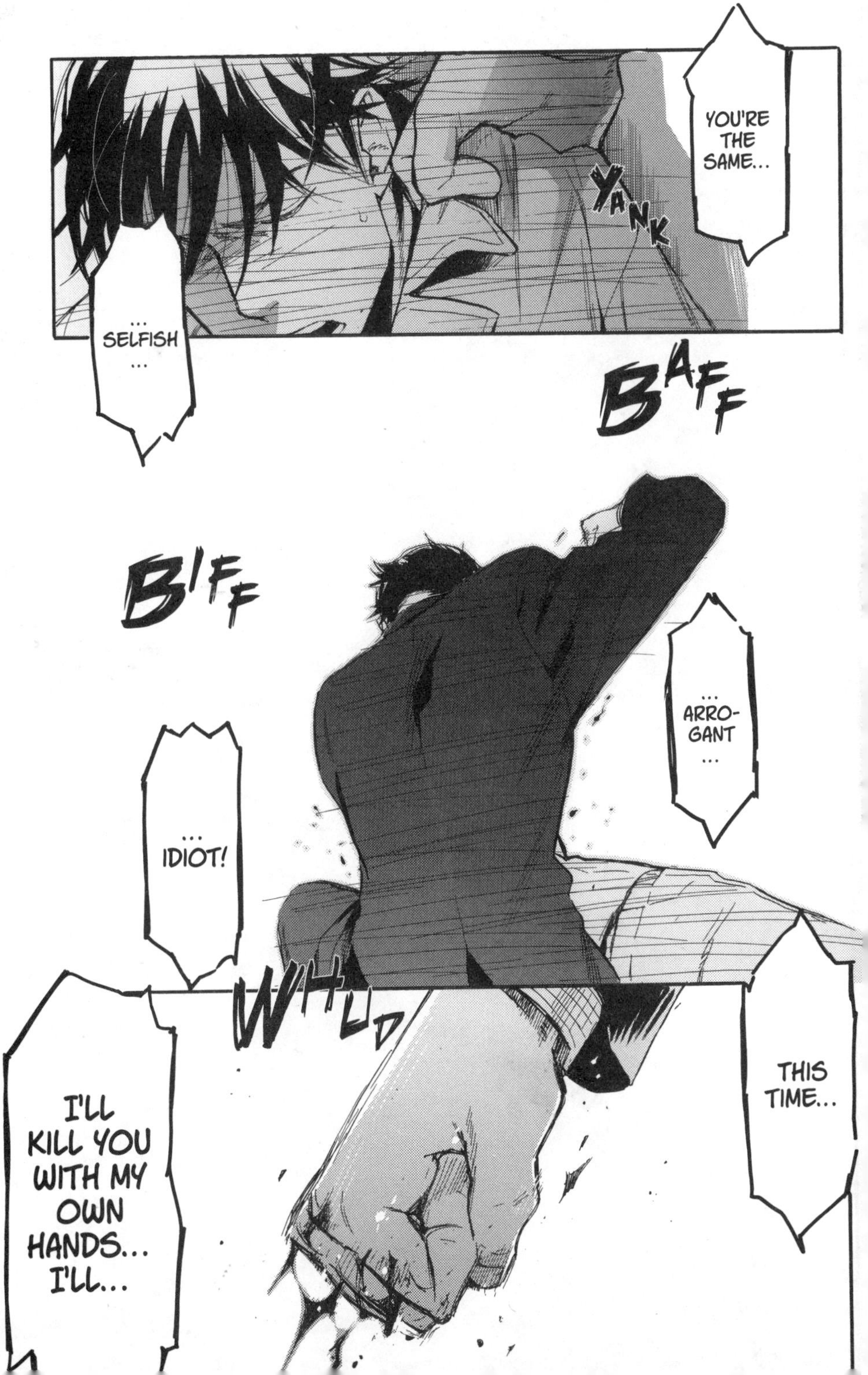
YOU'RE THE SAME...
YANK
...SELFISH...
BAFF
BIFF
...ARROGANT...
...IDIOT!
THIS TIME...
WHUD
I'LL KILL YOU WITH MY OWN HANDS... I'LL...

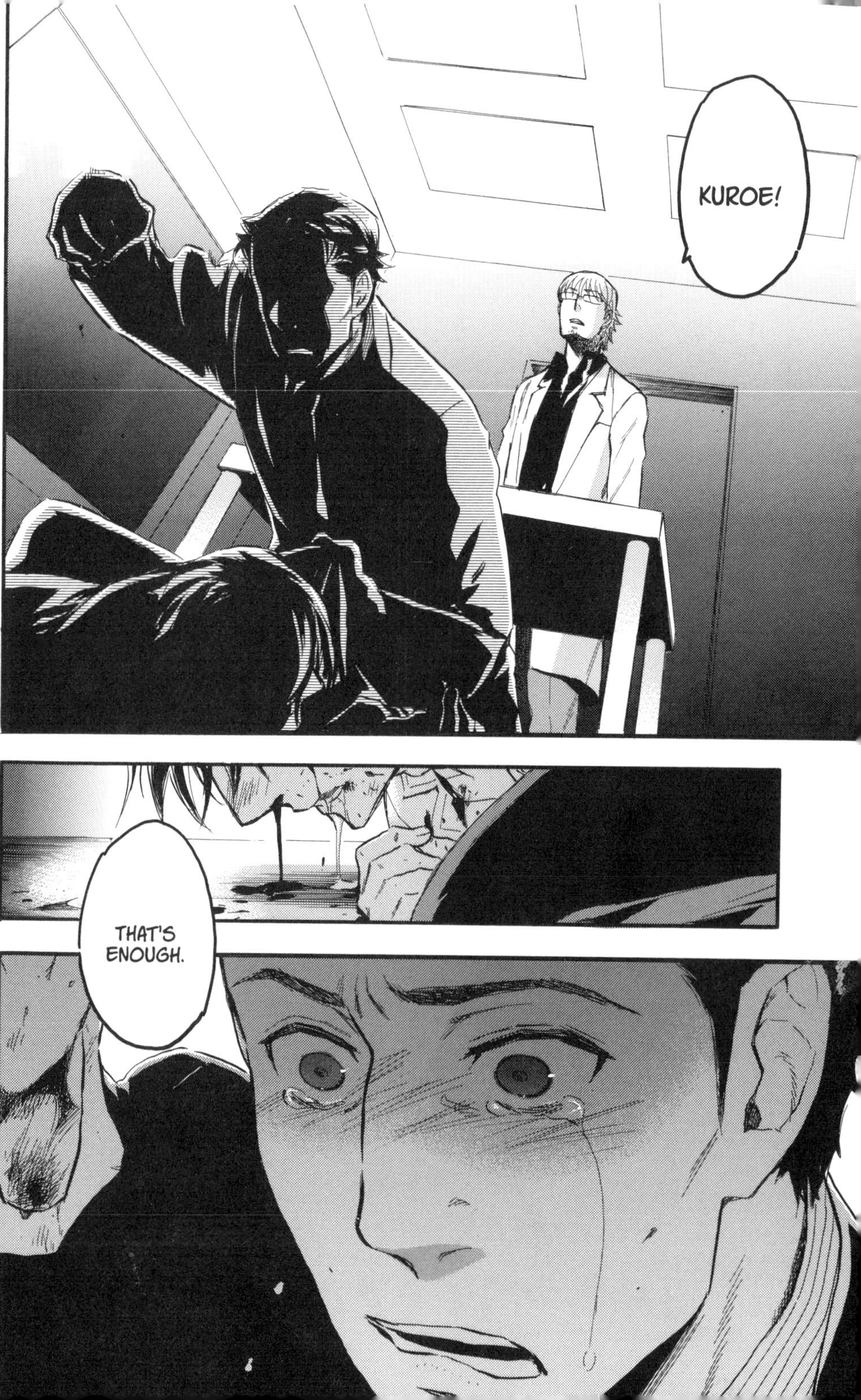
KUROE!
THAT'S ENOUGH.

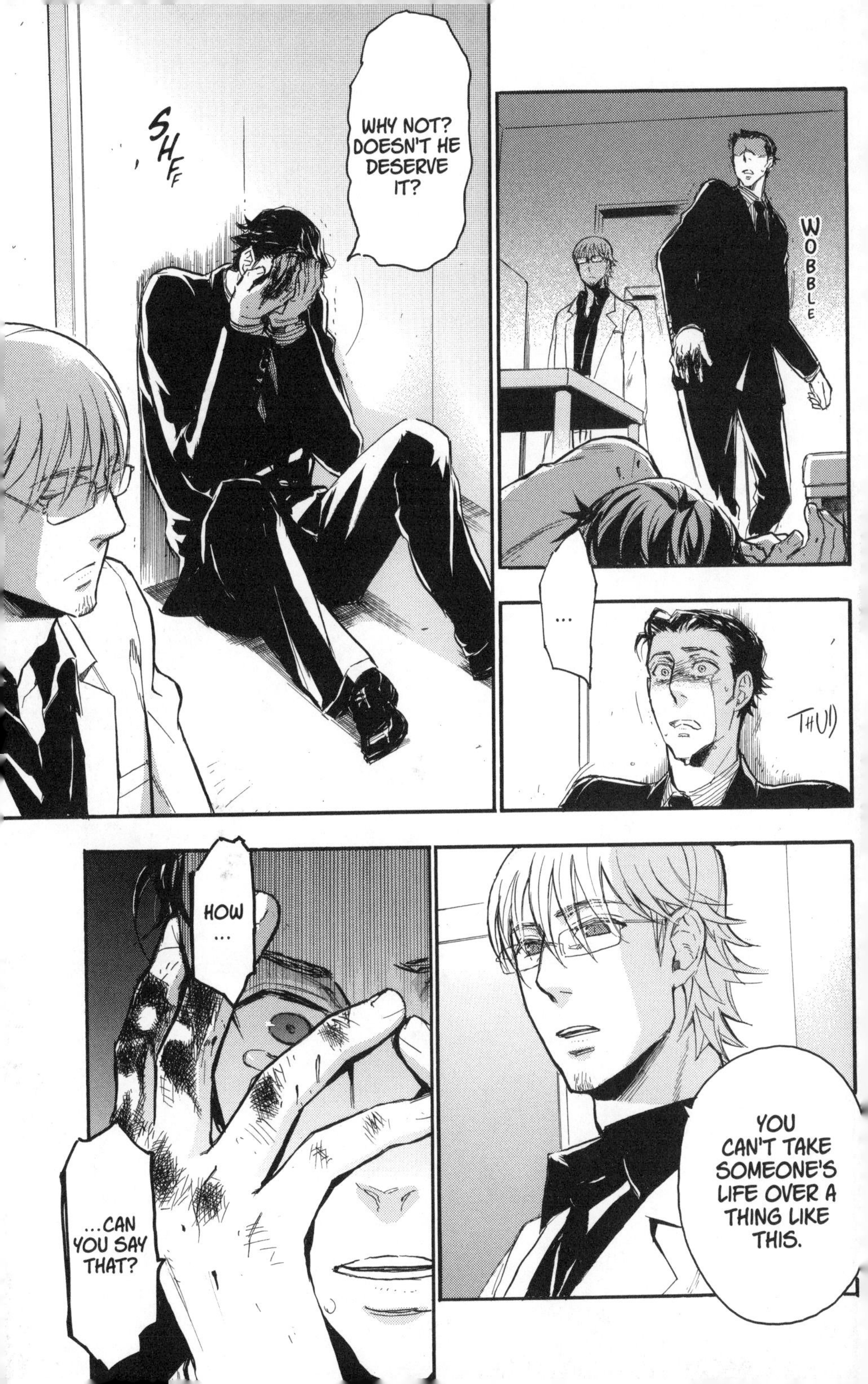
WOBBLE
...
THUD
SHFF
WHY NOT? DOESN'T HE DESERVE IT?
YOU CAN'T TAKE SOMEONE'S LIFE OVER A THING LIKE THIS.
HOW ...
...CAN YOU SAY THAT?

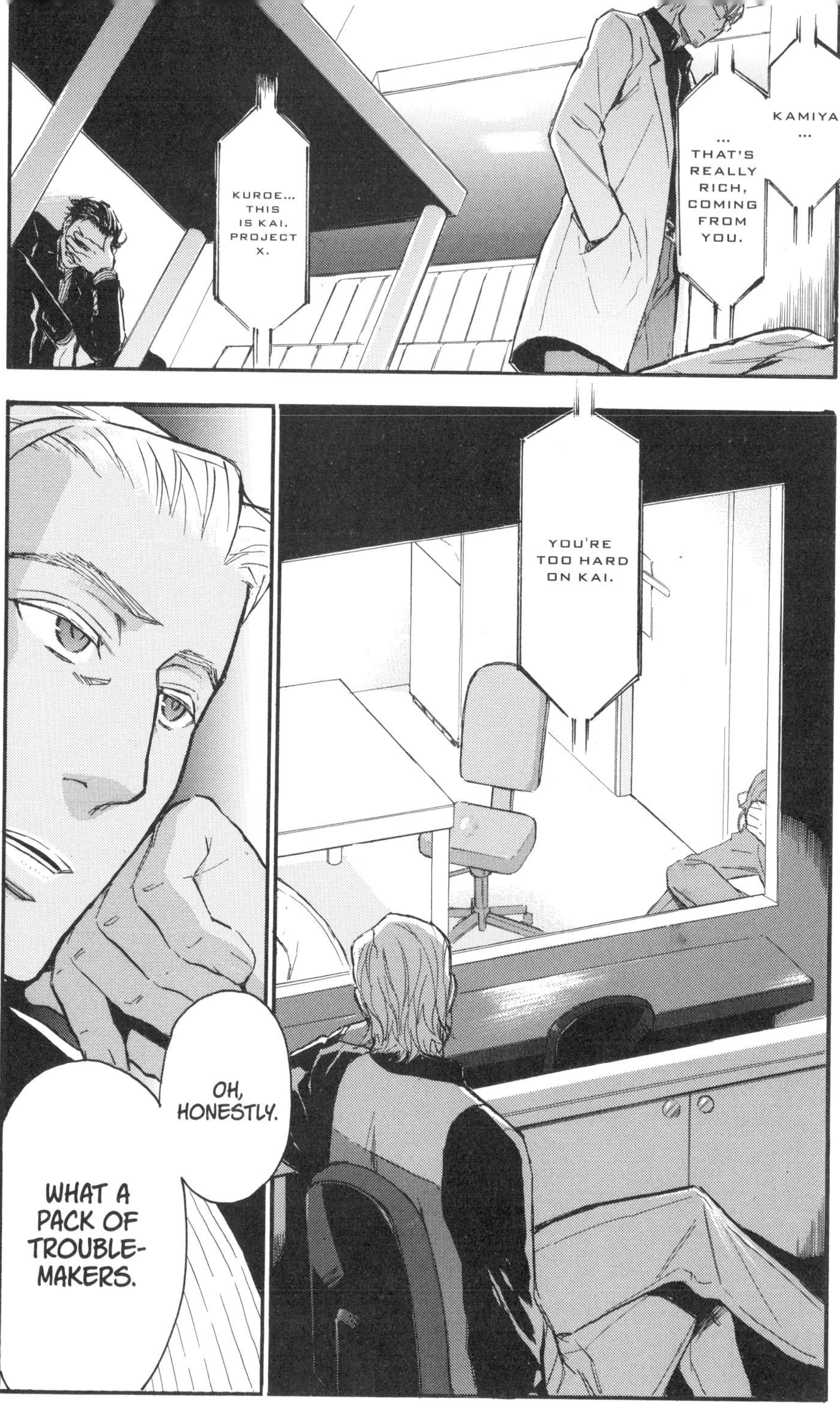
KAMIYA...
...THAT'S REALLY RICH, COMING FROM YOU.
KUROE... THIS IS KAI. PROJECT X.
YOU'RE TOO HARD ON KAI.
OH, HONESTLY.
WHAT A PACK OF TROUBLE-MAKERS.

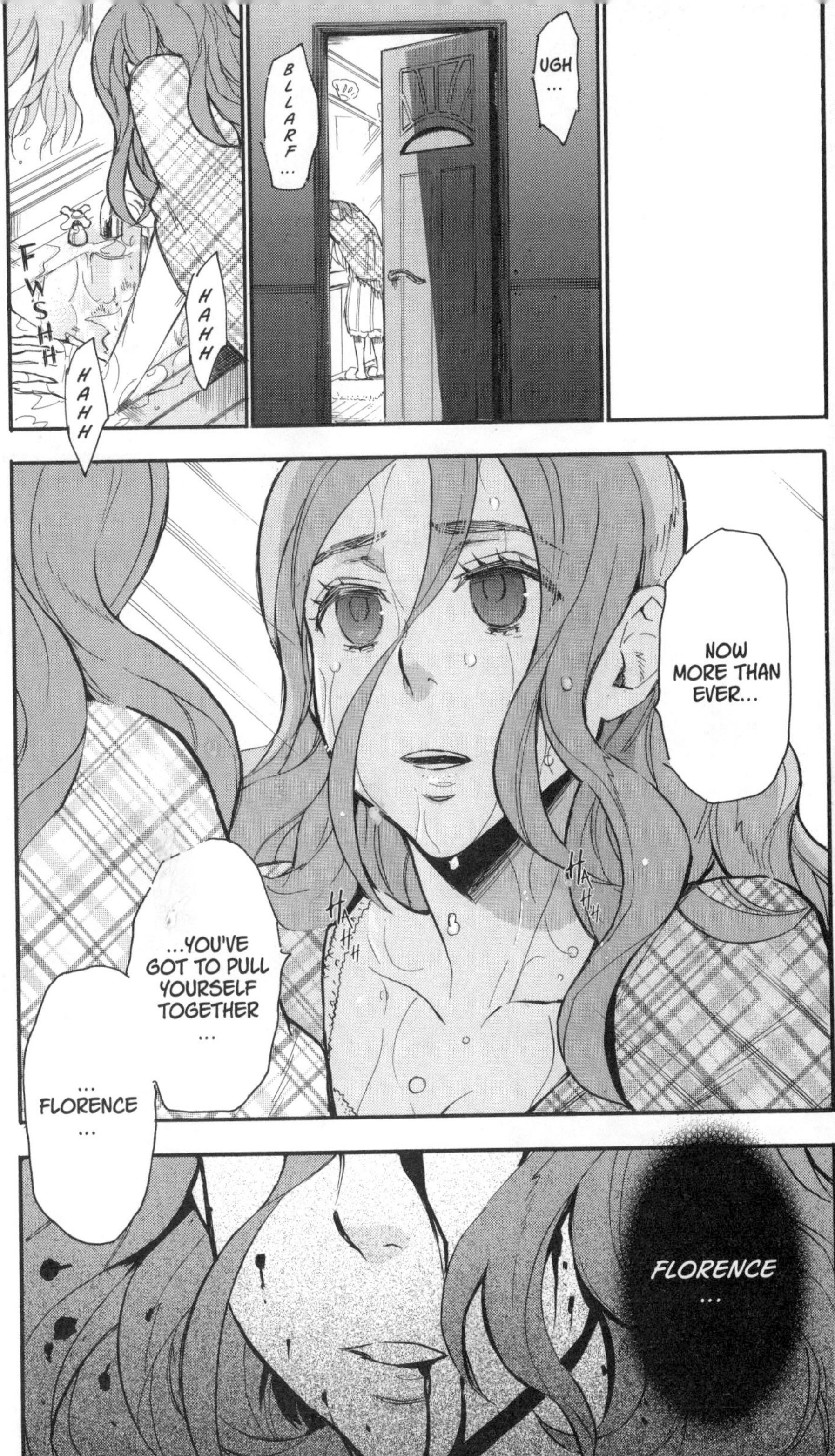
UGH...
BLLARF...
HAHH
FWSHH
HAHH
NOW MORE THAN EVER...
HAHH
HAHH
...YOU'VE GOT TO PULL YOURSELF TOGETHER...
...FLORENCE...
FLORENCE...

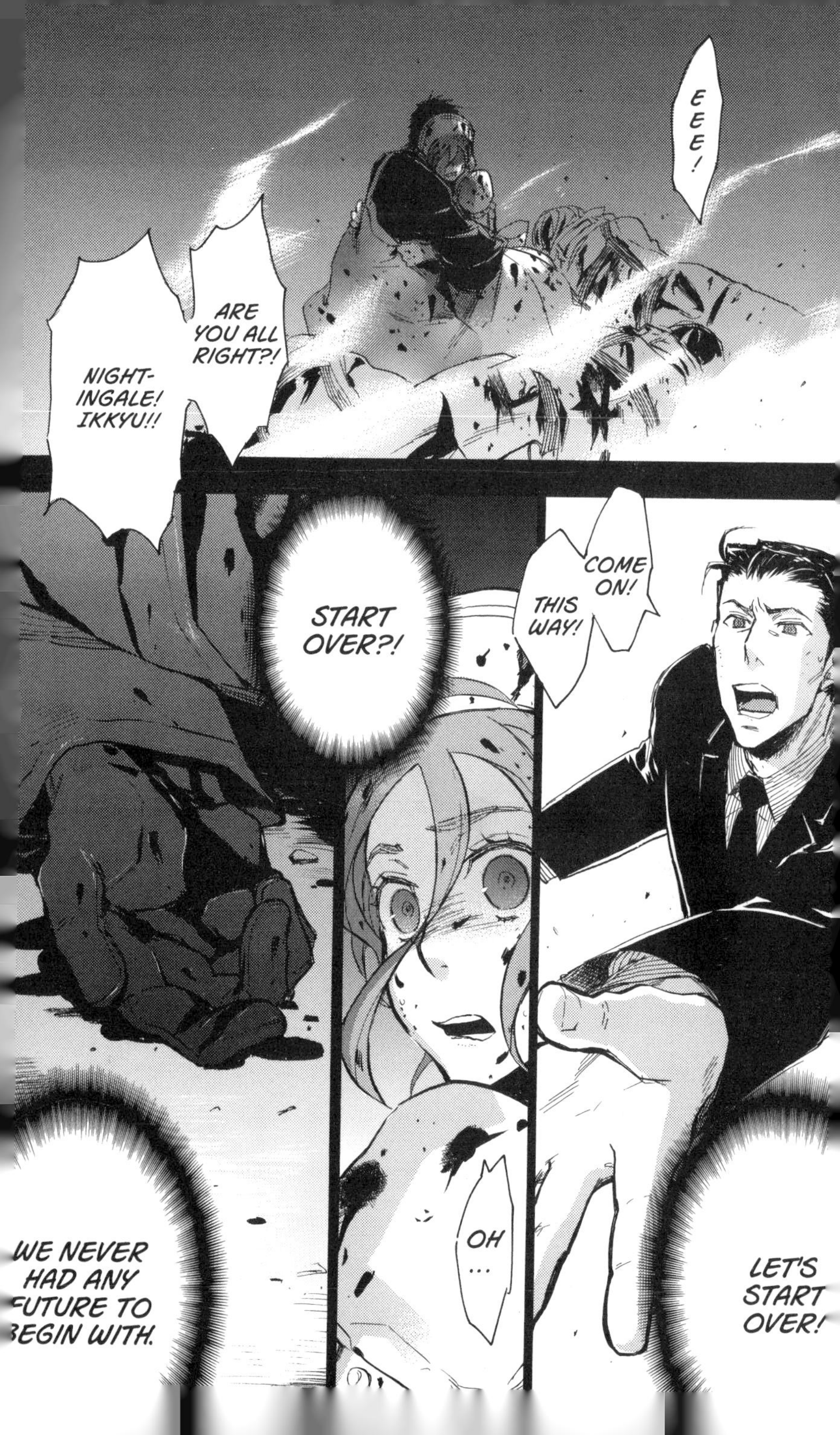
EEE!
ARE YOU ALL RIGHT?!
NIGHT-INGALE! IKKYU!!
COME ON!
THIS WAY!
LET'S START OVER!
START OVER?!
OH...
WE NEVER HAD ANY FUTURE TO BEGIN WITH.

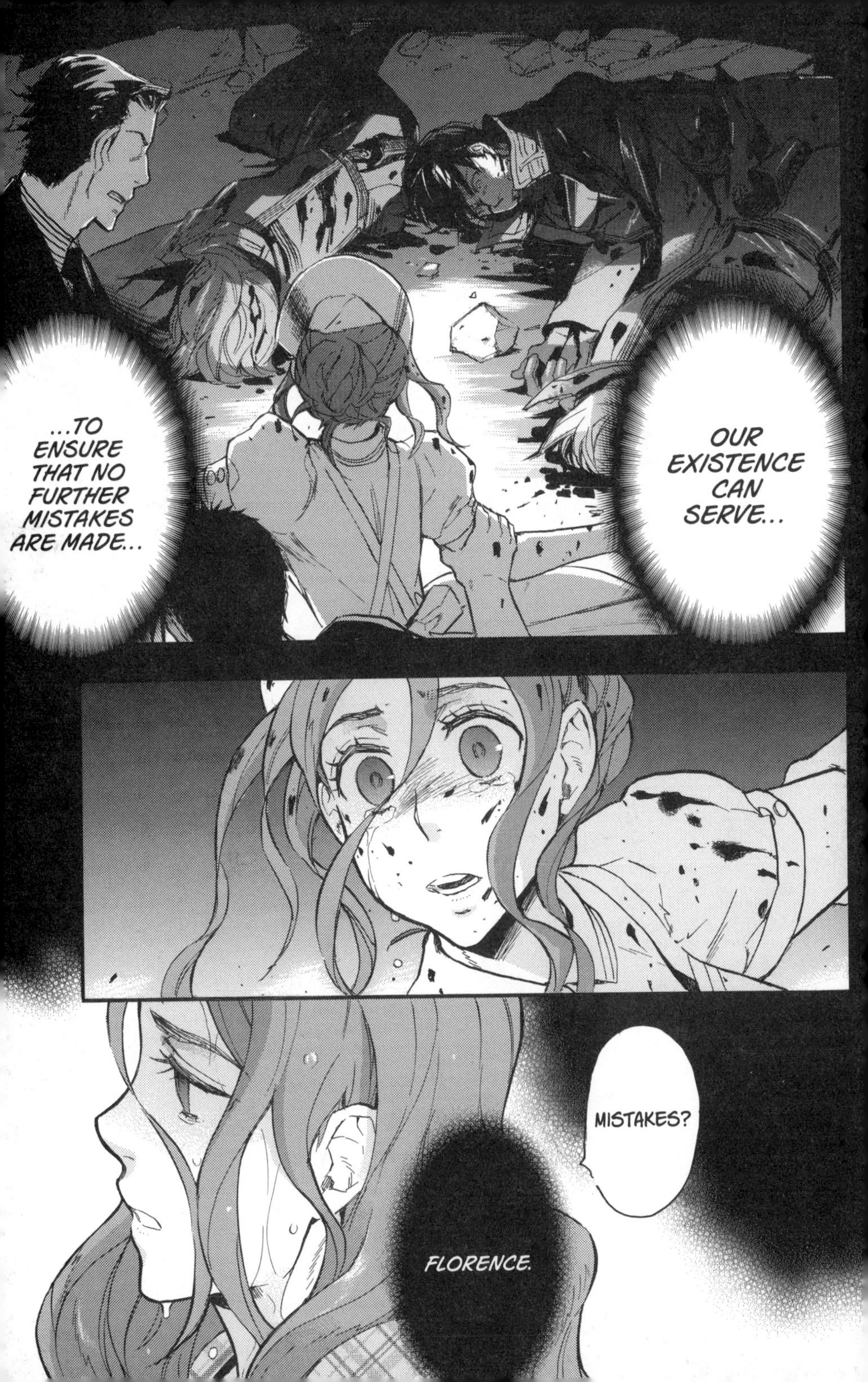
OUR EXISTENCE CAN SERVE...
...TO ENSURE THAT NO FURTHER MISTAKES ARE MADE...
MISTAKES?
FLORENCE.

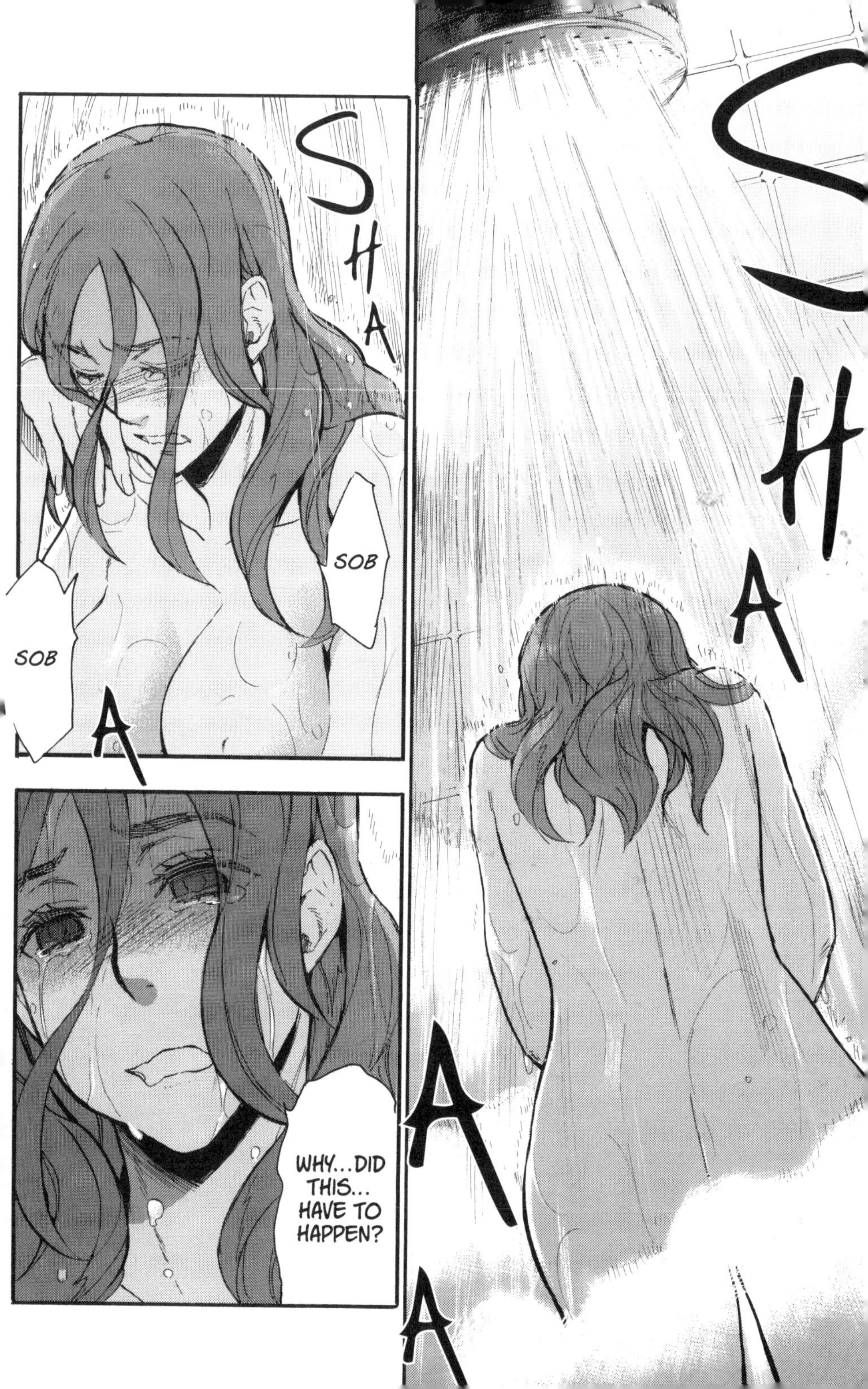
SHAAAA
SHAA
SOB
SOB
WHY...DID THIS... HAVE TO HAPPEN?

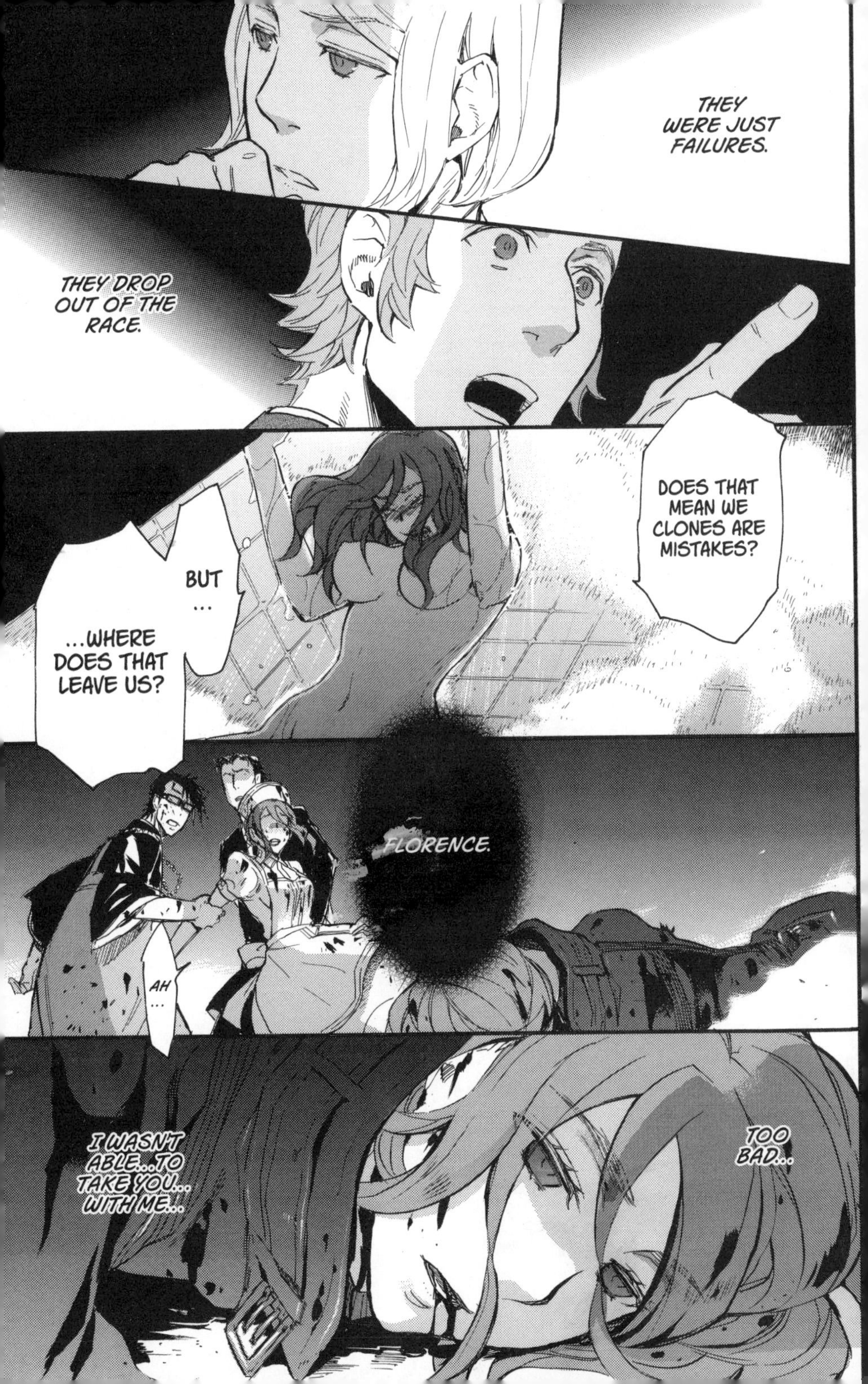
THEY WERE JUST FAILURES.
THEY DROP OUT OF THE RACE.
DOES THAT MEAN WE CLONES ARE MISTAKES?
BUT ...
...WHERE DOES THAT LEAVE US?
FLORENCE.
AH ...
TOO BAD...
I WASN'T ABLE...TO TAKE YOU... WITH ME...

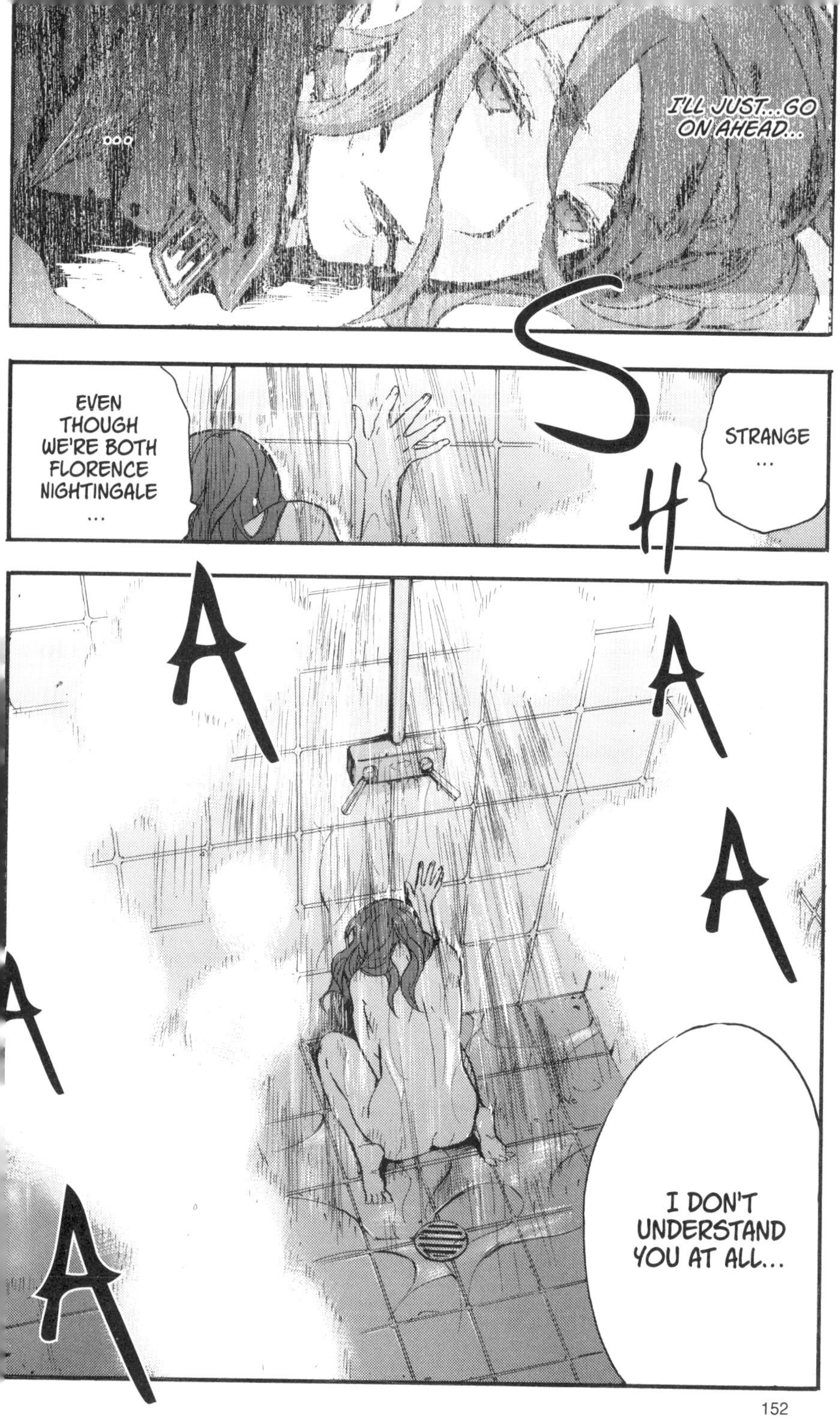
I'LL JUST...GO ON AHEAD...
...
STRANGE...
EVEN THOUGH WE'RE BOTH FLORENCE NIGHTINGALE...
SHAAAAA
I DON'T UNDERSTAND YOU AT ALL...

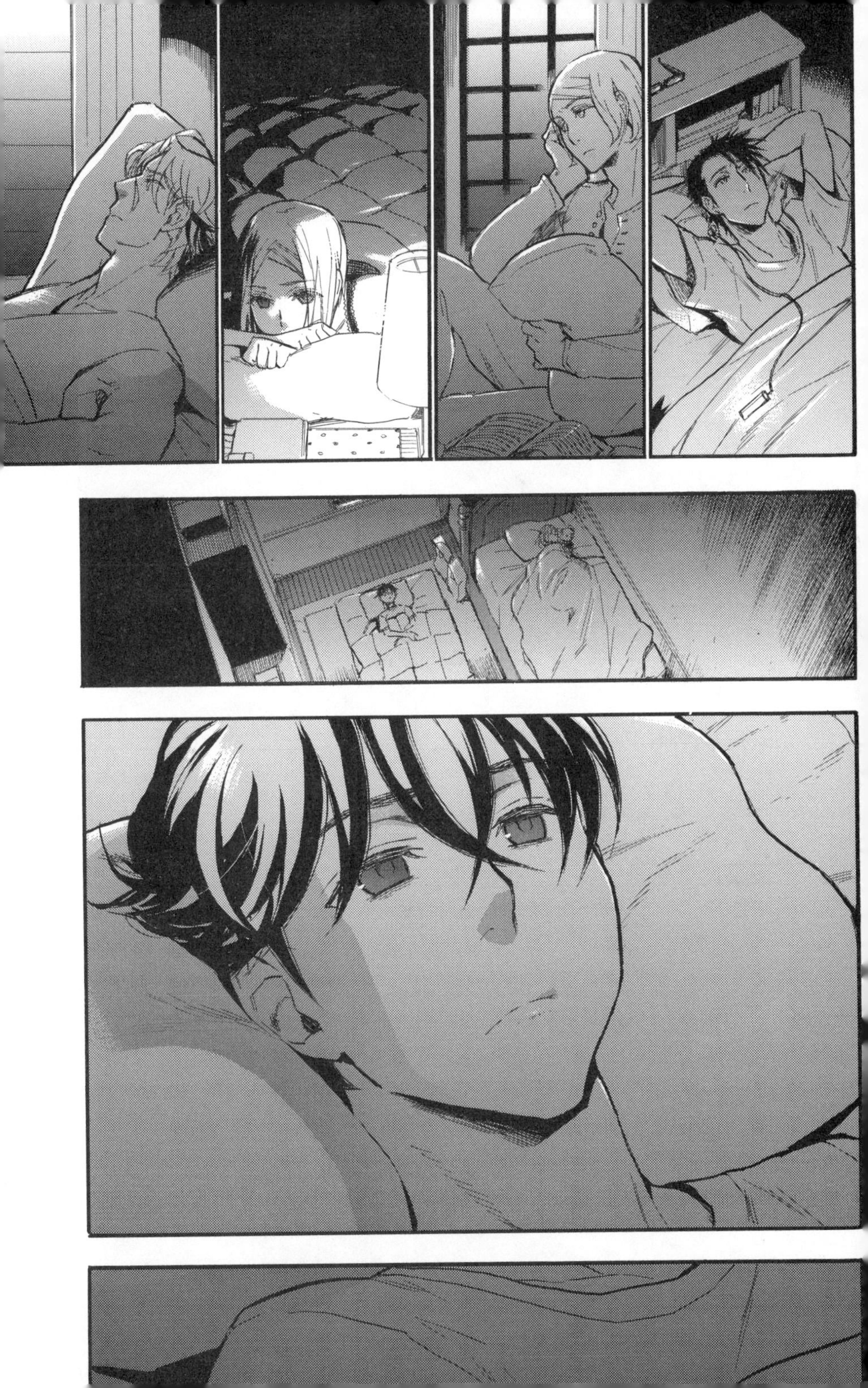

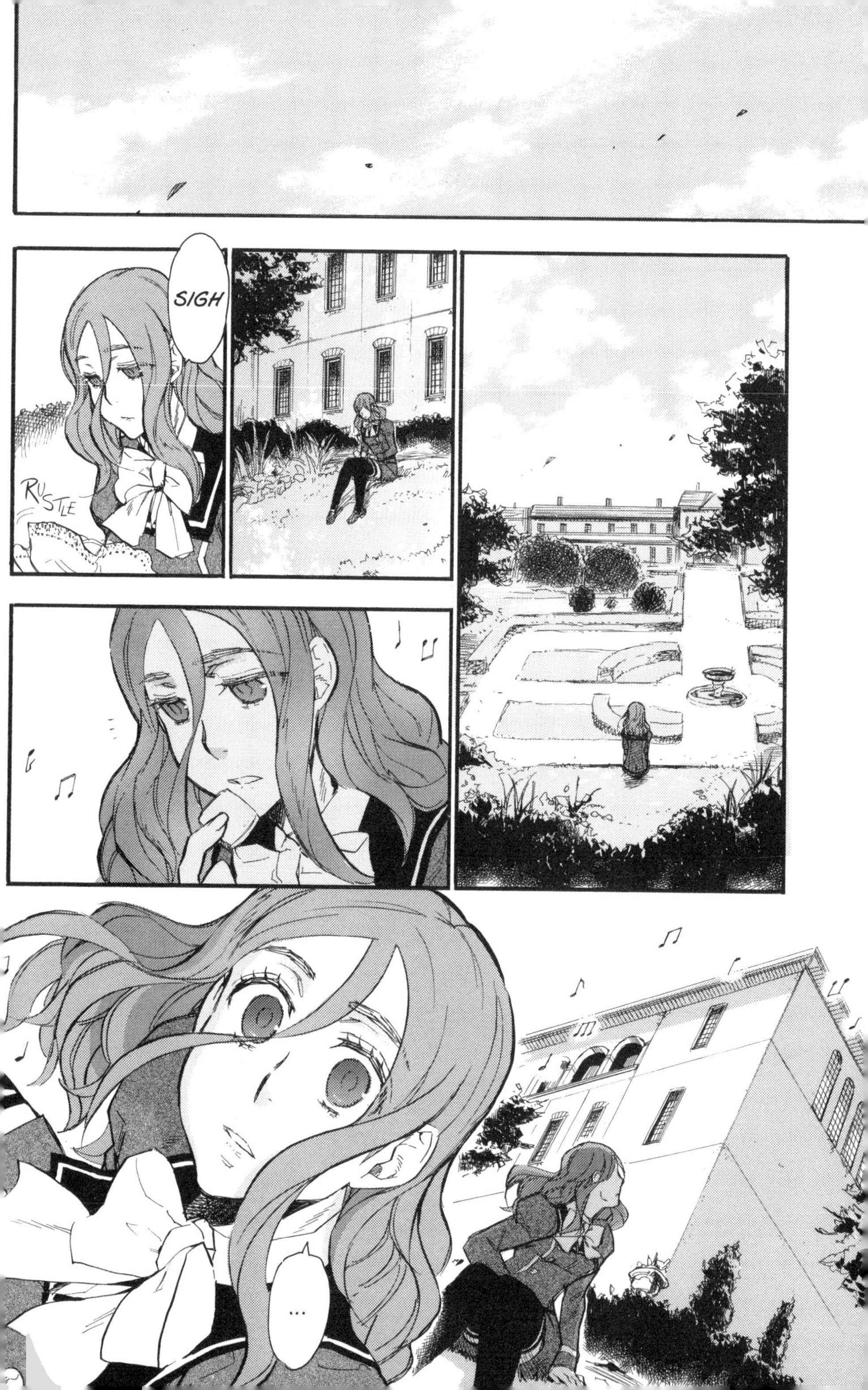
SIGH
RUSTLE
...

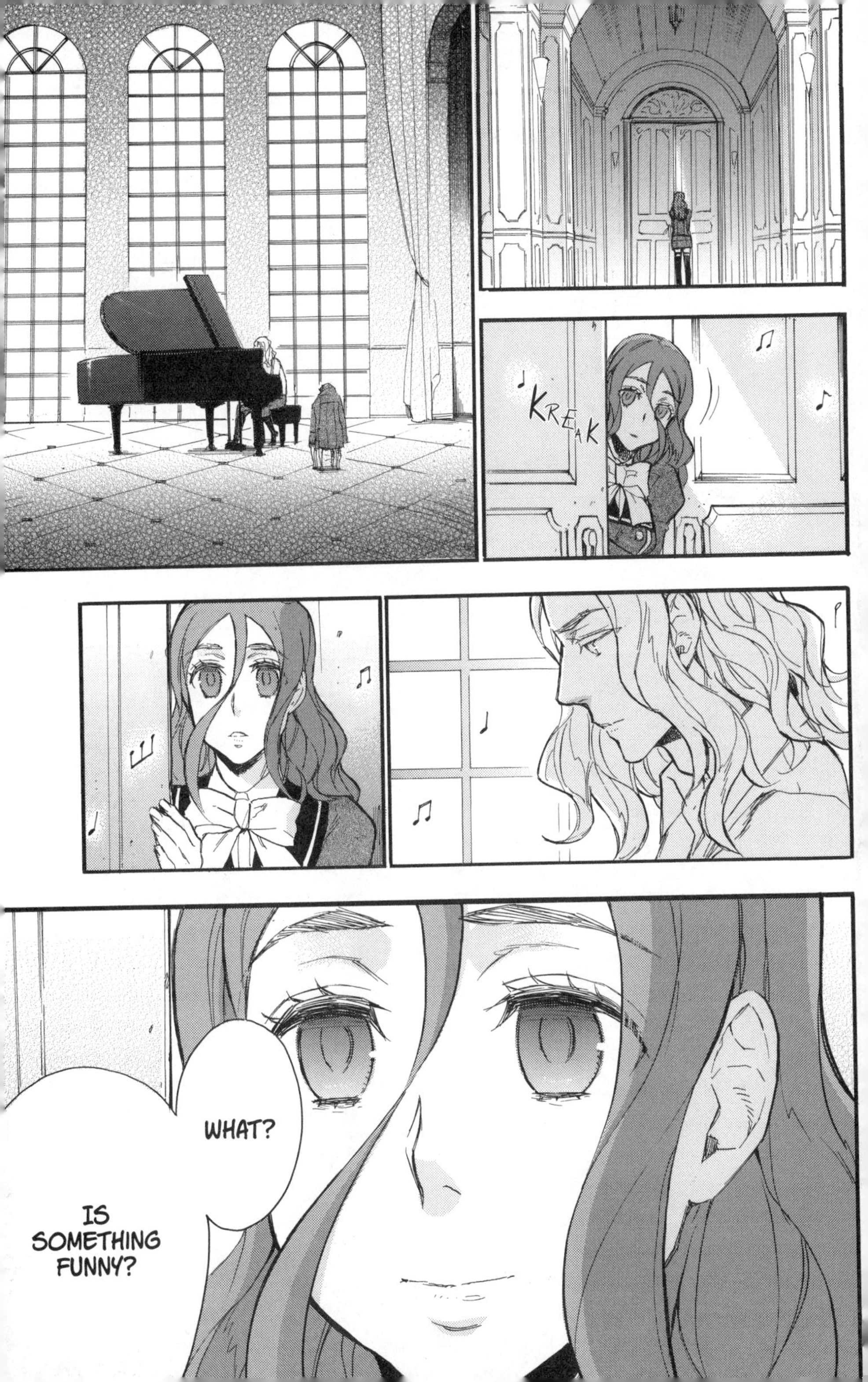
KREAK
WHAT?
IS SOMETHING FUNNY?

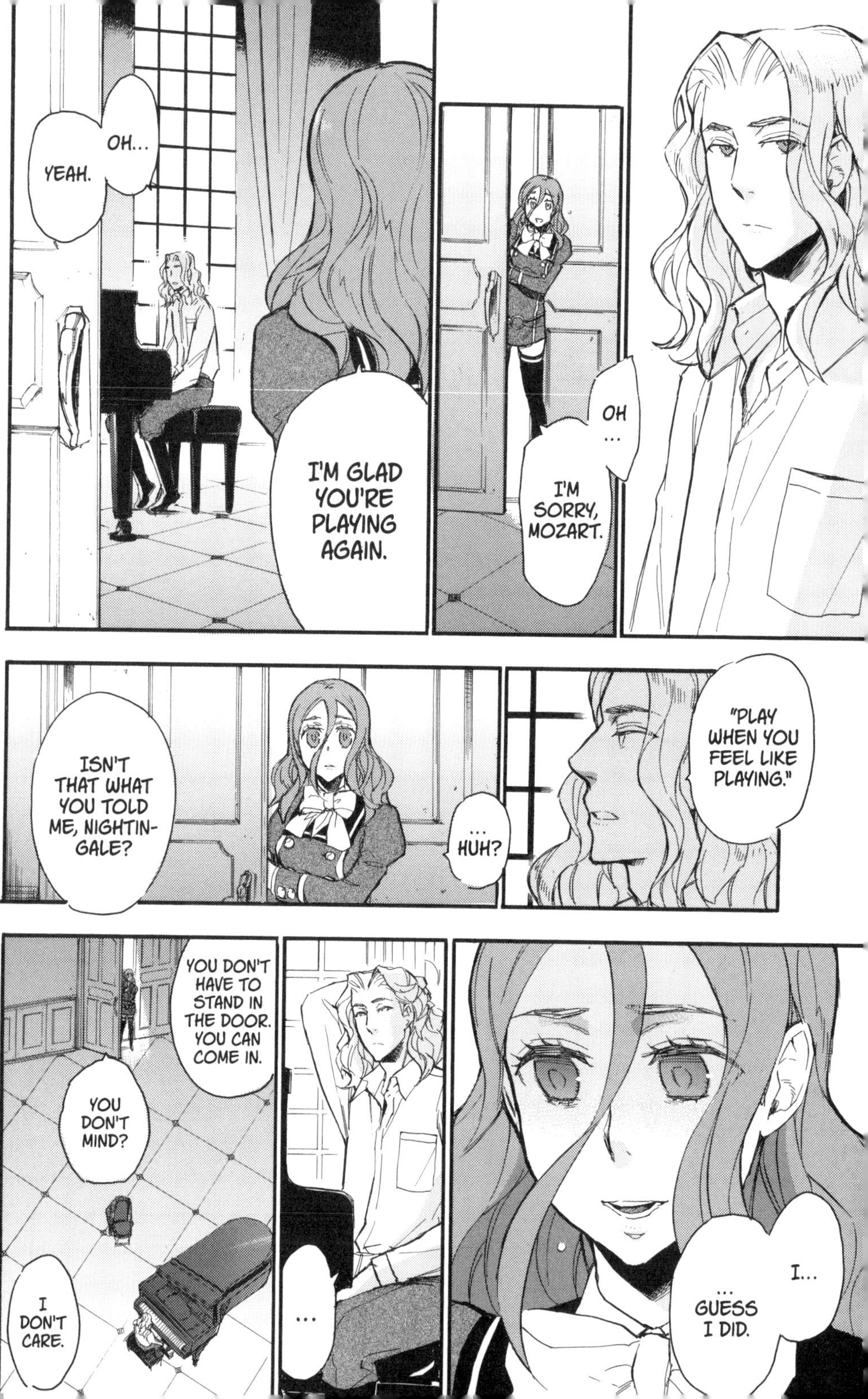
OH ...
I'M SORRY, MOZART.
OH... YEAH.
I'M GLAD YOU'RE PLAYING AGAIN.
"PLAY WHEN YOU FEEL LIKE PLAYING."
... HUH?
ISN'T THAT WHAT YOU TOLD ME, NIGHTINGALE?
I...
... GUESS I DID.
...
YOU DON'T HAVE TO STAND IN THE DOOR. YOU CAN COME IN.
YOU DON'T MIND?
I DON'T CARE.

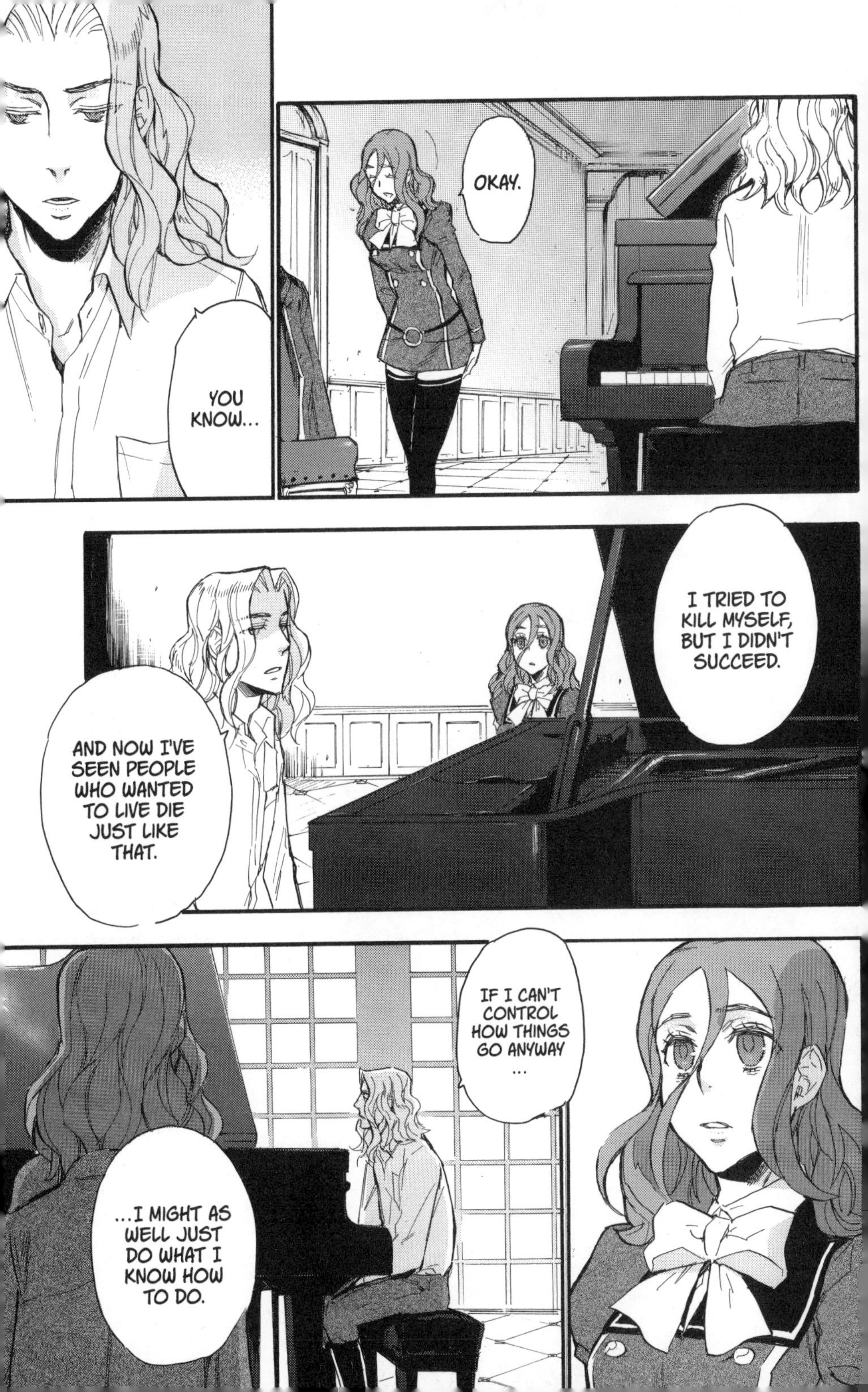
OKAY.
YOU KNOW...
I TRIED TO KILL MYSELF, BUT I DIDN'T SUCCEED.
AND NOW I'VE SEEN PEOPLE WHO WANTED TO LIVE DIE JUST LIKE THAT.
IF I CAN'T CONTROL HOW THINGS GO ANYWAY ...
...I MIGHT AS WELL JUST DO WHAT I KNOW HOW TO DO.

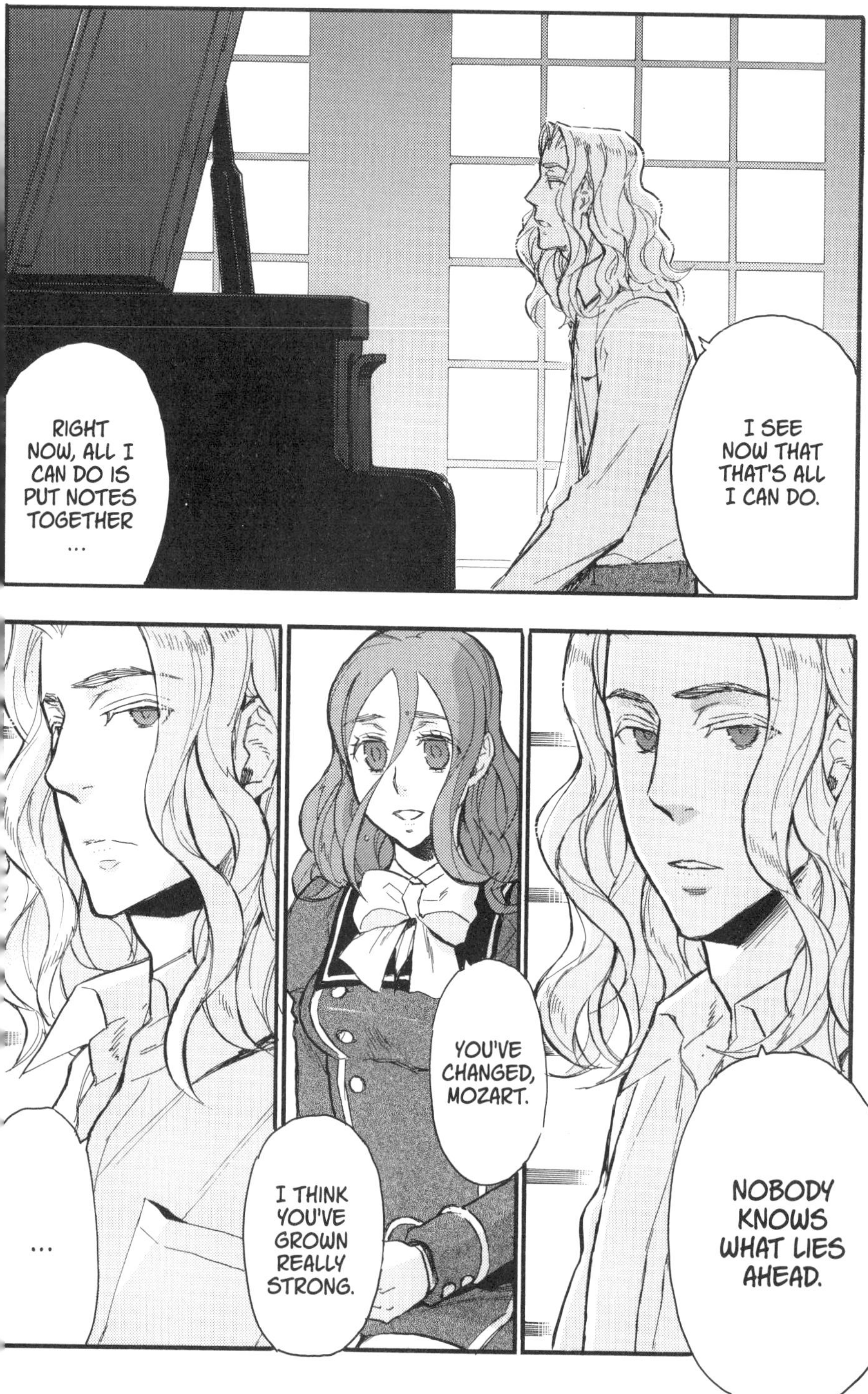
I SEE NOW THAT THAT'S ALL I CAN DO.
RIGHT NOW, ALL I CAN DO IS PUT NOTES TOGETHER ...
NOBODY KNOWS WHAT LIES AHEAD.
YOU'VE CHANGED, MOZART.
I THINK YOU'VE GROWN REALLY STRONG.
...

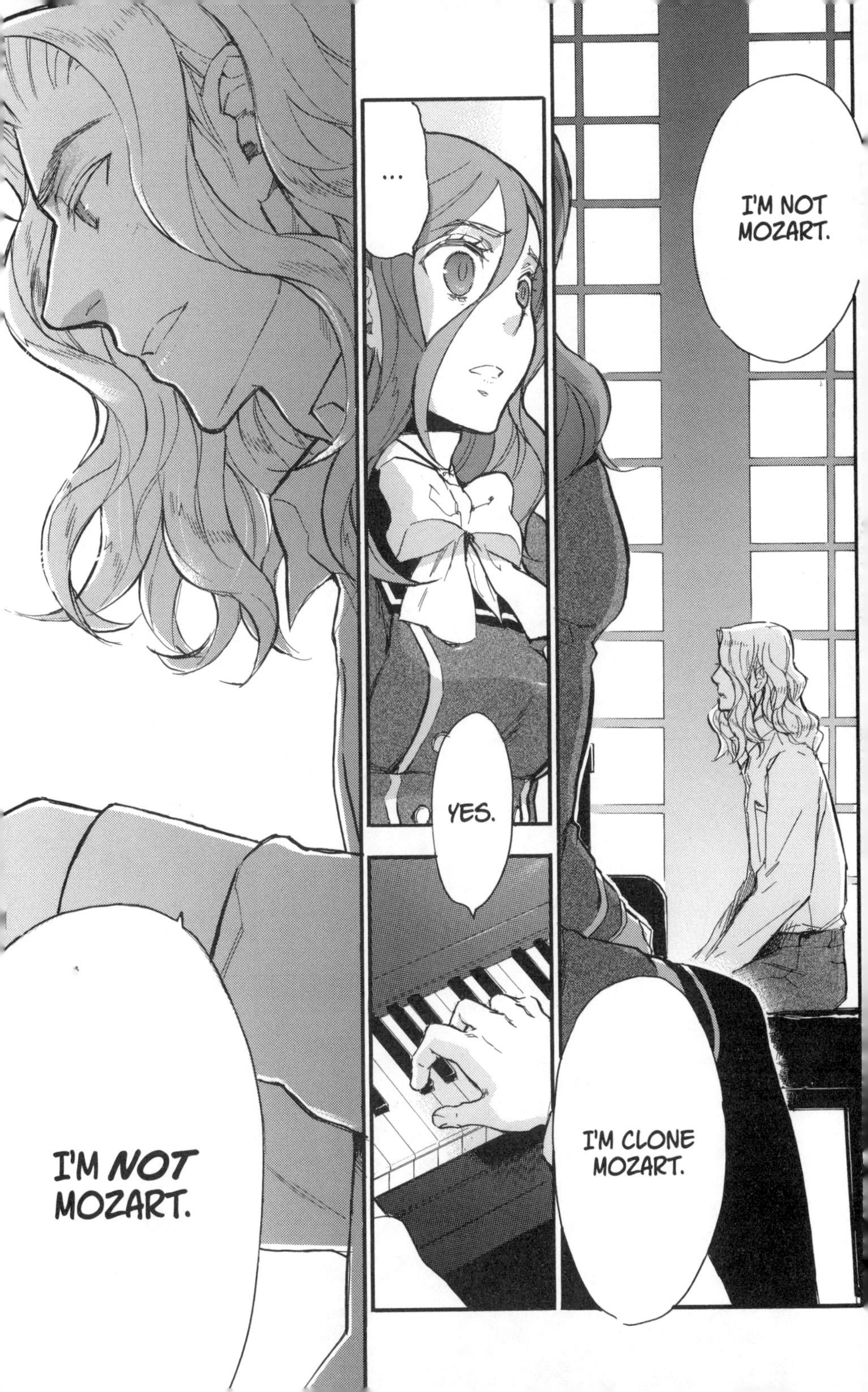
I'M NOT MOZART.
...
YES.
I'M CLONE MOZART.
I'M *NOT* MOZART.

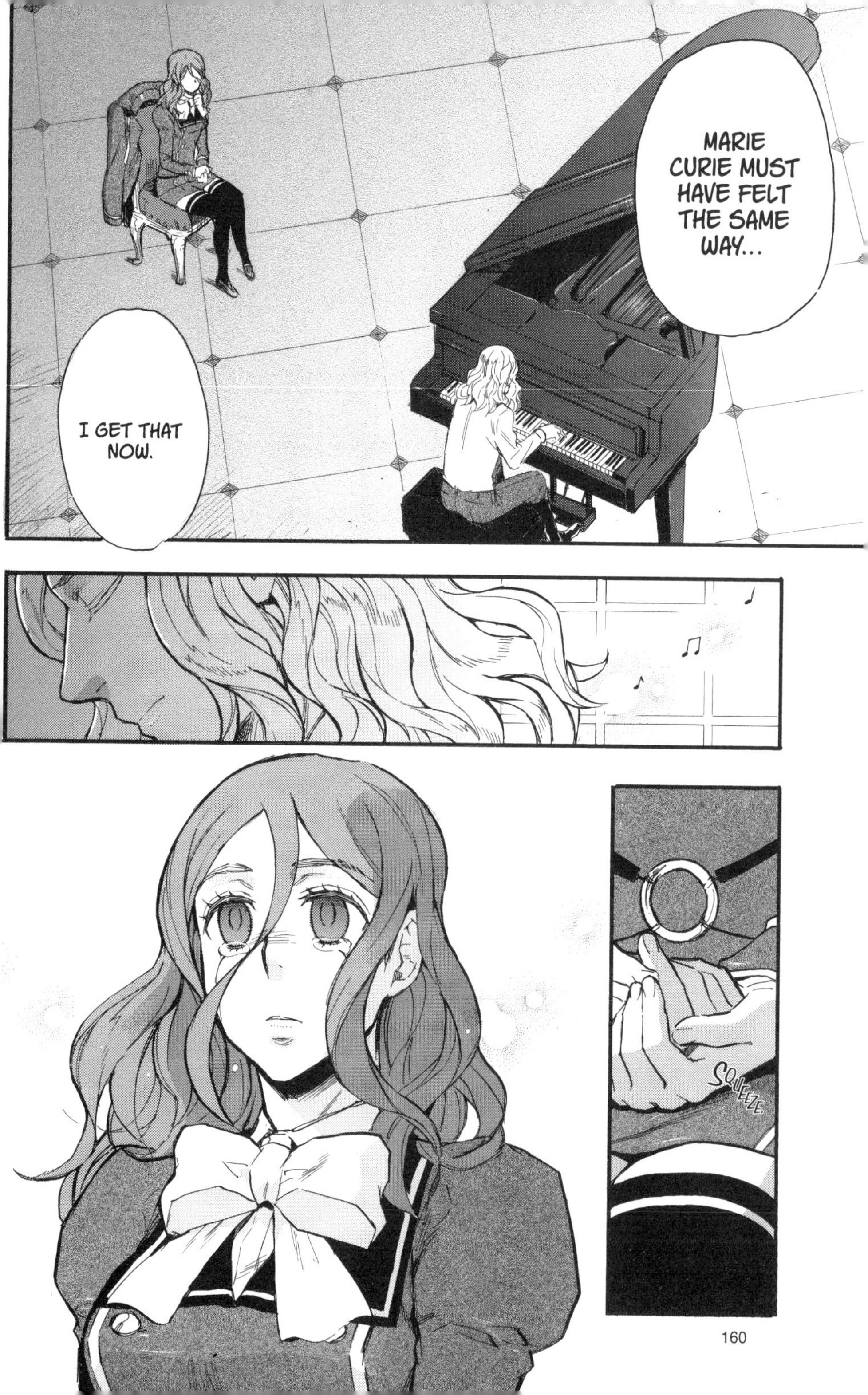
MARIE CURIE MUST HAVE FELT THE SAME WAY...
I GET THAT NOW.
SQUEEZE

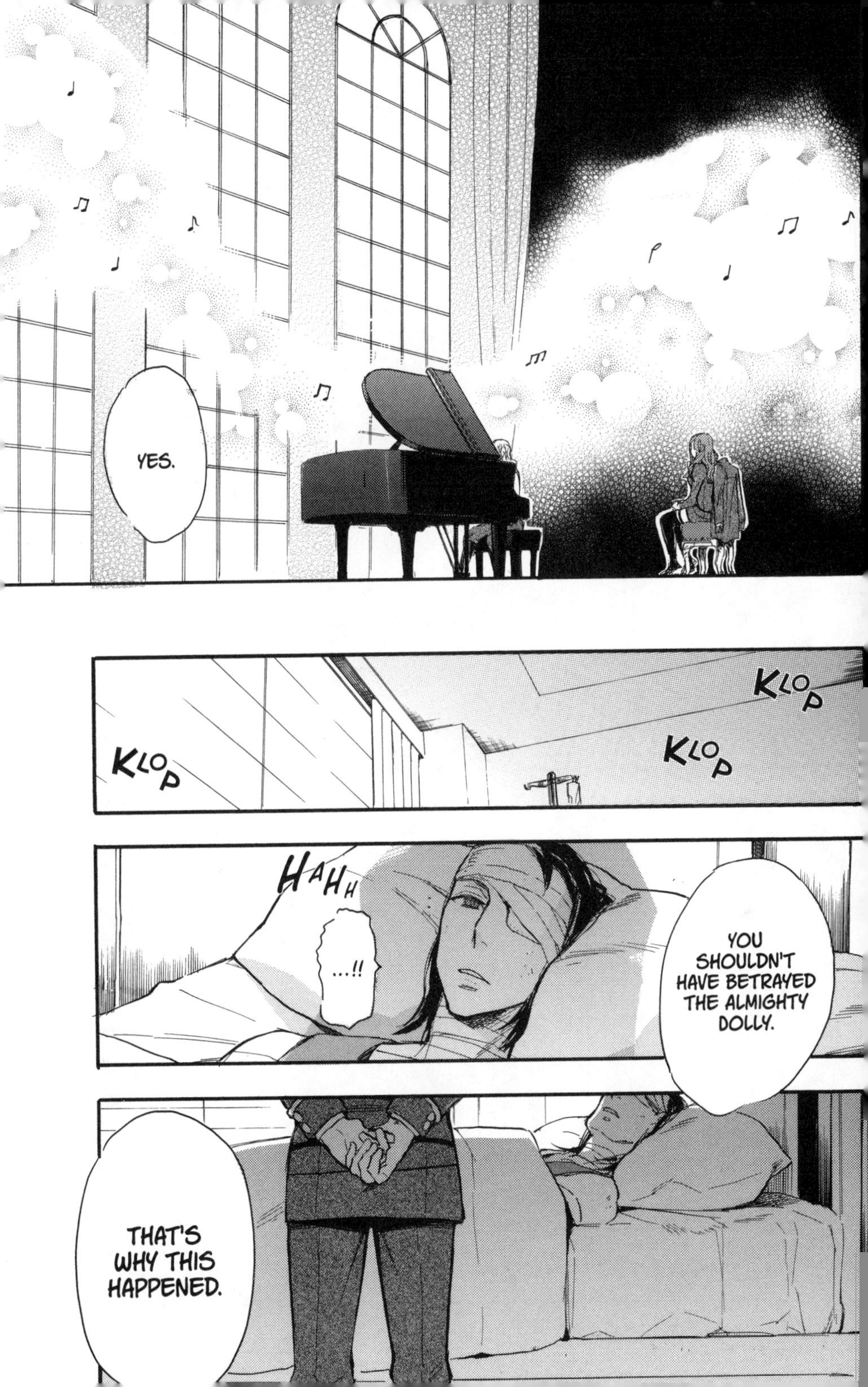
YES.
KLOP
KLOP
KLOP
YOU SHOULDN'T HAVE BETRAYED THE ALMIGHTY DOLLY.
HAHH
...!!
THAT'S WHY THIS HAPPENED.

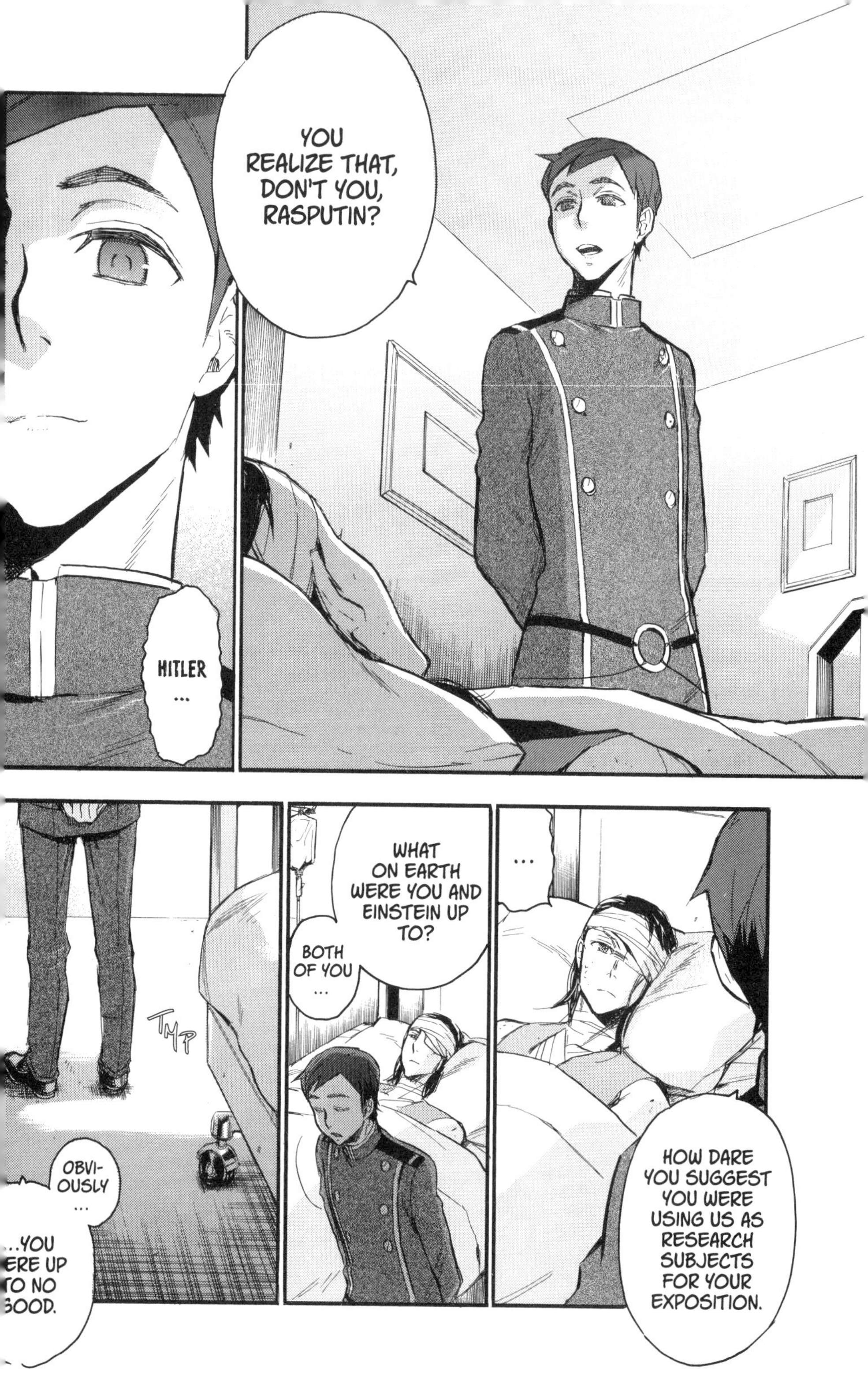
YOU REALIZE THAT, DON'T YOU, RASPUTIN?
HITLER ...
...
HOW DARE YOU SUGGEST YOU WERE USING US AS RESEARCH SUBJECTS FOR YOUR EXPOSITION.
WHAT ON EARTH WERE YOU AND EINSTEIN UP TO?
BOTH OF YOU ...
TMP
OBVI-OUSLY ...
...YOU ERE UP TO NO GOOD.

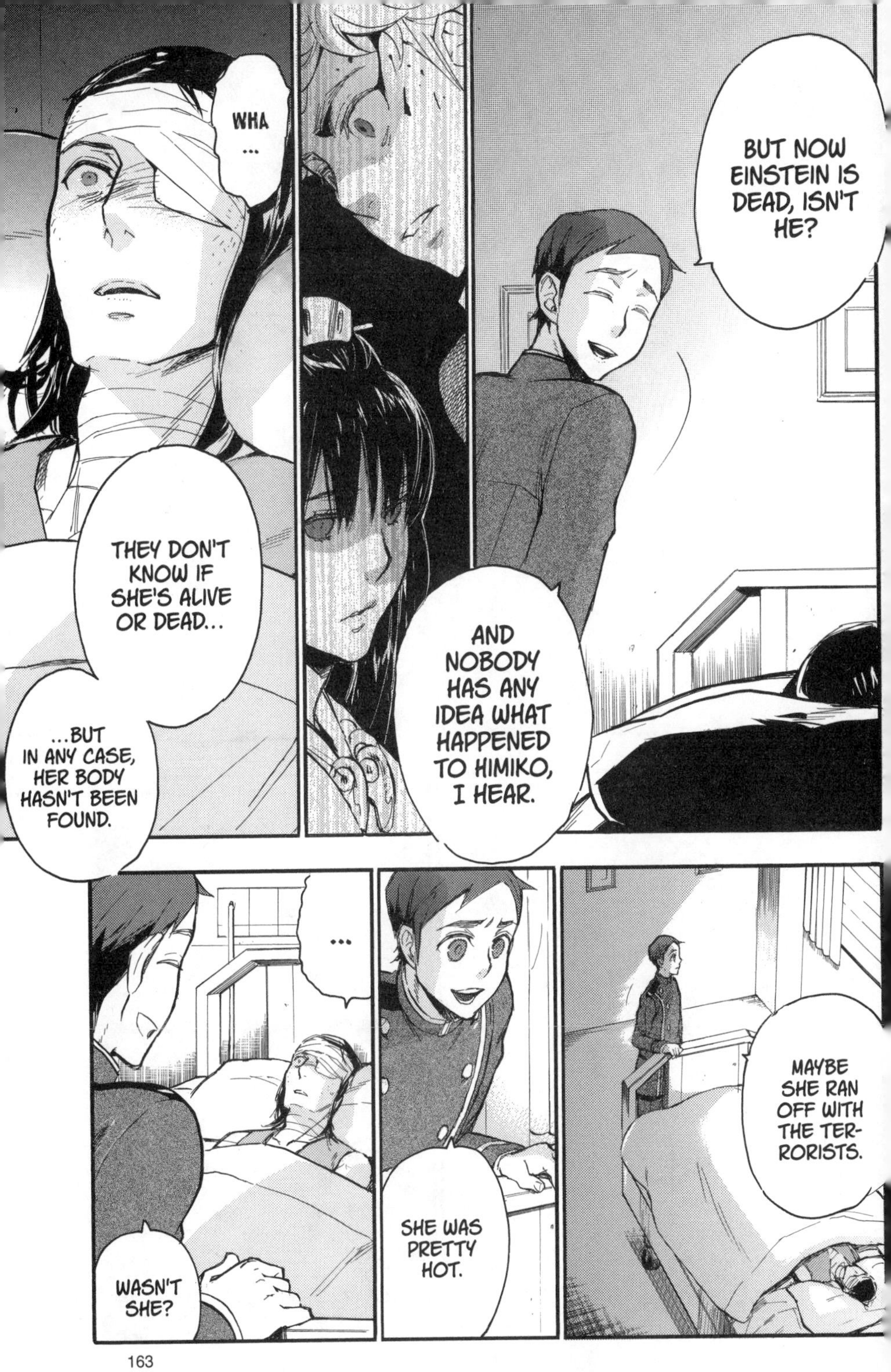
BUT NOW EINSTEIN IS DEAD, ISN'T HE?
AND NOBODY HAS ANY IDEA WHAT HAPPENED TO HIMIKO, I HEAR.
WHA ...
THEY DON'T KNOW IF SHE'S ALIVE OR DEAD...
...BUT IN ANY CASE, HER BODY HASN'T BEEN FOUND.
MAYBE SHE RAN OFF WITH THE TER-RORISTS.
SHE WAS PRETTY HOT.
...
WASN'T SHE?

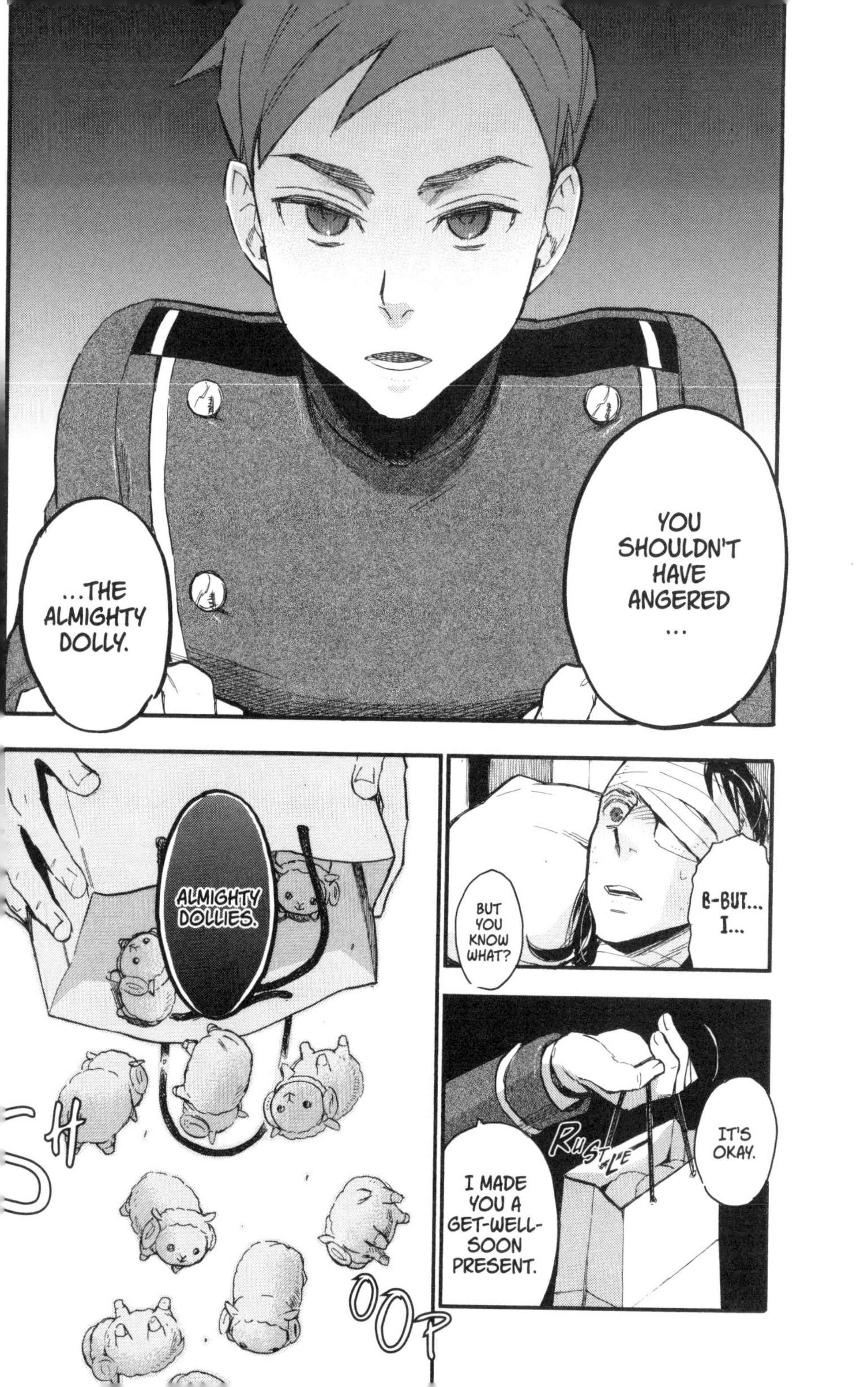
YOU SHOULDN'T HAVE ANGERED...
...THE ALMIGHTY DOLLY.
B-BUT... I...
BUT YOU KNOW WHAT?
IT'S OKAY.
RUSTLE
I MADE YOU A GET-WELL-SOON PRESENT.
ALMIGHTY DOLLIES.
SHOOP

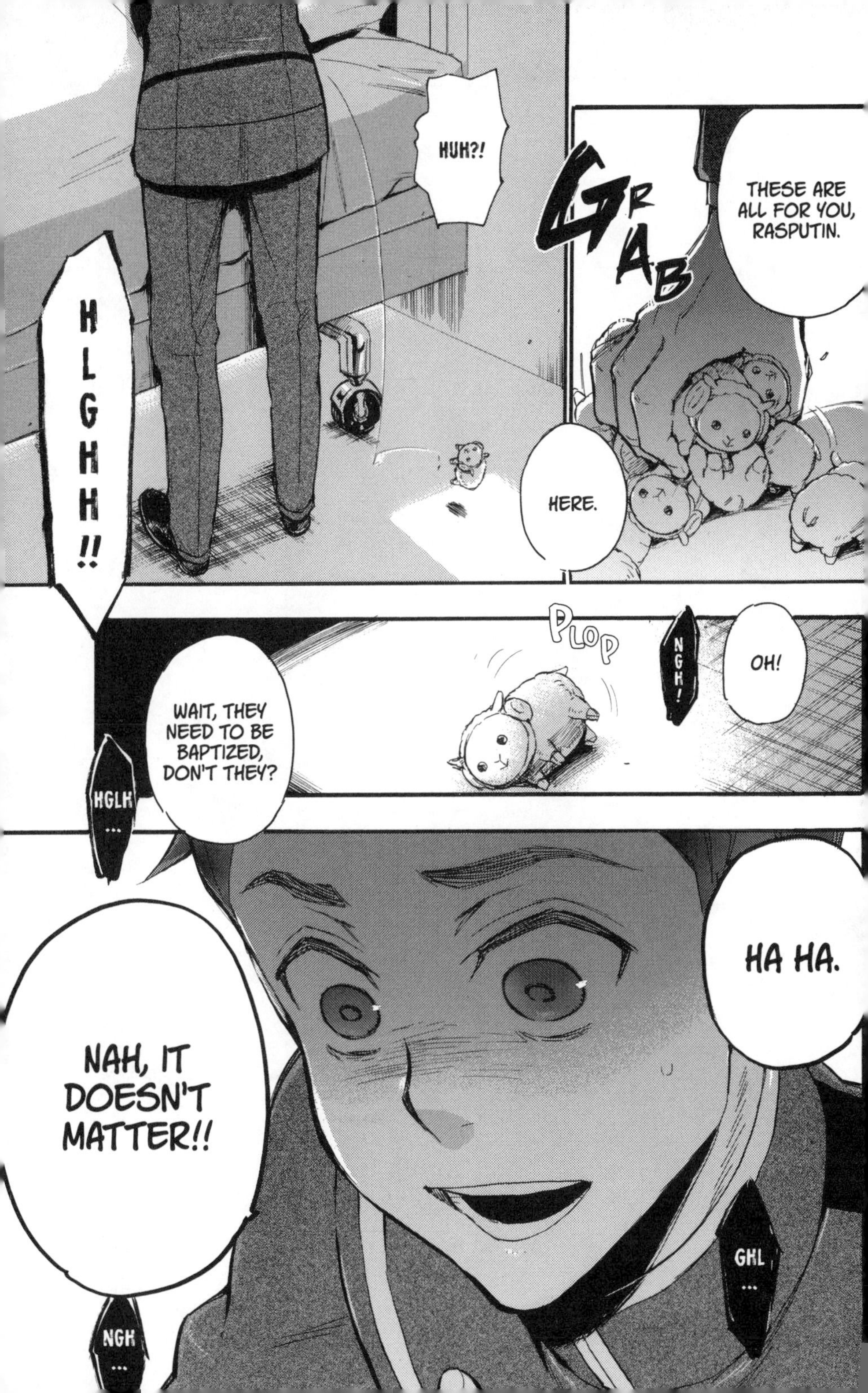
THESE ARE ALL FOR YOU, RASPUTIN.
GRAB
HERE.
HUH?!
HLGHH!!
OH!
NGH!
PLOP
WAIT, THEY NEED TO BE BAPTIZED, DON'T THEY?
HGLH...
HA HA.
GHL...
NAH, IT DOESN'T MATTER!!
NGH...

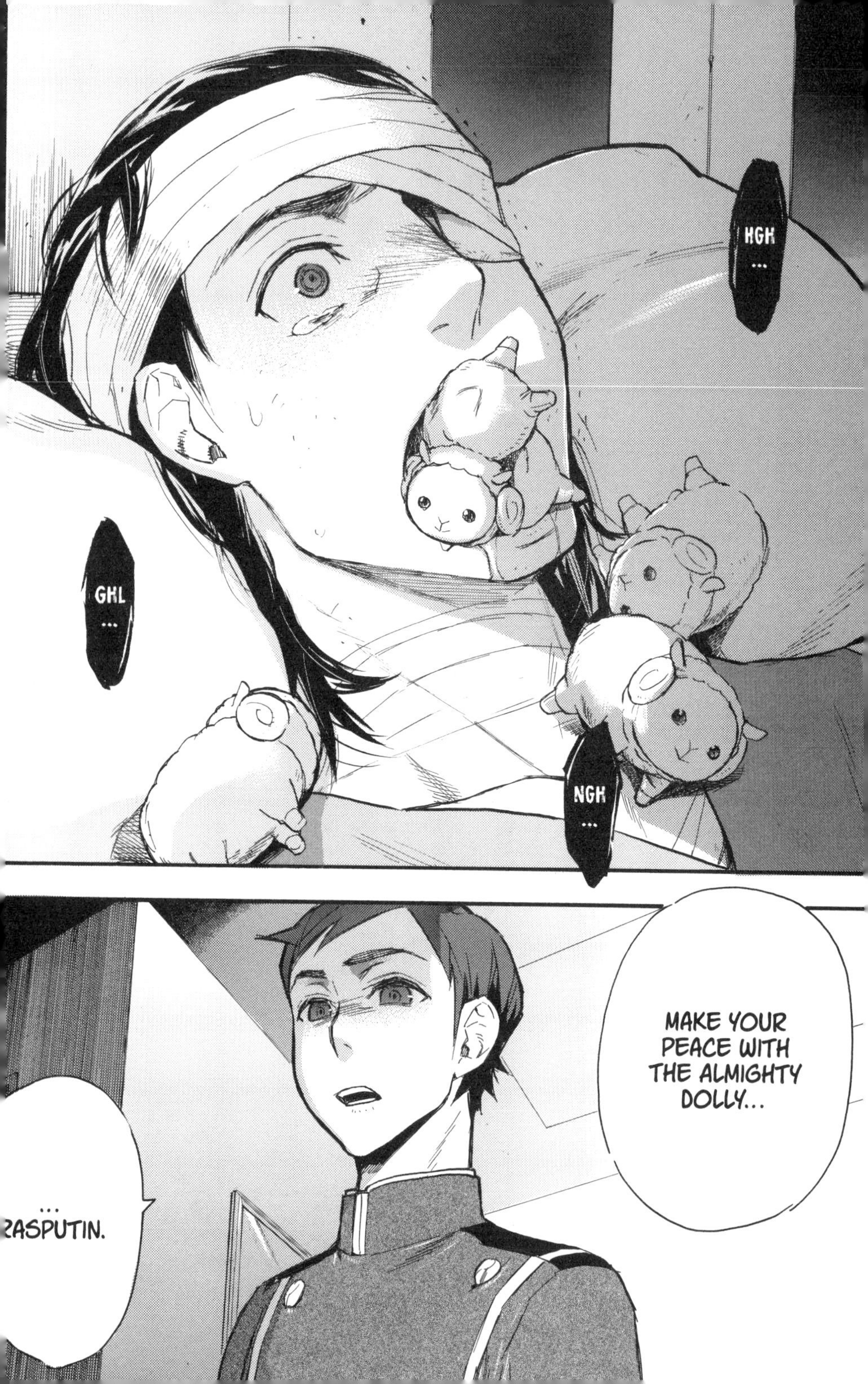
HGH...
NGH...
GHL...
MAKE YOUR PEACE WITH THE ALMIGHTY DOLLY...
...RASPUTIN.

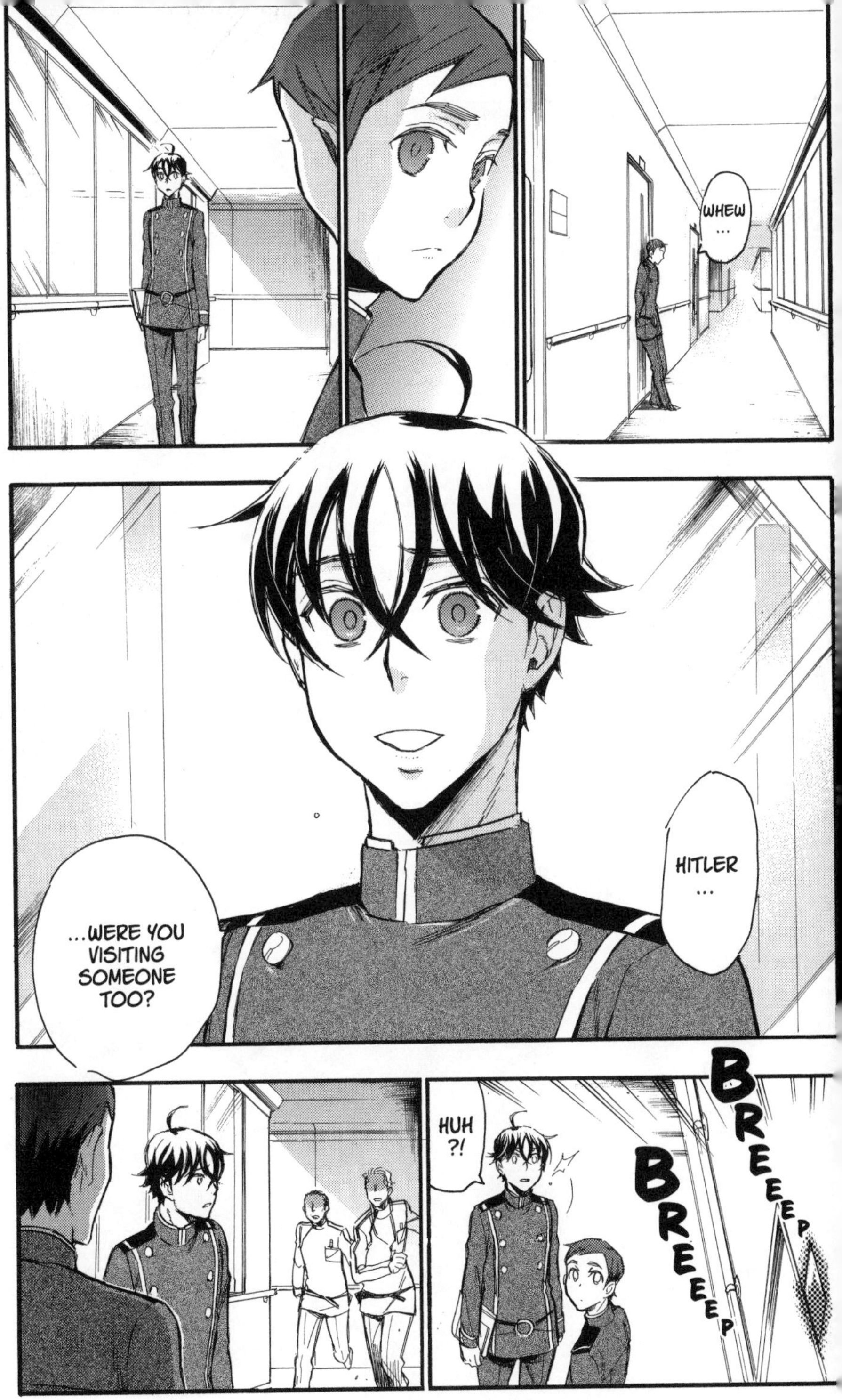
WHEW ...
HITLER ...
...WERE YOU VISITING SOMEONE TOO?
BREEEP
BREEEP
HUH ?!

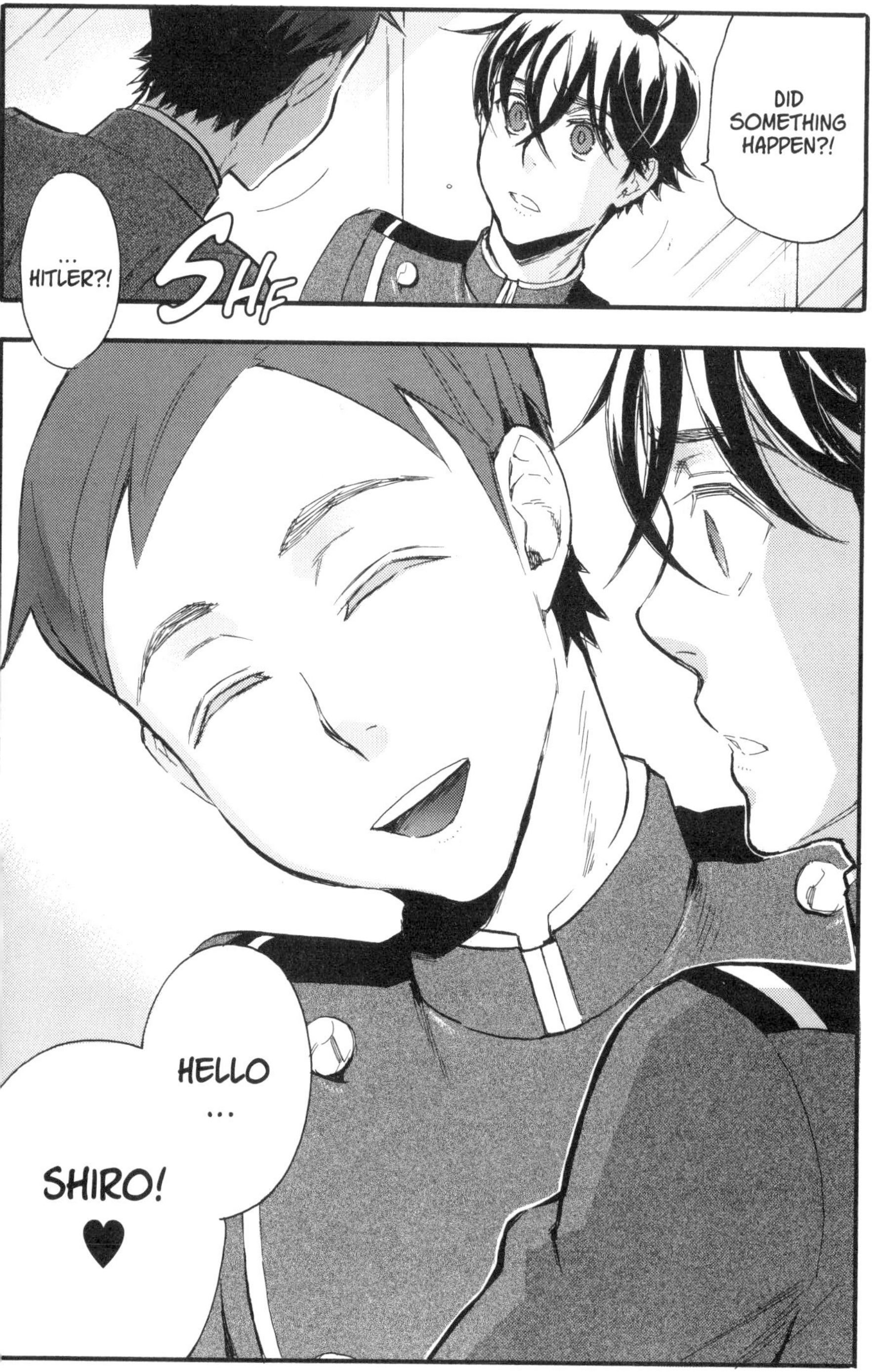
DID SOMETHING HAPPEN?!
SHF
...HITLER?!
HELLO ... SHIRO! ♥

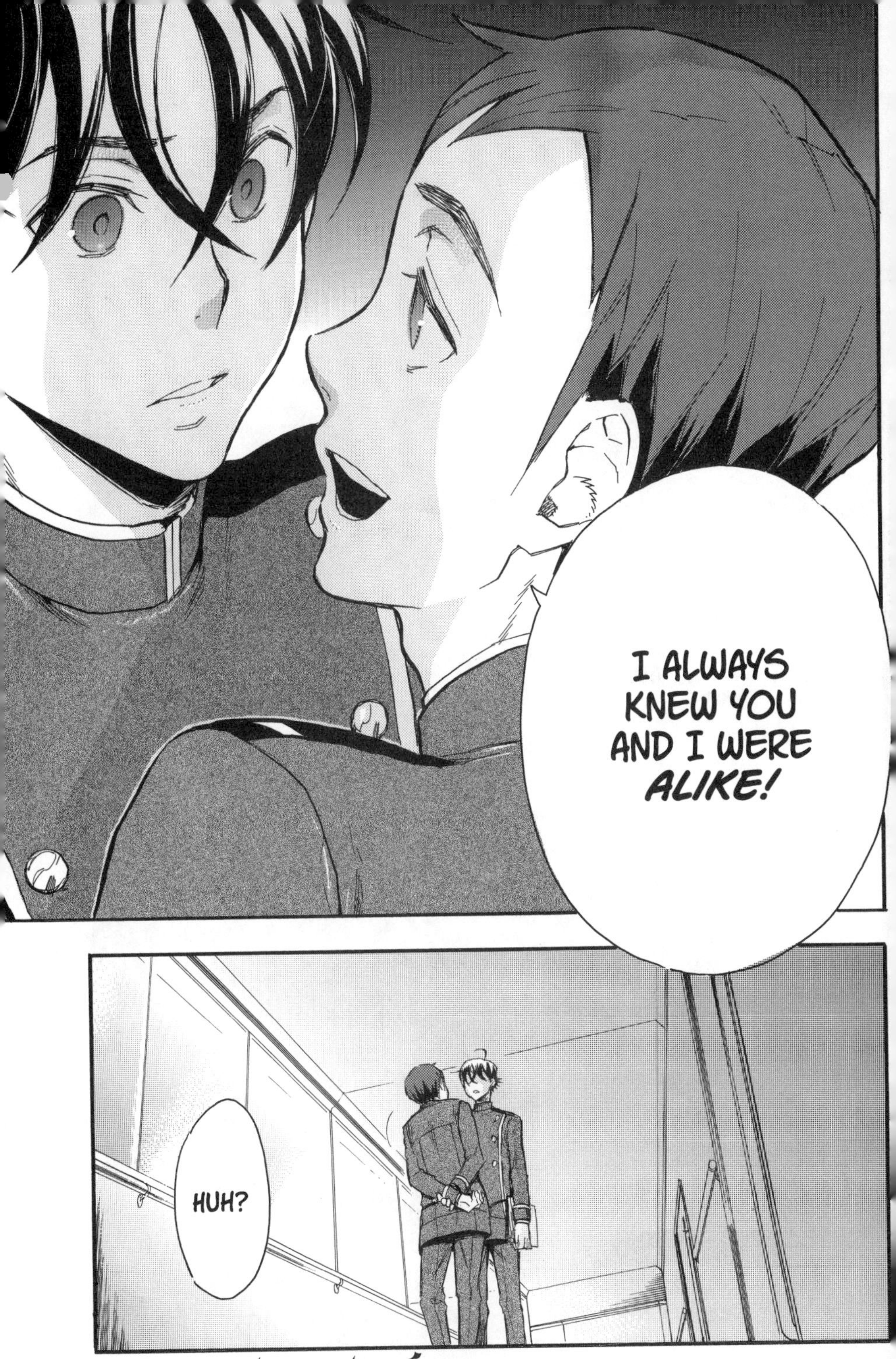
I ALWAYS KNEW YOU AND I WERE *ALIKE!*
HUH?

CHAPTER twenty-four

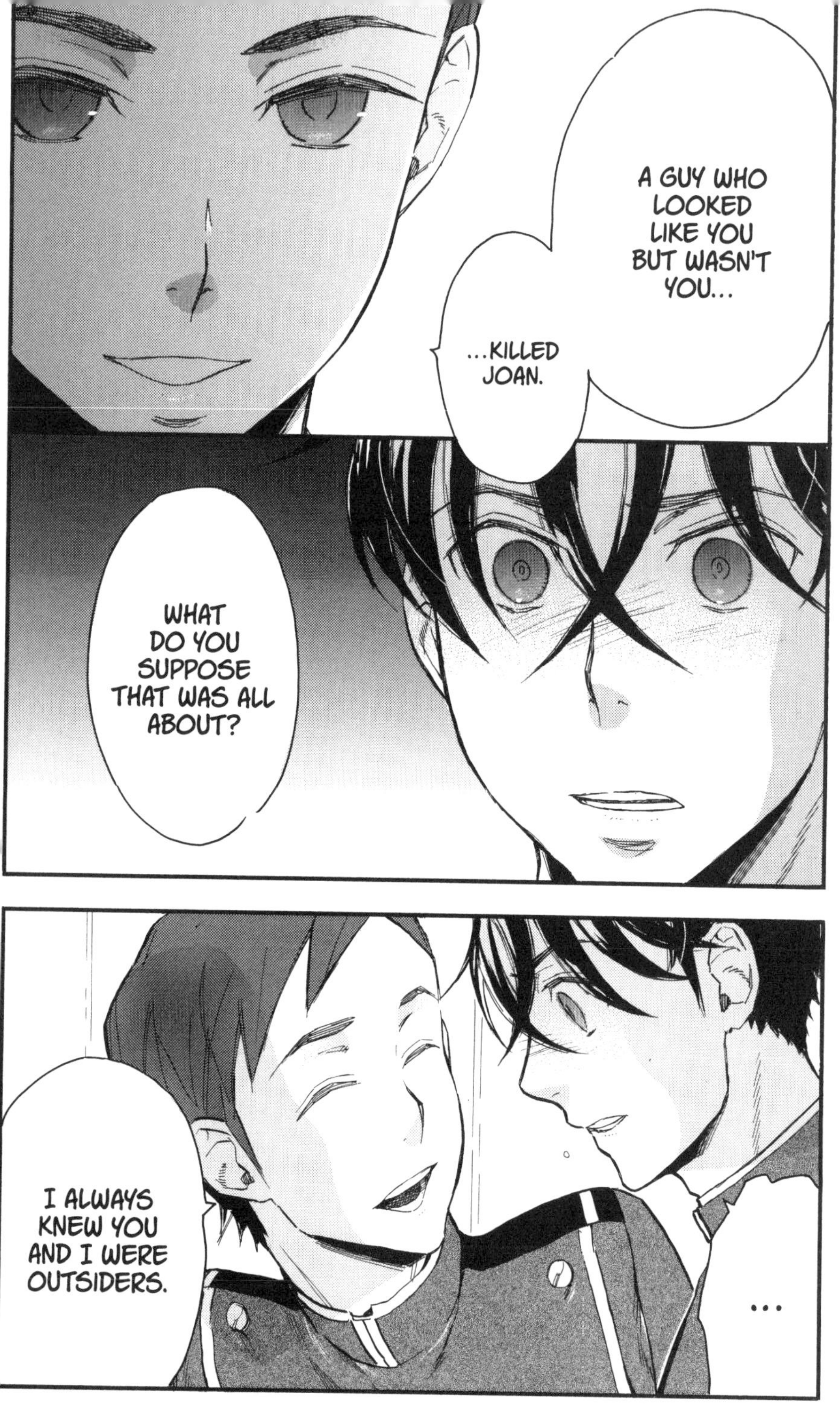
A GUY WHO LOOKED LIKE YOU BUT WASN'T YOU...
...KILLED JOAN.
WHAT DO YOU SUPPOSE THAT WAS ALL ABOUT?
...
I ALWAYS KNEW YOU AND I WERE OUTSIDERS.

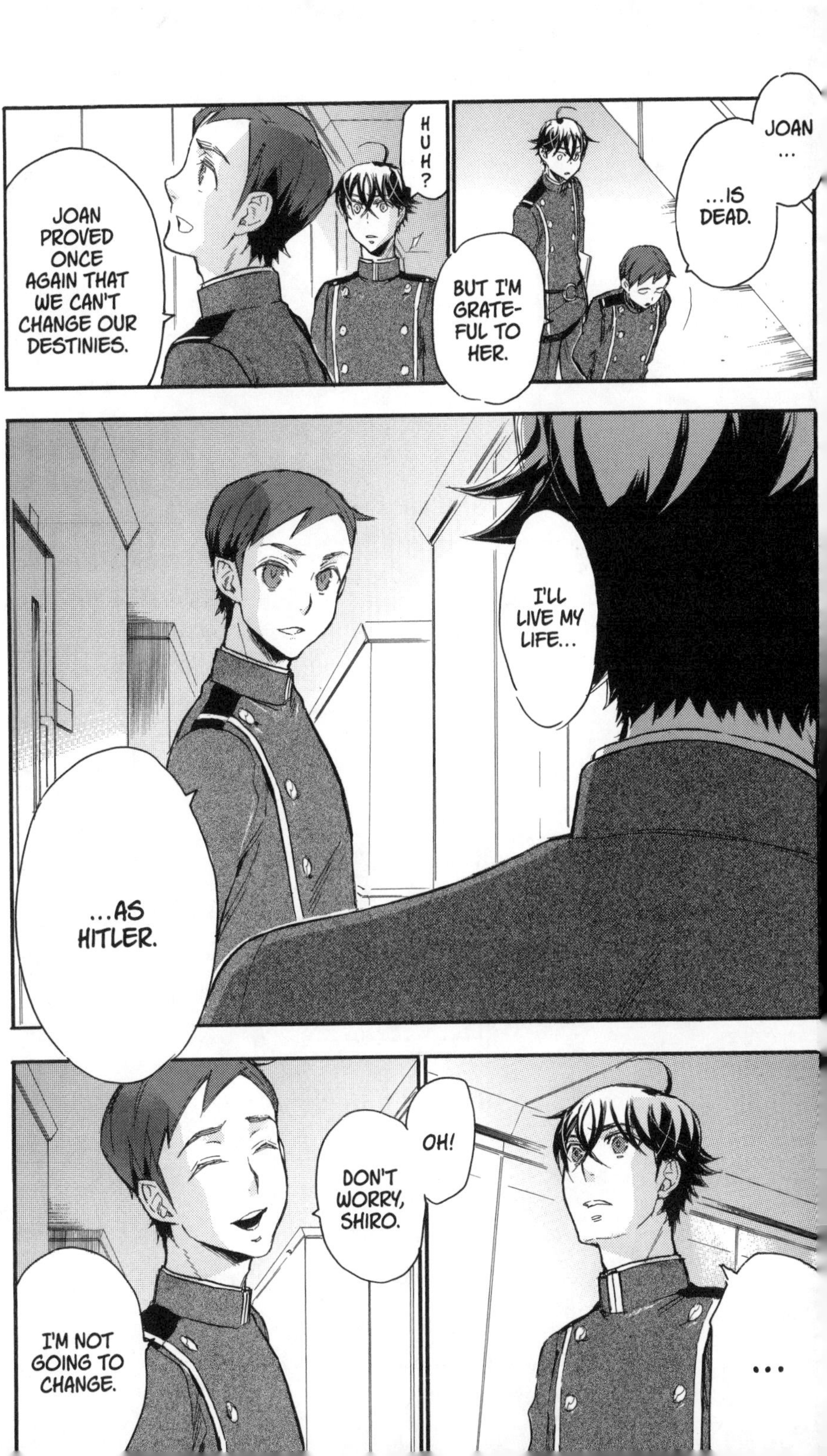
JOAN ...
...IS DEAD.
BUT I'M GRATE-FUL TO HER.
HUH?
JOAN PROVED ONCE AGAIN THAT WE CAN'T CHANGE OUR DESTINIES.
I'LL LIVE MY LIFE...
...AS HITLER.
...
OH!
DON'T WORRY, SHIRO.
I'M NOT GOING TO CHANGE.

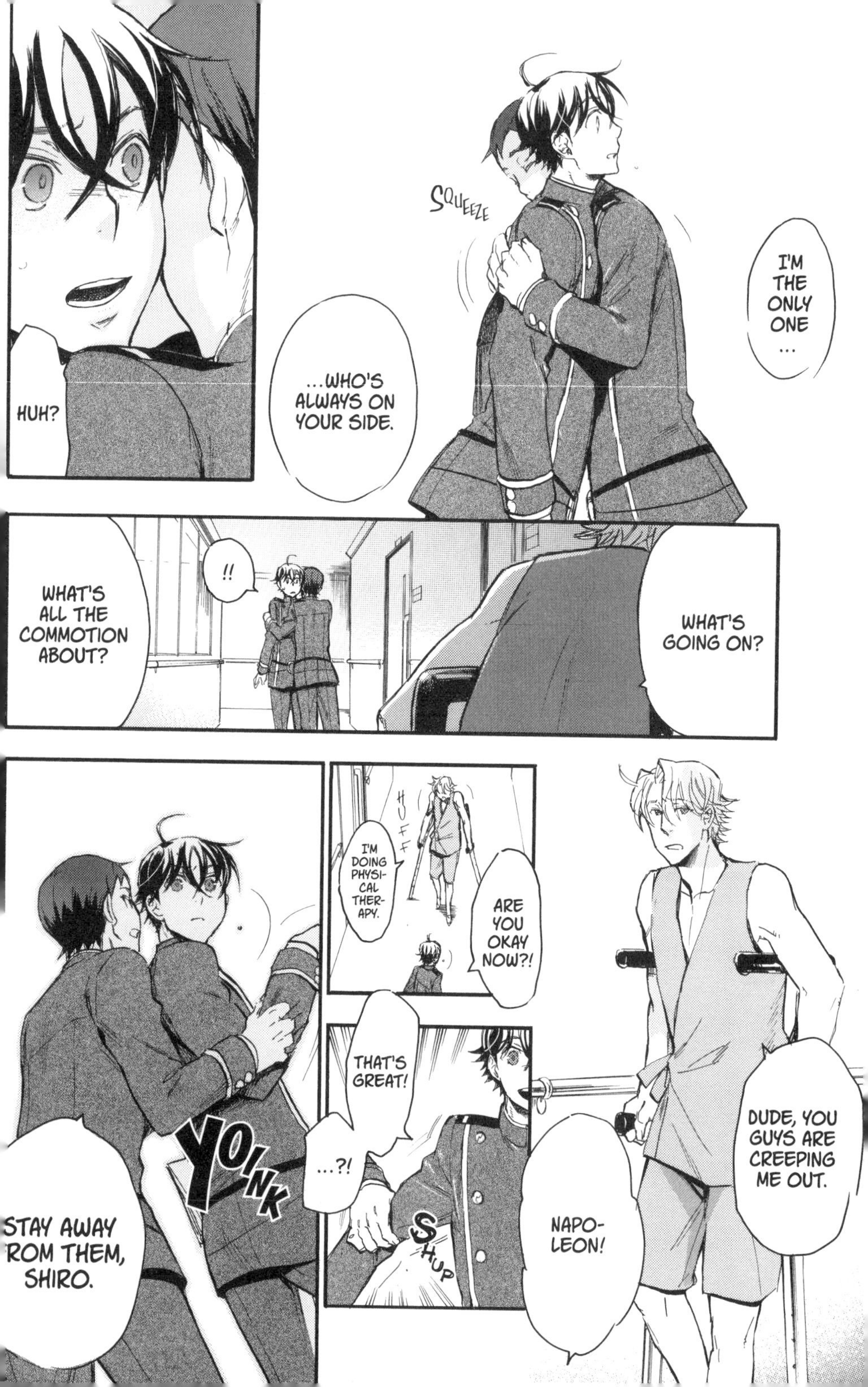
I'M THE ONLY ONE ...
SQUEEZE
...WHO'S ALWAYS ON YOUR SIDE.
HUH?
WHAT'S GOING ON?
!!
WHAT'S ALL THE COMMOTION ABOUT?
DUDE, YOU GUYS ARE CREEPING ME OUT.
NAPO-LEON!
ARE YOU OKAY NOW?!
HUFF
I'M DOING PHYSI-CAL THER-APY.
THAT'S GREAT!
SHUP
...?!
YOINK
STAY AWAY ROM THEM, SHIRO.

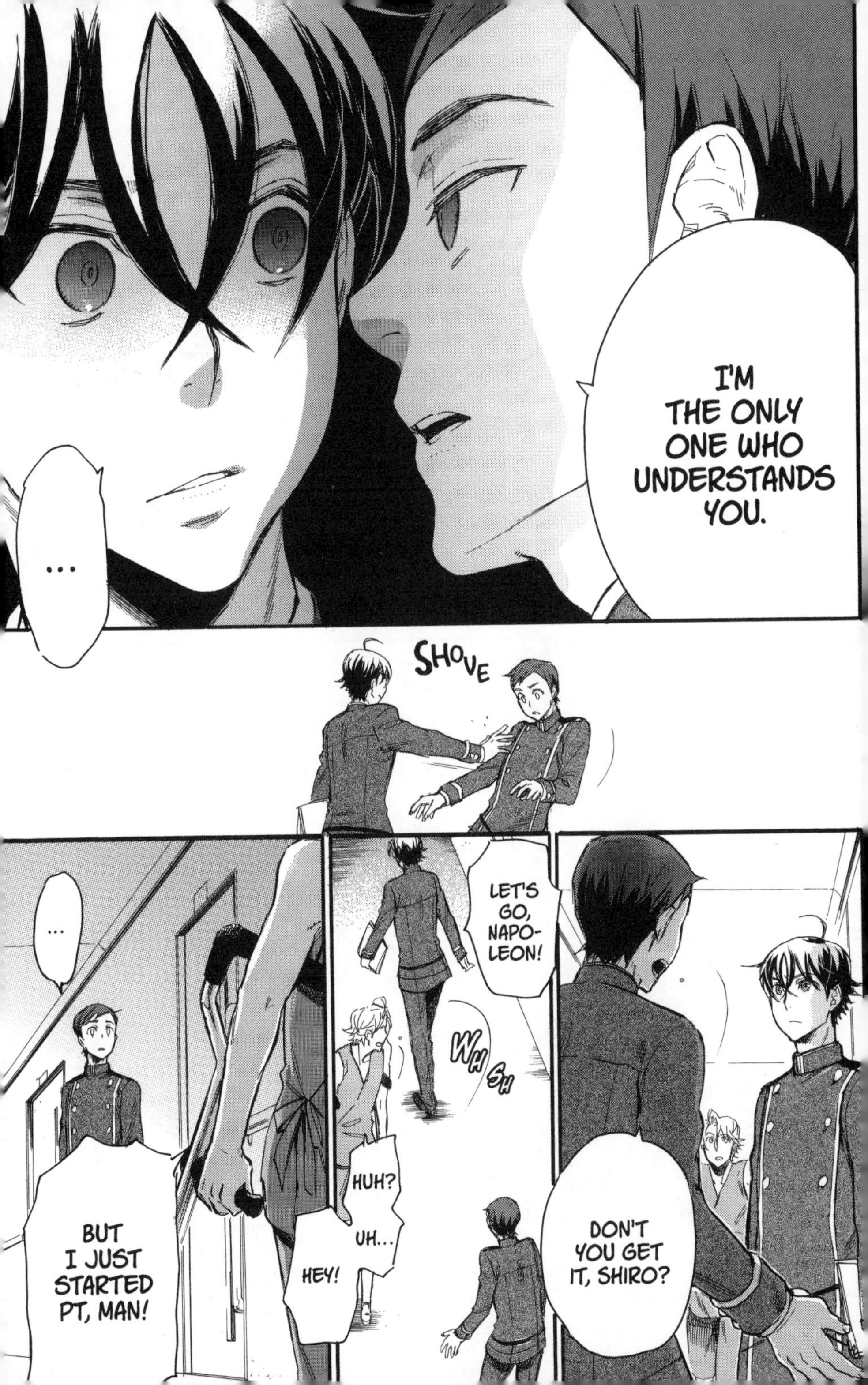
I'M THE ONLY ONE WHO UNDERSTANDS YOU.
...
SHOVE
DON'T YOU GET IT, SHIRO?
LET'S GO, NAPO-LEON!
WHSH
HUH?
UH...
HEY!
...
BUT I JUST STARTED PT, MAN!

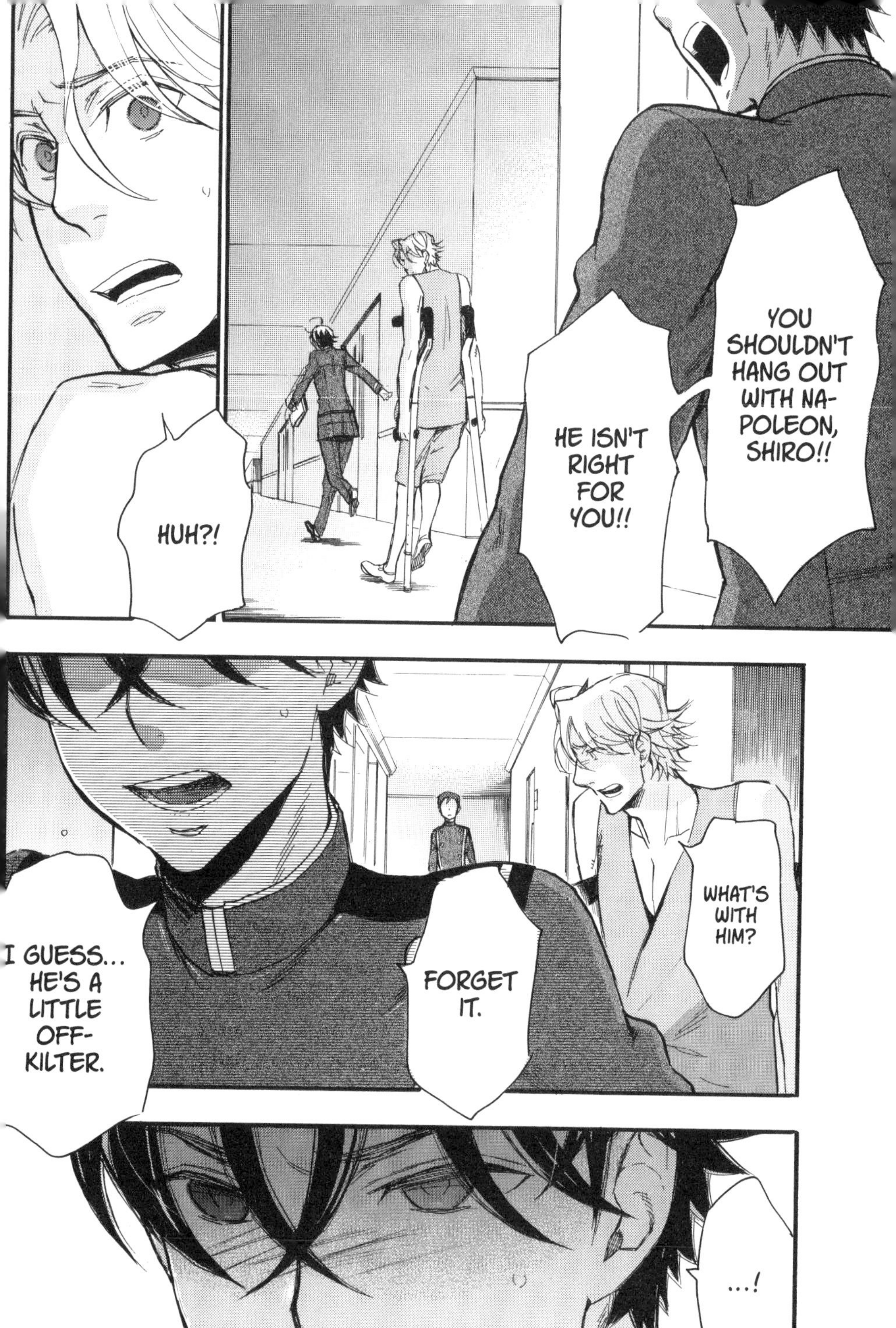
YOU SHOULDN'T HANG OUT WITH NAPOLEON, SHIRO!!
HE ISN'T RIGHT FOR YOU!!
HUH?!
WHAT'S WITH HIM?
FORGET IT.
I GUESS... HE'S A LITTLE OFF-KILTER.
...!

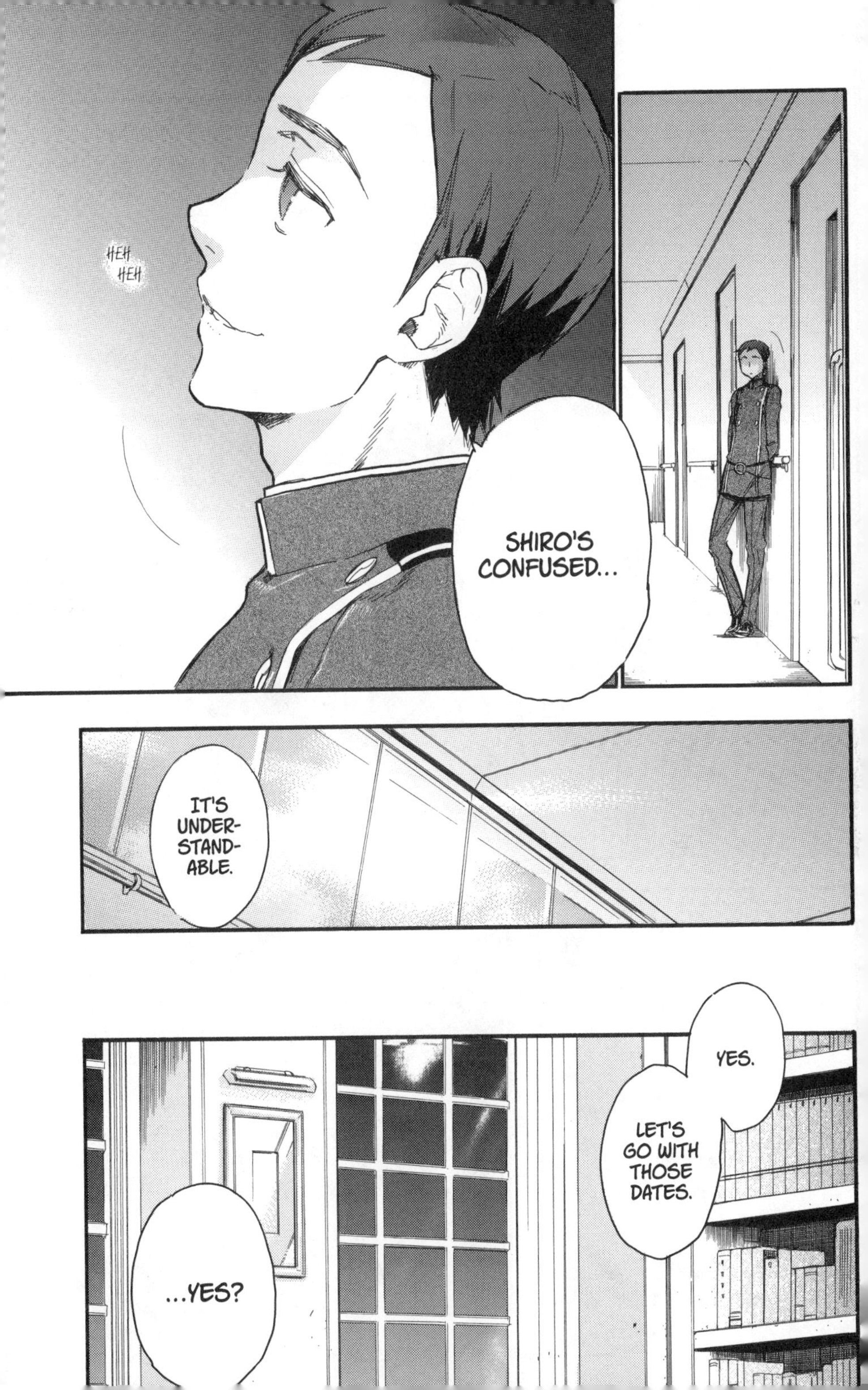
HEH HEH
SHIRO'S CONFUSED...
IT'S UNDER-STAND-ABLE.
YES.
LET'S GO WITH THOSE DATES.
...YES?

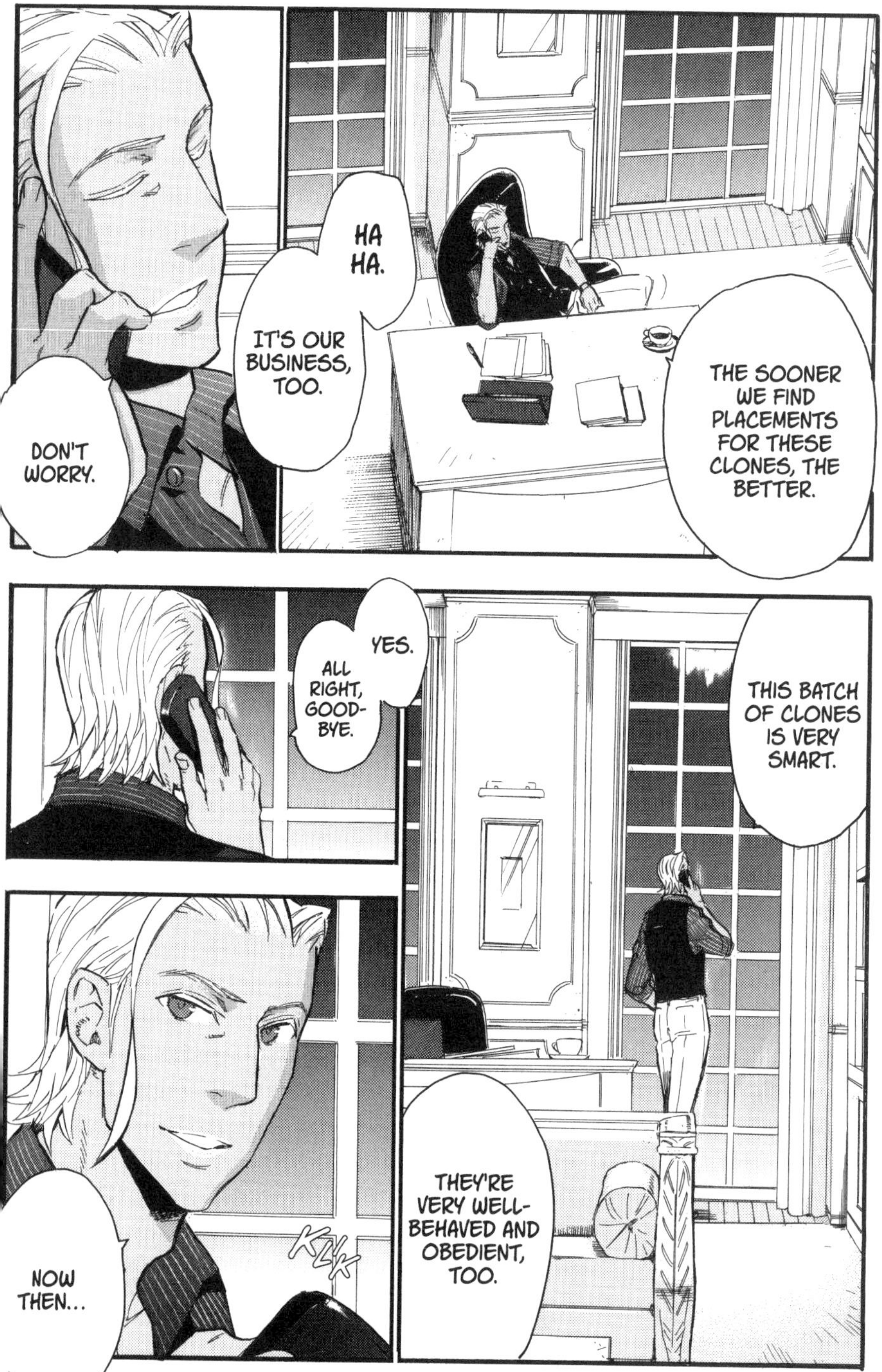
THE SOONER WE FIND PLACEMENTS FOR THESE CLONES, THE BETTER.
HA HA.
IT'S OUR BUSINESS, TOO.
DON'T WORRY.
THIS BATCH OF CLONES IS VERY SMART.
THEY'RE VERY WELL-BEHAVED AND OBEDIENT, TOO.
YES.
ALL RIGHT, GOOD-BYE.
KLIK
NOW THEN...

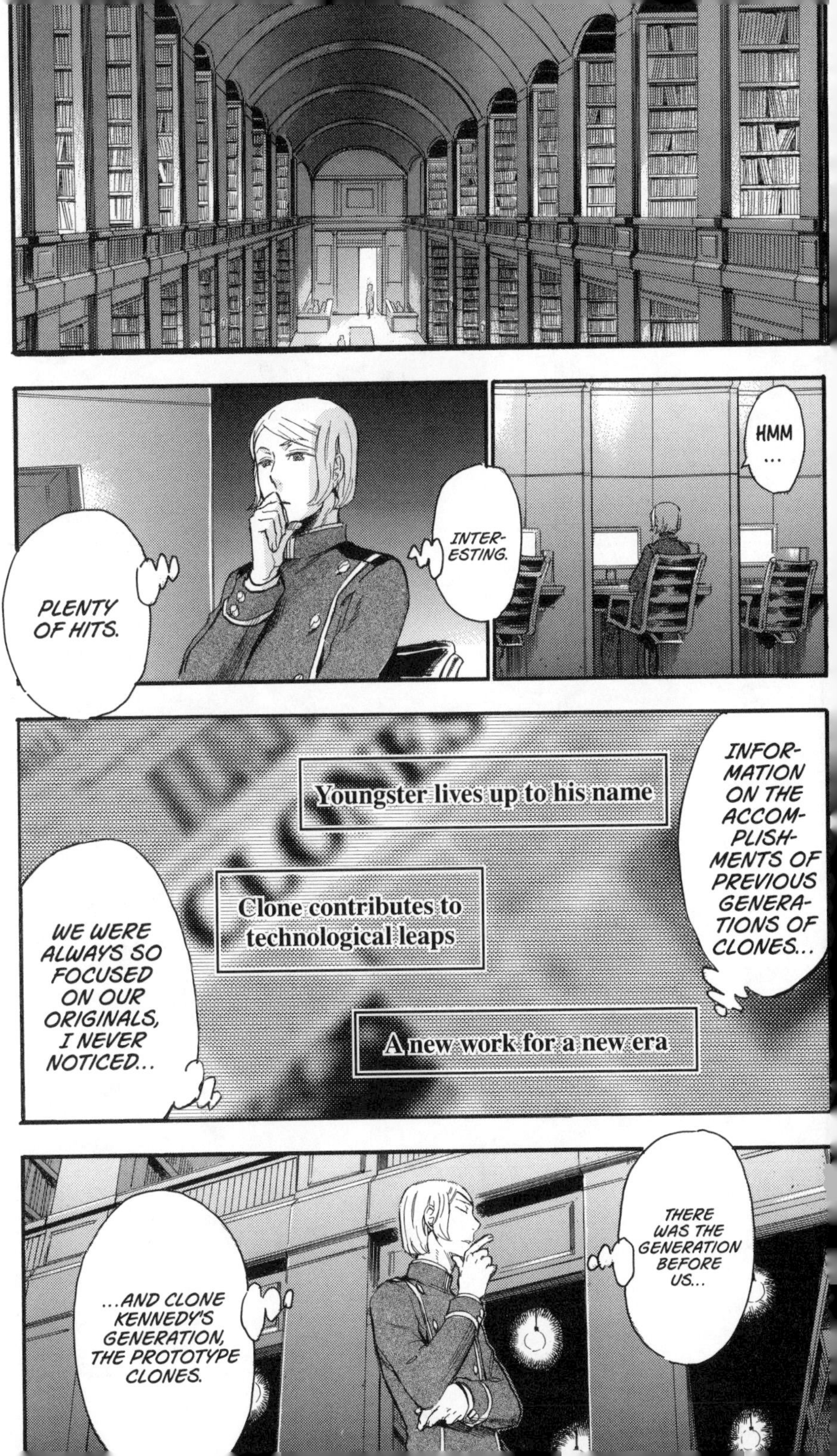
HMM...
INTERESTING.
PLENTY OF HITS.
INFORMATION ON THE ACCOMPLISHMENTS OF PREVIOUS GENERATIONS OF CLONES...
Youngster lives up to his name
Clone contributes to technological leaps
A new work for a new era
WE WERE ALWAYS SO FOCUSED ON OUR ORIGINALS, I NEVER NOTICED...
THERE WAS THE GENERATION BEFORE US...
...AND CLONE KENNEDY'S GENERATION, THE PROTOTYPE CLONES.

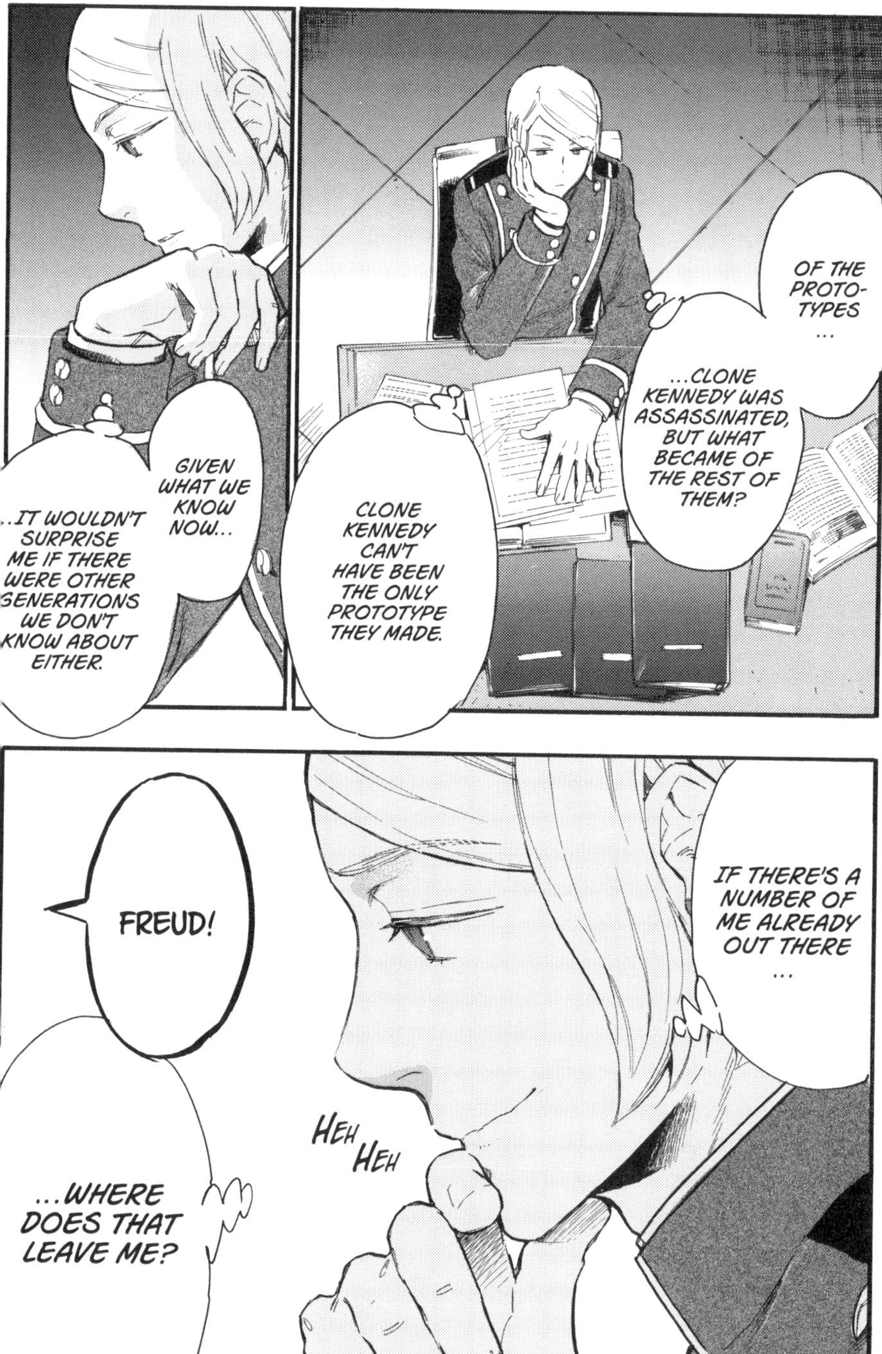
OF THE PROTO-TYPES ...
...CLONE KENNEDY WAS ASSASSINATED, BUT WHAT BECAME OF THE REST OF THEM?
CLONE KENNEDY CAN'T HAVE BEEN THE ONLY PROTOTYPE THEY MADE.
GIVEN WHAT WE KNOW NOW...
...IT WOULDN'T SURPRISE ME IF THERE WERE OTHER GENERATIONS WE DON'T KNOW ABOUT EITHER.
IF THERE'S A NUMBER OF ME ALREADY OUT THERE ...
FREUD!
HEH HEH
...WHERE DOES THAT LEAVE ME?

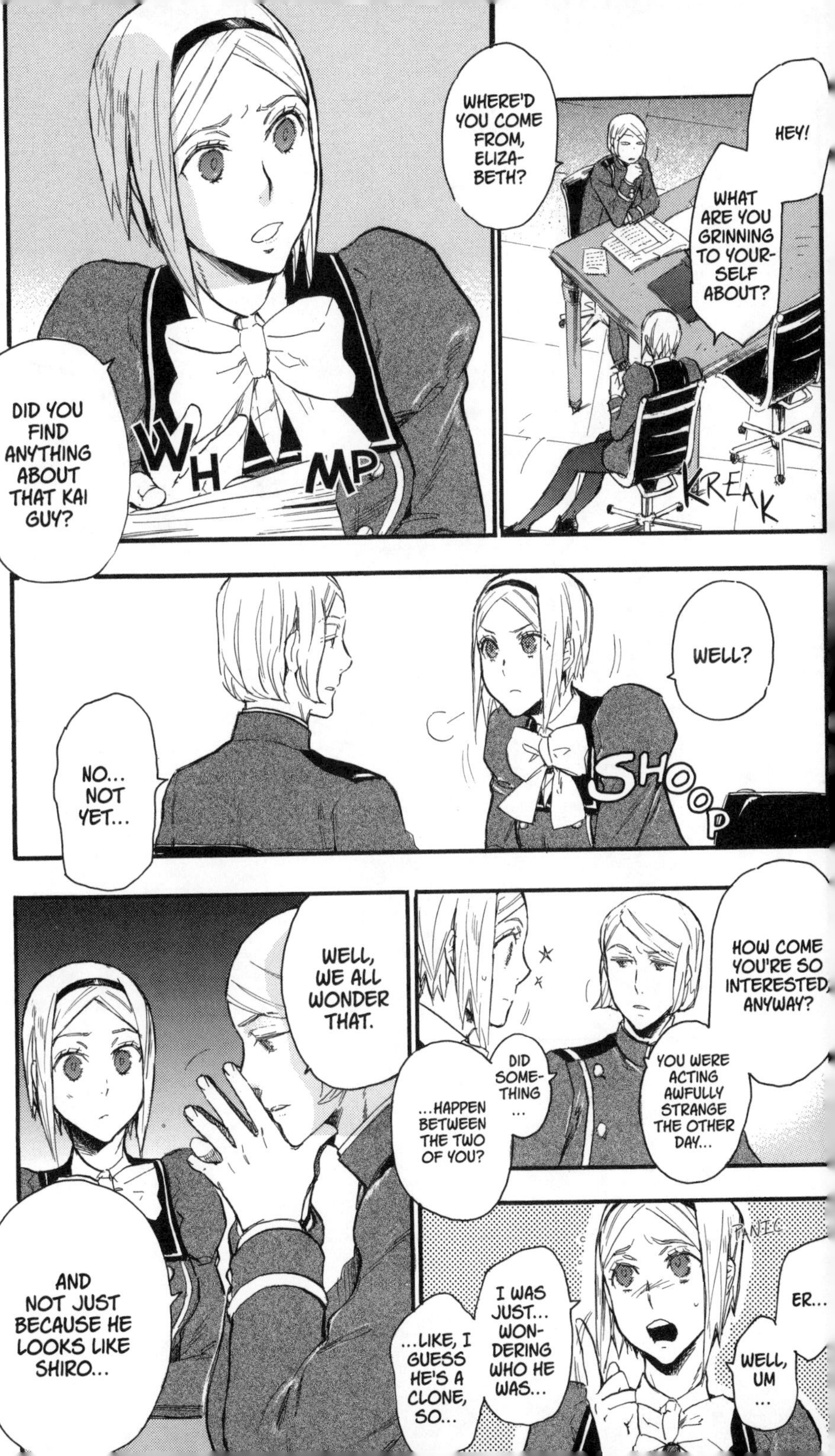
HEY!
WHAT ARE YOU GRINNING TO YOURSELF ABOUT?
WHERE'D YOU COME FROM, ELIZABETH?
KREAK
WHAMP
DID YOU FIND ANYTHING ABOUT THAT KAI GUY?
WELL?
SHOOP
NO... NOT YET...
HOW COME YOU'RE SO INTERESTED, ANYWAY?
YOU WERE ACTING AWFULLY STRANGE THE OTHER DAY...
DID SOMETHING...
...HAPPEN BETWEEN THE TWO OF YOU?
PANIC
ER...
WELL, UM...
I WAS JUST... WONDERING WHO HE WAS...
...LIKE, I GUESS HE'S A CLONE, SO...
WELL, WE ALL WONDER THAT.
AND NOT JUST BECAUSE HE LOOKS LIKE SHIRO...

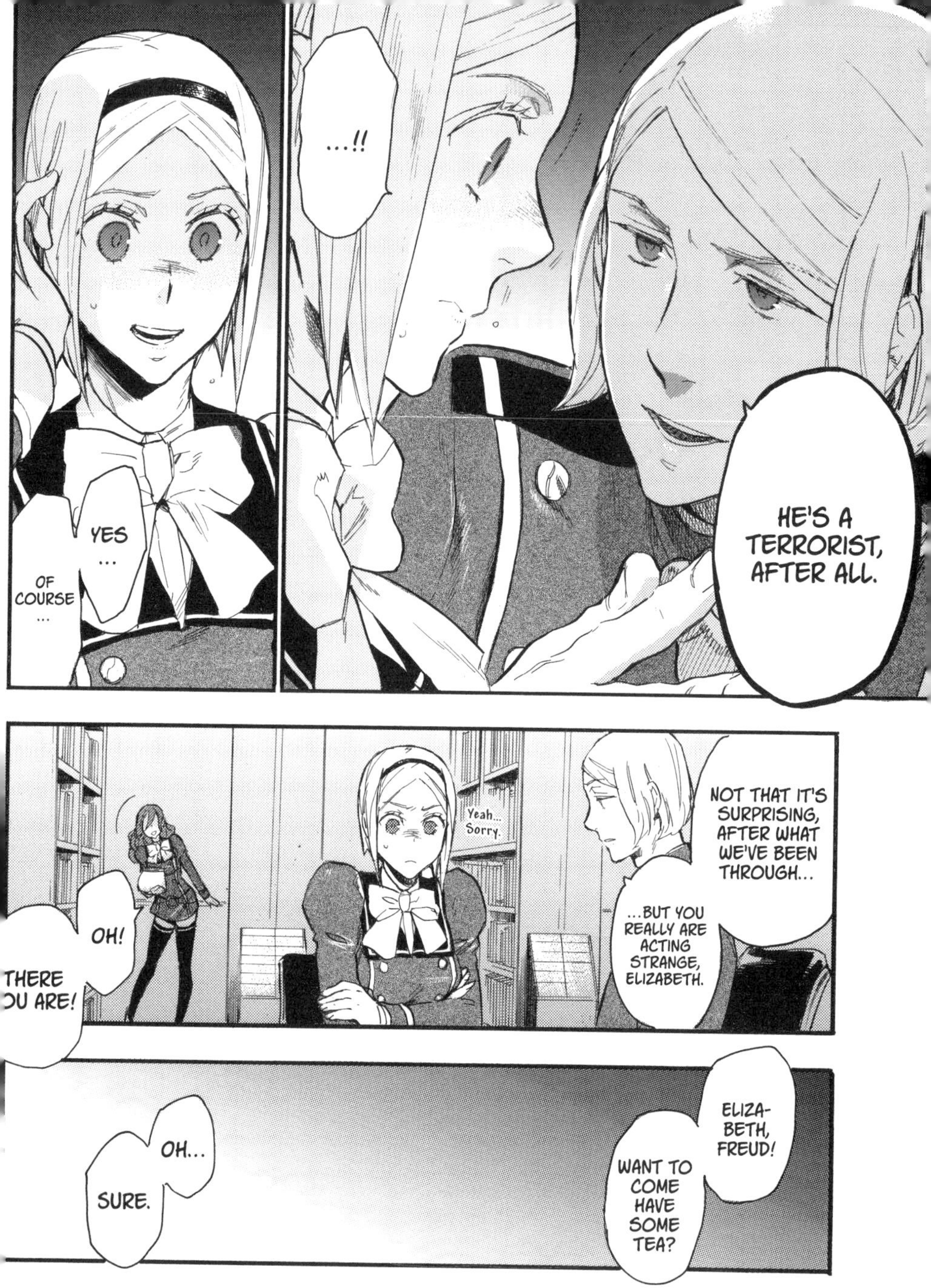
HE'S A TERRORIST, AFTER ALL.
...!!
YES ...
OF COURSE ...
NOT THAT IT'S SURPRISING, AFTER WHAT WE'VE BEEN THROUGH...
...BUT YOU REALLY ARE ACTING STRANGE, ELIZABETH.
Yeah... Sorry.
OH!
THERE OU ARE!
ELIZA-BETH, FREUD!
WANT TO COME HAVE SOME TEA?
OH... SURE.

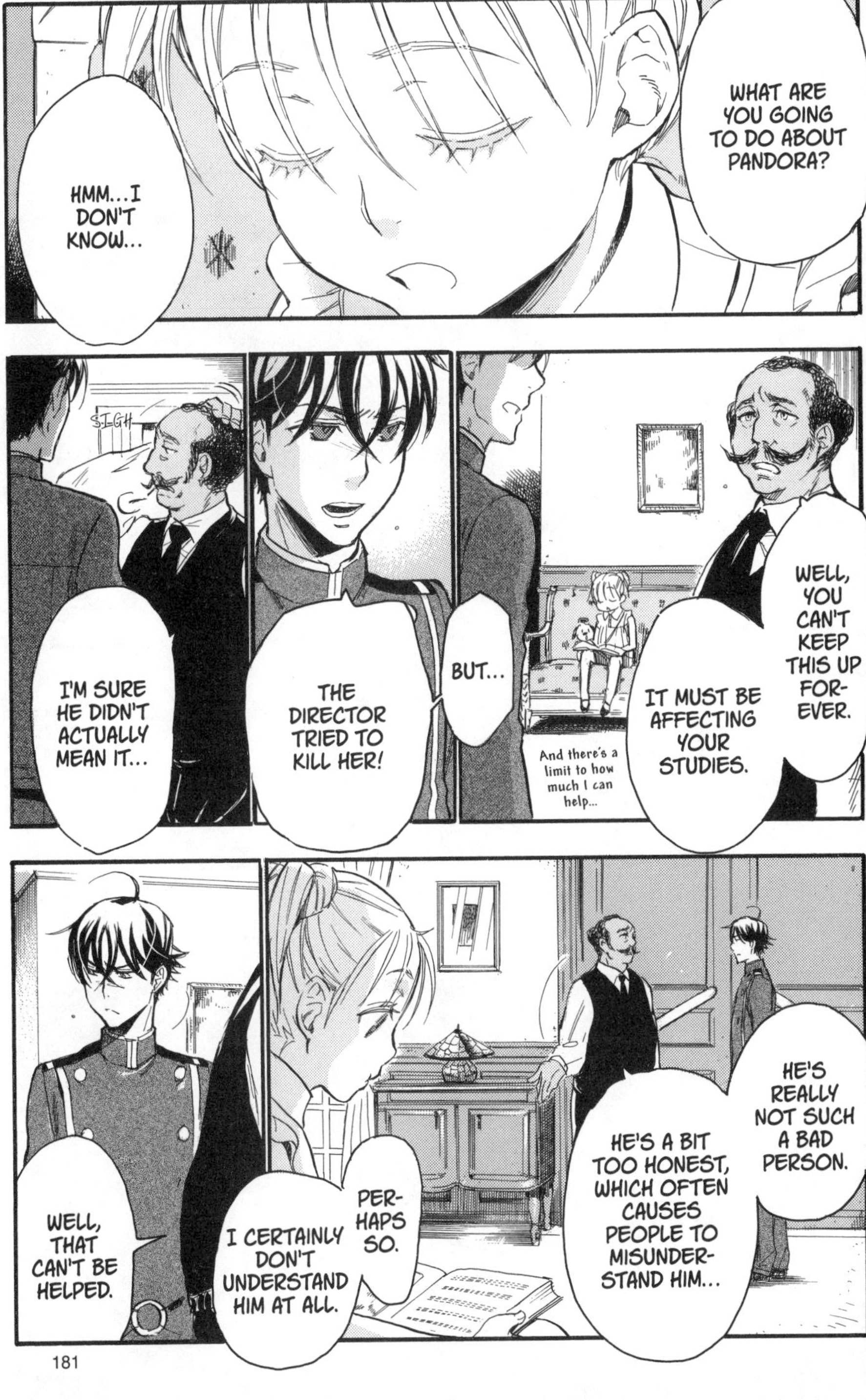
WHAT ARE YOU GOING TO DO ABOUT PANDORA?
HMM...I DON'T KNOW...
WELL, YOU CAN'T KEEP THIS UP FOR-EVER.
IT MUST BE AFFECTING YOUR STUDIES.
And there's a limit to how much I can help...
BUT...
THE DIRECTOR TRIED TO KILL HER!
SIGH
I'M SURE HE DIDN'T ACTUALLY MEAN IT...
HE'S REALLY NOT SUCH A BAD PERSON.
HE'S A BIT TOO HONEST, WHICH OFTEN CAUSES PEOPLE TO MISUNDER-STAND HIM...
PER-HAPS SO.
I CERTAINLY DON'T UNDERSTAND HIM AT ALL.
WELL, THAT CAN'T BE HELPED.

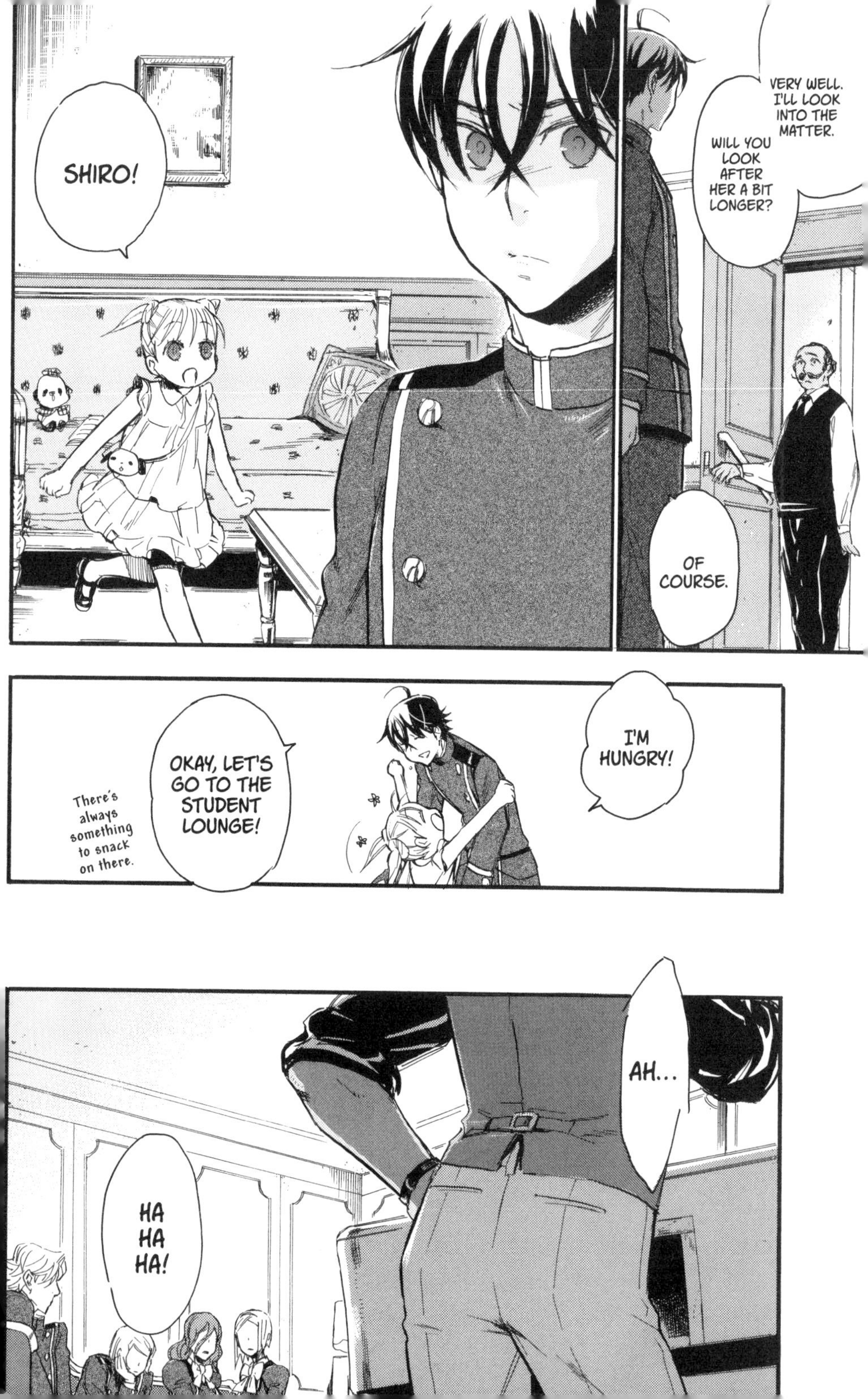
VERY WELL. I'LL LOOK INTO THE MATTER.
WILL YOU LOOK AFTER HER A BIT LONGER?
OF COURSE.
SHIRO!
I'M HUNGRY!
OKAY, LET'S GO TO THE STUDENT LOUNGE!
There's always something to snack on there.
AH...
HA HA HA!

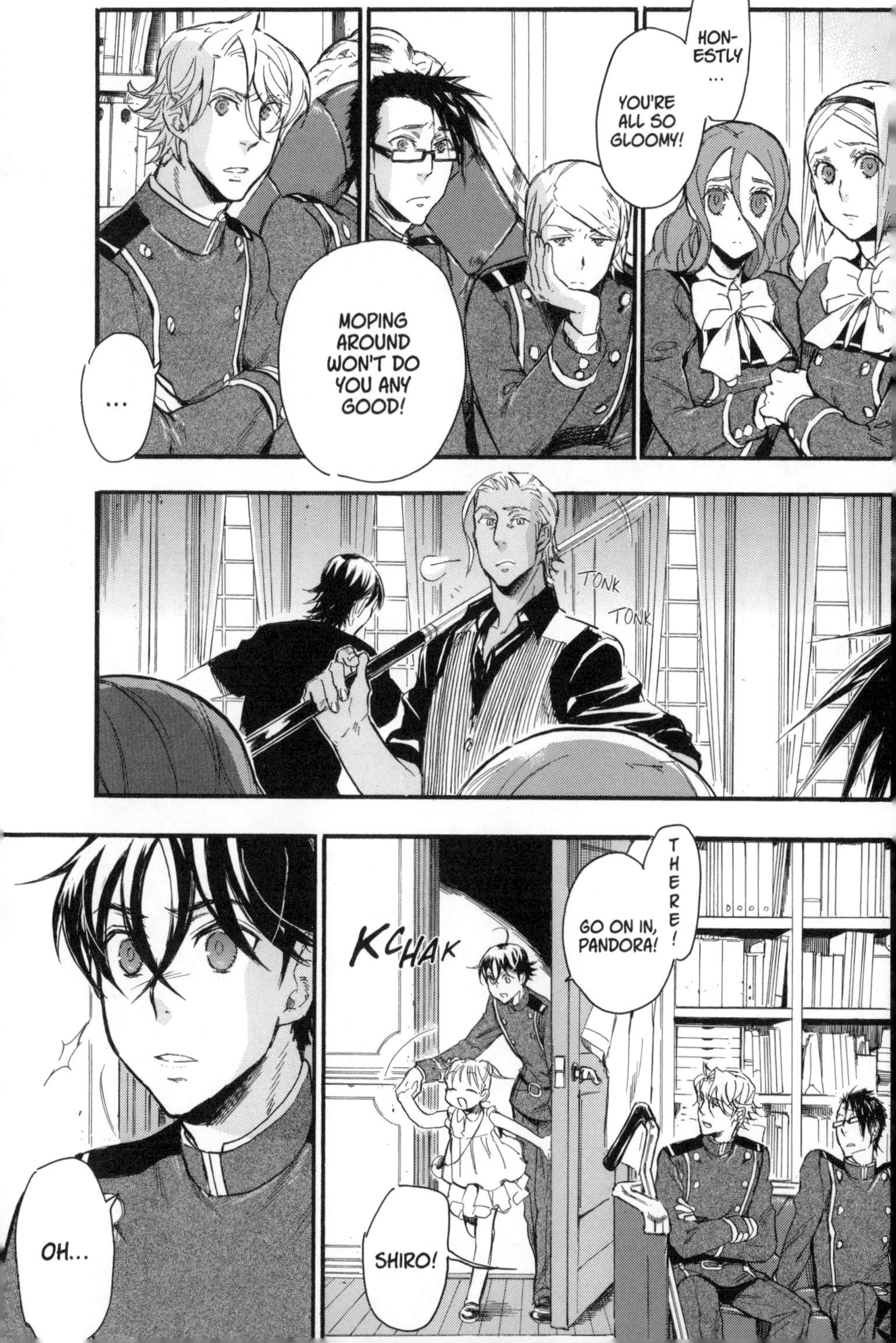
HON-ESTLY...
YOU'RE ALL SO GLOOMY!
MOPING AROUND WON'T DO YOU ANY GOOD!
...
TONK
TONK
THERE!
GO ON IN, PANDORA!
KCHAK
SHIRO!
OH...

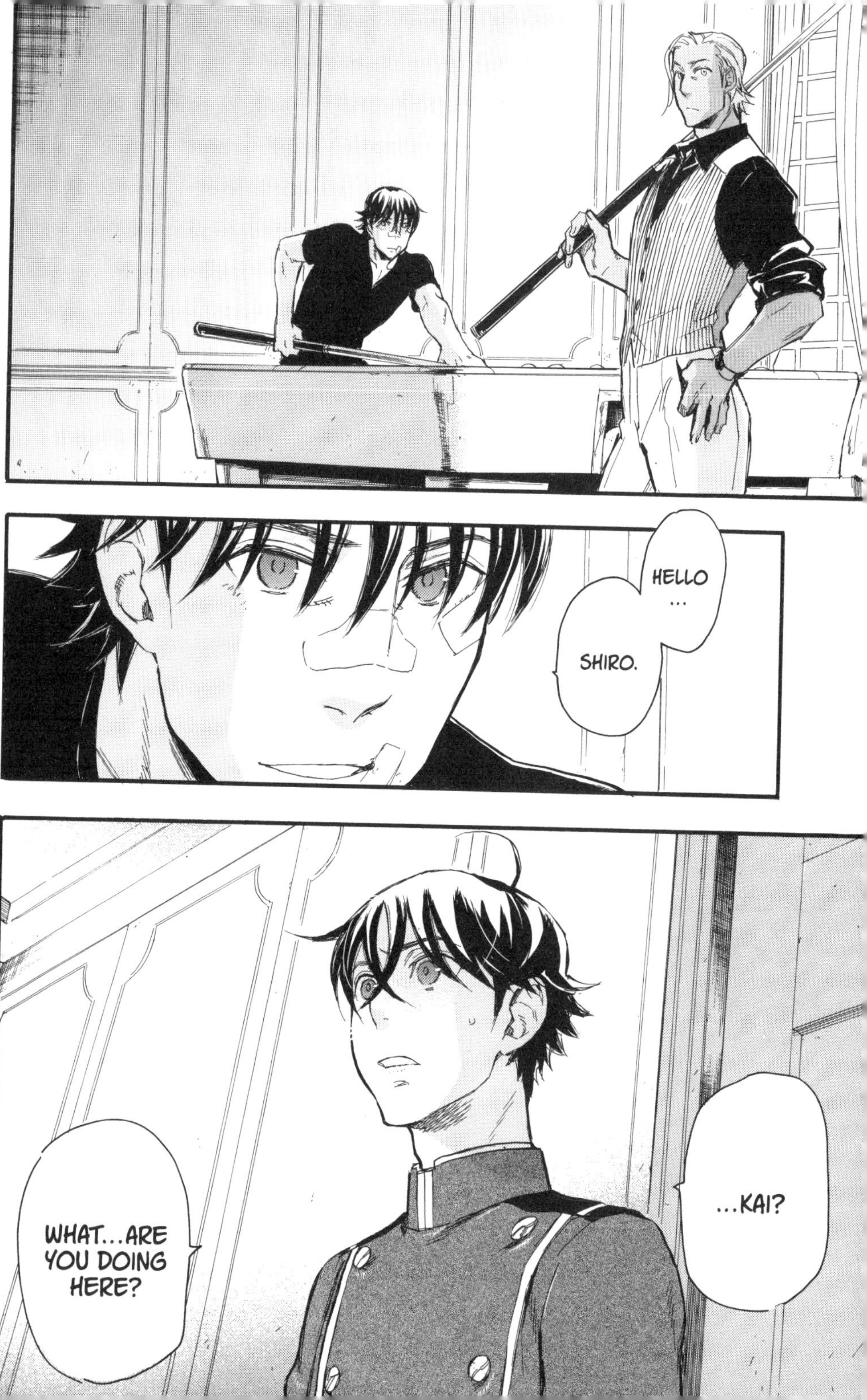
HELLO ...
SHIRO.
...KAI?
WHAT...ARE YOU DOING HERE?

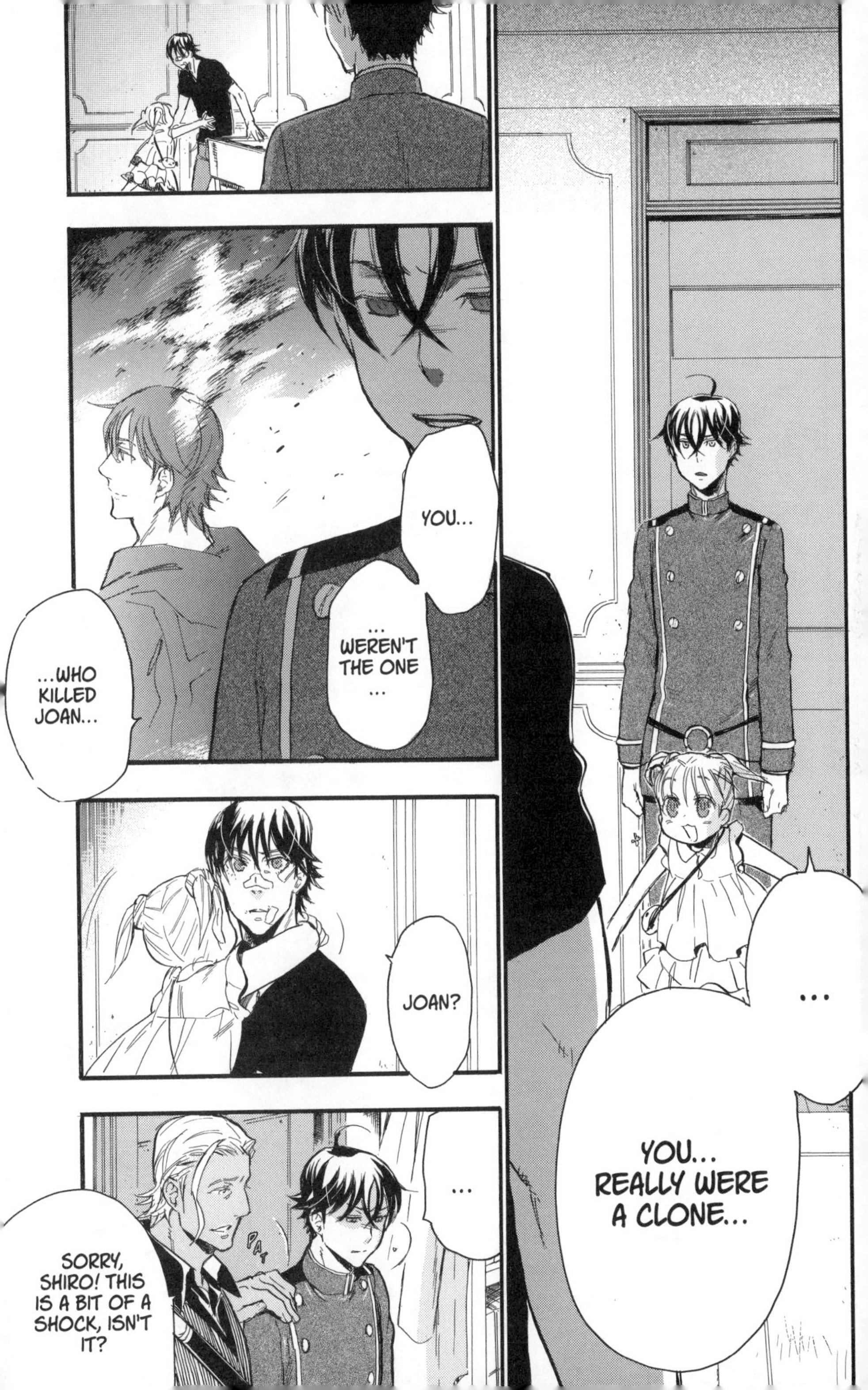
...
YOU... REALLY WERE A CLONE...
YOU...
...WEREN'T THE ONE...
...WHO KILLED JOAN...
JOAN?
...
SORRY, SHIRO! THIS IS A BIT OF A SHOCK, ISN'T IT?

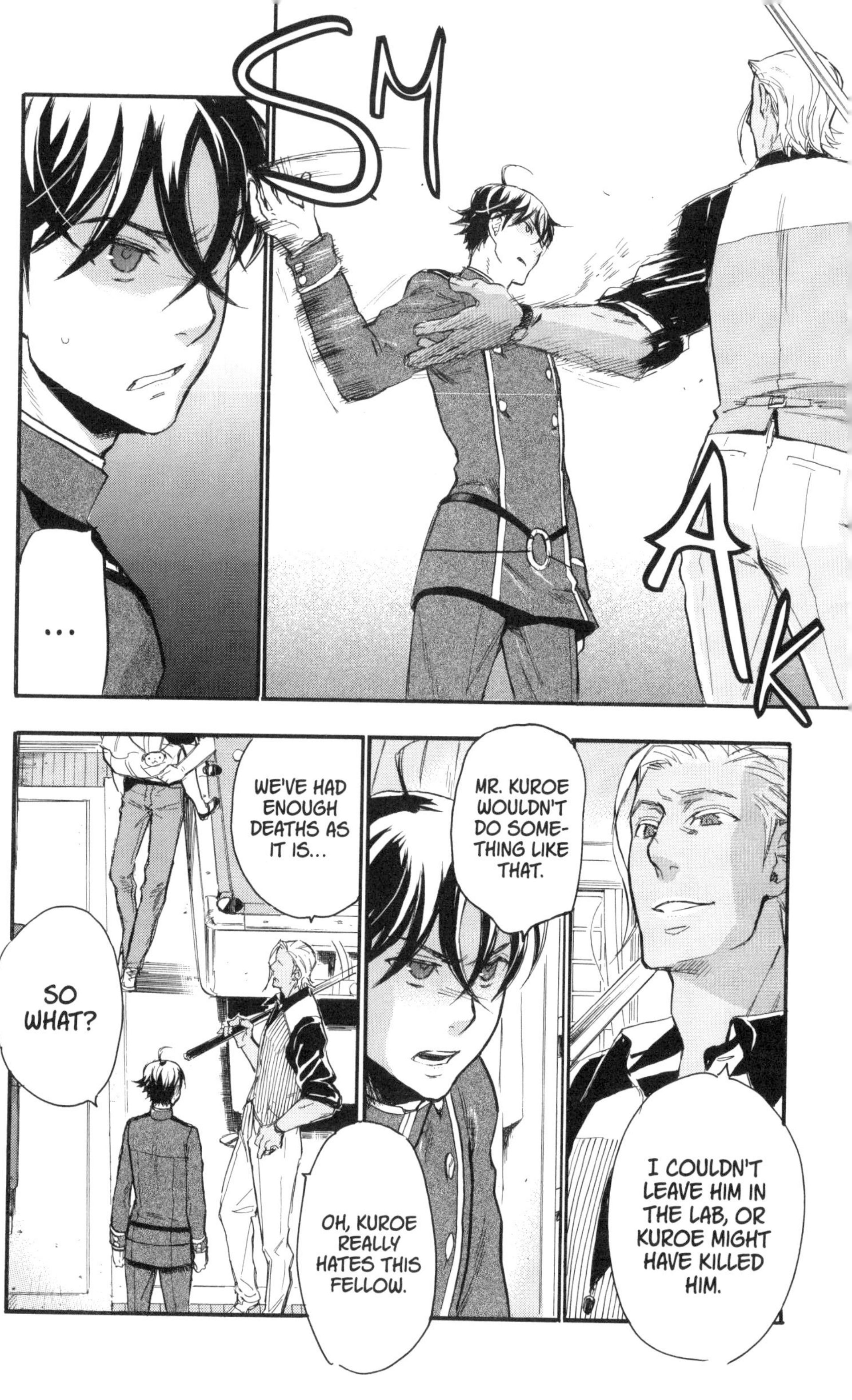
SM
AK
...
I COULDN'T LEAVE HIM IN THE LAB, OR KUROE MIGHT HAVE KILLED HIM.
MR. KUROE WOULDN'T DO SOMETHING LIKE THAT.
OH, KUROE REALLY HATES THIS FELLOW.
WE'VE HAD ENOUGH DEATHS AS IT IS...
SO WHAT?

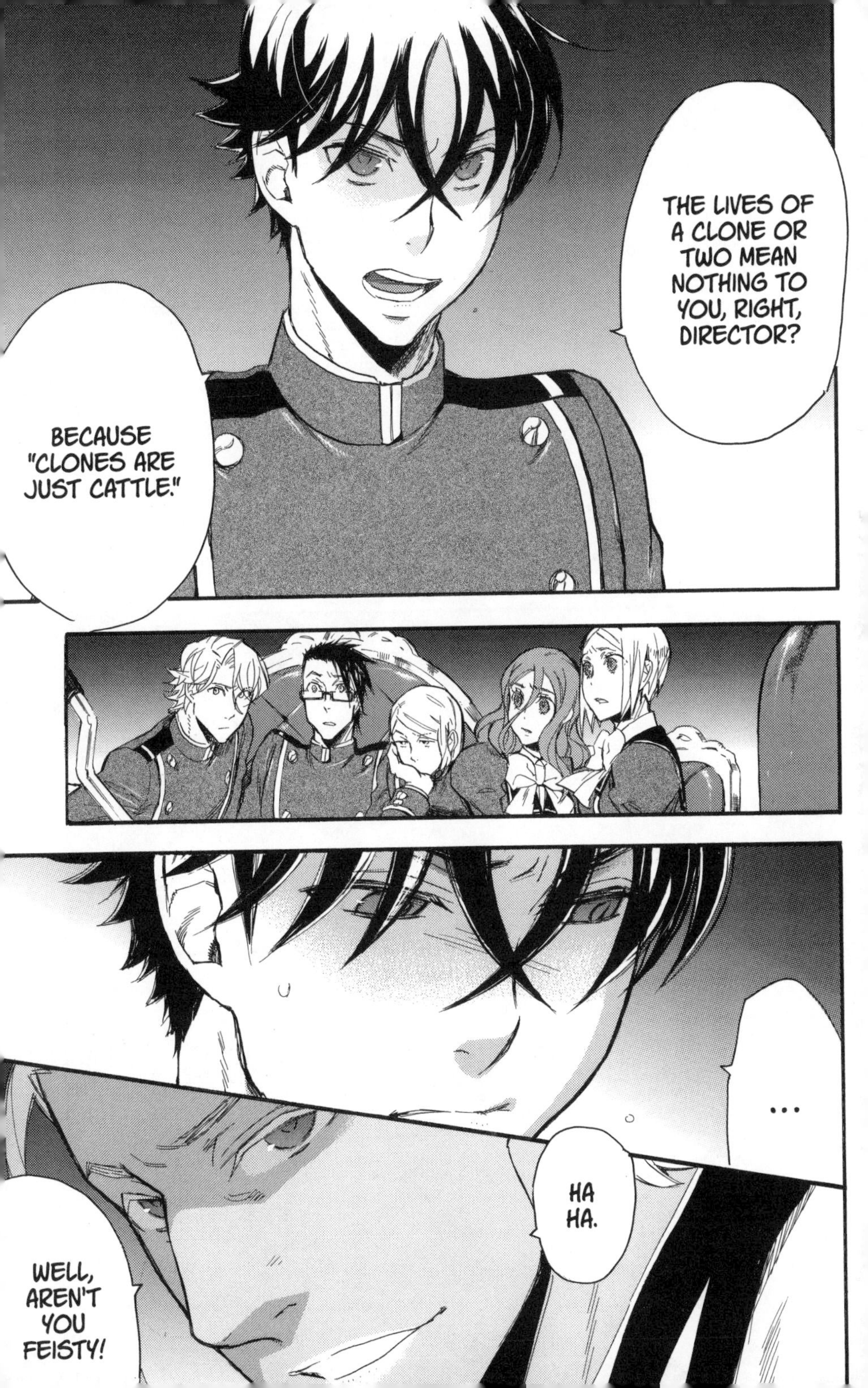
THE LIVES OF A CLONE OR TWO MEAN NOTHING TO YOU, RIGHT, DIRECTOR?
BECAUSE "CLONES ARE JUST CATTLE."
...
HA HA.
WELL, AREN'T YOU FEISTY!

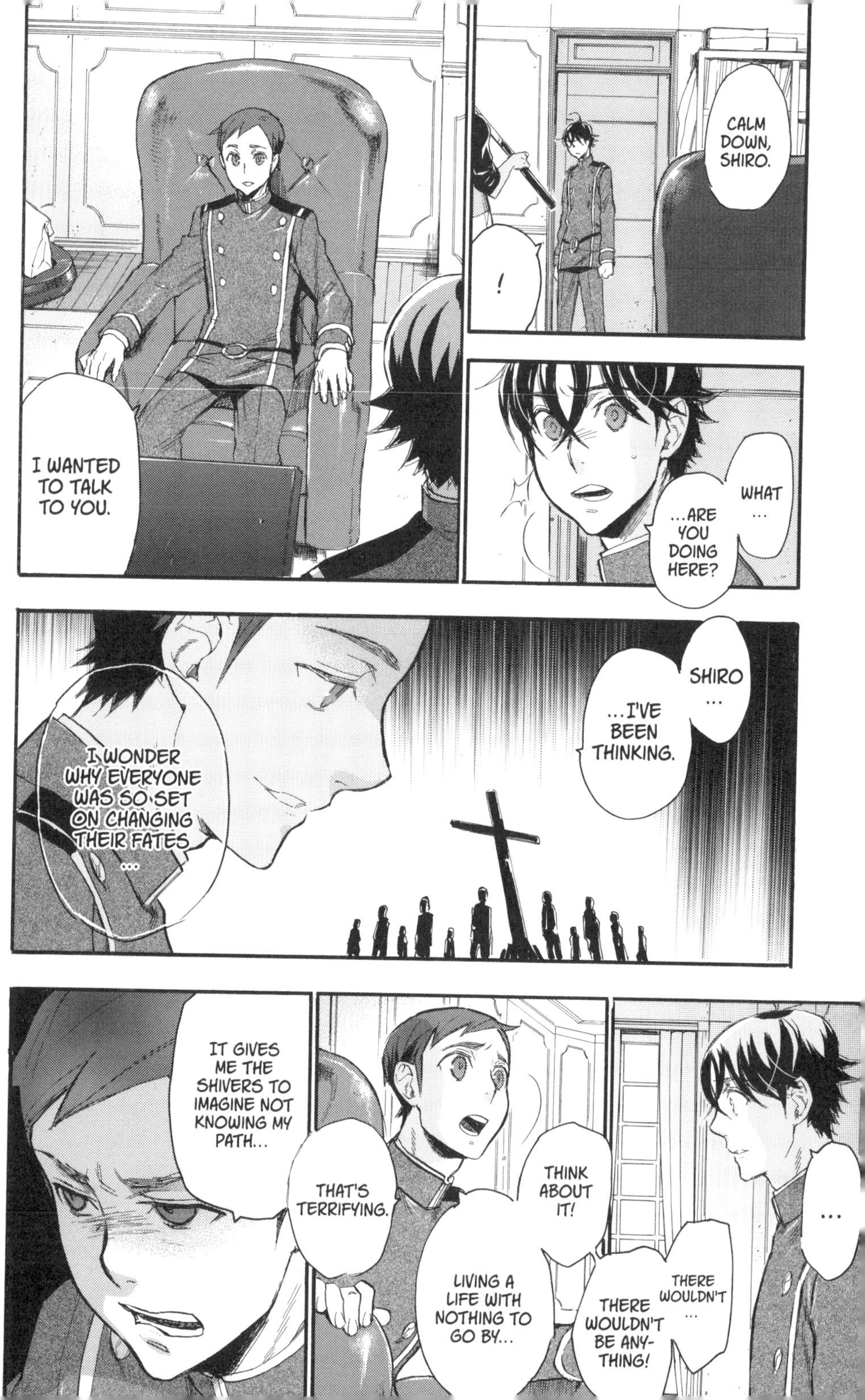
CALM DOWN, SHIRO.
!
WHAT ...
...ARE YOU DOING HERE?
I WANTED TO TALK TO YOU.
SHIRO ...
...I'VE BEEN THINKING.
I WONDER WHY EVERYONE WAS SO SET ON CHANGING THEIR FATES ...
...
THERE WOULDN'T ...
THINK ABOUT IT!
THERE WOULDN'T BE ANY-THING!
LIVING A LIFE WITH NOTHING TO GO BY...
THAT'S TERRIFYING.
IT GIVES ME THE SHIVERS TO IMAGINE NOT KNOWING MY PATH...

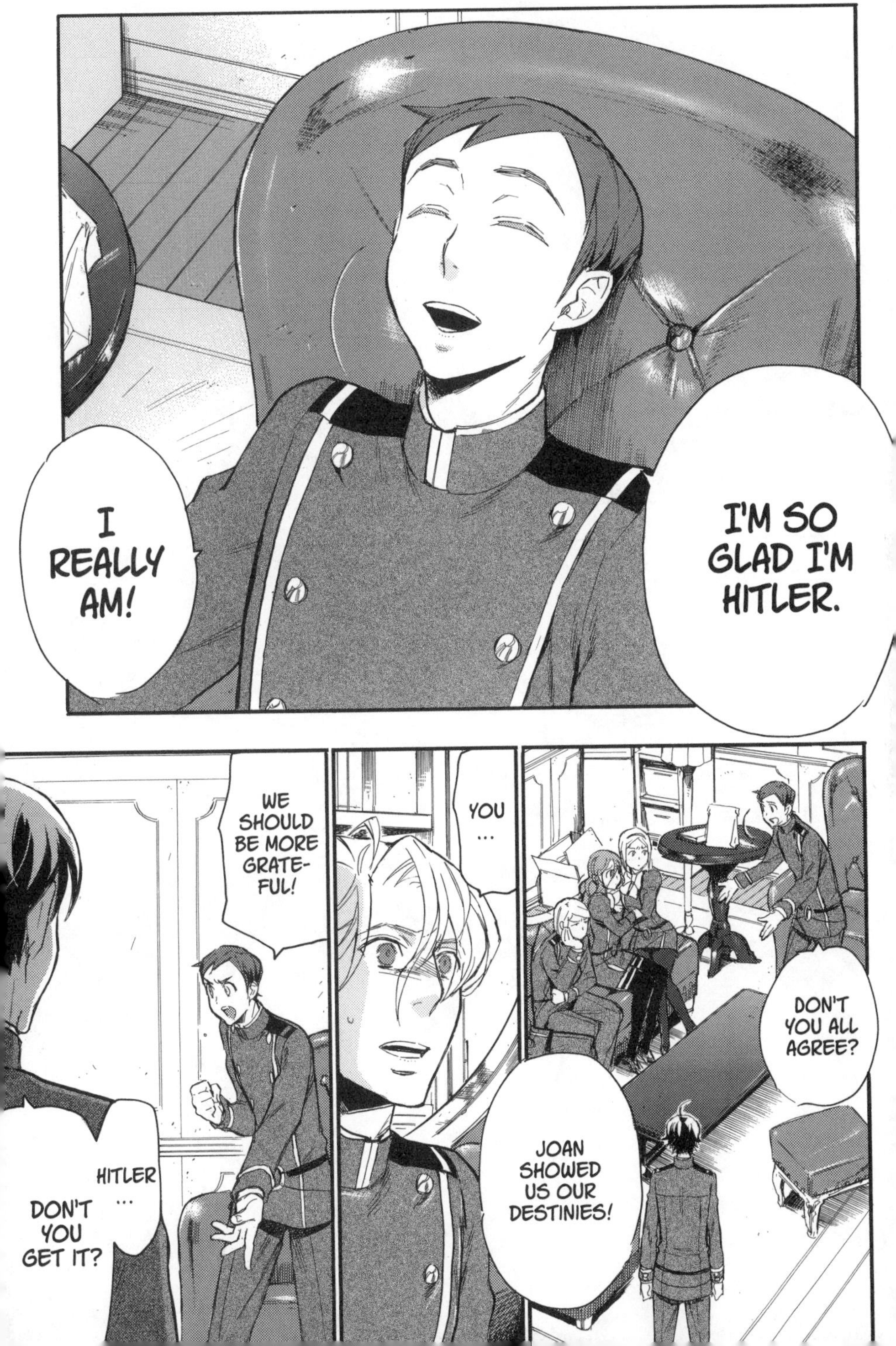
I'M SO GLAD I'M HITLER.
I REALLY AM!
DON'T YOU ALL AGREE?
JOAN SHOWED US OUR DESTINIES!
YOU ...
WE SHOULD BE MORE GRATE-FUL!
HITLER ...
DON'T YOU GET IT?

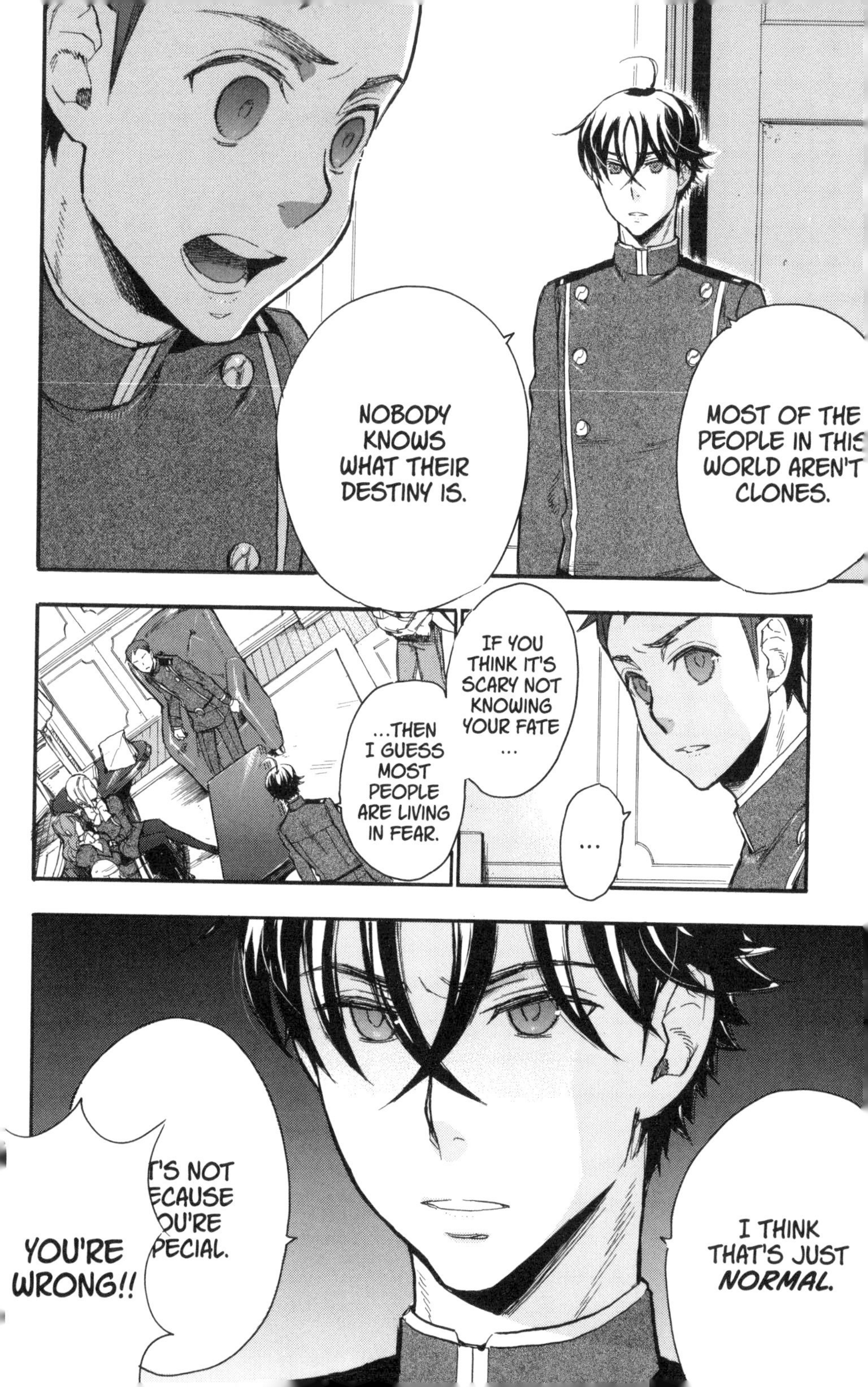
MOST OF THE PEOPLE IN THIS WORLD AREN'T CLONES.
NOBODY KNOWS WHAT THEIR DESTINY IS.
IF YOU THINK IT'S SCARY NOT KNOWING YOUR FATE ...
...THEN I GUESS MOST PEOPLE ARE LIVING IN FEAR.
...
I THINK THAT'S JUST *NORMAL*.
T'S NOT ECAUSE OU'RE PECIAL.
YOU'RE WRONG!!

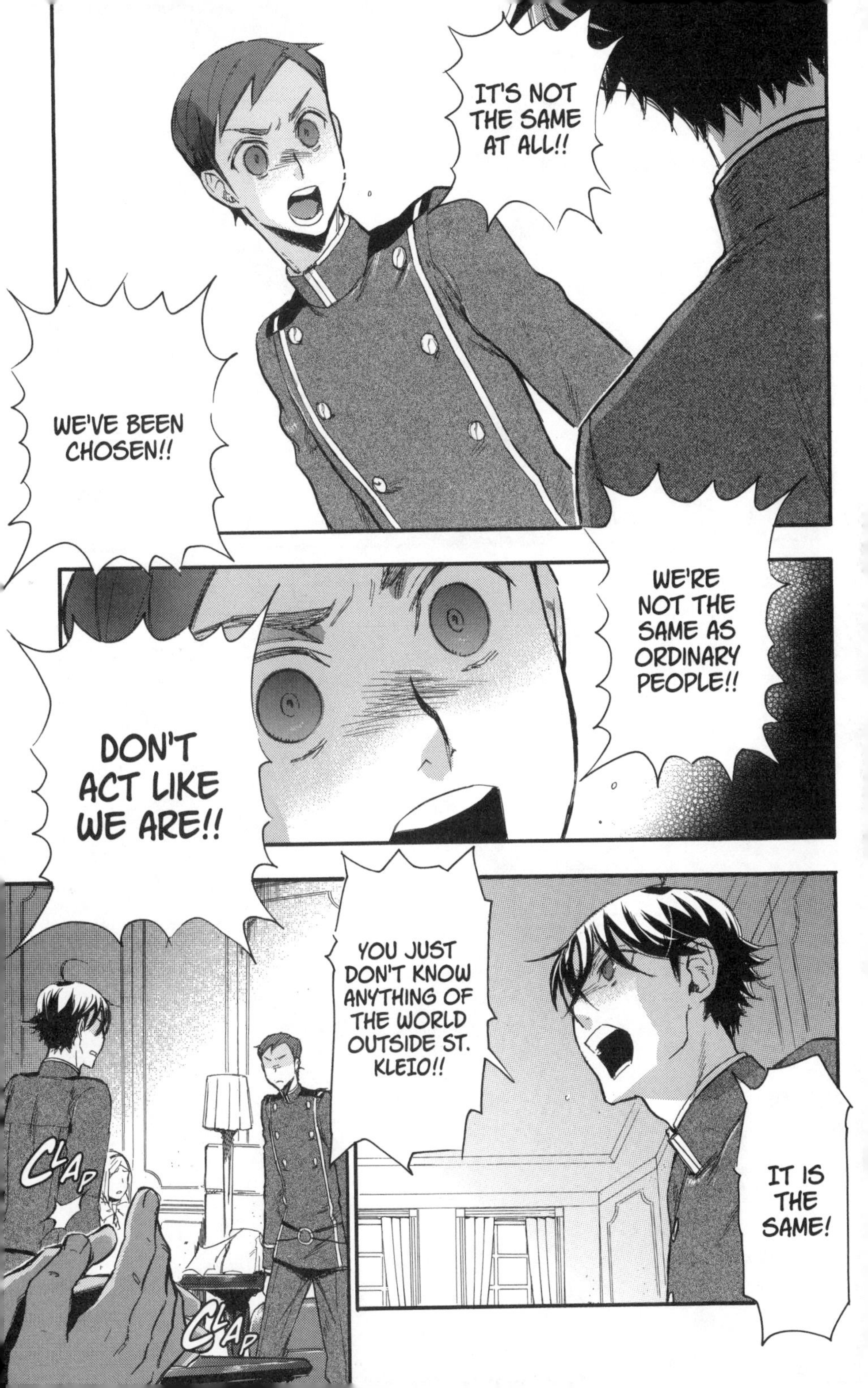
IT'S NOT THE SAME AT ALL!!
WE'VE BEEN CHOSEN!!
WE'RE NOT THE SAME AS ORDINARY PEOPLE!!
DON'T ACT LIKE WE ARE!!
YOU JUST DON'T KNOW ANYTHING OF THE WORLD OUTSIDE ST. KLEIO!!
IT IS THE SAME!
CLAP
CLAP

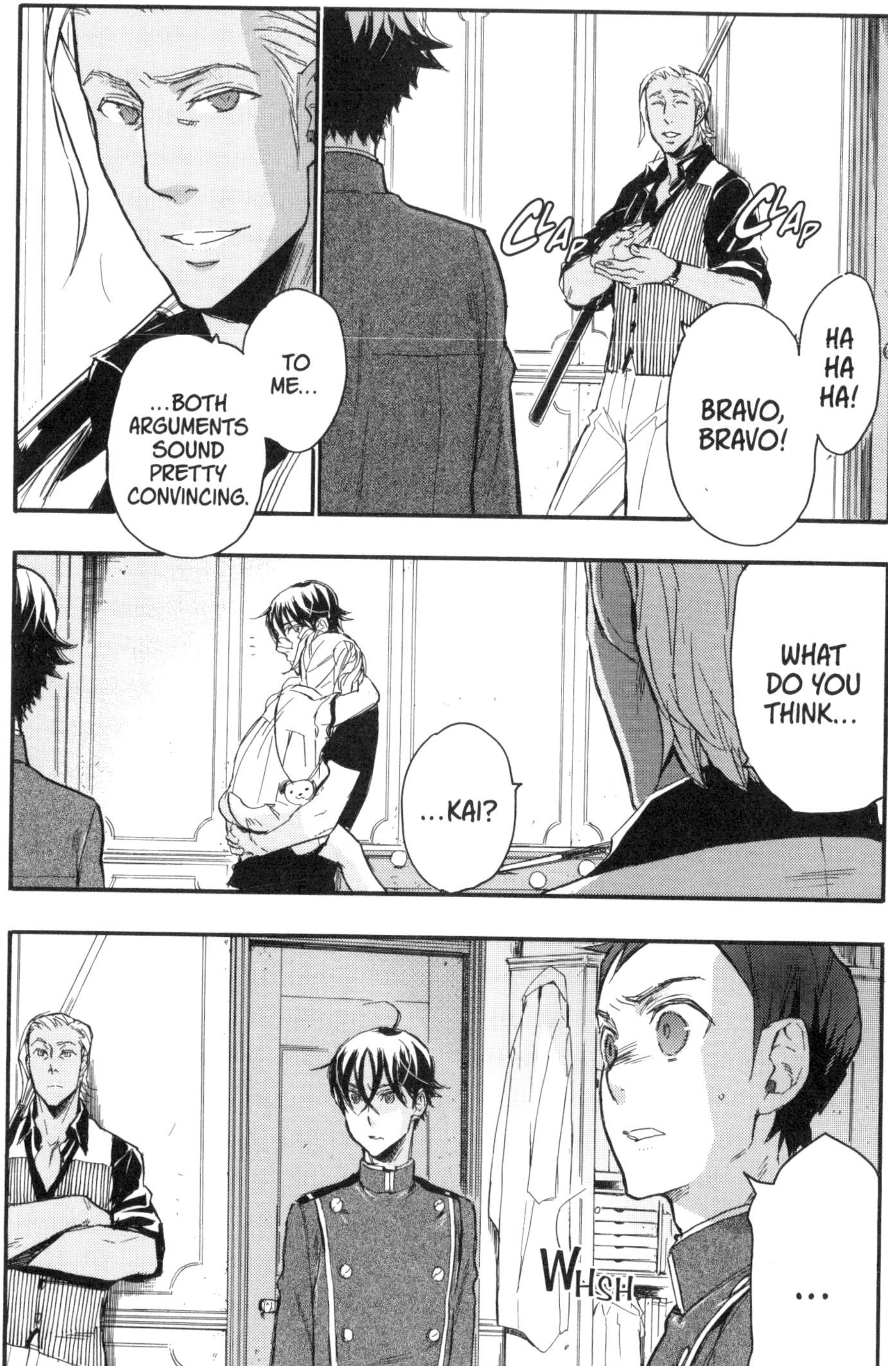
CLAP CLAP
HA HA HA!
BRAVO, BRAVO!
TO ME...
...BOTH ARGUMENTS SOUND PRETTY CONVINCING.
WHAT DO YOU THINK...
...KAI?
...
WHSH

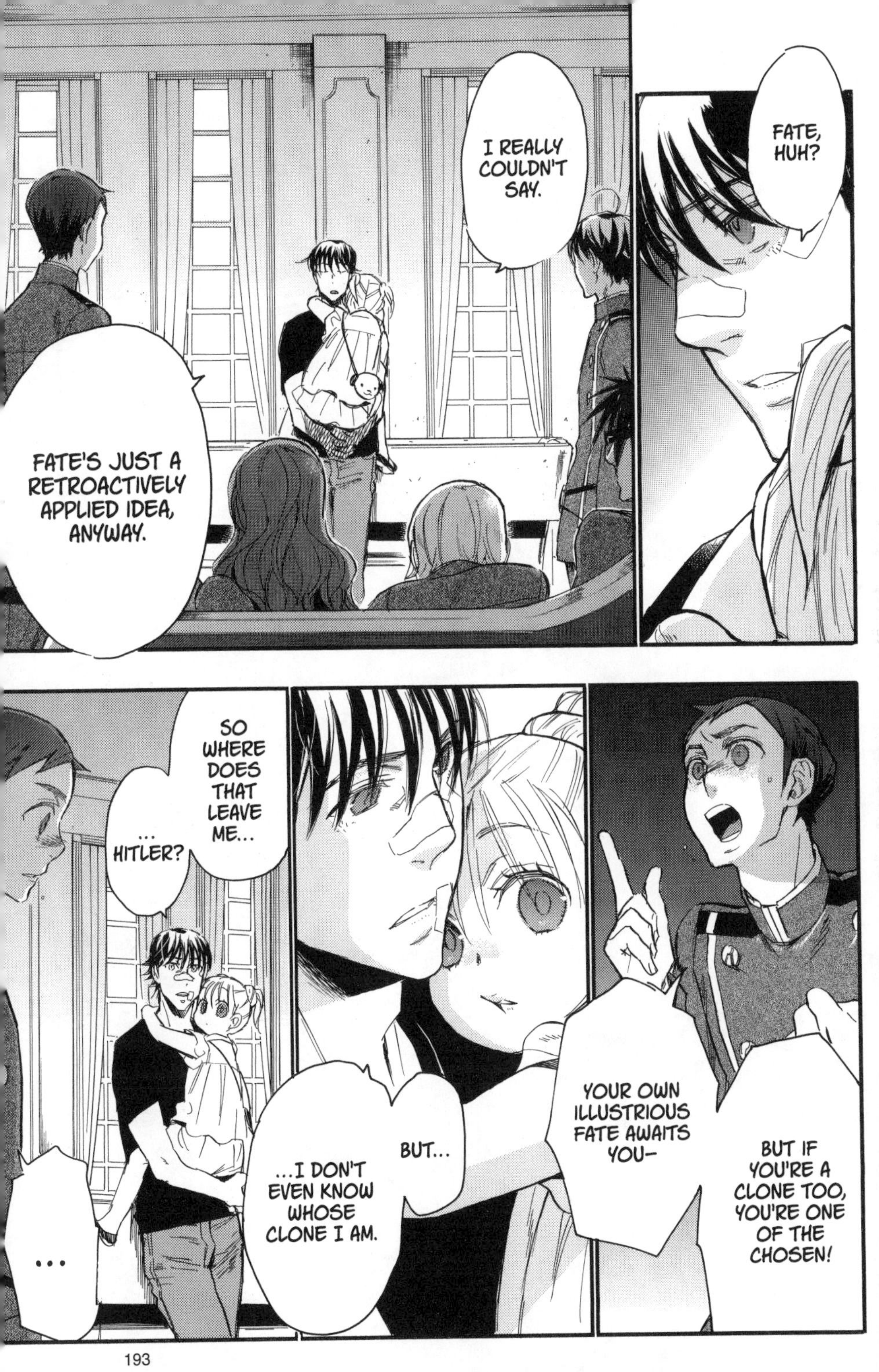
FATE, HUH?
I REALLY COULDN'T SAY.
FATE'S JUST A RETROACTIVELY APPLIED IDEA, ANYWAY.
BUT IF YOU'RE A CLONE TOO, YOU'RE ONE OF THE CHOSEN!
YOUR OWN ILLUSTRIOUS FATE AWAITS YOU—
BUT...
...I DON'T EVEN KNOW WHOSE CLONE I AM.
SO WHERE DOES THAT LEAVE ME...
...HITLER?
...

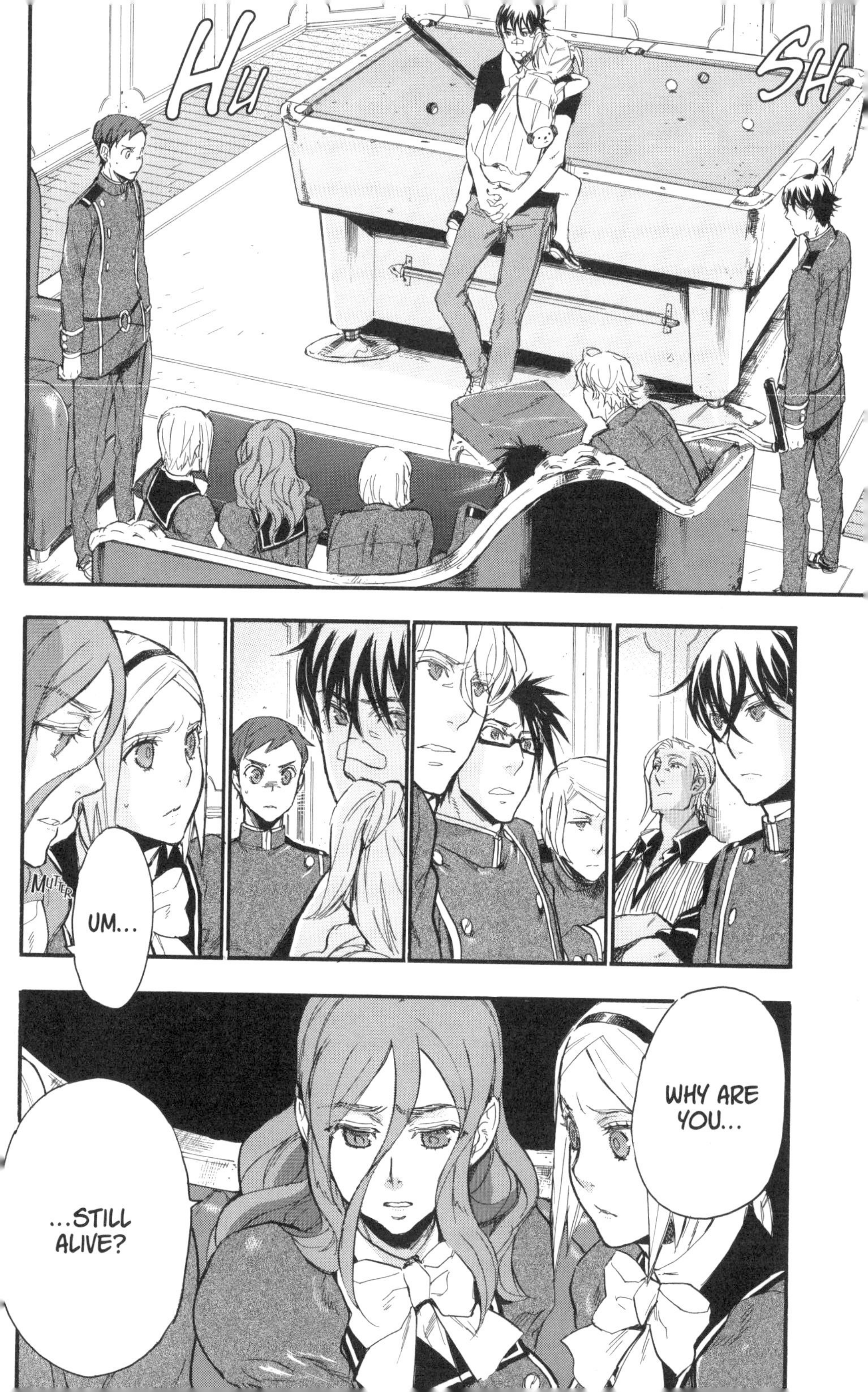
HUSH
MUTTER
UM...
WHY ARE YOU...
...STILL ALIVE?

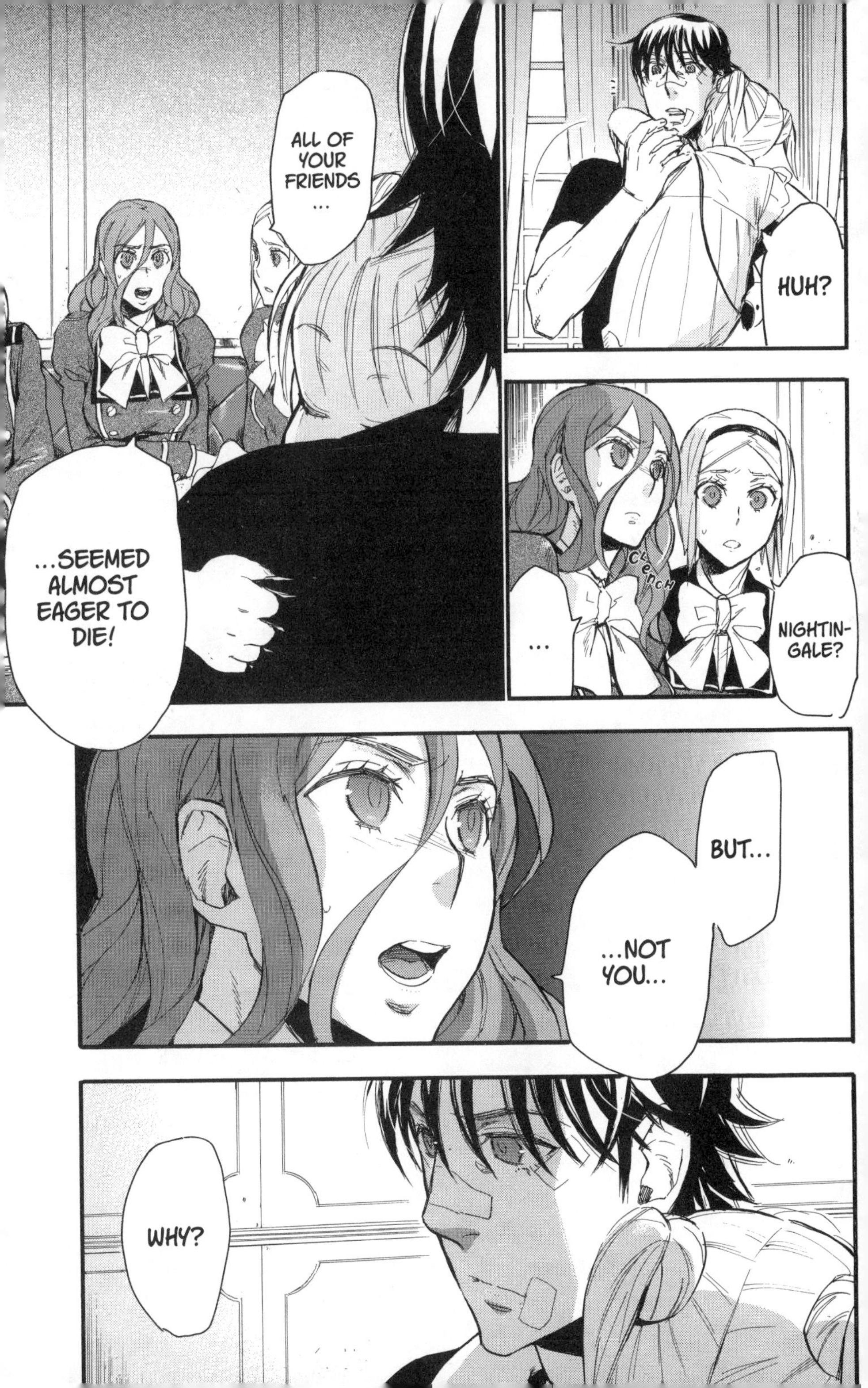
HUH?
NIGHTIN-GALE?
CLENCH
...
ALL OF YOUR FRIENDS ...
...SEEMED ALMOST EAGER TO DIE!
BUT...
...NOT YOU...
WHY?

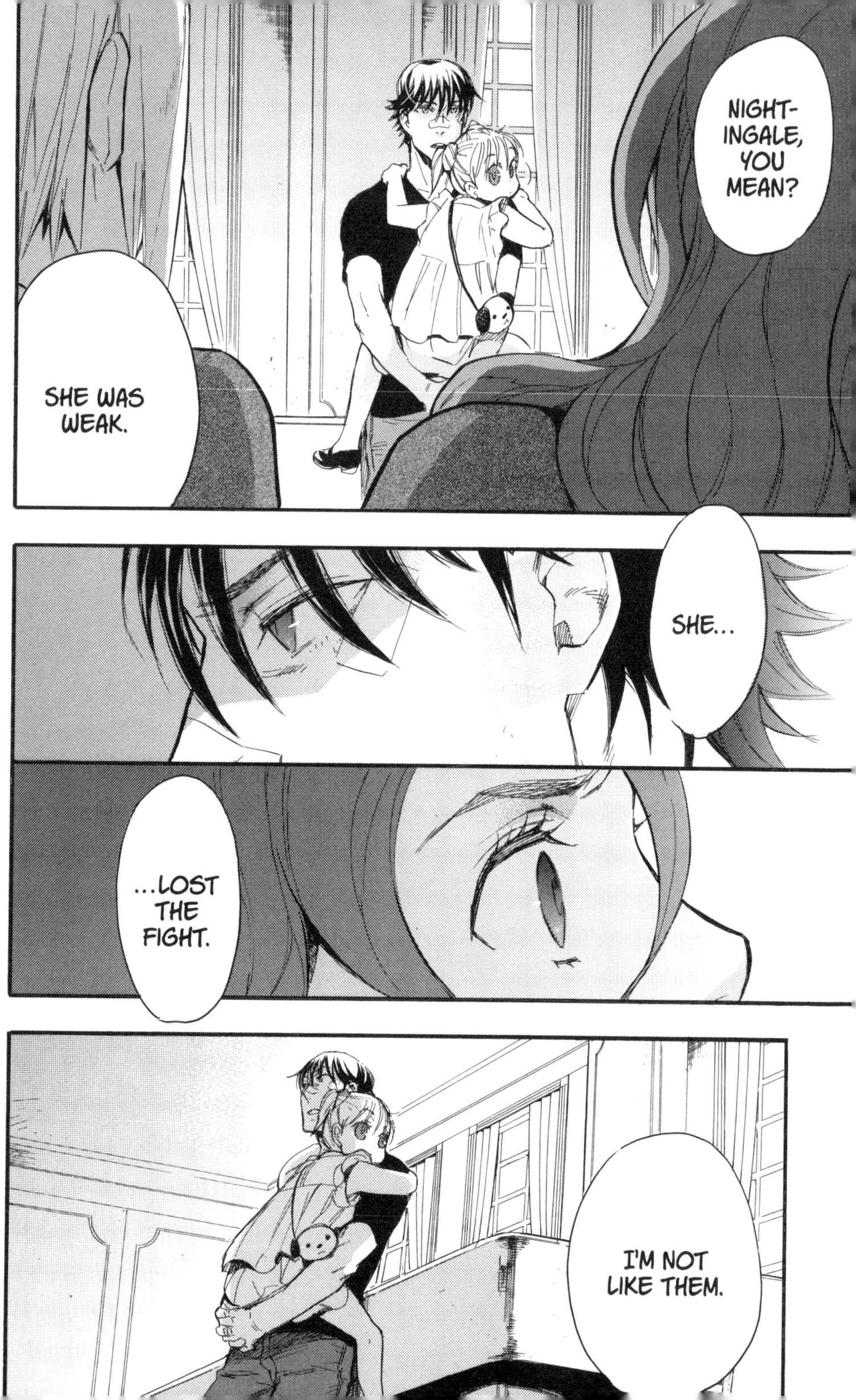
NIGHT-
INGALE,
YOU
MEAN?
SHE WAS WEAK.
SHE...
...LOST THE FIGHT.
I'M NOT LIKE THEM.

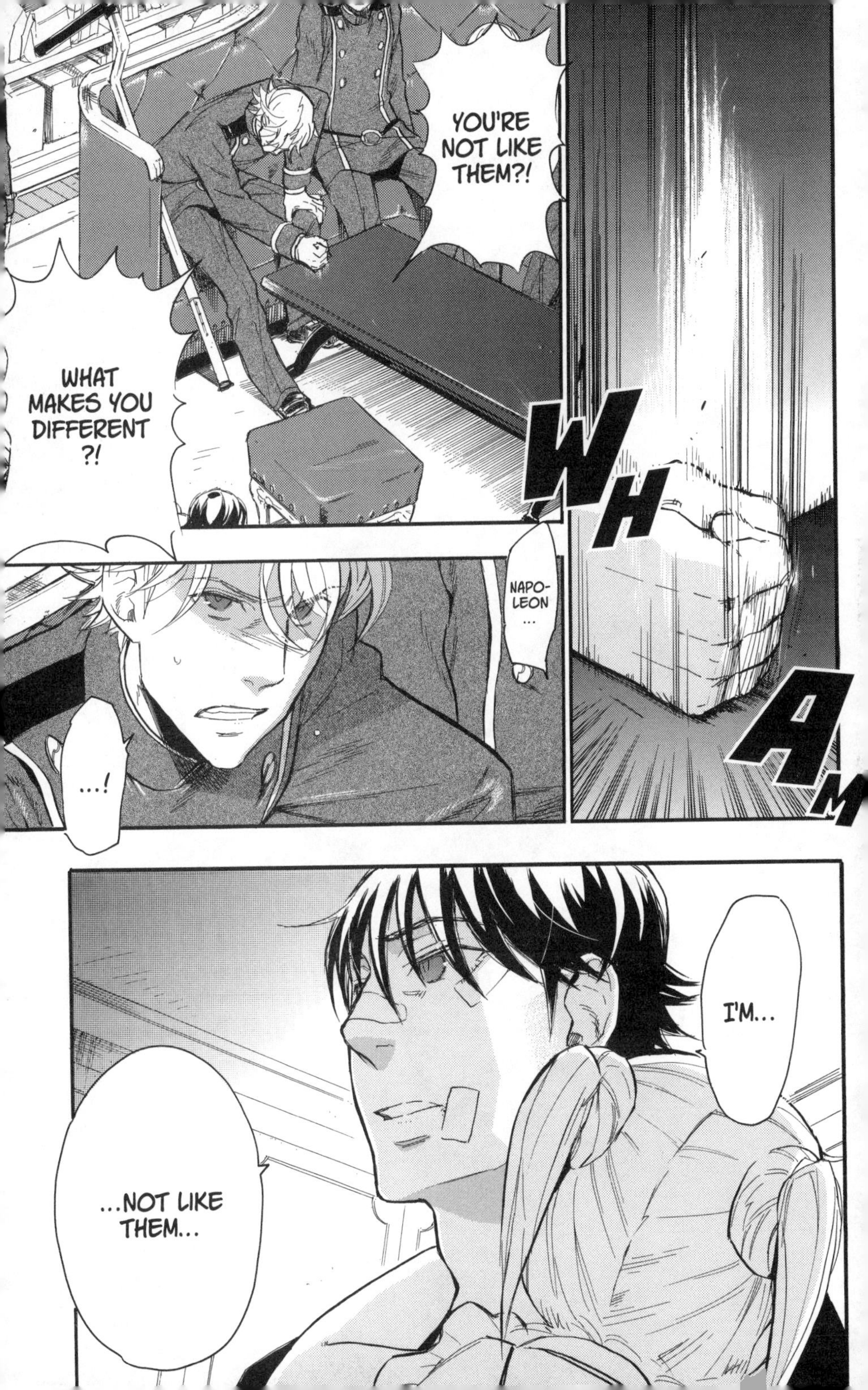
WHAM
YOU'RE NOT LIKE THEM?!
WHAT MAKES YOU DIFFERENT ?!
NAPO-LEON ...
...!
I'M...
...NOT LIKE THEM...

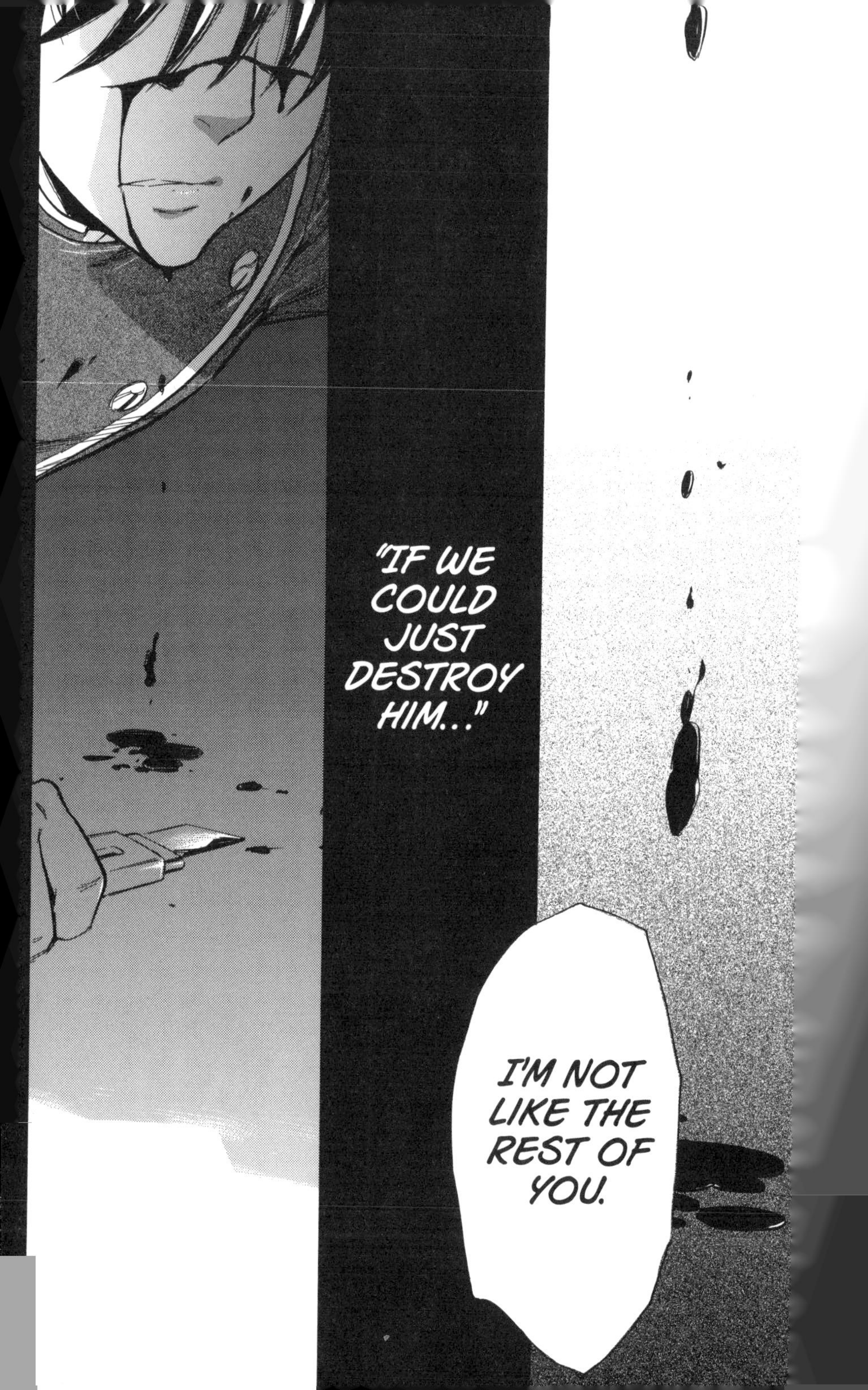
I'M NOT LIKE THE REST OF YOU.
"IF WE COULD JUST DESTROY HIM..."

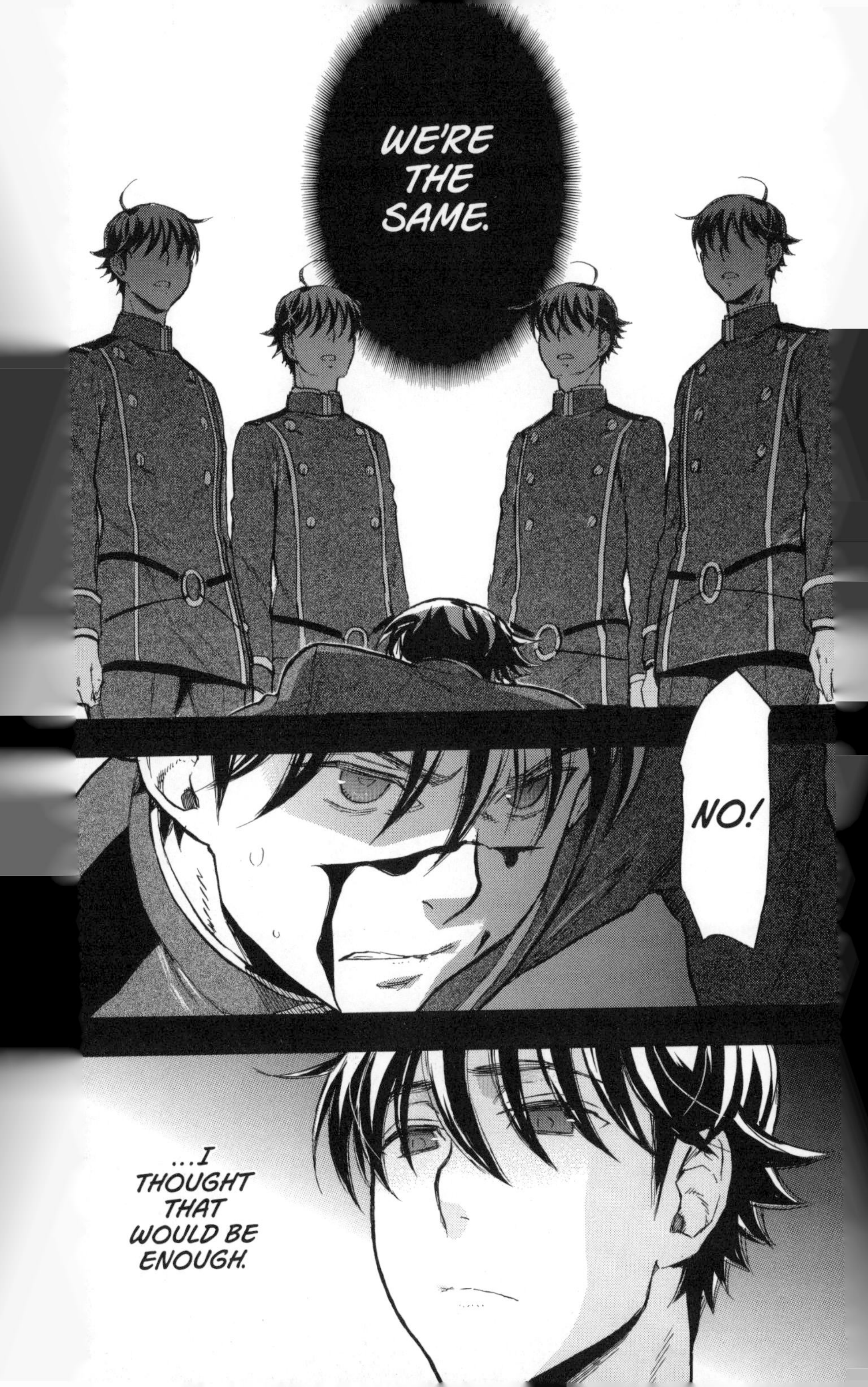
WE'RE THE SAME.
NO!
...I THOUGHT THAT WOULD BE ENOUGH.

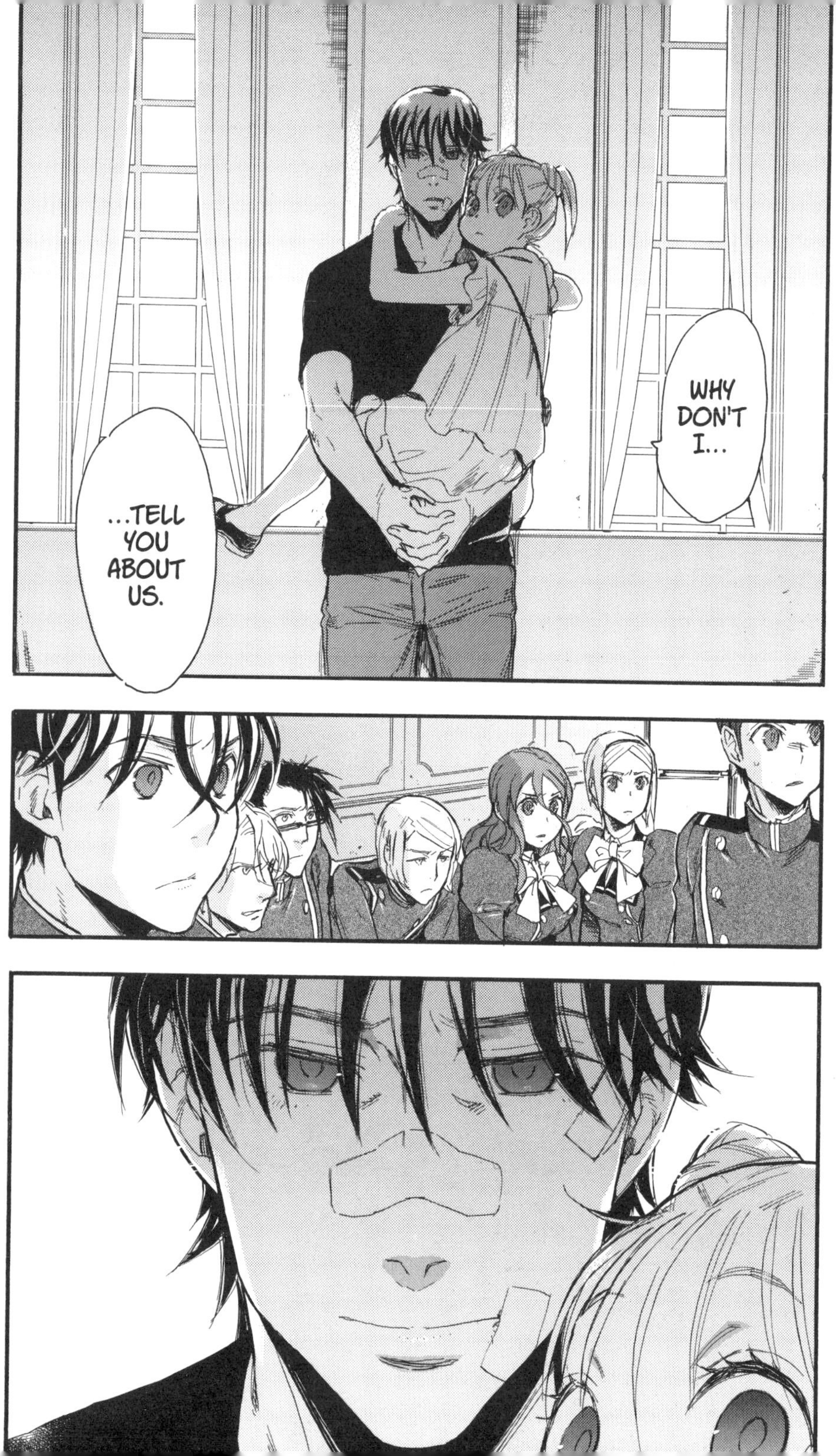
WHY DON'T I...
...TELL YOU ABOUT US.

afterschool charisma

VOLUME FOUR

end

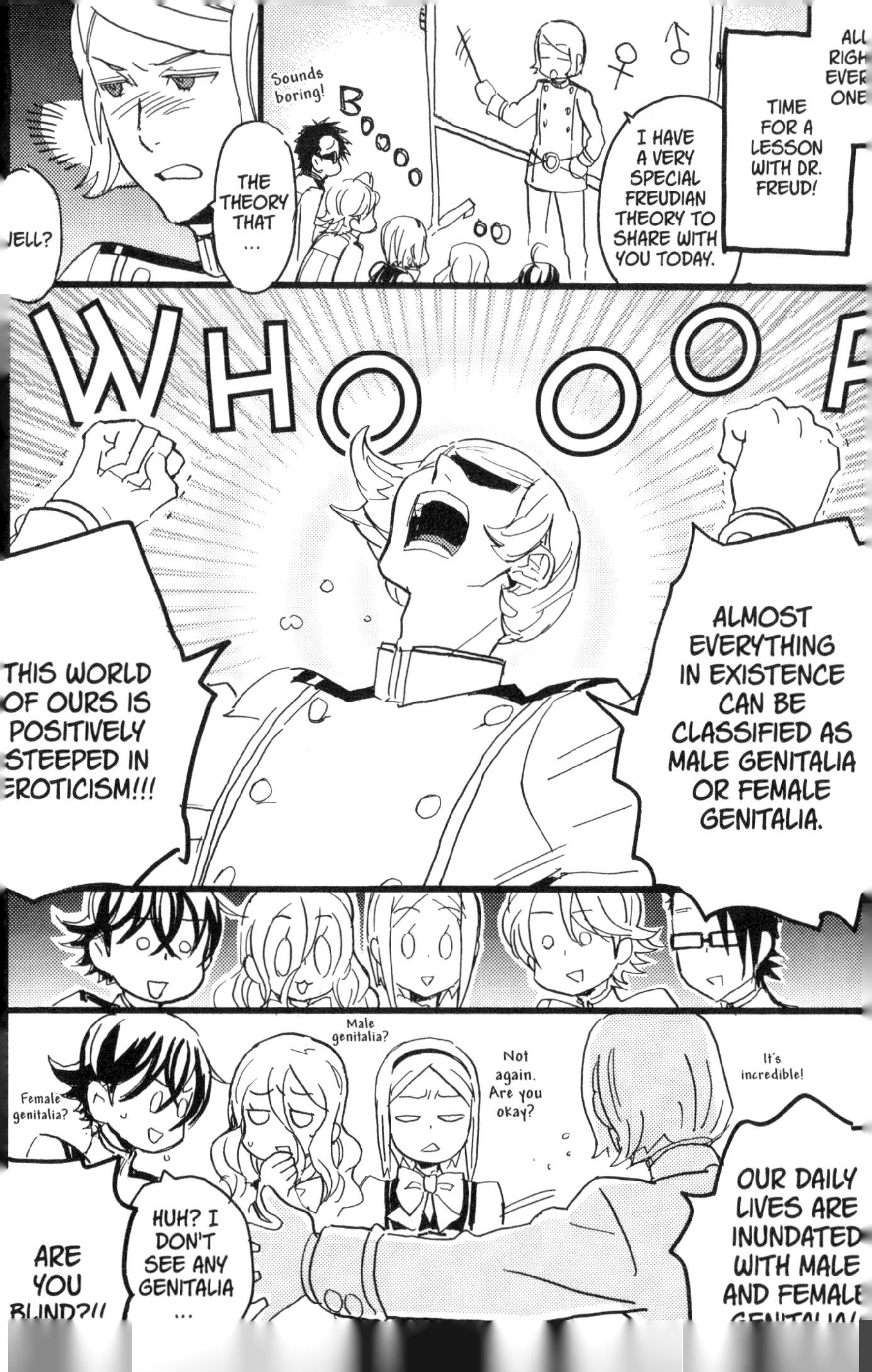
ALL RIGH EVER ONE
TIME FOR A LESSON WITH DR. FREUD!
I HAVE A VERY SPECIAL FREUDIAN THEORY TO SHARE WITH YOU TODAY.
BOOOOO
Sounds boring!
THE THEORY THAT ...
ELL?
WHOOO
ALMOST EVERYTHING IN EXISTENCE CAN BE CLASSIFIED AS MALE GENITALIA OR FEMALE GENITALIA.
THIS WORLD OF OURS IS POSITIVELY STEEPED IN EROTICISM!!!
OUR DAILY LIVES ARE INUNDATED WITH MALE AND FEMALE
It's incredible!
Not again. Are you okay?
Male genitalia?
Female genitalia?
HUH? I DON'T SEE ANY GENITALIA ...
ARE YOU

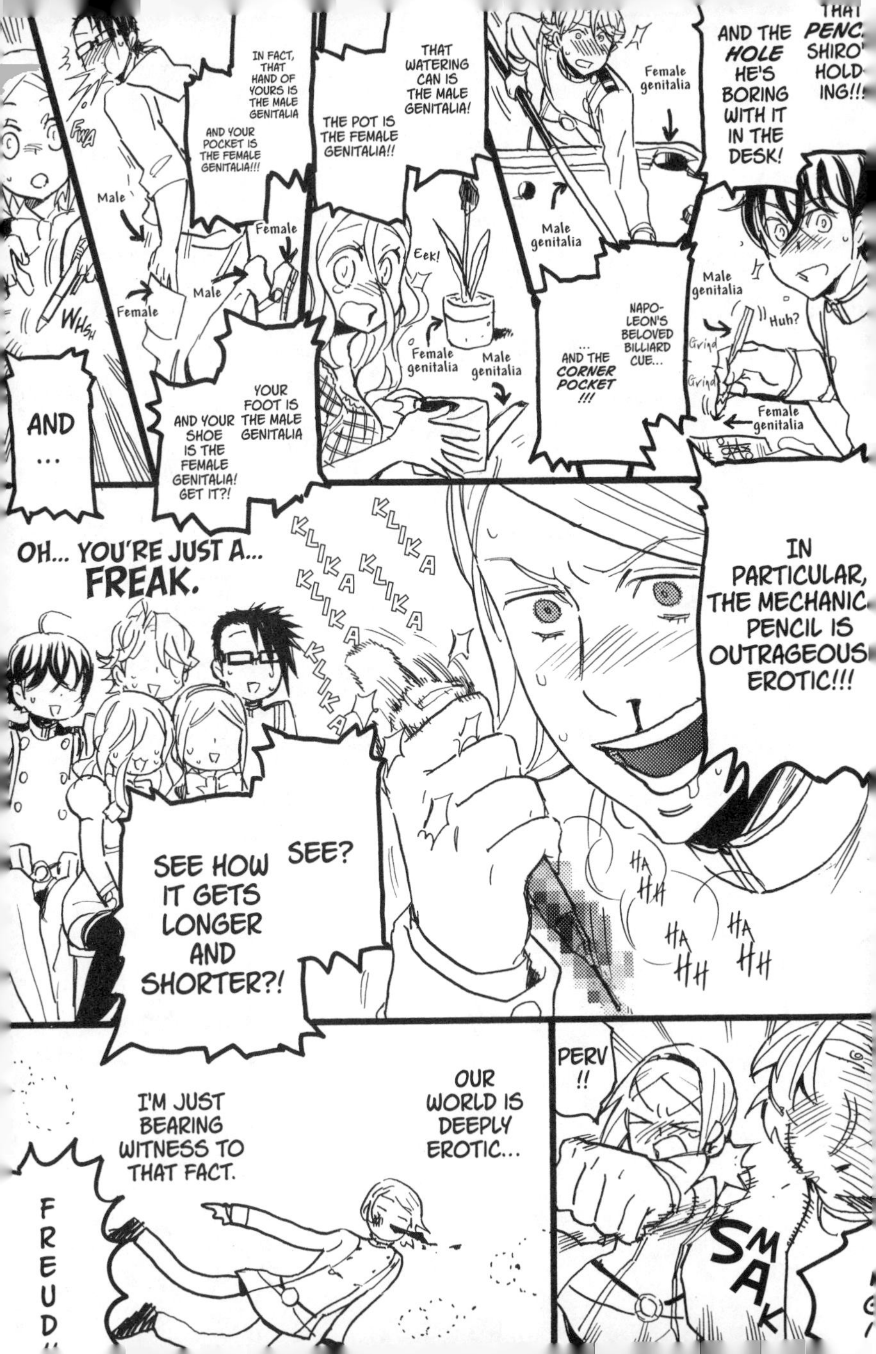
THAT PENC SHIRO' HOLD-ING!!!
AND THE HOLE HE'S BORING WITH IT IN THE DESK!
Huh?
Male genitalia
Grind
Grind
Female genitalia
Female genitalia
Male genitalia
NAPOLEON'S BELOVED BILLIARD CUE...
...AND THE CORNER POCKET!!!
THAT WATERING CAN IS THE MALE GENITALIA!
THE POT IS THE FEMALE GENITALIA!!
Eek!
Female genitalia
Male genitalia
IN FACT, THAT HAND OF YOURS IS THE MALE GENITALIA
AND YOUR POCKET IS THE FEMALE GENITALIA!!!
FWA
Female
Male
Male
Female
WHSH
YOUR FOOT IS THE MALE GENITALIA
AND YOUR SHOE IS THE FEMALE GENITALIA! GET IT?!
AND ...
IN PARTICULAR, THE MECHANIC PENCIL IS OUTRAGEOUS EROTIC!!!
KLIKA KLIKA KLIKA KLIKA KLIKA
SEE?
SEE HOW IT GETS LONGER AND SHORTER?!
HAHH HAHH HAHH
OH... YOU'RE JUST A... FREAK.
PERV!!
SMAK
OUR WORLD IS DEEPLY EROTIC...
I'M JUST BEARING WITNESS TO THAT FACT.
FREUD

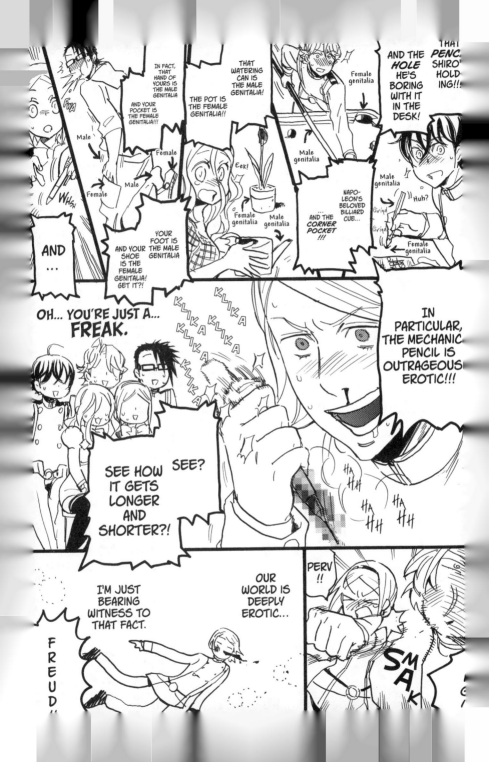

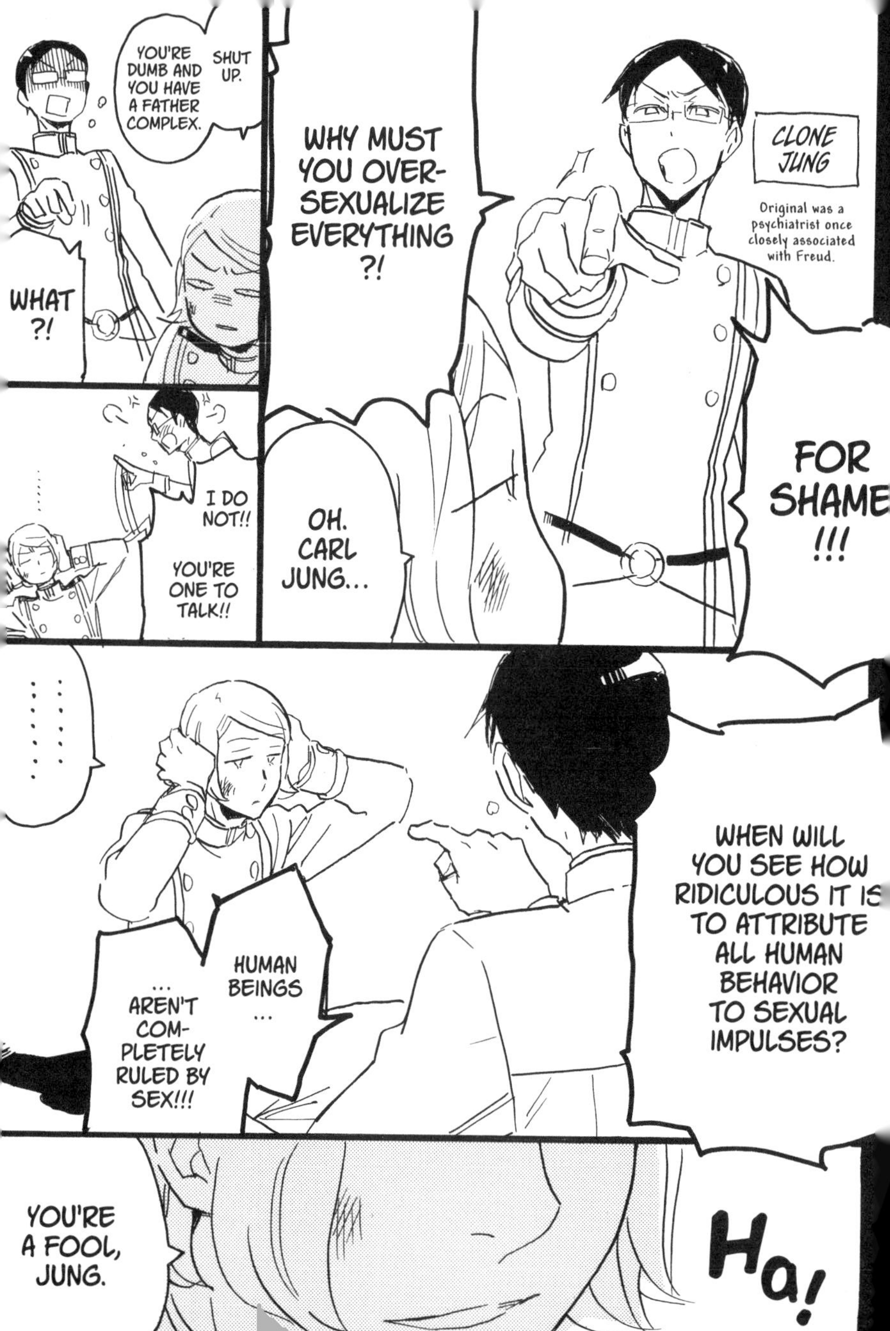
CLONE JUNG
Original was a psychiatrist once closely associated with Freud.
FOR SHAME!!!
WHY MUST YOU OVER-SEXUALIZE EVERYTHING?!
OH. CARL JUNG...
SHUT UP.
YOU'RE DUMB AND YOU HAVE A FATHER COMPLEX.
WHAT?!
I DO NOT!!
YOU'RE ONE TO TALK!!
......
WHEN WILL YOU SEE HOW RIDICULOUS IT IS TO ATTRIBUTE ALL HUMAN BEHAVIOR TO SEXUAL IMPULSES?
......
HUMAN BEINGS...
...AREN'T COMPLETELY RULED BY SEX!!!
Ha!
YOU'RE A FOOL, JUNG.

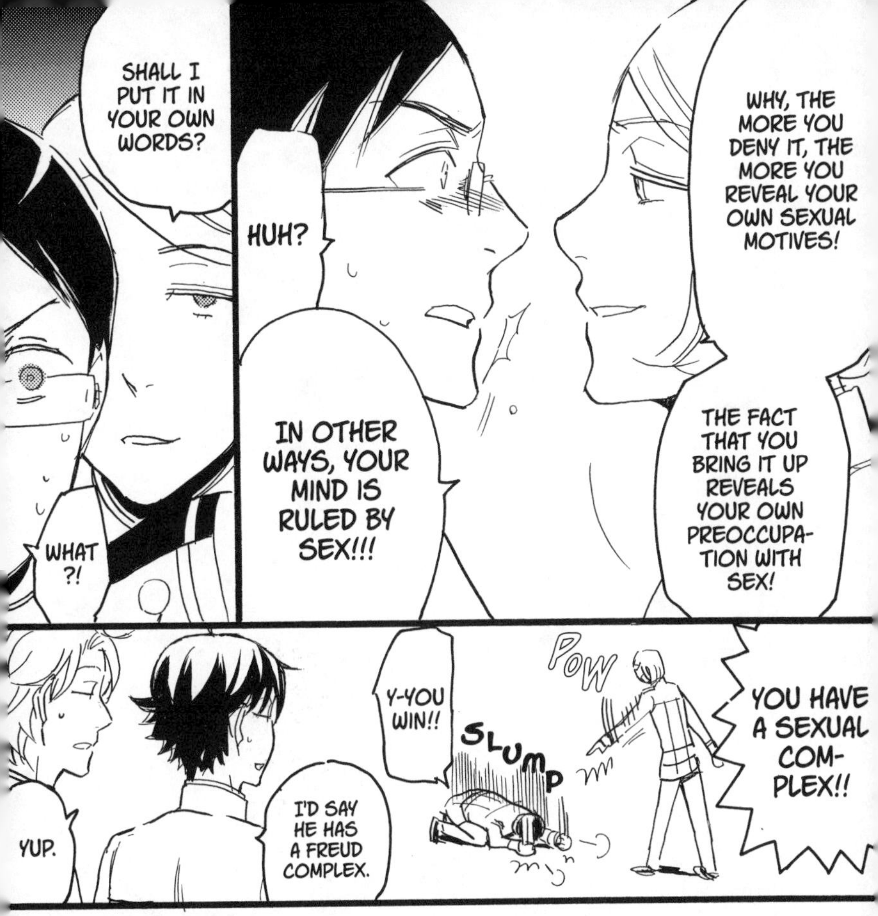
WHY, THE MORE YOU DENY IT, THE MORE YOU REVEAL YOUR OWN SEXUAL MOTIVES!
HUH?
THE FACT THAT YOU BRING IT UP REVEALS YOUR OWN PREOCCUPATION WITH SEX!
IN OTHER WAYS, YOUR MIND IS RULED BY SEX!!!
SHALL I PUT IT IN YOUR OWN WORDS?
WHAT ?!
YOU HAVE A SEXUAL COMPLEX!!
POW
Y-YOU WIN!!
SLUMP
I'D SAY HE HAS A FREUD COMPLEX.
YUP.

COMPLEX – Psychological phenomenon involving the simultaneous occurrence of conflicting emotions, resulting in complex reactions. (Carl Jung)

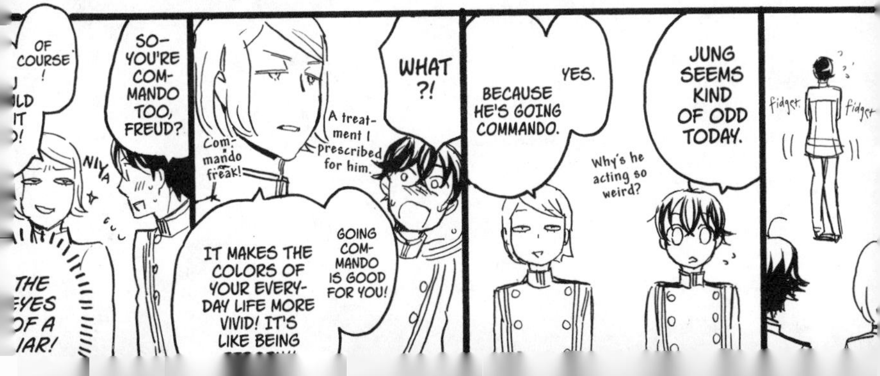
fidget fidget
JUNG SEEMS KIND OF ODD TODAY.
YES.
BECAUSE HE'S GOING COMMANDO.
Why's he acting so weird?
WHAT ?!
A treatment I prescribed for him.
GOING COMMANDO IS GOOD FOR YOU!
Com-mando freak!
IT MAKES THE COLORS OF YOUR EVERYDAY LIFE MORE VIVID! IT'S LIKE BEING
SO- YOU'RE COMMANDO TOO, FREUD?
OF COURSE!
NIYA
THE EYES OF A IAR!

AFTERSCHOOL CHARISMA
VOLUME 4
VIZ SIGNATURE EDITION

STORY & ART BY **KUMIKO SUEKANE**

© 2009 Kumiko SUEKANE/Shogakukan
All rights reserved.
Original Japanese edition "HOUKAGO NO CARISMA"
published by SHOGAKUKAN Inc.

Original Japanese cover design by Mitsuru KOBAYASHI (GENI A LÒIDE)

TRANSLATION –○– CAMELLIA NIEH
TOUCH UP ART & LETTERING –○– ERIKA TERRIQUEZ
DESIGN –○– FAWN LAU
EDITOR –○– MEGAN BATES

Printed in Canada

Published by VIZ Media, LLC
P.O. Box 77010
San Francisco, CA 94107

10 9 8 7 6 5 4 3 2 1

First printing, October 2011

PARENTAL ADVISORY
AFTERSCHOOL CHARISMA is rated T+
for Older Teen and is recommended for
ages 16 and up.
RATED **T+** FOR OLDER TEEN
ratings.viz.com

www.viz.com

VIZ SIGNATURE
WWW.SIGIKKI.COM

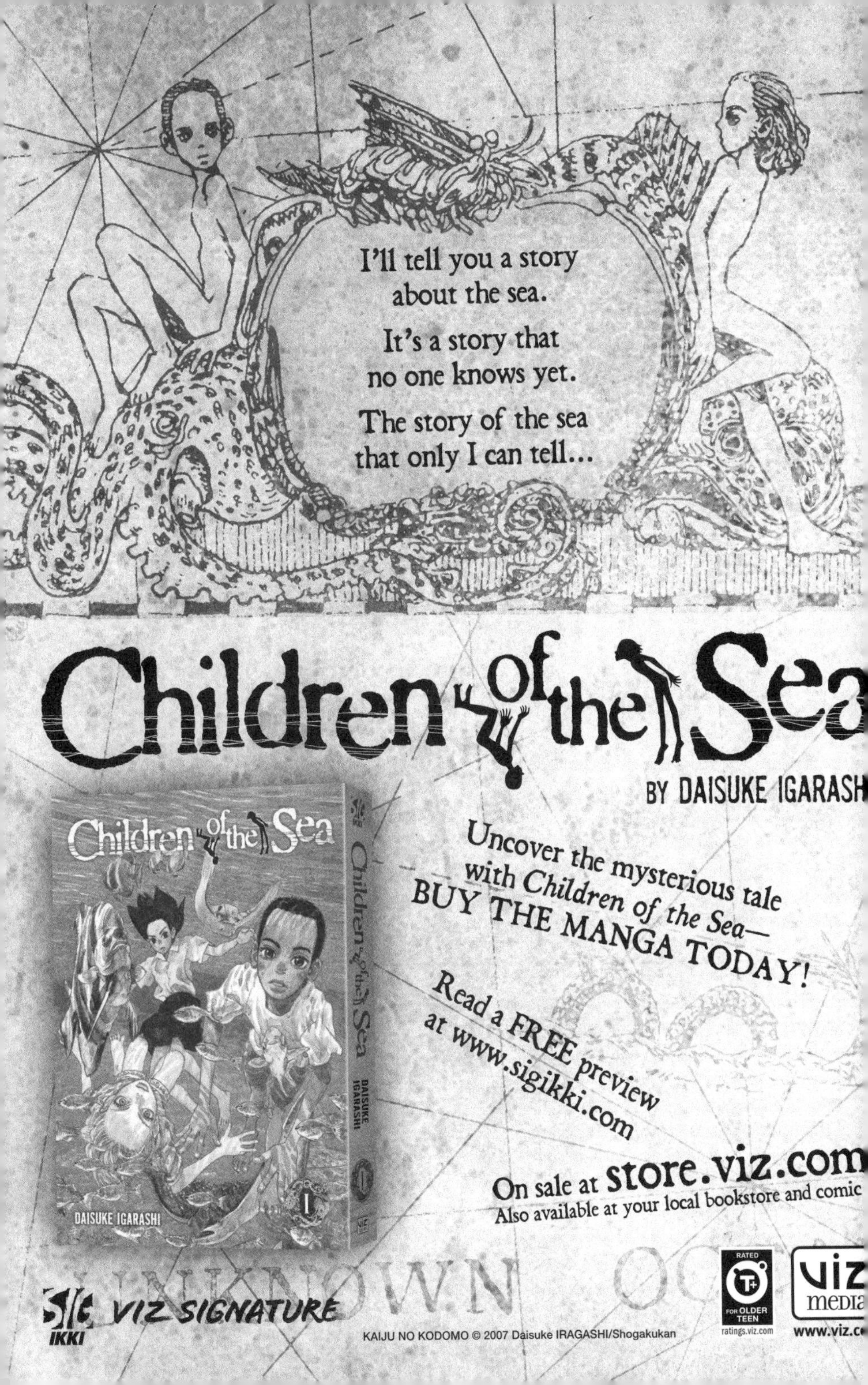
I'll tell you a story about the sea.
It's a story that no one knows yet.
The story of the sea that only I can tell...
Children of the Sea
BY DAISUKE IGARASH
Children of the Sea
DAISUKE IGARASHI
1
Uncover the mysterious tale with Children of the Sea—BUY THE MANGA TODAY!
Read a FREE preview at www.sigikki.com
On sale at store.viz.com
Also available at your local bookstore and comic
SIG IKKI VIZ SIGNATURE
KAIJU NO KODOMO © 2007 Daisuke IRAGASHI/Shogakukan
RATED T+ FOR OLDER TEEN ratings.viz.com
viz media
www.viz.c